INTERNATIONAL LAW *FOR* INTERNATIONAL RELATIONS

INTERNATIONAL LAW *FOR* INTERNATIONAL RELATIONS

Edited by
Başak Çalı

OXFORD
UNIVERSITY PRESS

OXFORD
UNIVERSITY PRESS

Great Clarendon Street, Oxford OX2 6DP

Oxford University Press is a department of the University of Oxford.
It furthers the University's objective of excellence in research, scholarship,
and education by publishing worldwide in

Oxford New York

Auckland Cape Town Dar es Salaam Hong Kong Karachi
Kuala Lumpur Madrid Melbourne Mexico City Nairobi
New Delhi Shanghai Taipei Toronto

With offices in

Argentina Austria Brazil Chile Czech Republic France Greece
Guatemala Hungary Italy Japan Poland Portugal Singapore
South Korea Switzerland Thailand Turkey Ukraine Vietnam

Oxford is a registered trade mark of Oxford University Press
in the UK and in certain other countries

Published in the United States
by Oxford University Press Inc., New York

British Library Cataloguing in Publication Data

Data available

Library of Congress Cataloging in Publication Data

International law for international relations / Başak Çali.
  p. cm.
ISBN 978-0-19-955842-1
1. International law. 2. International relations. I. Çali, Başak, 1974–
KZ3410.I5794 2010
341–dc22

2009042108

Typeset by MPS Limited, A Macmillan Company
Printed in Great Britain
on acid-free paper by
CPI Antony Rowe

ISBN 978–0–19–955842–1

1 3 5 7 9 10 8 6 4 2

Preface

International law has become a key element of any politics and international relations degree. The existing range of international law textbooks for the student of law, while excellent, is inadequate for the student of international relations who has no prior legal background and comes to the field with more knowledge and understanding of how states behave rather than what rules regulate state behaviour. The breadth of international law and institutions in contemporary global politics means that it is no longer possible to make sense of international politics without understanding international law and the complex regulatory frameworks that exist in international relations. This textbook gives the student that understanding for use in the real world or in further academic study.

This textbook provides the international relations student with what he or she needs to understand about international law in three ways. It maps out the different ways to approach the study of international law, explains the main sources of international law-making, and identifies the key topics of international law. Throughout, the book balances the technical, legal knowledge necessary to understand the nuances of international law with the broader political processes that shape both the content and effectiveness of international law. The intricacies of international law are presented accessibly to animate both the learning of international law and its evaluation. With this approach, *International Law for International Relations* aims to introduce the student to the international law perspective of international relations and how this perspective differs from other approaches in international relations.

This book has been lucky to have benefited from submissions from an exceptional group of academics and practitioners in the fields of international law and international relations. For their hard work and effort I thank them. Every author is an expert in his or her field and has either experience teaching international law to politics students or using international law in real-world political situations. The contributors have made the subject matter accessible and have reflected carefully on the bearing international law has on the international issues it addresses. This means that the book draws a very rich and diverse picture of international law and enables the student to see the different patterns of interaction between law and politics in each topic.

Finally, thanks have to be given to Sabina Appelt. Everything the contributors wrote was reviewed by Sabina and what started out as a student perspective soon turned into full-blown editing. It is a credit to Sabina that every chapter has substantively improved throughout the editorial process. Her speed, hard work, and sense of humour kept the process on track. I would also like to thank Elizabeth Griffin and the editors at OUP for their help and support and, of course, Sam for casting a layman's eye over the text and making the coffee.

Başak Çalı

Contents—Summary

PART I STUDYING INTERNATIONAL LAW

PART II IDENTIFYING INTERNATIONAL LAW

9   States and international law: the problems of self-determination,
    secession, and recognition   191
    Christopher J. Borgen

10 Use of force in international law   213
    Nigel Rodley and Başak Çalı

11 International humanitarian law   234
    Elizabeth Griffin and Başak Çalı

12 International criminal law   258
    Paola Gaeta

13 International human rights law   281
    Başak Çalı

14 International law for environmental protection   306
    David M. Ong

15 World trade and international law   330
    Thomas Sebastian

16 Global social justice and international law   351
    Saladin Meckled-Garcia

CONCLUSION

17 International law in international relations: what are
    the prospects for the future?   379
    Başak Çalı

    Table of cases   395

    Table of major multilateral international treaties and documents 397

    Glossary   399

    References   409

    Index   421

Detailed contents

PART I STUDYING INTERNATIONAL LAW

CONCLUSION

Guided Tour of Learning Features

This book is enriched with a range of learning tools to help you navigate the text and reinforce your knowledge of International Law. This guided tour shows you how to get the most out of your textbook package.

CHAPTER CONTENTS

- Introduction
- What is international law?
- The relationship between international law and international relat
- Why study international law?
- Conclusion

Chapter Overviews

Brief overviews at the beginning of every chapter set the scene for upcoming themes and issues to be discussed, and indicate the scope of coverage within each chapter.

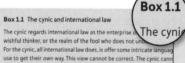

Box 1.1 The cynic and international law

The cynic regards international law as the enterprise o wishful thinker, or the realm of the fool who does not un For the cynic, all international law does, is offer some intricate languag use to get their own way. This view cannot be correct. The cynic cann continuing existence of international law as an idea and as a practice. that international law is merely a means of manipulation, why was int

Boxes, Tables and Case Studies

Throughout the book boxes, tables, and case studies provide you with extra information on particular topics that complement your understanding of the main chapter text.

hergence as a means for states to reach cooperation ommon interests. International norms and rules crea d transparency, and the possibilities of iterated intera o overcome problems of **collective action**. Liberals are th lists to focus on **international regimes** as important features o ational regimes have been classically defined by Stephen Krasner s, norms, rules, and decision-making procedures around which nverge in a given issue-area'. Notice that this definition might

Glossary Terms

Key terms appear in bold in the text and are defined in a glossary at the end of the book to aid you in exam revision.

Questions

Questions

1. What is international law and how is it different fro[...]
2. What are the areas regulated by international law?
3. What does the sceptic say about international law?
4. What do you think is the most significant difference between inte[...]
   and international law?

Questions

A set of carefully devised questions has been provided to help you assess your understanding of core themes, and may also be used as the basis of seminar discussion or coursework.

Further reading

Simmons, B. and Steinberg, R. H. (2006) (eds.), *International Law and International Relations* (Cambridge: Cambridge University Press). *An excellent collection of essays on different permutations of the relationship between the disciplines of international law and international relations.*

intern[...]
significa[...]
Ku, C., Diehl, P. F., Simmo[...]
and Jacobson, H.K. (2[...]
national Law: Opportu[...]
for Political Science [...]
ble' International Stu[...]

Further Reading

Reading lists have been provided as a guide to finding out more about the issues raised within each chapter and to help you locate the key academic literature in the field.

Websites

http://www.chathamhouse.org.uk *The website of the Roya[...] vides an interesting overview of what—from a UK perspective— and pressing contemporary topics in the area of international relations.*

http://www2.etown.edu/vl/ *This internet directory brings together over 2[...] sources of information and analysis in a wide range of international affairs, in[...] international relations topics.*

Important Websites

At the end most chapters you will find an annotated summary of useful websites, which will be instrumental in further research.

Guided Tour of the Online Resource Centre

www.oxfordtextbooks.co.uk/orc/cali/

The Online Resource Centre that accompanies this book provides students and instructors with ready-to-use teaching and learning materials. These resources are free of charge and designed to maximize the learning experience.

FOR STUDENTS:

Flashcard Glossary

A series of interactive flashcards containing key terms and concepts have been provided to test your understanding of the terminology of International Law.

Problem-solving Questions

For each International Law topic a problem-question is posed, together with a list of key considerations and a guide to sources of information to help you go about solving it.

Revision Tips

A checklist of the key points from each chapter is provided to help you to focus your revision.

Web Links

A series of annotated web links have been provided to point you in the direction of different theoretical debates, important treaties, working papers, articles and other relevant sources of information.

FOR INSTRUCTORS:

PowerPoint® Presentations

These complement each chapter of the book and are a useful resource for preparing lectures and handouts. They allow lecturers to guide students through the key concepts and can be fully customized to meet the needs of the course.

Contributors

Meghna Abraham is the Head of the Economic, Social and Cultural Rights Team at the International Secretariat of Amnesty International. She has previously worked with a number of NGOs and academic centres in India, Switzerland, and the United Kingdom.

Fiona B. Adamson is a Senior Lecturer (Associate Professor) of International Relations in the Department of Politics and International Studies at SOAS, University of London. Her work has appeared in *International Security*, *European Journal of International Relations*, *International Studies Review*, *Cambridge Review of International Affairs*, and a number of edited volumes.

Juan M. Amaya-Castro is Assistant Professor and Academic Head of the Department of International Law and Human Rights at the United Nations Mandated University for Peace in Costa Rica.

Antony Anghie is the Samuel D. Thurman Professor of International Law at the S.J. Quinney School of Law, University of Utah. He is the author of *Imperialism, Sovereignty and the Making of International Law* (2005).

Jason Beckett is a Lecturer in the Law School of the University of Leicester, where he teaches and researches in the fields of legal method, legal theory, political theory, critical theory, and Public International Law. His work has appeared in the *European Journal of International Law*, *German Law Journal*, and a number of edited volumes.

Christopher J. Borgen is Associate Dean for International Studies and Professor of Law at St. John's University School of Law in New York City. He is the principle author of *Thawing a Frozen Conflict: Legal Aspects of the Separatist Crisis in Moldova*, a report issued by the Special Committee on European Affairs of the New York City Bar, and he is the co-founder of *Opinio Juris*, a website devoted to debate and discussion on issues of international law and politics.

Başak Çalı is Lecturer of International Law and Human Rights at the Department of Political Science, University College London. Her work has appeared in the *Human Rights Quarterly*, *European Journal of International Law*, and a number of edited volumes.

Paola Gaeta is Professor in International Law at Florence University, Professor of International Criminal Law at the Law Faculty of the University of Geneva and the Director of the LLM Programme of the Geneva Academy of International Humanitarian Law and Human Rights. Her most recent book is *The UN Convention on Genocide: a Commentary* (ed.) (2009).

Elizabeth Griffin is an academic and practitioner with a specialization in international humanitarian and human rights law applicable in conflict and post-conflict situations. She is Adjunct Professor, George Washington University and Director of the Human Rights Center, UN Mandated University for Peace. Elizabeth serves as a consultant to Amnesty International and the UN Office for the High Commissioner for Human Rights. She has extensive field experience working for NGOs and the UN in Kosovo, Afghanistan, Bosnia Herzegovina, and Central America.

Saladin Meckled-Garcia is Lecturer in Human Rights and Political Theory and Director of the Human Rights Programme at the Department of Political Science, University College London. He has published a number of works in the field of political philosophy, including works on justice theory, political authority, and human rights.

David M. Ong is Reader in International and Environmental Law at the University of Essex, Law School. His work has appeared in the *American Journal of International Law*, the *European Journal of International Law*, the *Irish Yearbook of International Law*, and the *Yearbook of International Environmental Law*.

Sir Nigel Rodley KBE is Professor of Law and Chair of the Human Rights Centre, University of Essex. He is a Member (since 2001) and Vice-Chair (2003–2004, 2009–2010) of the UN Human Rights Committee and was UN Commission on Human Rights Special Rapporteur on Torture (1993–2001). Several of his articles and book chapters have dealt with aspects of the use of force in international law. He is the author of *The Treatment of Prisoners in International Law* (1999).

Thomas Sebastian is Counsel at the Advisory Centre on WTO Law in Geneva. In that capacity he represents developing and least developed countries in proceedings before the WTO dispute settlement system and provides advice on issues of WTO law.

Chandra Lekha Sriram is Professor of Human Rights and Director of the Centre on Human Rights in Conflict at the University of East London School of Law. Her most recent book is *Peace as Governance: Power-sharing, Armed Groups, and Contemporary Peace Negotiations* (2008).

Emmanuel Voyiakis is a Lecturer at Brunel Law School, UK. His research focuses on the theory and sources of international law and the theory of private law. His work has appeared in *International and Comparative Law Quarterly,* and in a number of edited volumes.

List of boxes

List of tables

List of case studies

Abbreviations

AI Amnesty International

ASEAN Association of South East Asian Nations

BYBIL British Year Book of International Law

CACJ Central American Court of Justice

CAN Computer Network Attack

CEDAW Committee on the Elimination of Discrimination against Women

CERCLA Comprehensive Environmental Response, Compensation and Liability Act

CIL Customary International Law

CLS Critical Legal Studies

CoE Council of Europe

CSCE Conference for Security and Cooperation in Europe

ECE Economic Commission for Europe

ECJ European Court of Justice

ECOSOC Economic and Social Council

ECOWAS Economic Community of West African States

EEZ Exclusive Economic Zones

EFTA European Free Trade Association

EHS Environmental, Health and Safety

EIA Environmental Impact Assessment

EU European Union

GATS General Agreement on Trade in Services

GATT General Agreement on Tariffs and Trade

HGA Host Government Agreement

ICC International Criminal Court

ICCPR International Covenant on Civil and Political Rights

ICESCR International Covenant on Economic, Social and Cultural Rights

ICJ International Court of Justice

ICRC International Committee of the Red Cross

ICTR International Criminal Tribunal for Rwanda

ICTY International Criminal Tribunal for the Former Yugoslavia

IFC International Finance Corporation

IGO Inter-Governmental Organizations

IHL International Humanitarian Law

IHRL International Human Rights Law

IL International Law

IMF International Monetary Fund

IMO International Maritime Organization

IMT International Military Tribunal at Nuremberg

IO International Organization

IR International Relations

ITLOS International Tribunal for the Law of the Sea

MAI Multilateral Agreement on Investment

MEA Multilateral Environmental Agreement

MFN Most-Favoured Nation

NATO North Atlantic Treaty Organization

NGO Non-Governmental Organization

NPT Nuclear Non-Proliferation Treaty

OAS Organization of American States

ONUB United Nations Operation in Burundi

OSCE Organization for Security and Cooperation in Europe

PCIL Permanent Court of International Justice

PIL Public International Law

PKK Parti Karkerani Kurdistan (Kurdistan Workers' Party)

PLO Palestinian Liberation Organization

PMC Private Military Company

SACU South African Customs Union

SC Security Council

SCM Agreement Agreement on Subsidies and Countervailing Measures

SEA Strategic Environmental Assessment

SPS Agreement Sanitary and Phytosanitary Agreement

TBT Agreement Technical Barriers to Trade Agreement

TIA Transnational Investment Agreement

TMR Transnistrian Moldovan Republic

TNC Transnational Corporation

TRIPS Trade-Related Aspects of Intellectual Property Rights

TRNC Turkish Republic of Northern Cyprus

TWAIL Third World Approaches to International Law

UDHR Universal Declaration of Human Rights

UKMIL United Kingdom Materials in International Law

UN United Nations

UNCHE United Nations Convention on the Human Environment

UNCLOS United Nations Convention on the Law of the Sea

UNDP United Nations Development Programme

UNEF United Nations Emergency Force

UNGA United Nations General Assembly

UNMIK United Nations Mission in Kosovo

USSR Union of Soviet Socialist Republics

VCLT Vienna Convention on the Law of Treaties

WCED World Commission on Environment and Development

WTO World Trade Organization

WWI World War One

WWII World War Two

PART I

STUDYING INTERNATIONAL LAW

This part of the book provides you with theoretical perspectives on and about international law and locates international law within the broader world historical context. There are three main aims: *first*, we want you to think about the relationship between international relations and international law as two fields of inquiry in order to assess similarities and differences between adopting an international relations approach and an international law approach to any topic. Our *second* aim is to systematically go through international relations theories in order to discuss how they view the place of international law in international relations. The *third* aim is to locate international law and its institutional and theoretical development within larger processes of world history. We finally introduce theories about international law itself and how international lawyers theorize the complex relationship between law, politics, and morality. The overview of theoretical perspectives about international law gives you grounding in the central concepts used to study international law. It further shows that theoretical perspectives are addressing different types of inquiries towards the role and nature of international law and enables you to identify the different ways in which international law is theorized.

Chapter 1

International law for international relations: foundations for interdisciplinary study

Başak Çalı

CHAPTER CONTENTS

- Introduction
- What is international law?
- The relationship between international law and international relations
- Why study international law?
- Conclusion

CHAPTER OVERVIEW

This chapter is about the relationship between international relations and international law—and aims to sketch out the most appropriate way to understand this relationship. The two disciplines are overlapping, but distinct, and this chapter will discuss the ways in which they converge and diverge in terms of disciplinary commitments and the types of knowledge they produce. The chapter will explain how international relations and international law can be interested in the same phenomena—sometimes for the same reasons and sometimes for different reasons. The chapter will then show how international law informs our understanding of single events in international affairs as well as change and continuity in the international system. The chapter will conclude by providing six important reasons to study international law for students of international relations.

Introduction

This textbook is intended primarily for the use of international relations and politics students. Its aim is to give an outline of the most important questions in international law and the significance of these questions for studying international relations. The textbook does not assume any background in law or international law. The book also does not pursue what may be termed a 'purely legal approach'. It aims to ground the study of international law within broader international political concerns and theoretical frameworks. It pays attention to the kinds of aims pursued by or through international law in international relations. It discusses the extent to which some international laws are foundations of international political interactions. It asks whether international law is in need of reform to meet the demands of current and future international politics.

Debates about the roles, functions, and purposes of international law in international relations are rich and complex. These debates require a clear approach in order to understand the relationship between international relations and international law. This introductory chapter aims to develop a methodology for approaching the relationship between these two disciplines and the focus of their inquiry.

The first question for a student of politics or international relations who sets out to study international law is 'What is international law and why study it?' Students

---

Box 1.1 The cynic and international law

The cynic regards international law as the enterprise of the naïve, the occupation of the wishful thinker, or the realm of the fool who does not understand international politics. For the cynic, all international law does, is offer some intricate language which politicians use to get their own way. This view cannot be correct. The cynic cannot account for the continuing existence of international law as an idea and as a practice. If everyone knows that international law is merely a means of manipulation, why was international law not abandoned some hundred years ago? Why, after each of the twentieth century's world wars, did we build institutions which have further entrenched international law? The problem with the cynic is that he or she grossly underestimates the intelligence of everyone who has worked for international institutions and their cooperation. This is not to say that international law is not used in a manipulative way in everyday politics. However, the survival of the idea and practice of international law after hundreds of years of manipulation shows us that there is something more to it than mere rhetoric. The real disagreement about international law, therefore, must be about how relevant it is in specific contexts and circumstances, not about whether it is relevant at all.

of international law, we can say, know what international law is—it is the law that regulates the relations between states—and study it because they see an intrinsic value in the subject. Students of politics and international relations may find this definition and motivation naïve. Are the relations between states *really* regulated? Why study rules, which are disputed and not regularly respected? So, a textbook on international law has to motivate the very keen international relations student as well as the very cynical. It has to clarify what international law is and the purpose of studying it.

What is international law?

The textbook definition that international law is the law that regulates relations between states gives us two important aspects of a definition of international law, namely that it is concerned with interstate regulation and that international law is different from other types of law. *Regulation* is an important general characteristic of all law. Law is *prescriptive* and it commands how all people ought to act in their relations with others. It also enables us to predict how actors may behave towards us. However, this definition is misleading in so far as international law can regulate other forms of relationships that states agree to regulate.

International law is different from other law such as *domestic law* and *conflict of laws* (or *private international law*). The former regulates relationships between natural and legal persons within a single country and the law that is applied is determined by the legislation of that country. The latter regulates relationships between natural and legal persons that happen to be in more than one country, such as relationships between companies in two different countries or between parents from two different countries over the custody of children. In such cases, courts have to decide the law of which country should be applied. It is for this reason that international law is sometimes also called *public international law*. This is to emphasize that its focus is interstate relations and not relations between private entities and domestic laws of any country cannot tell us what international laws are. Private entities, such as companies or individuals, however, can be *subjects* of international law. For example, international aviation is governed by international law because there are international treaties between states about it. Similarly, individuals can be prosecuted under international criminal law or claim rights against states under international human rights law because there are interstate treaties that make these possible. International law, therefore, regulates more than just interstate relations. It also regulates other forms of relationships that states agree to regulate internationally. International law regulates the conduct of actors that make up contemporary international society. International society is primarily made up of states. It is also made up of international organizations and non-state actors—such as armed groups or business enterprises and individuals—but only in so far as their status, powers, and responsibilities are recognized by states through international law.

An essential element of the definition of international law, therefore, is not its subject matter or the type of entities it regulates, but that it is law that is made by states collectively. No single state acting unilaterally can make international law; neither can a collection of corporations or individuals. In other words, the authority to make

---

Box 1.2 Areas of contemporary international law

This list is not exhaustive, but gives us an idea about the diversity of areas that international law relates to:

Airspace
Development
Bio-diversity
Climate change
Conduct of armed conflicts
Diplomatic and consular relations
Extradition
Finance
Fisheries
Human rights
Indigenous rights
Intellectual property
International crimes
Minority rights
Natural resources
Outer space
Ozone layer
Postal matters
Peace and security
Science and security
Sea
Trade
Use of force
Weapons

international law rests with states acting together. International organizations, individuals, and corporations can all become subjects of international law and have limited powers and international personality recognized under international law. They can also help clarify what international law is by interpreting it or they can appear in international courts. But they cannot make international law. This means that there are no predetermined limits as to what areas international law does or should regulate. This can only be determined through collective agreement amongst states.

The relationship between international law and international relations

International relations is interested in much broader phenomena than just the legal regulation of international affairs. International relations is interested in understanding how and why states and other actors on the international plane behave in the ways that they do, the nature of the international system, and the role of international actors, processes and discourses (see Chapter 2). International relations is more interested in what does in fact happen under certain conditions and how we can explain interactions and behaviour in international relations (although some international scholars may also propose how international relations should be conducted and what international institutions we should have).

Given this difference in focus in approaching international affairs, three preliminary questions are helpful to think about the relationship between international law and international relations.

These are:

1. Are international relations and international law two separate disciplines or are they different approaches within a single discipline?

2. How does the knowledge produced in international relations and international law overlap, conflict, and co-depend?

3. At what point and in what way does international law enter into international relations research?

Are international relations and international law two separate disciplines?

International relations and international law are two separate, but overlapping disciplines. Disciplines are a collection of a number of ground rules on how a subject matter is identified and there are invariably disagreements among the members of a discipline about what these ground rules are. How distinct the two disciplines are, therefore, depends on points of view within each discipline.

International law and international relations have common concerns as well as key differences. There is not, however, a straightforward answer or definitive list of differences and similarities. Students of both disciplines disagree about the proper boundaries between international law and international relations. More accurately, therefore, there are a number of lists (as we shall see in Chapters 2 and 3).

Let's start with the most basic similarity. International relations and international law are concerned with international phenomena. They share a curiosity about how we may identify international phenomena and how such phenomena relate to or affect domestic affairs and how domestic affairs inform international phenomena. Consider the following questions:

- How does a new state enter into the international system?

- What guides the behaviour of actors in the everyday life of international relations?

- Why do international organizations exist?

- Why have states created and signed up to international treaties in virtually every area of public policy?

- What is the significance of one or a collection of powerful states disregarding some established rule of international law?

- What are the differences between the powers and capacities of states and non-state actors in international law?

These questions are all about international phenomena. They focus on the significance, the role, the added value, and the future of international organizations, international cooperation and international regulation in international relations. It is easy to see why these questions are of interest to both disciplines. International relations seeks to understand and explain existing arrangements and institutions at the international level. It also aims to identify patterns or generalizations about behaviour in international relations. Normative branches of international relations aim to identify what duties, rights, and obligations states have towards each other and towards individuals or groups and what principles should govern international institutions and interactions. It is also necessary for international law to understand these because they raise important questions of appropriate boundaries of international regulation. That the two disciplines share an interest in the same phenomena does not necessarily mean, however, that the interest is shared for the same reasons.

Nor does it mean that the two disciplines attempt to address the phenomena in the same way (Ku et al. 2001).

International relations and international law can differ or overlap in their motivations for asking the questions above. They can also go about answering them in different, or overlapping ways. International relations and international law can be interested in the same phenomena for different reasons. They could also be interested in the same phenomena for the same reasons. Each of these reveals a different type of disciplinary relationship. The more divergent the reasons for interest in international phenomena, the more separate the two disciplines become. Conversely, the more similar the questions about the same phenomenon become, the more the disciplines overlap. Whether the two disciplines are distinct or not is dependent on how the research questions are framed.

There are two central independent variables that determine the nature of the relationship between international relations and international law.

1. Reasons motivating the asking of a question.

2. Reasons motivating the selection of procedures in order to answer a question.

The former indicates differences in terms of *approaches*. The latter indicates differences in *methodology*.

Differences in approach and methodology are key to understanding how different outcomes in terms of findings, views, and opinions are formulated with respect to the same subject matter. Approaches and methodologies, in this respect, are broader concepts than the concept of discipline. There will be, however, a core concentration of similar approaches and methodologies in every discipline, which will give the discipline its dominant colour. For example, realism (Chapter 2) in international relations and legal positivism (Chapter 4) in international law have been regarded as the most dominant approaches for a long time. International relations and international law contain a number of approaches and methodologies, which are discussed in greater detail in Chapters 2 and 4. Proponents of different approaches and methodologies in each discipline have strong disagreements about how the discipline should proceed to enhance its understanding of the subject matter. That is

Table 1.1 Approach, methodology, discipline

Approach	Methodology	Discipline
Ideas intended to deal with a subject	Justification of procedures to answer a question within a subject	A branch of knowledge that hosts a number of approaches and methodologies

Table 1.2 Interdisciplinary engagement

Scenario 1	Scenario 2	Scenario 3
Two separate approaches, some separate methodologies	Two separate approaches, but a single methodology	Two similar approaches with similar methodologies
Very different disciplines, hard to have anything common	Different disciplines, some common points	Full overlap between research agendas

why it is equally possible to have strong alliances between the disciplines of international relations and international law as well as a complete lack of interest in what goes on in the neighbouring discipline.

We can now start to understand what interdisciplinary disagreements are usually about. They can be between: any approach in international relations against another approach in international law or any methodology in international relations against another methodology in international law. This also tells us that it is not necessary that the relationship between two disciplines will always be about disagreements. Provided that the approaches or the methodologies overlap, the relationship can be one of mutual interest in the same type of questions for the same kind of reasons. For example, students of international relations who study the conditions of international cooperation may be thought as international lawyers in disguise or vice versa.

What is the most dominant disciplinary characteristic of international relations and international law? From what we have said so far, it is clear that not everyone will agree on a particular answer to this question. We may still find a distinction that most will agree on: international law is primarily interested in the *regulation* of international affairs. International relations is more interested in *understanding and explaining* them. The legal element has a more significant weight in international law, while in international relations it is the political element that takes centre stage. International lawyers ask when we have international law. International relations scholars ask how international actors behave.

These dominant characteristics guide which questions are viewed as worthy of higher or priority interest. For the international lawyer, for example, the central question is: what are the rules and principles that govern international relations and how do we identify such rules? For the international relations scholar, more

Table 1.3 Disciplinary differences

International relations	International law
Understanding and explaining international affairs	Regulation of international affairs

important is: what makes states support a particular norm in international relations and how do we know when support for that norm erodes or increases? We can see that these questions tackle the same type of issues, but have different concerns, approaches, and methodologies in mind. This may not, however, look as straightforward after further scrutiny. We can equally say that international relations students are interested in understanding international affairs and its politics because they are interested in how best to regulate it. They hope to propose prescriptions based on the general patterns of behaviour and structural generalizations. Conversely, international law cannot successfully regulate international affairs without understanding how a particular norm came to be accepted in the first place. Each discipline needs to inform the other in order to be successful. This shows us that international law and international relations can ask the same questions for different reasons.

In conclusion, it is possible to offer a qualified answer to the question of whether international law and international relations are two separate disciplines. Easy or simplistic answers will not do. The answer has more to do with identifying shared *attitudes* to international affairs in each discipline.

Final verdict: separate or the same?

1. International relations and international law are concerned with the same kind of phenomena: relationships, processes, institutions, events that take place in the international sphere.

2. Whether they are two separate disciplines or not is sensitive to the different approaches and methodologies that are hosted in these disciplines.

3. The two are not necessarily in fundamental conflict with each other in terms of positions they hold about international affairs. They may or may not be in conflict.

4. They are dependent on each other given that understanding or explaining international affairs may take its cue from the very regulation of these affairs and vice versa.

Table 1.4 Disciplinary convergences

International relations	International law
Understanding and explaining international affairs with the aim of its better regulation	Regulation of international affairs based on a grounded understanding of current international affairs

5. If there is an overlap in the approaches and methodologies, it is not possible to differentiate between the two.

6. The relationship between international relations and international law is generally understood in terms of the positions of the most dominant approach in both disciplines. This does not mean, however, that there is only one way of conceiving the relationship.

How does the knowledge produced in international relations and international law overlap, conflict, and co-depend?

This is a more concrete and practical kind of question. It can help us appreciate what use international law knowledge has when we are interested in a particular subject, such as use of force, nuclear weapons, war crimes tribunals, or international trade. We need to develop a similar kind of attitude here, as we did to the discipline question. The added value of international law knowledge in international relations depends on what kind of knowledge is generated in these disciplines.

Types of knowledge generated by international relations and international law

All forms of academic study concern knowledge generation. Knowledge generation is both an end in itself and a means of enhancing the practical world. Different types of knowledge are generated within disciplines. It would not be surprising to note that the different types of knowledge produced are sensitive to the approaches and methodologies one adopts.

It is possible to differentiate between four types of knowledge in the fields of international relations and international law. These are factual knowledge, empirical knowledge, conceptual knowledge, and normative knowledge. The emphasis placed on these types of knowledge, however, is different in international relations and international law.

Factual knowledge entails knowing something is the case. The current number of states, the number of international treaties, which states have signed up to a particular treaty are all factual types of knowledge. Given the interest of international law in the regulation of international affairs, accurate information about international treaties, the mandates and composition of international organizations, the relationship between different organizations at the international level, and the way in which international institutions operate matters to international law.

A factual statement such as 'The United Nations protects human rights' is not inaccurate for a student of international relations. For a student of international law, however, it is not completely accurate as it lacks both detail and appropriate differentiation. For the international lawyer, a factual statement would be: 'The United Nations Charter in its Articles 1, 55, and 56 has provisions for the protection of human rights. All organs of the UN have the duty to give effect to these provisions, but the specialized protection mechanism is the Human Rights Council which reports to the Economic and Social Council.'

The difference between the two statements captures the sensitivity to detail and precision in international law when talking about institutional arrangements. This is because different types of arrangements have different kinds of legal significance and they may point to different types of responsibility. A great advantage of studying international law in this respect is to acquire detailed knowledge of the workings of international organizations and their practices. Chapters in Part 3: Topics in international law provide legal-factual presentations of the most important topics in international law.

Empirical knowledge comes in qualitative or in quantitative ways. The more qualitative the knowledge, the more contextual and particular it is about a social event. The more quantitative it gets the more the knowledge will be subject to generalization and it will be inferred from a large number of events (Landman 2006). International relations generates both qualitative and quantitative empirical knowledge. Qualitative approaches utilize techniques such as single case studies and small comparative case studies. They could focus on how a particular set of actors understand or perceive the practices they are engaged in. Quantitative approaches focus on larger sets of data and try to uncover causal relationships or patterns. There are disagreements between quantitative and qualitative knowledge producers across the whole spectrum of social sciences (Creswell 2003). Qualitative empiricists think that the aim of producing generalizations does not capture the deep complexities embedded in each case. Quantitative empiricists think that qualitative empirical knowledge is unable to capture the big picture.

International law is an outsider to the vocabulary of qualitative and quantitative research techniques. It does, however, use both techniques to generate international legal knowledge. Some international lawyers believe that international law should overlap with the practice of states as much as possible. In order to locate international law they carry out quantitative analysis of state practice with the aim of discerning patterns in state behaviour. Some international lawyers see this as futile. International law can also be a consumer of quantitative knowledge produced in international relations.

It is also possible to qualify some types of knowledge in international law as qualitative. International lawyers, for example, focus on single case studies in terms of their significance in clarifying the status of international law (Rodley and Cali 2007). They also carry out comparative analysis (Crawford 1979). The key distinction between knowledge produced in international relations and international law in the empirical sense is *attitude* towards data collection and interpretation. International law is primarily interested in data that is defined as having legal significance (see Chapter 6). When international lawyers carry out case studies or comparative analyses, they filter the information they collect based on some criteria of legal significance and interpret the data in the light of its coherence with international law principles. This means that they are interested in empirical data in terms of its heuristic (interpretative) implications. International relations, however, has a much broader focus. It uses empirical data to test causal hypotheses as well as to understand social reality classified as practices, discourses, events, or processes.

Conceptual knowledge is about understanding the very concepts that are used to ground a systematic inquiry. It aims to identify the relevant concepts for inquiry as well as the hierarchy, categorization, and relationship between different concepts. The generation of conceptual knowledge extends to questioning the adequacy of existing concepts that ground the inquiry. It revises them and proposes new ones. Conceptual analysis is not about inquiring into what happens in practice. It is an inquiry into the *very idea* of the concepts as abstract categories. This form of knowledge may, of course, be sensitive to the practical meaning of concepts, but it nevertheless has to rise above practice for the concept to frame an inquiry. It, therefore, concerns itself with logical generalizations, distinctions, and categories that would help ground all types of queries. Conceptual knowledge is an indispensable component of any research design.

International relations and international law strongly overlap in the domain of production of conceptual knowledge. International relations borrows more from international law at this level of inquiry. Consider some of the central concepts for international relations such as state, consent, international society, war, peace, self-defence, self-determination, or humanitarian intervention. International law is an important resource in understanding the history and practical usage of these concepts in international affairs. It would be impossible, for example, to talk about international peace and security without reference to the collective security system of the United Nations Charter, which, after all, is a piece of international law. And we all know that Westphalia state system refers to two treaties signed in 1648—surprisingly neither in Westphalia—between the Holy Roman Emperor Ferdinand III of the Habsburg Dynasty, the Kingdoms of Spain, France, and Sweden, and the Dutch Republic (see Chapter 3).

An important reminder here is that international law is only one source of conceptual knowledge for international relations. International relations, for instance, also turns to political philosophy (Kratochwill 1989). At times, concepts grounded in international law will be different from those grounded in a particular strand of political philosophy (Meckled-Garcia and Cali 2006). Political philosophers and international lawyers will point to different definitions for the correct use of concepts (Buchanan 2004). But again, such issues are also the domain of conceptual knowledge to consider and debate.

Normative knowledge is the fourth category of knowledge that is produced in international relations and international law. It is concerned with what the state of affairs *ought to be*. This is generally opposed to factual or empirical knowledge which is concerned with what the state of affairs *is*. Normative research generates knowledge for 'ought' or 'should' type of questions. Consider, for example, the question 'How should we understand the legitimacy of international organizations?' This question does not aim to find out whether international organizations are regarded as legitimate. It instead aims to identify evaluative standards independent of any agent's perception that will ground the legitimacy of international organizations. Normative knowledge relies heavily on conceptual knowledge and less on empirical and factual knowledge.

In international relations, specialists in the domain of international ethics or international political theory generally define themselves as interested in normative knowledge. Some normative knowledge is purely idealist. It will only concern the ideal conditions of, for instance, legitimacy in international relations. Some normative knowledge can also incorporate what must be done to reach a certain state of desirable normative affairs (Buchanan and Keohane 2006). It will therefore be concerned not only with desirability, but also with feasibility. These types of normative projects will be more sensitive to factual and empirical knowledge.

One of the central modes of knowledge production in international law is normative. We could regard international law as producing legal normative knowledge about international affairs. The very idea of regulation is inevitably interested in what the content of the rules are and what reasons there are to follow them. International law is simultaneously interested in desirable and feasible forms of international conduct and organizational framework. This is because international lawyers are not concerned with the question of what norms *should* govern international affairs, but actually what norms *do* govern international affairs. International lawyers, therefore, assume that international law provides a distinct legal reason to act or to refrain from acting in particular ways for all states. For this reason, international law is a separate discipline from international morality. Most

Table 1.5　The knowledge production chart

International relations	Factual	Qualitative Quantitative	Conceptual	Normative (idealist/ realist)
International law	Factual/detailed in establishing legal facts	Qualitative Quantitative	Conceptual	Normative Realist

international law scholars think that international law is sandwiched between normative and factual-empirical type inquiries (Koskenniemi 1989). In other words, the question of what rules govern international affairs is at once normative, factual, and empirical.

In this light, it is possible to see why some normative international relations students may regard international law as disappointing, conservative and not progressive enough. They may be disappointed when they find out how international law addresses some of the most important contemporary challenges such as armed conflicts, climate change, nuclear proliferation, or human rights. But international law creates realistic normative knowledge. It would be pointless to have an international law that has no chance of being accepted or implemented by states or other actors. International law, therefore, thinks that it has to be grounded in the practice of states (the disagreements about what this means will be addressed in Chapters 4 and 6). Therefore, the student of international relations has to be as wary of the idealist as s/he has to be of the cynic.

At what point and in what way does international law enter into international relations research?

We have so far looked at what types of knowledge are generated by international law and international relations and the extent to which these types of knowledge overlap, differ and co-depend. There is one further element we need to consider: when does the knowledge produced in international law become relevant in international relations? There are at least two views. According to the practical view, international law can enter into international relations analysis with its ability to offer practical insight into assigning meanings to the events in everyday international affairs. Another view, the systemic view, is an argument about the value of international law knowledge to better understand the international system, how different parts of the system fit together and what the bigger picture of international affairs looks like.

The single event lens

The practical insight of international law comes when we are analysing a single event in international relations. One of the important aspects of international relations and international law is the training both disciplines give students on how to best produce informed commentary about ongoing political affairs. A very important reason for any student signing up to courses on international relations or international law is to learn how to better understand contemporary international affairs and particular problems within them. For example, how should we approach the declarations of independence by East Timor and Kosovo? What do these mean? Are they lawful? Are they desirable? What sorts of effects do they have for other groups? What role did international law have in facilitating support for the independence? When faced with a specific event, international law differs in approaching it because it selects and processes facts and evidence in a different way. It focuses on the legal significance or legal consequences of events. It provides reasons for explaining why states have acted in a certain way, for example, why they have recognized East Timor unanimously and why unanimous recognition was not forthcoming in the case of Kosovo. Through studying international law we are able to better understand the instances when international law is not followed and why.

In everyday life it is common to hear commentators referring to what is called the 'international law' perspective or the 'international relations' perspective. When a military intervention takes place or when a state refuses to extradite a terrorist suspect to another country it is common to ask 'what does international law say on the matter?' This question tells us that people in general assume that a regulatory view about international affairs exists. It also tells us that this view is valued as worth knowing. Experts on international relations are asked to comment on different aspects of issues. What would be the reactions of other states to a military intervention? What would the political consequences of this event be? Some common questions may also be asked of both experts: 'Would the international law

Table 1.6 Description and evaluation of single events

International relations	International law
Political qualification of events, acts, processes	Legal qualification of events, acts, processes
Assessment of consequences of events, acts, processes in terms of their broader political significance	Assessment of events, acts, processes in terms of their broader legal significance
Assessment of compliance with regulatory frameworks	Assessment of compliance with regulatory frameworks

framework be followed on this matter by states? What would happen if states act contrary to international law?'

International law enables the student of international relations to identify the normative rules and principles that are thought to govern a particular event in international affairs. Once this framework is identified, it is possible to analyse the extent to which states are complying or conforming. In a single event lens, international law gives states reasons to act or refrain from acting in a certain way. International relations is then able to analyse why these are strong or weak reasons in particular instances.

International law invites students to process empirical facts in a different way than international relations. International law enables us: (1) to process the facts in terms of their international legal significance and (2) to comment on the legal consequences of acts and events. International relations is able to show: (1) the political significance of the events or acts and (2) possible consequences of the events or acts for the future in terms of the actors that are concerned. Both disciplines use descriptive and evaluative schemes. The same event can be described and evaluated in different ways within each discipline. Depending on the approach one adopts, international law and international relations students may pay attention to how an event is classified in the other discipline. This is, however, not necessary and only approach-sensitive. It is perfectly possible for a student of international relations to hold that, neither (1) the legal qualification, nor (2) the legal consequences are relevant or that both are crucial to understanding the political qualification or consequences. The same holds for a student of international law.

International law, therefore:

1. sets out what the rules governing an event are;
2. gives reasons for actors to act in a certain ways; and
3. evaluates what the legal consequences of acting or refraining from acting in a certain way are.

Whilst international relations:

1. evaluates the relevance and importance of reasons provided by international law;
2. explains why they are or not followed in specific instances; and
3. evaluates the political consequences of acting or refraining from acting in a certain way.

The systemic lens

A common concern that runs through both disciplines is identifying the systemic characteristics of international affairs. This concern comes in many shapes. First, who are the central actors in the international system? Is the emphasis on states as the main players and law-makers adequate? How should we understand the role of international organizations, global governance regimes, and non-state actors in international affairs? Focusing on actors beyond the state affects how research questions are formulated in both disciplines. For example, what is the role of private military companies in current conflicts? Do we need to regulate the activities of these companies in international law? Should we hold non-state actors accountable in international law?

A second concern is how we go about identifying and understanding the systemic values of the international system. What are the constitutive values upon which international relations are based? How do we identify what these values are? Which discipline is better equipped to understand and expose the value system of international affairs? In what ways do international relations and international law differ in their identification of systemic values?

Third, there is a concern about how we may evaluate the system-wide changes in the international system. What have been the greatest achievements of the international system? Has there been an increase in international cooperation? Should international relations be assessed in terms of the expansion of values such as justice, human rights, self-determination, or democracy? Is there an increase in cooperation and regulation in the international system over the years? Is it better regulated? What has been the contribution of international law to system-wide changes in international relations? These, as one would expect, are very important and contested grand debates, within and across the two disciplines.

If we leave aside the sceptic's objection that international law has nothing to contribute to understanding the systemic values in international relations, there are at least two ways in which international law enters into system-wide debates in international relations. First, international law may represent the ideals of the international system, such as peaceful coexistence and effective cooperation. Actors in international affairs may be viewed as under a duty to work towards these ideals, even though they may not always succeed in everyday politics.

Table 1.7 Common concerns

The central role of the state as an analytical category	Values that underlie the international system	System-wide changes in international relations
Institutional design	Compliance with international law	Providing solutions to common problems

This is an idealist approach to international law. A second view holds that international law may represent the background values of international politics. The basic political ideas of the international system, such as non-intervention, political equality of states, and state sovereignty are embedded in international law. International law contributes to international relations by hosting its basic and constitutive ideas. This is a constitutive approach to international law. On both accounts international law offers starting points and critical tools to the student of international relations to understand the change and continuity of system-wide values.

Why study international law?

It is now time to go back to the question we started with: Why study international law? We have emphasized two main claims in this chapter to lay the groundwork for this question. First, although international relations and international law appear to be separate disciplines, their degree of separation very much depends on how participants in these disciplines define their research interests and concerns. International law can be studied from any of the perspectives within international relations and different theoretical frameworks will assign different kinds of significance to international law. Second, we suggested that the types of knowledge production might overlap in international relations and international law. What we have found is that there are different ways in which a student of international relations may be motivated in studying international law. Here is a list of six reasons for crossing from international relations to international law.

1. International law can be appealed to when developing views within international relations

International law is an institutional practice with a long history and presence in the international system, as we shall see in Chapter 3. It has undergone a number of changes, and these changes have increased tremendously since 1945 with the emergence of international human rights law, international trade law, international criminal law, and international humanitarian law regimes. International law as a domain of institutional practice is important and exists as a matter of fact. Contemporary theories of international relations have to develop an account of what these networks and regimes mean for the state of the international system and its future and how dense they are.

2. International law can be studied in order to have an understanding of the operation of international organizations and institutions

All international organizations appeal to basic principles of international law in their operations. International organizations, in this respect, exist by virtue of international law. The workings of the United Nations (UN) General Assembly, the UN Security Council, the UN Peace-building Commission, the UN Human Rights Council only become clear after a study of the UN Charter and relevant decisions, declarations, resolutions of these bodies. There are also an increasing number of institutional arrangements that we cannot analyse without a clear understanding of their status and mandate in international law. Consider for example, peacekeeping or peace enforcement missions authorized by the Security Council or the refugee camps run by the UN High Commission for Refugees or the International Red Cross and Red Crescent, which is recognized to have a special mandate under international humanitarian law treaties and domestic laws.

3. International law can be studied to understand the history of interstate practice over the years

International law has a memory of state practice in a historical context. We can compare the amount and kinds of cooperation states had in previous centuries with the current situation by studying the international treaties in a historical perspective. International law gives us an idea about the acceptable basis of interstate cooperation and how states deal with the most pressing issues of their times through international law. A comparison, for example, between the League of Nations and the UN offer us an understanding of international affairs in terms of which ideas have been institutionalized and how effective such institutionalization has proved. This is also very important when we talk about the reform of the international system. International law enables us to have a historically informed attitude towards what may be feasible for the future of international law.

4. International law can be studied to find out what the distinct international law position is on any aspect of international affairs

There are a number of views that can be offered on a particular debate in international affairs. There could be the subjective view, i.e. an account of what any stakeholder thinks is the case. There could be the normative view, i.e. an account of what would be the best position to be adopted by anyone. Finally, there could be the international law view, i.e. an account of what would be the correct conduct or outcome in international law. For the student of international relations interested in understanding how international actors conduct themselves, the international law perspective is indispensable as international law aims to offer established standards of conduct. For the future policy-maker or politician, it is imperative to be able to critically appraise whether the current rules of international law are worth following or supporting or whether they are in need of fundamental revision. International law, therefore, is particularly important for international relations students who wish to criticize the actual conduct of states or would like to propose changes to existing arrangements.

5. International law can be studied with the purpose of understanding the power of its norms and the rise and fall of international legal frameworks

A central reason to engage with international law is to assess the extent to which the norms embedded in international law guide and control state behaviour. There are a number of scenarios that may emerge in any area of international relations at any time. One scenario is that some new development may take place, for example, the possibility of exploitation of resources on the moon. It would then be necessary to assess whether there are already a number of norms that govern this area or whether different norms emerge that are able to address the concerns in a more specific way. Another scenario would be the case of states withdrawing their support from an international law rule. This would lead us to question what made the rule inadequate and what replaces it instead. Yet another scenario is the sphere of contested norms and how a student of international relations can distinguish between a norm with weak support and a contested norm. A final systematic issue would be the circumstances under which a fundamental international legal norm may undergo change or reform. International law not only provides indicators about where the most pressing problems lie with respect to the power of norms, it also offers perspectives to international relations students about how to assess the rise and demise of international law.

6. International law is worth studying because it is a site where we can engage with both ideas and practice about international affairs

The final answer to the *Why international law?* question is one about developing a certain kind of attitude to international affairs. International law contributes to how we think about international relations as a whole and the basic aims of international society. This is a different orientation of thinking, especially as opposed to thinking about the basic aims of states. More significantly, contemporary international law, with its focus stretching beyond interstate relations to areas such as the environment, human rights, trade, development, allows students of international relations to engage with questions about a fair international system and the possibility of such a system under contemporary political conditions. International law with one foot in the practice of international affairs and another one in principles and norms is a perfect location to think about the future of international relations.

Conclusion

This chapter gave an account of how to approach the relationship between international relations and international law. It showed that there is no single answer in conceiving this relationship and that it all depends on the approaches and methodologies adopted in both disciplines. The ways to understand the relationship between these two disciplines are as many as the approaches and methodologies hosted in them. One way to distinguish the two is to suggest that international relations is concerned with explaining and describing international affairs as they stand whilst international law regulates these affairs by setting standards of conduct. But, we have also seen that even this simple distinction has to be accepted with caution.

A sound way of understanding how international relations and international law contribute to each other is to become aware of the type of knowledge provided in these disciplines. Again, we saw that saying that international relations is in the business of empirical knowledge and international law in normative knowledge is simplistic. Both disciplines produce factual, empirical, conceptual, and normative knowledge. They, however, are interested in facts and empirical knowledge in different ways. We saw that the disciplines come very close to each other in the production of conceptual knowledge. In the domain of normative knowledge, international law can be classified as a special branch of normative international relations theories, as it produces normative knowledge based on realistic and practically grounded premises.

International law makes a unique contribution to our understanding of day-to-day international affairs by offering standards of conduct to evaluate the behaviour of international actors. At the level of system-wide analysis, international law is an important resource for students of international relations. Studying international law is an important way to grasp the facts of international life, as well as the values underpinning it. More importantly, studying international law requires disciplinary awareness for a student of international relations. A systematic study of international law is a way to become a better student of international relations.

Questions

1. What is international law and how is it different from domestic law?
2. What are the areas regulated by international law?
3. What does the sceptic say about international law?
4. What do you think is the most significant difference between international relations and international law?
5. What is factual knowledge? Can you give an example?
6. What is empirical knowledge? Can you given an example?
7. What is conceptual knowledge? Can you give an example?
8. What is normative knowledge? Can you give an example?
9. How do international relations and international law differ in assessing a single event?
10. What can international law contribute to international relations in understanding system-wide changes?
11. Why should a student of international relations study international law?

Further reading

Abbott, K. W., Keohane, R. O., Moravscik, A., Slaughter, A.-M., and Snidal, D. (2000) 'The Concept of Legalisation', *International Organization* 54/3: 401–19 and compare it to Finnemore, M. and Toope, J. (2001) 'Alternatives to "Legalisation": Richer Views of Law and Politics' *International Organization* 55/3: 741–56. *A good example of two groups of international relations scholars disagreeing on the definition of international law and international legal frameworks and their significance in international law.*

Buchanan, A. and Keohane, R. (2006) 'The Legitimacy of Global Governance Institutions' *Ethics and International Affairs* 20/4: 405–37. *An example of a normative and reform-oriented analysis of legitimacy in international relations.*

Ku, C., Diehl, P. F., Simmons, B., Dallmeyer, D. G., and Jacobson, H.K. (2001) 'Exploring International Law: Opportunities and Challenges for Political Science Research: *A Roundtable' International Studies Review* 3/1: 3–23. *A collection of essays on why international relations students have neglected international law and how they can increase the quality and quantity of research on international law.*

Simmons, B. and Steinberg, R. H. (2006) (eds.), *International Law and International Relations* (Cambridge: Cambridge University Press). *An excellent collection of essays on different permutations of the relationship between the disciplines of international law and international relations.*

Websites

Visit the Online Resource Centre that accompanies this book to access more learning resources
www.oxfordtextbooks.co.uk/orc/cali/

Chapter 2

Perspectives on international law in international relations

Fiona B. Adamson and Chandra Lekha Sriram

CHAPTER CONTENTS

- Introduction
- Realism
- Liberalism
- Institutionalism
- Constructivism
- Marxism, Feminism, and Critical Theory
- Conclusion

CHAPTER OVERVIEW

This chapter examines how international relations (IR) scholarship perceives international law (IL). International law often appears to be relatively invisible in theories of IR, and thus students of IR may question the need to study international law. This chapter argues nevertheless that much of IR theory engages implicitly, if not explicitly, with international law. It does so, however, by using very different terminology, language, and approaches. IR scholarship which directly engages with international legal agreements and legally constituted institutions often approaches them through the language of norms, institutions, and regimes, rather than through the language of law. In this chapter we explore some of the dominant theoretical paradigms in IR, and consider in turn how each views the role of international law in international politics. For each paradigm, we present its general theoretical assumptions, its key actors and processes and how it perceives international law.

Introduction

What perspectives on international law (IL) are found in the field of international relations (IR)? In the previous chapter, we learned that IR and IL can be thought of as overlapping, yet distinct, disciplines which concern themselves with similar phenomena. Both IR and IL are interested in questions relating to international order and state behaviour in world politics. Yet they may ask different types of questions, employ very different starting assumptions, and use different approaches and methodologies in their inquiries.

The discipline of international relations is organized into different *paradigms*. Paradigms are philosophical and theoretical frameworks that guide intellectual inquiry by suggesting what subject matter should be focused on and how the subject matter should be approached and understood. Most students of international relations are familiar with some of the major paradigms or theoretical approaches in the field, such as Realism and Liberalism. They will have noticed, perhaps, that theoretical approaches and debates in international relations rarely refer to international law, or that when they do, they often treat it as of little or no significance. It therefore might be easy to conclude that an understanding of international law would be irrelevant to students of international relations.

This chapter takes a different position. It argues that each of the major paradigms in IR engages with questions relating to international law. The study of international law therefore adds to one's understanding of international relations. Much of the engagement with international law by IR theory, however, is implicit rather than explicit. Many objects of study in international relations are heavily legal in content, but are described using the language, terminology, and assumptions of IR theory. In order to understand the ways in which IR and IL address common concerns, it is important to become familiar with the different language and approaches used in the two disciplines.

IR scholars, for example, speak about institutions, regimes, norms, and organizations, rather than treaties, conventions, customary law, or legally created institutions. IR scholars, like IL scholars, are concerned with major issues of importance in global politics, such as human rights and the environment. However, in their work IR scholars will speak about international human rights or international environmental *regimes*, whereas IL scholars will refer to international human rights law or international environmental *law*. This may be what Anne-Marie Slaughter Burley has referred to as IR scholars '[re]discovering international law (and refusing to recognize it)' (Slaughter Burley 1993: 219).

IR scholars rarely focus on international legal standards per se, but rather on the shared understandings, agreements, and institutions that make up the international legal order. IR scholars are thus likely to address international law concerns by studying the development and maintenance of, and the compliance with international 'norms, rules and regimes'. Nevertheless, even within IR there is great disagreement as to the origins and evolution of international legal norms, rules, and institutions. This disagreement reflects the different starting assumptions and emphases of the different theories that define IR.

In this chapter, we address how IR views and studies international law through a discussion of some of the major paradigms, or theoretical approaches, in the discipline. We discuss Realism, Liberalism, Institutionalism, Constructivism, Marxism, Feminism, and Critical Theory—and examine how they each view international law. As we discuss each theory, we focus on its general view of the international system, the key actors in it, and key processes related to the creation and maintenance of, and compliance with, rules and laws. In so doing, we elaborate upon each theory's view of the relevance and influence of international law in general, as well as suggesting how theories of IR seek to explain rules, institutions, and processes which are legalized in nature. We provide some concrete examples in each section of issue areas in which IR engages with IL, such as regulating the use of force, or protecting human rights. Many of these issues will be discussed in far greater detail in the individual chapters to come in this volume.

Realism

Theory

Realism is an approach to IR that emphasizes state power, national security, and the threat or use of force as the most important elements for understanding world politics. Realists often trace their origins back to classical theorists such as *Thucydides* (460 B.C.–395 B.C.), *Machiavelli* (1469–1527), and *Hobbes* (1568–1679) who all emphasized how power and self-interest shape politics.

Realists are arguably the most cynical of IR scholars with respect to the value of studying IL. Many realists would argue that most of international law is *epiphenomenal* to state power, in other words that the contours of international law and its effectiveness are a product of the interests of powerful states or the balance of power amongst states, but that international law does not exert an independent effect on states: powerful states will follow international law when it is in their national interest and will ignore it when it is not; weak states will comply with international law when they are compelled to by powerful states. This view of international law reflects the famous dictum proposed by Thucydides, 'The strong do what they can, and the weak suffer what they must.'

Realists have traditionally argued that they seek to understand world politics as it is, rather than as it should be. They have contrasted themselves with 'Idealists' who seek to build a better world through institutions and rule of law. International law is then viewed by some realists as a type of 'Idealism' and is critiqued for its naïve view of power. Yet, this division is too simplistic. Most approaches to international law are very sensitive to state power relations and many realists recognize the need for international law. Early realist IR scholars, such as E.H. Carr (1939), argued that one needs a good dose of both 'realism' and 'utopianism' to properly understand international politics. Some contemporary realists employ realist assumptions and principles in their critique of international law in order to identify the limits of its efficacy such that it might be improved. An example of this is the work of Jack Snyder and Leslie Vinjamuri (2003/4) on human rights and transitional justice, who have argued that political stability and strong institutions should take short-term precedence over legal norms in achieving justice in post-conflict situations in order to strengthen the rule of law over the long term.

Actors

Realists view states as the primary actors in the international system. In other words, states are treated as natural actors in world politics. In fact, IR scholars often discuss sovereign states interacting in an institutional and legal void that is described as a 'state of nature' or **anarchy** (meaning a lack of sovereign authority or government). Kenneth Waltz, in his influential book *Theory of International Politics* (1979), famously viewed states as the only relevant units for understanding the structure of world politics. Waltz and other realists argue that state behaviour is best explained by the **balance of power** in the international system, as measured by material factors, such as size of territory and population, and the strength of the military and economy. If one wishes to understand world politics, according to this perspective, the important factor is to understand which states have the most power in the international system. Within this context, international law is largely irrelevant. States do not respond primarily to legal rules, but rather to practical considerations determined by the amount of power they have vis-à-vis other states. Ultimately, the contours of the international system are shaped by power and the use of force, and not by international law.

Such approaches make it difficult for realist IR scholars to analyse developments in international organizations and international law in which states voluntarily comply with international law, give up aspects of their sovereignty, or share sovereignty with other actors. It also means that realists have a difficult time studying international organizations or international legal orders as anything more than the outcome of state interests. A key example here would be the emergence of the European Union as an entity in which states have pooled their authority and have delegated aspects of their sovereignty to a supranational organization. Such institutional arrangements are difficult to understand from a purely state-centric and power politics perspective. For example, the introduction of the Euro as a common currency in many EU states, and the emergence of a European common monetary policy, poses a puzzle to realists, as it suggests a willingness of EU states to relinquish national autonomy and sovereignty in a key area of domestic economic policy.

Processes

A realist perspective on the emergence and maintenance of international norms, many of which are legalized, follows from its understanding of the key actors in international politics and the nature of the international system. Realists, with their focus on state power and their scepticism of legal approaches to world politics, would understand the emergence of legal norms, rules, and institutions as being largely a product of the interest and influence of powerful states. In its most cynical form, international law and its application can be viewed as a form of *victors' justice* that reflects the interests of the powerful. In this view, the laws of war codified in the late nineteenth century represent the interests and views of the powerful Christian states; norms of decolonization and self-determination can be viewed as emerging out of the US challenge to the old order of European empires; the international legal order embedded in the United Nations can be viewed as a codification of both the power structure (membership of the UN Security Council) and normative commitments (liberal individualism as a focus of human rights law) that reflected US interests at the end of World War II.

Thus a realist would view the creation, maintenance, and frequent compliance by states with international legal rules regarding, for example, the use of force, as a matter of power and self-interest. Realists would argue that states create rules limiting use of force and conduct during armed conflict for self-interested reasons and will similarly feel no compunction about violating those rules when they cease to be in their interest. If a state sees a benefit in breaking the rules against the use of force, perhaps because it doesn't expect any sanction to be imposed and is sufficiently powerful to use force successfully, they would argue that it is likely to do so. Similarly, realists argue that states only agree to international humanitarian law (IHL) when it coincides with their own interests. States agree to the **Geneva Conventions** (see Chapter 11) (the four treaties forming the basis of international humanitarian law) in order to avoid having their own soldiers tortured, or civilians intentionally targeted. However, they would argue that powerful states are just as quick to violate such rules when they view it as being in their own self-interest to do so. From a realist perspective, this might explain why the United States would appear to have ignored international humanitarian law in its pursuit of the 'war on terror' during the years of the Bush administration.

Realists make similar arguments about the creation of international legal institutions to respond to war crimes and atrocities. For example, they might explain prosecutions after World War II in the Nuremberg Trials as 'victors' justice'. Similarly, realists could argue that the creation of a tribunal to prosecute crimes in the former Yugoslavia stemmed primarily from the interests of Western states in a stable Europe rather than the pursuit of justice. Some realists claim that states only sign on to human rights obligations when they serve their interests, or impose no real constraints. For example, simply reporting levels of human rights compliance to monitoring committees may not be viewed as a particularly onerous obligation for states and this would explain why it is relatively widespread.

Liberalism

Theory

Liberal and institutionalist arguments in international relations (discussed in the next section below) are often intertwined, as liberal institutionalism, and have often been offered by the same IR scholars. However, it is useful to disaggregate the two and identify elements of liberal IR theory, beyond those linked to institutionalism (Moravcsik 1997).

Liberal IR theory makes a number of assumptions which contradict at least in part the realist view of the international system. They disagree, first, that the structure of the international system (in other words, international anarchy or lack of world government, and the balance of power) is the primary determinant of state behaviour. They instead point to internal facts including the type of government and constitutional order that states have, as well as other factors such as domestic politics, civil society, and individual beliefs. Liberals focus on the interests and preferences of actors, and how preferences are aggregated and negotiated.[1] Thus, governments represent the interests of at least some segment of the domestic polity, even if they are not demo-cratic. Therefore, their behaviour in the international system reflects to some degree the preferences of internal actors. Individual states may each pursue their own self-interest, but they do not necessarily conceive of that interest identically or behave identically.

A central argument of liberal IR theory is that the nature of the domestic political and constitutional order matters for understanding state behaviour. Liberal and democratic states, on this logic, are more likely to comply with international law and to conduct their relations, at least with other liberal democratic states, in a legally ordered fashion. This is in part due to the adherence to the rule of law present in the domestic order, and the constraining effect of a democratically empowered electorate and civil society. This is related to arguments that some liberals make regarding the *democratic peace*.

Much as the democratic peace theory argues that democracies fight each other less, for reasons both normative and structural, some liberal IR scholars suggest that liberal democracies are more likely to adhere to international obligations. This is again for reasons that are both normative and structural: countries that purport to adhere to the rule of law domestically may see similar virtues in supporting it internationally; similarly, domestic legal structures in democratic states may be better adapted to incorporate international obligations, or may even be shaped so as to require it. This of course ought not be overstated: the US, as the world's most powerful democracy, has not only 'unsigned' the ICC treaty, and publicly cam-paigned against it, but has failed to ratify international legal agreements such as the Kyoto Protocol or the United Nations Convention on the Rights of the Child. Moravcsik (2000) suggests that it is not necessarily strong democracies that sign on to human rights agreements, but rather newly democratizing countries, which use such agreements as a safeguard against returning to old authoritarian ways.

Box 2.1 The democratic peace thesis

The democratic peace thesis claims that democracies are unlikely to fight each other. Prominent liberal IR scholars who have advanced the democratic peace thesis are Michael Doyle (1983) and Bruce Russett (1994). A number of different explanations have been given for the finding that democratic states are unlikely to go to war with each other. Some explanations emphasize the role played by shared liberal norms and values. Other expla-nations focus on the institutional constraints on war found in democratic systems, the transparency of information provided by a free press, or other factors such as trade ties and interdependence.

Liberal IR scholars in general are arguably much more sympathetic to the role played by international law in world politics than realists are. Their focus on the interests of actors and how those are aggregated by domestic institutions and constitutional structures resonates with a legal perspective on political order. In other words, both liberal IR theorists and international legal scholars share a focus on the roles played by institutions and rules in creating political order. An additional characteristic of liberalism that resonates with an international law perspective is the liberal belief in progress in international relations. Whereas realists tend to view international politics as an unchanging and ongoing power struggle amongst states, liberals generally are optimistic about the role that rules and institutions can play in creating international order, reducing conflict, and fostering greater levels of cooperation between states.

Actors

Liberal IR scholars do not reject the realist premise that states are important actors in the international system, but they do reject the claim that they are the only units of analysis worth studying. They argue for the need to open the supposed black box of the state, and understand that states behave differently in the international system even though they all have a similar interest in survival. This, they argue, is due to variations in regime type, and the influence of domestic actors in international politics.

In addition, liberals give a greater weight than realists do to the role played by *international organizations* (IOs) and **non-governmental organizations** (NGOs) as actors in world politics. Liberals' concern with interests and institutions at the domestic level of states lead them to also pay attention to how interests are articulated and how institutions function at the global level. In addition to the international states system, liberals are concerned with the functioning of international organizations as political institutions, which act as arenas for state interaction and interest articulation. Just as liberals are concerned with constitutional orders and the rule of law at the level of the state, they acknowledge the role that international legal institutions play in international politics, including regional and international courts. Similarly, liberals place a greater weight on the importance of non-governmental organizations (NGOs) in world politics than realists do. NGOs are viewed by liberals as being part of a *global civil society* of non-state actors and interest groups that exists in parallel to the state system. Thus, NGOs such as Amnesty International or Greenpeace represent international constituencies with interests in human rights or the environment, and play an important role in international politics in placing issues on the international agenda and in lobbying states and international organizations. Such dynamics, alongside traditional areas of realist concern, like interstate competition and power politics, are key aspects of world politics for liberals.

Processes

Liberals would explain the emergence of international legal norms and rules rather differently than realists. Instead of focusing on international legal norms as the outcome of power relations in the international system, they might focus on how norms and rules emerge in domestic contexts (see above) and then spread to the international sphere. Liberals, in contrast to realists, argue that states often comply with UN rules regarding the use of force and with IHL for reasons beyond simple self-interest. Rather, there may be a set of domestic actors and interest groups which promote rule-governed behaviour: pressure groups, citizens, political parties, or the judiciary. As a corollary, some liberals have put forward the notion that liberal states based on the 'rule of law' domestically are more likely to comply with these obligations than non-liberal states which may be less constrained by judges or civil society.

Liberals also tend to focus on the functional role played by international law—understanding its emergence as a means for states to reach cooperation in areas in which they have common interests. International norms and rules create shared expectations, increased transparency, and the possibilities of iterated interaction—all of which help states to overcome problems of **collective action**. Liberals are therefore more likely than realists to focus on **international regimes** as important features of world politics. International regimes have been classically defined by Stephen Krasner (1983: 1) as 'principles, norms, rules, and decision-making procedures around which actor expectations converge in a given issue-area'. Notice that this definition might include, but is not confined to, international law. Furthermore, the definition does not explicitly refer to international law, legal norms or institutions, and nor, for the most part, does the body of IR literature on international regimes.

This is a key difference in the approach, language, and terminology of IR scholars that distinguishes it from international legal scholarship. It means that IR scholars interested in the use of force, humanitarianism, human rights, refugees, trade, and the environment will refer to the international regime that exists in each of these areas rather than referring to bodies of international human rights law or international environmental law as such. There are some exceptions to this, such as the growing international relations literature that explicitly examines the question of *legalization* in world politics (Goldstein et al. 2000). However, students of international relations can gain much from having an understanding of international legal scholarship on international human rights law, international refugee law, international trade law, or international environmental law as elaborating on key components of the IR literature on the international human rights regime, the international refugee regime, international trade regime, or international environmental regime.

Institutionalism

Theory

International relations scholars who view themselves as institutionalists have developed a rational actor, functionalist approach to the development of international law or institutions that is consistent with both realist and liberal tenets. Scholars such as Robert Keohane have argued that states create institutions out of self-interest in order to facilitate cooperation, to help them to achieve goals and aims which they could not do singly (Keohane and Martin 1995). Institutions, then, are not created so much to bind and limit states as to enable them to pursue their interests. Institutionalists combine realist and liberal perspectives on international law by focusing on the *rational self-interest* of states. The perspective taken by most institutionalists has become known as *rationalism*, which can be contrasted with social constructivism, which is discussed in the next section.

Actors

For institutionalists, states are still key actors in the international system, but so too are the institutions which they create, which can come to have an autonomous agency of their own. Institutionalists recognize that states often create organizations and regimes in large part for self-interested reasons: states create institutions that facilitate activities in which they wish to engage, such as trade, or that ease the risks of interstate negotiations, such as those over arms control. Informal institutions and regimes can become more deeply institutionalized and formalized over time, eventually resulting in a formal international organization (IO). Classic examples of this are the General Agreement on Tariffs and Trade (GATT), which developed into the more formalized World Trade Organization (WTO) in 1995 (see Chapter 15), or the Conference for Security and Cooperation in Europe (CSCE) which eventually became the Organization for Security and Cooperation in Europe (OSCE).

Institutionalists argue that because institutions or regimes facilitate transparency, reduce transactions costs, and reduce the risks of cheating, states will create rules and abide by them. International institutions foster iterated interactions among states, thus increasing what **game theorists** refer to as *the shadow of the future*. This simply means that, when states interact repeatedly with one another in institutions, they begin to take a long-term rather than short-term perspective on their relationships. This encourages greater levels of *reciprocity*, leading to higher levels of cooperation and stability.

Box 2.2 Game theory and international cooperation

Because of its focus on rational self-interest, institutionalism lends itself to the formal modelling of game theoretic approaches. Game theory uses mathematics to model strategic interactions based on the preferences of actors. It has been widely used in some branches of international relations to understand the dynamics of interstate cooperation. Game theory experiments have shown that actors who interact repeatedly may obtain cooperation over time by using a tit-for-tat strategy of reciprocating their opponent's behaviour (Axelrod 1984). Since international institutions help to create stable expectations and foster long-term interaction, they can, through a similar logic, help to create cooperation among states.

Many institutionalists will also argue that once created, institutions develop an identity and power of their own, constraining state behaviour even where states may wish to deviate from agreed rules. Path dependency ensures that institutions are easier to maintain than they are to create. Institutions and regimes, once created, may have more enduring power than states initially anticipate. They may be set up initially because of the self-interested concerns of states, but because of their ability to reduce transaction costs, increase transparency, and enable regularity and stability, they can come to constrain state behaviour even well after they cease to serve state interests. Regimes therefore serve not just the needs of the powerful but also the rational calculations of all states. Institutionalists argue that states are usually more concerned with achieving *absolute gains* than *relative gains*, and thus will

---

Box 2.3 Relative versus absolute gains

The debate over whether states are more concerned with absolute gains (i.e. doing better than previously) or relative gains (i.e. how they fare compared with other states) when they cooperate, was an important debate between realists and liberals in the field of international relations in the 1990s. The debate has converged into a common rationalist perspective on state behaviour that focuses increasingly on the importance of institutional design in creating mixes of incentives and constraints that affect states' rational calculations.

value the role that institutions play in facilitating collective action and cooperation, leading all states to be better off over time.

Processes

Institutionalists argue that institutions create stable expectations, facilitate cooperation and linkages, and help set standards of legitimate behaviour. These theorists have also come to focus on questions of rational institutional design and function, and how compliance with international norms—and/or international law—is achieved. In other words, why do states comply with international norms and political agreements? Why do states comply with international law? A key argument here is that even without coercion and central enforcement, legal rules and procedures can help shape the structure of international politics by creating incentives for rational self-interested states to engage in sustained cooperation with one another. By fostering iterated interaction, international institutions help states to come to value long-term mutual engagement on issues, allowing them to develop patterns of reciprocity and stable expectations about the behaviour of other states.

Institutionalist theory is, at its core, about explaining the creation and main-tenance of, and compliance with, more or less formalized rules and institutions in the international system. They may seldom describe them as legal, but much of what they discuss are legally created and regulated institutions. This phenom-enon occurs across a range of issue areas in international politics. States agree collectively to self-restrain by limiting whaling, or banning trade in endangered species, because, over the long term, they have individual and shared interests in the protection of species and the environment. Similarly, over the long term, states may arguably benefit by removing restrictions on free trade, allowing for the free-flow of goods across borders, even if particular segments of domes-tic economies are exposed to the painful consequences of this process in the short term.

The rationalist perspective used by institutionalists to understand why states comply with legal obligations in the absence of enforcement mechanisms is not based on formal legal reasoning but rather focuses on how institutions can be designed to encourage states to pursue their own self-interest in ways that facili-tate long-term cooperation over time. This of course may also be a concern in international law, yet it is rarely addressed so explicitly in the rationalist, stra-tegic and game-theoretic language and approach that dominates much of the international relations literature on state compliance with international norms and legal obligations.

Constructivism

Theory

Constructivism is an approach to international relations that focuses broadly on the roles that norms, ideas, and culture play in world politics. From a constructivist perspective, these non-material factors are often more important to understanding world politics than material factors, such as how many weapons a state has or the strength of its economy (traditional measures of power for realists). One prominent constructivist, Alexander Wendt, famously said that international politics is about 'ideas all the way down'. In other words, we cannot understand world politics without understanding the identity and self-understanding of the actors that make up world politics (Wendt 1999). States may not always act out of a concern for raw power and self-interest—they are social entities that can be 'other-regarding' and concerned with what is appropriate behaviour in world politics. They often make decisions and determine their actions based on the *logic of appropriateness* (concern with what is socially appropriate) rather than a rationalist *logic of consequences* (concern with an instrumental outcome). Constructivism thus provides a clear contrast to rationalist approaches to international politics.

States' priorities might be shaped by their own national identity, which is in turn informed by a unique set of cultural, historical, and institutional traditions. As social actors, states are influenced by **international norms** that prescribe what is considered to be appropriate and inappropriate behaviour. States are concerned with status and world opinion. They care about the definition of what it means to be a 'good state' and their decisions to sign on to international legal instruments and to comply with international law is based as much or more on normative concerns regarding the logic of appropriateness as it is on rational concerns of narrow self-interest.

Many social constructivists thus share a number of concerns with IL scholars; however, they use a different language and approach. Whereas international human rights lawyers view states as being embedded in an international legal order of human rights obligations, and focus on the specific institutions, conventions, and treaties that legally oblige states to uphold human rights laws and principles, social constructivists may focus more on the strength of human rights norms more generally, and would examine acceptance and implementation of human rights norms as a social process, rather than simply a legal obligation. Social constructivists also use a different set of terminology from international legal scholars. While IL scholars are interested in the 'evolution of international law', social constructivists are interested in processes of socialization and in the emergence, spread, and deepening of 'international norms'.

The English School

The IR–IL divide has appeared most distinctly in the United States, although this is not to say that it isn't present elsewhere. In the United Kingdom, however, one tradition of IR theory has continued to view international law as an important part of international politics: the so-called English School, which shares some features with constructivist theories. Scholars of the English School embrace the role of law, rules, and norms in international society, with some describing their work as following in the 'Grotian tradition', referring to *Hugo Grotius*, a seventeenth-century international legal scholar. Writers such as Hedley Bull argue that they can accept realist premises regarding the nature of power in the international system and nonetheless identify a place for law and rule-governed behaviour (Bull 1977). Bull argues, for example, that even though international politics is anarchic, and lacks the hierarchy and structure of domestic politics, this does not mean that rules and indeed law cannot govern state behaviour. He argues rather that international society is an anarchical society, in that there is no single hierarchical supranational power, but that it is a *society* nonetheless that is based on shared institutions and conventions. He identifies international law as an important institution in world politics, along with other institutions, such as state sovereignty, international diplomacy, warfare and the balance of power. The English School perspective on international law can thus be seen as combining some of the views of both realists and constructivists.

The English School is also an important approach because it is one of the few approaches in international relations to explicitly examine the origins of international society—and, by implication, the origins of the international legal order—in Europe and its spread to the rest of the world through empire and colonial rule. Much of realist or liberal theorizing, in contrast, tends to ignore the question of the origins of the current international order, taking instead a rather *ahistorical* approach to international relations.

Actors

Many constructivists and adherents of the English School concur with the realists' view that states are the primary actors in the international system. Overall, however, constructivists and English School theorists have a more nuanced and contextualized view of state identities and interests. Rather than viewing state interests as uniform or fixed, they view state identities and interests as malleable and subject to change. State identities and interests evolve over time, and this evolution can occur due to interaction with other states and processes of learning.

From a constructivist perspective, international institutions are not merely arenas for states to pursue their self-interests. Rather, they are sites of socialization and norm-promotion. State identities and interests are changed through their interaction with international institutions. International institutions are promoters of new norms and identities that can fundamentally reshape the preferences of state actors. States come to internalize new norms and develop new identities. International institutions can socialize states to take on new self-understandings and engage in new practices.

For example, when East European states joined NATO they had to develop new domestic understandings of civil-military relations (Gheciu 2005) and took on the identities of 'liberal democracies'. Similarly, states that become members of the European Union have to accept the *Copenhagen Criteria* (EU membership criteria that include democratic governance, human rights observance, and market economies) and then incorporate the *acquis communitaire*, or body of EU accumulated law, into their domestic legal systems.

Social constructivists would focus less on the legal process through which this occurs, and more on the effects this process has on the identity and self-understanding of states. Constructivists, like other IR theorists, rarely speak directly of international law as part of this process, preferring instead to study socialization processes, norm diffusion and identity change. Yet the relevance to international law is clear: a focus on the internalization of new norms and changing identities suggests that states comply with international legal obligations not simply out of fear or narrow self-interest, but rather that values, beliefs, and normative affinities play an important role in achieving compliance.

In addition to international organizations, such as NATO or the EU, constructivists pay a great deal of attention to the role of transnational actors who may influence the behaviour of states through their norm promoting activities. These include NGOs, transnational advocacy networks, or individual 'norm entrepreneurs'. Constructivists, like liberals, place a strong emphasis on the role played by international civil society actors in shaping the normative environment in which states operate.

Processes

Social constructivists are keenly interested in the emergence and evolution of international norms. Alexander Wendt, for example, argues that international order is shaped by the shared understanding of states regarding 'cultures of anarchy'. He subsumes realist and liberal perspectives on world politics, arguing that particular cultures of anarchy socialize states into particular forms of behaviour. A realist 'Hobbesian' anarchy is based on competing power relations and portrays other states as enemies; an institutionalist 'Lockean' anarchy is based on competing interests and portrays other states as rivals; whereas a 'Kantian' anarchy is based on shared values and portrays other states as friends. Ultimately, international order is determined by 'what states make of it' (Wendt 1999; 1992).

While this dovetails with some concerns of international legal scholars in strengthening an international legal order, the language and framework used by a constructivist such as Wendt is very different from the language and framework employed by a scholar of international law. On the other hand, there are some constructivists who take a more legalistic approach, such as Christian Reus-Smit (2004), who have been more sympathetic to explicitly examining the relationship between international law and international politics through a reflection on the feedback effects of law on politics, rather than just politics on law.

Other social constructivists such as Martha Finnemore and Kathryn Sikkink (2005) have focused on the role that individual 'norm entrepreneurs' play in promoting and institutionalizing new international norms. They argue that international norms emerge in life cycles that generally begin with norm promotion by individuals, and progress to norm institutionalization within international organizations and institutions, followed by socialization and acceptance of norms by state actors that begins with a few state actors and then spreads until it reaches a tipping point and creates a 'norms cascade'. This can, they argue, lead to a general acceptance, internalization, and the naturalization and institutionalization of the new norm. Within this framework, international law plays an important role in promoting normative change. The signing on to international conventions and treaties marks an important stage in the 'norm cascade' pattern. Whereas states may initially sign on to international human rights or other conventions for instrumental reasons, this may initiate a process that eventually leads to a change in behaviour, and internalization of new norms, and perhaps an eventual change in a state's own self-identity. Again, the terminology used here is very different from that used by IL scholars, but parallels processes of state acceptance of and compliance with international law, and the ways in which international law can insert itself into a state, reshaping domestic legal practice.

With regard to the creation of and compliance with limitations on resort to the use of force or conduct of armed conflict, constructivists point to the normative power of the UN Charter, International Humanitarian Law and other international treaties. State leaders may comply with these legal regimes because they believe them to have value in themselves, and because they conceive of their states to be law-abiding members of the international community. The social constructivist Nina Tannenwald, for example, has argued that states have not used nuclear weapons and largely comply with the Nuclear Non-Proliferation Treaty (NPT) because they have internalized a strong 'nuclear taboo' that makes it normatively unacceptable to use or openly pursue nuclear weaponry (see also Chapter 6). This is a very different argument from that made by realists who would focus instead on the role of power, threats, coercive diplomacy, and security guarantees in limiting the use and spread of nuclear weapons since World War II.

Marxism, Feminism, and Critical Theory

Theory

There are many additional paradigms in international relations that present alternative views on world politics. Robert Cox once famously made the distinction between 'problem-solving theories' and 'critical theories', with problem-solving theories taking the world as it is, and critical theories envisioning the world as it could be (Cox 1981). There are many varieties of critical approaches to world politics, which are linked by a focus on critiquing the status quo in world politics and placing an emphasis on the relationship between theory and praxis.

Marxist approaches to international relations include *world systems theory* and *neo-Gramscian* approaches. World systems theory (Wallerstein 1974; Hobson 2000) emphasizes the role that capitalism has played in shaping a world order that is divided into powerful core states and less powerful states on the periphery. It examines the fusion between state and class power, with an emphasis on how economic elites in both the core and the periphery are linked in a common interest in maintaining an unequal and exploitative status quo. Neo-Gramscian approaches to world politics (Cox 1981; Gill 1992) similarly emphasize inequality but point to the role that the ideas of the powerful, such as neoliberalism, play in maintaining inequality. They would argue that such hegemonic perspectives structure the international order in subtle ways that benefit elites. International law is therefore not a neutral force in world politics, but reflects the ideologies and interests of global elites.

Other critical perspectives on world politics would similarly view the international legal order as reflection of particularistic interests. Feminist theorists, many of whom view the international state system as a reflection of gendered power relations which prioritize public institutions over the private sphere, and which trace many of the institutions of international public life to gendered considerations of power and interest, would similarly view international law as reflective of a gendered international order.

Actors

Critical approaches to world politics include a more diverse range of actors as significant players in international relations; they do not assume the primacy of the state. Marxist approaches to world politics place an emphasis on the interests of global capital: the power of multinational corporations, it is argued, often outweighs the power of small or weak states. Powerful economic interests converge in forums such as the *World Economic Forum* (an annual meeting of business, government, and other elites in Davos, Switzerland) and are arguably reflected in a global order in which neoliberal ideologies provide a system of meaning in which powerful states, global economic elites, and international institutions such as the World Bank and the IMF share common economic interests.

Feminist approaches to international relations would focus on the extent to which women are often treated as invisible actors in world politics. While realists focus on the role of US military bases in maintaining US hegemony, or liberals focus on how United Nations peacekeepers are deployed to resolve collective security concerns, feminist approaches would examine the gendered nature of these arrangements and would point to how both military bases and peacekeeping operations are often closely linked to local sex industries or sex trafficking (Enloe 1992).

Processes

Marxists will tend to interpret the emergence and maintenance of international legal agreements and regimes as reflective of the interests of capital within powerful countries or across countries. Thus, for example, the self-constraints states create through free trade agreements are not a puzzle, even in the face of significant domestic opposition from labour or environmental movements. Rather, they represent the interests of domestic and multinational corporations in relatively unfettered transfer of goods, capital, and labour. Feminist critiques of international legal processes have in some ways also effected change in the functioning of them: while traditionally females were often overlooked as specific subjects of international law, the rapid progressive development of international humanitarian law and international criminal law has seen increased recognition of the distinct harms which women may suffer disproportionately. Thus, for example, the *ad hoc* criminal tribunals for the former Yugoslavia and Rwanda have elaborated upon rape as a war crime and as an element of genocide.

Conclusion

In this chapter, we have seen that different theories of international relations have very different assumptions about the underlying nature of world politics, and the relevant actors and processes that make up international political life. These in turn affect their views—implicitly, if not explicitly—of the relevance and function of international law. Each of these theories: Realism, Liberalism, Institutionalism, Constructivism, Marxism, Feminism, and Critical Theory, places a different degree of emphasis on the relative importance of state power, rational self-interest, institutions, and ideas and culture—which shapes the perspectives they bring to understanding international law.

We have seen that IR scholars are interested in important IL questions, such as the origins and evolution of international law, and why states do or don't comply with international law. However, their emphasis may be less upon the legal nature of the object of study than on explaining behaviour in the international system—of states, institutions and individuals—and where or why these actors create norms, support and maintain them, or comply with them. We have provided some specific examples of substantive areas in which one finds convergence between international relations and international law—many of which will be explored in much greater detail in some of the chapters to come.

Many of the theoretical perspectives presented in this chapter will be familiar to students of international relations; however, often the relationship the various IR paradigms have to the study of international law is difficult to discern. Perspectives on international law in international relations are often implicit, rather than explicit. Theories of international relations approach the study of world politics with a different language and terminology from international law. Often there is a great deal of overlap between the two disciplines in the substantive interests and questions that are addressed, but the terminology employed and the perspective taken make it difficult for the two disciplines to maintain a sustained dialogue. Nevertheless, for students of international relations, obtaining an understanding of international law is not only a valuable exercise in and of itself, but can also ultimately help the student to have a better understanding of international relations.

Questions

1. Why should students of international relations study international law?
2. Why has much of international relations theory historically dismissed the importance of international law?
3. How do realists understand the place, if any, of law in international politics?
4. How do liberals understand the place of law in international politics?
5. How do institutionalists understand the place of law in international politics?
6. How do constructivists or English School scholars understand the place of law in international politics?
7. What is meant by the 'logic of appropriateness' and the 'logic of consequences' and what are the main differences between a rationalist and social constructivist perspective on international law?
8. How do Marxists, critical theorists, or feminists understand the place of law in international politics?
9. If the international system is anarchical, what role do you think that institutions, norms, or law play in constraining state behaviour, if any? If they do play a role, why and how?
10. Select one of the theoretical paradigms discussed here, identifying the theoretical explanation, key actors, and processes. Use it to explain a contemporary international regime (human rights, environmental, or other).

Further reading

Abbott, K. (1989) 'Modern International Relations Theory: A Prospectus for International Lawyers' *Yale Journal of International Law* 14/2: 335–411. *A helpful summary of relevant IR theories and their approaches to international law.*

Biersteker, T., Spiro, P., Sriram, C. L., and Raffo, V. (2006) (eds.) *International Law and International Relations: Bridging Theory and Practice (London: Routledge). Contributions seek to examine the relation between international relations and international law in specific international political challenges .*

Franck, T. (1990), *The Power of Legitimacy Among Nations* (Oxford: Oxford University Press). *A prominent international lawyer considers why states might comply with international legal obligations, focusing upon their legitimacy.*

Goldstein, J., Kahler, M., Keohane, R., and Slaughter, A. (2000) (eds.) Special issue devoted to 'Legalization' of *International Organization,* 54/3. *Contributions examine the concept of legalization in international politics.*

Keohane, R. (1984) *After Hegemony: Cooperation and Discord in the World Political Economy* (Princeton, NJ: Princeton University Press). *Leading institutionalist IR scholar presents his arguments about how regimes function in the absence of a global hegemon.*

Krasner, S. (1983) (ed.) *International Regimes* (Ithaca, NY: Cornell University

Press). *Contributions consider the concept and impact of international regimes.*

Moravcsik, A. (1997) 'Taking Preference Seriously: A Liberal Theory of International Politics' *International Organization* 51/4: 513–53. *A leading liberal IR scholar makes a case for liberalism as a distinctive approach to world politics.*

Slaughter, A., Tulumello, A., and Wood, S. A. (1998) 'International Law and International Relations Theory: A New Generation of Interdisciplinary Scholarship' *American Journal of International Law* 92/3: 367–97. *Developing on Slaughter Burley's classic piece, a consideration of scholarship engaging both IL and IR.*

Waltz, K. (1979) *Theory of International Politics* (New York, NY: McGraw-Hill). *Leading realist IR scholar presents his theoretical arguments.*

Wight, M. (1992) *International Theory: The Three Traditions* (London: Holmes and Meier). *A leading representative of the English School presents approaches to international politics.*

Websites

http://www.chathamhouse.org.uk *The website of the Royal Institute of International Affairs provides an interesting overview of what—from a UK perspective—are perceived to be the most relevant and pressing contemporary topics in the area of international relations.*

http://www2.etown.edu/vl/ *This internet directory brings together over 2,000 annotated links to sources of information and analysis in a wide range of international affairs, international studies, and international relations topics.*

http://www.g7.utoronto.ca *This website offers up-to-date information on meetings, summits, conferences, and research related to G8 activity.*

http://www.iiss.org *The International Institute for Strategic Studies conducts research focused on military and political conflict and offers publications on a wide range of topics.*

http://www.opendemocracy.net *This is an open source of view and opinion pieces written by experts all around the world on democratic, international, and global politics.*

Visit the Online Resource Centre that accompanies this book to access more learning resources www.oxfordtextbooks.co.uk/orc/cali/

Chapter endnote

1. The terms 'liberal' and 'liberalism' here refer to both Liberal International Relations Theory (liberalism, liberal IR scholars) and, in the context of domestic government, political systems based on principles of liberalism (i.e. liberal democracy, constitutional liberalism). This dual usage is standard in international relations literature.

Chapter 3

Basic principles of international law: a historical perspective

Antony Anghie

CHAPTER CONTENTS

- Introduction
- The birth of modern international law: the sixteenth century
- The Congress of Vienna: international law from 1815–1914
- The League of Nations: international law from 1919–1939
- The United Nations: 1945 to the present
- Conclusion

CHAPTER OVERVIEW

This chapter provides an outline of the modern history of international law, commencing in the sixteenth century and extending to the present. It begins by considering the issues of the subject matter of the history of international law, the different ways in which this history has been approached, and the broad question of why an understanding of the history of international law is important for a study of international law and international relations. The chapter identifies some of the basic concerns of international law—such as the prevention of war—and illustrates the ways in which international law has attempted, over the centuries, to deal with a rapidly changing international system. The history of international law is traditionally divided into different phases—usually separated by a major European war—and this chapter outlines the key developments that occurred in each phase. It adopts a historical perspective in examining how some of the foundational concepts of international law, most prominently, sovereignty, have developed over time and suggests how the history of sovereignty may be approached in very different ways. It covers the role of imperialism, both in terms of international relations and the development of international law. It sketches the historical evolution of international institutions such as the League of Nations and United Nations, and concludes by pointing to some of the major contemporary issues in international law, and the continuing relevance of an historical approach to the discipline.

Introduction

International law can be broadly defined as the law that regulates relations among sovereign states. International relations scholars have long been interested in the question of whether international law has any impact on state behaviour. It is argued that states—especially powerful states—ignore international law when it does not correspond with their own interests. Given that the international system lacks a world police force that punishes states that violate international law, it would seem that international law is of little use. Despite this, over the centuries, international law has been astonishingly adaptable and resilient; it continues to feature prominently in international relations even though it has been incessantly violated. International law now regulates a far greater range of issues than was the case even twenty years ago (see Chapter 1). The basic question then arises as to why states expend so much effort to create international law—to negotiate treaties in a diverse range of areas, for instance—if it is so ineffective. In order to address these issues, careful attention must be paid to the continuously changing relationship between those two complex entities that might be termed 'power'—traditionally the major focus of international relations (see Chapter 2) scholars—and 'law'.

The subject matter of a history of international law

The study of the history of international law might provide some insights into this apparent paradox by enabling an overview of the attempts made by international law to regulate state behaviour in relation to matters ranging from war to the environment to human rights to commercial relations, and the strengths and weaknesses of the discipline as it has endeavoured to adapt to a complex and rapidly changing international system.

The history of international law can be approached in a number of different ways. In the first place, it can be the study of the interaction between states over time. International law is created by states—whether through treaties or through a repeated practice which is inspired by a sense of legal obligation and which gives rise to customary international law. Thus any study of international law, including the history of international law, involves a close study of state behaviour and the attempts by states to manage international relations among themselves—often through wars and, on other occasions, through the creation of new institutions or legal regimes dealing with major issues such as international trade and foreign investment. Second, the history of international law includes an examination of the theories about international law—what it is, how it is made, why it is binding on states. Third, histories of international law are in many ways histories of broader ideas—about, for example, the nature of man, the essence of international society, the means of achieving international peace, the relations between diverse peoples. The ideas of international law propounded by many great scholars cannot be properly appreciated without considering them in the context of these larger concerns. Finally, a study of the history of international law raises the question of how a particular history is written. What is the perspective of the author, what issues are regarded as more or less important, what peoples and cultures are more or less important, what values are being advanced, and what assumptions are made? What follows is an attempt to sketch a history of international law which touches upon all these different themes and elements.

Any history of international law involves tracing the complex relationships between events, such as wars, and the legal rules and institutions that are devised to address the challenges and problems that these events reveal. As we shall see, many of the most important developments in international legal doctrine and institutions have occurred following major wars. In many instances, leaders and statesmen attempt, after such massive catastrophes, to create a better and different international system, often accompanied by new political principles and appropriate laws and institutions, to make sure that history does not repeat itself and that instead a new era of peace, stability, and prosperity is ushered in. Developments in international legal jurisprudence that is, theories about the character and operation of international law, constitute an equally important dimension of the history of international law. The international lawyer's basic task is to identify and apply the international law that is relevant to a particular dispute or situation, whether it has to do with title to territory or commercial matters, and assess what actions the law permits.

These questions are not always easy to answer as the international system lacks a single, defined, legislative body and states may well disagree as to what the applicable and relevant law is. As a result, these questions inevitably involve dealing with important issues of international legal theory such as: where do we find international law? How is international law made? What makes international law binding on states? These questions have preoccupied international lawyers over the centuries. In attempting to answer them, jurists have developed theories about the character of sovereignty, the sources of international law, and the nature of the international system. In many cases, the jurists formulating these theories were affected by contemporaneous international events, and tried to explain such events as an illustration of a larger theory about how states behave or about the character of international law.

Almost invariably, these jurists aspired to act as advisors and to present theories of international law that would be taken into account by the state—the foreign policy of the Bush administration, for instance, was significantly influenced by neo-conservative thinkers and their particular vision of the world and the role of the United States within it.

Thus the history of international law is a history of events and doctrines and state practices and theories about law (see Chapter 4); but it is also a history of ideas, the attempts of scholars and jurists over the centuries to present coherent accounts of how states behave, how international law is made, how the system works and, sometimes, more ambitiously, how peace, international stability, and justice are achieved.[1] This chapter will discuss how particular problems and events have contributed to the development of international law. This has been the traditional approach to studying international law.

Box 3.1 Critical approaches to international legal history

It should be pointed out that the writing of the history of international law has itself been the subject of controversy. In recent times, attempts have been made to present 'histories' of international law rather than elaborate on one traditional story. Critical scholars of international law have presented perspectives that involve reinterpreting central historical events—by questioning and reinterpreting the importance, for instance, of the Peace of Westphalia, for international law. Critical scholarship seeks to identify and contest the 'Eurocentric' character of conventional histories and to focus instead on peoples and societies that have been profoundly affected by international law, but whose voices and experiences have not been incorporated into the telling of its history.

A history of international law written from the perspective of a powerful European state such as the United Kingdom, it is argued, would be very different from a history written by the native peoples of the Americas or Australasia whose dispossession was justified by the international law of the time.

These are important developments, as a particular vision of the history of any discipline almost inevitably affects its study because it is the problems and challenges, the values and attitudes revealed by that history that often inspire further inquiry and the techniques and methods of solving even contemporary problems depend in various ways on what has already been formulated.

A more complex understanding of international law is emerging as a consequence of this work, one that suggests that international law cannot be seen only as a gallant attempt to prevent the ravages of war and protect human beings against depredations of tyrants and disasters. Rather, these new histories suggest that international law itself has enabled the suppression and conquest of peoples and can even justify large-scale violence. In short, international law may not only further the cause of international justice, but even undermine it. These critical perspectives on the history of international law may prompt a more subtle appreciation of the character and uses of international law.

The birth of modern international law: the sixteenth century

Throughout history, interaction between different entities—whether characterized as empires or societies or tribes—has resulted in the formulation of principles that facilitate and regularize such encounters. Seen in this way, a version of international law has existed for thousands of years. Studies of the history of Mesopotamia, ancient Greece, the Roman Empire, ancient China, and ancient India reveal the existence of city-states that formulated rules to govern relations between members of their own system—including provisions for the treatment of diplomats, the making and enforcement of treaties, and principles governing the declaration and conduct of war (Bederman 2001).

The beginnings of Empire

Whatever these antecedents, the modern discipline of international law, as it is traditionally presented traces its beginnings to the sixteenth and seventeenth centuries, and with various developments occurring within Europe, principally those connected with the emergence of the sovereign state, and the particular political and theoretical problems associated with these developments. The Peace of Westphalia of 1648 may be seen as the crucial moment which gave rise to the modern system of international relations based on the sovereign state. But the Westphalian system itself might be regarded as one response to a much broader and more fundamental question which scholars and sovereigns had attempted to resolve since ancient times: how to develop a set of principles that would govern relations between very diverse peoples. This issue engaged the most prominent European jurists of the sixteenth century, including Spanish scholars such as Francisco de Vitoria (1486–1546) and Suarez (1548–1617). It was an issue that emerged in a very powerful form in the colonial confrontation between European and non-European peoples. This was the age of discovery for the explorers in Europe who journeyed in search of gold and trade into the Americas, Africa, and Asia, where they often encountered rich and complex civilizations. Legal scholars of the time attempted to articulate doctrines that would account for dealings between European and non-European peoples who belonged to entirely different cultural systems. What was the law that governed relations between such disparate societies? How was such a law to be identified or created? What was the legal status of these non-European territories, and what rights and responsibilities followed? Much of Vitoria's jurisprudence grapples with these fundamental questions as he examines the claims made by the Spanish to acquire sovereignty over the lands and peoples of the West Indies following the voyages of Columbus. Vitoria's analysis of the legal issues generated by this encounter also included a presentation of the intricate relationship between divine law, as prescribed by the Pope, and secular power, represented by the Emperor. Vitoria also examined issues such as whether there was one law universally binding on both Spanish and Indians—despite their very different cultures—and the legal identity of the Indians in this system. His examination of when it is legal to go to war, and what rules should be observed in going to war occurs in the particular historical context of the wars conducted by the Spanish against the Indians.

Box 3.2 Religion and law

Theology was inextricably intertwined with law in this period. It is commonplace for works of this period to cite scripture—especially from the gospels and letters of St. Paul—as authority for their jurisprudence. Christianity prescribed a set of principles that was universally applicable both to relations within states and between states and indeed, the distinction between what we now call 'domestic' and 'international' law was not very well developed at this time. All these jurists were preoccupied by a question that had been deeply examined centuries earlier by the greatest of Catholic political philosophers, Augustine: when was it legal to go to war and use violence. This issue was especially problematic to these early scholars because Christianity had repeatedly proclaimed itself to be a religion of peace.

The Peace of Westphalia and Westphalian sovereignty: 1648

Within Christian Europe the splitting of the church following the Reformation led to deep hatred between states on either side of the resulting divide, states that were each absolutely convinced of the truth and validity of their own position and intent on converting all non-believers by force, if necessary, in order to establish the universal validity of the one 'true' religion. Wars that were especially ferocious and bloody resulted because the issue at stake was more than merely territory; it had to do with God. And, invariably in these wars, the enemy was thought of as less than human, as an abomination against whom any violence could be legally directed.

The Thirty Years War (1618–1648) resulted in the devastation of much of Europe from Sweden to the Balkans. It was in the midst of these conflicts that the great Dutch scholar, Hugo Grotius (1583–1645), often thought of as the founder of modern international law, wrote his monumental work, *The Rights of War and Peace* (first published in 1625). His major achievement lay in shifting the basis of law from religion to natural law, by arguing that the great principles of law—whether in relation to war, commerce, or the formation of treaties—could be derived from nature or reason, rather than God (although, on the whole, he was careful to argue that this corresponded with God's law as well). The important point was that natural law was binding on all people, regardless of their religion.

> **Box 3.3** *Pacta sunt servanda*
>
> One of the fundamental principles of this natural law, Grotius further asserted, was the principle of *pacta sunt servanda*; treaties must be obeyed—a principle of international law that is still regarded as a foundation of the modern discipline. In this way, Grotius, like his great contemporary, Thomas Hobbes (1588–1679) was responding to the alarming prospect of endless anarchy, a continuous war of all against all that seemed to be exemplified by the religious wars at the time.

The Thirty Years War was concluded by a peace settlement, the Peace of Westphalia, which sought to prevent further religious conflict by prescribing that each sovereign had absolute power within its own territory, and could therefore adopt whatever religion and political system it thought fit. No state was justified in attacking another state simply because that other state had a different ideology or religion. International law attempted to regulate relations between states, and it was only if a state violated its obligations to another state that liability could arise under international law.

Box 3.4 'Westphalian sovereignty'

'Westphalian sovereignty', as it is now popularly referred to in the literature, is traditionally understood to stand for the proposition that a sovereign has absolute legal power within its own territory. However, the Peace of Westphalia was established through a series of treaties and in fact included provisions that required states to protect the rights of religious minorities found within their territories. The disparity between the popular understanding of Westphalian sovereignty and the provisions of the actual texts provide a good example of the way in which general understandings may not withstand close historical scrutiny.

The idea that the sovereign was subject to no higher authority in its external relations has had an enduring significance and was manifested and entrenched in the practices, policies, institutions, indeed, the very identity of the state. Correspondingly, at least in Europe the international legal system was understood to comprise equal and sovereign states. Indeed, the history of international law is in many ways the history of sovereignty. Only sovereign entities have full standing in the international system—to bring claims, to make international law, and to create international institutions. A complex and continuously developing set of rules decides the crucial question of whether or not an entity is sovereign, and what the powers of the sovereign are. Sovereignty doctrine developed in two somewhat different geographical realms: first, in relations between European states that, despite their religious differences, were relatively homogenous culturally; and second, in encounters between European and non-European states, exemplified by the inaugural encounter between Europe and the West Indies. The history of sovereignty, then, must take into account developments in both these arenas.

In this respect it is noteworthy, that Grotius, the father of international law, was also the lawyer for the Dutch East India Company and wrote some of his earliest important works in an attempt to justify their expansion against Portuguese competition in the East Indies. Recent scholarship has pointed out the significant ways in which this work has influenced his masterpiece, *The Rights of War and Peace*.

The Peace of Westphalia can be seen, then, as the beginning of an historical process by which the state became more consolidated, the centre of absolute power, with its own rationality that was independent of religious considerations and ethics.

Box 3.5 Vattel and the development of 'sovereignty'

Scholars and jurists continuously refined these ideas of sovereignty. *The Law of Nations*, the great work of the Swiss jurist, Emer de Vattel (1714–67), was published in 1758. It was very widely read, not only in Europe, but, in time, in the United States and the Far East. Vattel acknowledged that states were bound by natural law. But he further argued that only states could interpret for themselves whether they had in fact breached natural law. Vattel himself presented this idea as a useful compromise between the theory of naturalism and the reality of the increasingly powerful nation state. But it led to a situation where, in effect, a state judged its own cause and rejected natural law as having any independent, binding authority. Then, as now, states were prone to assess events and the law in the light of their own interests and concerns, and like Vattel, scholars before and after him have attempted to provide solutions to the fundamental problem that the international system lacks a 'world government' which could enforce judgments on disputes between nations. Equally significantly, Vattel presented very influential rationalizations for colonialism. While he was opposed to the conquest of non-European states that had achieved what he regarded as a certain degree of advancement (which he equated with the practice of agriculture), he argued that societies that did not engage in agriculture were inferior, and that their lands could be taken over because they did not properly belong to anyone else. Vattel's arguments provided a semblance of legal justification for events such as the settlement of Australia by Europeans who claimed that the Aboriginal people who had lived there for thousands of years possessed no real rights to their lands. Once again, questions of sovereignty played a crucial role in this debate: were the indigenous peoples sovereign? If they were, on what basis could their lands be taken from them? If they were not sovereign, how was this decided?

The Congress of Vienna: international law from 1815–1914

Napoleon's defeat at Waterloo was followed by another effort to establish a new order in Europe. The Congress of Vienna in 1815 inaugurated not only a legal regime, but a new political order that was based on the concept of the 'balance of power'. The basic idea of the balance of power was that states would combine with each other to neutralize any state that threatened to acquire overwhelming and decisive power.

The consolidation of the power of the state was furthered in the nineteenth century, particularly as a result of the rise of nationalism, the demand by distinctive ethnic groups that they should become sovereign and thus achieve the highest status permitted by the international system.

The further ascendance of the sovereign state inevitably affected the jurisprudence of the nineteenth century. The theory of positivism, which claimed to be scientific and based on empirical, observable facts, was adapted by jurists to the field of international law (see Chapter 4). Naturalist jurisprudence had been severely criticized as being imprecise and subjective because different jurists and states could arrive at very different conclusions as to the content of rules dictated by 'nature' or 'reason'. By contrast, the nineteenth century positivists argued that international law was based on the observable actions of sovereign states—whether they took the form of treaties or state practice that gave rise to custom. In short, there was no system, whether based on religion or natural law that transcended and restrained the state. It was only if the state consented to a rule of international law that it was considered as bound by that rule. The sovereign state was supreme and could do as it wished in order to further its own interests. Within this system, it was legal for a sovereign to go to war whenever he decided to do so. Despite this, the balance of power system established by the Congress of Vienna succeeded in maintaining Europe in a relatively peaceful state during much of the nineteenth century. Stability was largely achieved by the fact that even though a state was legally permitted to go to war, it ran the risk of facing a formidable enemy made up of several opposing states intent on re-establishing a stable balance.

It was precisely during this time, also, that European states were engaged in fierce competition and rivalry for colonies. France, England, Russia, the Netherlands, Portugal, Spain, and the newly emergent Germany were intent on expanding their empires, and this project usually involved fighting savage wars against the peoples of Africa and Asia. The British Empire was the largest and most threatening in this Age of Empire, and other European states often allied with each other to negate British influence.

It was only in the late nineteenth century that Western international law became universally applicable, principally because the expansion of European empires through colonialism in effect imposed European international law on all societies—whether in the Pacific, Asia, Africa, or Latin America. International law played an important role in justifying the conquest and dispossession of non-European peoples, all this in the name of civilizing the barbarians. Natural law theory broadly held that all societies, whether in Europe or Asia or Africa, were governed by the same universal rules. By contrast, the dominant positivist international law of the nineteenth century decreed that non-European states were 'uncivilized' and therefore lacked sovereignty. This particular tenet of positivist jurisprudence derived in many ways from the racial theories—heavily influenced by Darwinism—that were emerging in Europe contemporaneously. As a consequence, these states had no legal standing to use international law against European states. Quite simply, uncivilized states were not sovereign and, consequently, lacked the legal personality to enable them to participate in the international system by making claims under international law, and indeed, engage themselves in the creation of international law by which they were still regarded as being bound.

Box 3.6 International law and the subordination of non-European peoples: the Berlin Conference

The Berlin Conference of 1885 provides one of the most dramatic examples of the role that international law played in the subordination of non-European peoples. The competition between European states for the riches of Africa—the scramble for Africa—threatened to result in war. The great powers of Europe met in Berlin in order to devise a system that would enable the 'orderly' exploitation of Africa without risking war. Africa was in effect carved up among the European states as a result of this conference and the agreements that followed it. Consequently, many African boundaries are straight lines which bear no connection with the ethnic groups living within them. The Conference established the large area of the Congo river basin as a 'free trade' area over which King Leopold II of Belgium was given effective administrative control. In addition, the Berlin Conference sought to end slavery and to ensure the well-being of the natives. Humanitarian sentiment was a prominent feature of this enterprise. What followed, however, was large-scale atrocity, as Leopold's attempts to exploit the riches of the Congo—which included ivory and rubber—caused the deaths of millions of Africans. The Belgian administrators punished Africans who failed to meet their quotas for gathering rubber by mutilations, by cutting off hands. The European powers who saw the Berlin Conference as a new and progressive development eventually relieved Leopold of his control over the Congo, which was then administered instead by the Belgian state. Violence and instability has been a constant feature of the region since at least this time.

One rationale underlying the positivist position that uncivilized states were not sovereign was that uncivilized states were considered so backward or culturally different that they were thought incapable of comprehending and adhering to the rules that had to be observed by members of the 'family of nations'. Some nations, such as Japan, were able to win entrance to the exclusive and largely Western family of nations by engaging in massive reform projects directed at modernizing their society and creating a correspondingly 'advanced' national legal system based on

Western models. More important, perhaps, was the fact that Japan defeated a major European power, Russia, in the battle of Tsushima in 1905. Even as Europe and the rest of the world were becoming more militaristic, states attempted to regulate the conduct of war. Of particular note in this regard were two conferences held at The Hague, in the Netherlands, in 1899 and 1907. These were devoted to creating laws that would operate in times of war. The law of war has been classically divided into two different categories: the law of war which deals with the question of when it is legal to go to war (*jus ad bello*); and the law of war which deals with the question of laws to be observed once the war has begun (*jus in bello*). This latter body of law developed notable principles such as the rule that it was illegal for armed forces to deliberately target civilians. The International Committee of the Red Cross, formed in 1863, played a crucial role in these proceedings despite the fact that it was not a state.

The League of Nations: international law from 1919–1939

The balance of power system that had succeeded in maintaining relative stability in nineteenth-century Europe compounded the magnitude and intensity of World War I, a war of such a massive scale and horror that it was termed 'The Great War' and 'The War to End All Wars'. It was hardly conceivable that another war of such a scope would take place again. The appalling death and destruction wrought by the war demonstrated the capabilities of modern weaponry, and made it imperative to create a new system of international order that would seek to prevent such a catastrophe from ever recurring. The efforts of the statesmen who gathered at the peace conference in Versailles in 1919 to achieve these ends resulted in the creation of a new international actor, the League of Nations, the first major international institution. The League was largely the product of the vision of President Woodrow Wilson of the United States—although the United States, not for the last time, refused to become a member of the institution it was instrumental in creating (see Chapter 12).

The League was established by sovereign states and was correspondingly limited by the fact that it could do little unless those states agreed among themselves on a particular course of action. Significantly, however, it was the first major attempt to coordinate the behaviour of states through an international actor that possessed its own legal personality and staff and set as its goal the advancement of international peace and security as opposed to the interests of individual member states.

Box 3.7 Collective security

The concept of 'collective security' was a crucial aspect of the League's attempts to create peace and security. Article 10 of its Covenant broadly required all member states to respect and preserve the territorial integrity and political independence of states against external aggression. Disarmament was another major initiative, and Article 8 of the League Covenant noted that 'The Members of the League agree that the manufacture by private enterprise of munitions and implements of war is open to grave objections' and urged all member states to reduce their armaments to the extent compatible with their own security and international obligations. The Covenant also required member states to submit all disputes to some form of arbitration or judicial settlement, and to desist from war until three months after the decision of the body that heard the dispute.

Despite these efforts, the League proved helpless in preventing aggression. Italy invaded Abyssinia and Japan invaded Manchuria. Germany, which eventually joined the League became increasingly belligerent, and the League failed to respond effectively.

The demise of the League, which had been conceived of in terms of a new world order of peace and prosperity, dealt an enormous blow to the credibility of international organizations. Critics of the League argued that it was doomed to fail because it embodied a vision of international relations conducted according to an idealistic version of international law far removed from power, the real interests of states, and their views appeared to be justified by the collapse of the League.

The League's concern with war obscured its achievements and its large scale ambitions with regard to a number of other issues—in many respects, the achievements of the League were indeed considerable. The League, for instance, devised a set of institutional techniques that had an enduring influence on international law. The League established international committees to study numerous social and economic issues. For example, the International Labour Organization, which focused on questions of monitoring and improving labour standards throughout the world and was closely affiliated with the League, was created out of the recognition that world peace could only be achieved through the advancement of social justice.

In addition, the League engaged, in different ways, in the extraordinary project of creating and maintaining sovereign states, and developed an elaborate set of techniques for this purpose—some of which are still used by international organizations as they grapple with problems of governance and sovereignty in societies, such as Kosovo and East Timor, which have suffered intense conflict. The great League experiments in creating and stabilizing sovereign states occurred in two different contexts.

First, the problem of nationalism was seen as responsible in many ways for the outbreak of World War I. President Wilson attempted to resolve this complex issue by proclaiming the concept of 'self-determination', the idea that every nation should have its own state. Following this principle, new states—such as Poland—were created in Eastern Europe, under the auspices of the League. The redrawing of boundaries that resulted, however, meant that certain ethnic groups were now minorities within the newly formed states. The League attempted to protect these minority groups by means of a new treaty regime, the 'Minority Protection' system, which was unique in providing international guarantees for the rights of minorities. The Mandate System, created by Article 22 of the League of Nations Covenant, was an equally bold innovation in international law and institutions. This system was devised to protect the inhabitants of the territories that had belonged to Germany and the Ottoman Empire prior to the war. These territories extended from the Middle East to Africa and the Pacific, and included territories such as Palestine, Ruanda, and New Guinea. Under the old international law of the nineteenth century, these territories would have been distributed among the victorious powers. Wilson, however, insisted that a new international regime should be devised to protect non-European peoples, through international supervision, rather than subject them to a system of colonial exploitation. In the words of Article 22, 'the well-being and development of such peoples form a sacred trust of civilization'. The ultimate goal of the Mandate System was to promote self-government in these territories and indeed, in some cases, to ensure that they became sovereign states. The Mandate System was one response to events in the non-Western world, where nationalist movements were confronting the colonial powers. Anti-colonial protests—sometimes outright rebellions—had been launched in Asia and Africa, in India, Vietnam, Egypt, Iraq, and Kenya. Colonial rule was contested at a number of levels, and the Mandate System served the purpose of advancing the idea of a moral colonialism, one directed at protecting the people of the territories through international supervision and indeed, guiding them towards independence.

In these quite different regimes—one seeking to address the challenges of nationalism and the other the dilemmas of colonial rule—the League articulated a very rich and complex set of ideas about the character of the sovereign state and the role that the international community, through international organizations, could play in creating such states.

An equally important innovation of the League of Nations was the creation of the Permanent Court of International Justice (PCIJ). For many centuries states had created special tribunals to mediate and settle their disputes. However, the PCIJ was the first attempt to create a permanent court for the purpose of hearing any dispute relating to international law. There were strong arguments in favour of creating a system in which any state that had a grievance against another state could begin a case in the PCIJ and compel that other state to appear and defend itself. Once again, however, considerations of sovereignty prevailed. Thus, in the end, it was only if a state had agreed to appear before a Court by signing a treaty that it could be required to do so.

The United Nations: 1945 to the present

At the conclusion of World War II an international community that had been traumatized by a war that was, for the first time, truly global, attempted once again to create the laws and institutions necessary to ensure a lasting peace. The failed League of Nations was replaced by the United Nations, which, however, developed and elaborated on many of the institutional characteristics of the League.

Box 3.8 UN institutional structure

The UN Charter, in effect the constitution of the United Nations, created several different organs and outlined the specific powers of each organ. The General Assembly, as the name suggests, is the meeting place of the whole membership of the United Nations. While it may pass declarations about international issues, the Assembly has relatively limited powers. The Security Council, which is made up of five permanent members and ten non-permanent members who are periodically elected by the Assembly, is in effect the executive branch of the UN system. The permanent members are the US, France, China, Russia (formerly the Soviet Union), and France—the victors of World War II. Under the UN Charter, decisions of the Security Council are legally binding on all member states of the UN. However, all permanent members have the important power of vetoing any proposed decision. In this way, the United Nations acknowledges the simple fact that it would be ineffective in dealing with major issues without the support of the Great Powers, which have to be given a correspondingly special status in the system. The Council has the power to authorize the use of force—that is, to wage war. The UN lacks its own army. As a consequence, whenever the Council authorizes the use of force, it is in effect authorizing its member states to go to war under the auspices of the UN. A further organ, the Secretariat, supervises the day-to-day running of the UN bureaucracy, and is headed by the Secretary General. The Permanent Court of International Justice was replaced, in the UN Charter, by the International Court of Justice.

The preamble of the UN Charter begins with the powerful words 'to save succeeding generations from the scourge of war, which twice in our lifetime has brought untold sorrow to mankind', and towards this end, it declares war illegal except in two circumstances: first, a state can go to war in the event of self-defence, which is narrowly defined; and second, war can be authorized by the Security Council.

The horrors of World War II and in particular, the Holocaust, prompted the UN to begin a new and radical initiative—the international promotion of human rights. The individual had no real standing in international law up to that time. Thus, even if an individual visiting a foreign territory was harmed by the actions of the foreign government, she could only seek the protection of international law if her own government exercised the right of 'diplomatic protection' and claimed that the foreign government had infringed international law in the treatment of that person. In short, the wrong done to the individual was seen as a wrong done to the state of which that individual was a citizen. The individual had no independent standing, under international law, to bring a claim against the offending sovereign government. Further, under classical Westphalian ideas of sovereignty, a state could treat its own citizen in any way it pleased without implicating international law. One of the central tenets of international human rights law is that the manner in which a state treats its own citizen is a matter of international and not merely domestic concern. The relationship between a state and its citizen is now mediated by international law, in that all individuals within a state, including citizens, enjoy certain fundamental human rights that are provided by international law and any state which violates those rights is guilty of a breach of international law. As such, human rights law has had a profound impact on existing concepts of sovereignty (see Chapter 13). The Universal Declaration of Human Rights, adopted by the United Nations in 1948, outlines a variety of rights ranging from the right to 'life liberty and security of person' to 'the right to a standard of living adequate for the health and well-being of himself and of his family'. The Declaration was the foundation of a series of human rights treaties that subsequently came into existence, the most important of these being the International Covenant on Economic, Social and Cultural Rights and the International Covenant on Civil and Political Rights (see Chapter 13).

The period following the creation of the United Nations was dominated by two major international issues. A 'Cold War' took place between the Communist countries, led by the Soviet Union, and the West, led by the United States. UN work was greatly limited by the fact that these two adversaries played a prominent role in the UN system and both occupied permanent seats on the Security Council. Although no direct conflict occurred between the two great powers, proxy wars took place between them in various other territories, where the combatants were supported by one state or the other, as in the case of the civil war that broke out in Vietnam. The second major development was the intensifying campaign of colonized people to win their independence, as India did in 1947. Thus began a long and sometimes bloody process as the colonized people of Asia and Africa sought to win their freedom from European powers often reluctant to cede control over their possessions.

The United Nations was an important forum in this anti-colonial initiative. Newly independent states—as they were then called—became members of the United Nations, and used their numbers in the General Assembly to begin a series of campaigns directed at ending colonialism. One of the most important Declarations to be passed by the General Assembly asserted the 'right of peoples to self-determination', that is, to be free of colonial rule (see Chapter 9). Self-determination, which had been initially articulated as a means of dealing with the nationalist problems within Europe, was adapted to facilitate decolonization.

The new states confronted two major problems once they achieved independence. First, they had to consolidate their statehood; many of the new states were multi-ethnic in character, and had to ensure that the uniting nationalism that had been so powerful in the struggle for independence could then be harnessed to create a new and successful state that would be accepted by all its constituent groups. Secondly, as part of this process, they had to bring about real development to their populations which were largely impoverished and lacking the most basic living amenities.

The emergence of these new states profoundly changed the composition of the international community, and presented a major challenge to the international system, as they attributed their condition, in large part, to their experience of colonialism and economic exploitation that had been supported by an international law made by the colonial powers to further their own interests. The issue these states confronted was complex: could international law be used to dismantle the colonial relations it had legitimized in the first instance? The new states, having finally won sovereignty, now became intent on using their status to change this system. The term 'Third World' was sometimes used to describe this group of states—the 'First World' being the developed Western states and the 'Second World' the Socialist states. These states also formed what was termed the 'Non-Aligned Movement' in order to assert their aspiration to be independent of the Cold War rivalries that were prominent at the time.

In seeking to change the system by using international law, these states concentrated their energies on particular doctrines and areas of law that were of greatest significance to them: among these were the prevention of the use of force and prohibition of intervention; the creation of a New International Economic Order; and the Law of the Sea. They perceived their task as being that of reversing the effects of colonialism. The new states used their large numbers in the General Assembly to pass a series of wide-ranging resolutions that dealt with these issues. Many of the Western states either abstained or else opposed these resolutions that were nevertheless passed by large majorities. The Third World attempts to bring about such change, however, were largely unsuccessful. The developed states argued that they were not bound by the principles included in the various Declarations. In so doing they reverted to classical principles of international law, asserting first, that General Assembly resolutions had no binding power in any event and second, that they could not be bound by any rule unless they had agreed to be so bound. At the same time, the developed states argued that developing states were bound by customary law—relating to issues such as international economic law—even though developing states had not actively participated in the making of the custom by which they were ostensibly bound. In this way, the issue of the sources of international law and the manner in which international law is created and made binding on states became a crucial issue to the central debates of that time.

Third World attempts to transform international law were also hampered by changes in the international system. The efforts of many Third World states to bring about development proved to be failures, and often justified various forms of oppression by corrupt and authoritarian leaders. Civil wars broke out in many states, as different ethnic groups competed with each other for control of the state and all its resources. Although the Third World attempted in principle to remain independent of the Cold War, they often lacked the resources to do so, and local politicians sought to enhance their own power by claiming the support of one side or another, and relying on such support to repress their own people. The African dictator, Mobutu Sesu Seko of Zaire, is an example of this; he received massive support from the West despite the enormous suffering he inflicted on his people, as he was regarded as a key ally in the war against communism. One of the major decisions of the International Court of Justice during this period, *Nicaragua v the United States* was also a product of the Cold War, as the United States mined Nicaragua's harbour, claiming that it was defending other Central American states from subversion by Nicaragua's socialist government. The Court ruled that America's actions were illegal and reinforced the international legal norms of non-intervention and sovereignty.

The major doctrinal development of this period was the introduction of international human rights law. The new states strongly advocated the development of human rights law, and indeed presented the right to self-determination as a human right. Once again, however, disputes emerged between developed and developing states. Developed states focused principally on civil and political rights, such as the right to free speech and the right to a fair trial; developing countries, while accepting the importance of such rights, claimed that social and economic rights were equally important—including the right to health and the right to social welfare. Indeed, the developing states went further in arguing for a right to development and a right to peace, rights that the West largely disputed.

The end of the Cold War: international law from 1989

The dramatic and largely unforeseen collapse of the Soviet Union in 1989 promised to inaugurate 'A New World Order'. The character of that new order was quickly evident. Saddam Hussein invaded Kuwait in 1990, and this led to unprecedented action on the part of the United Nations which was now no longer so divided by cold war rivalry. Led by the United States, the UN immediately imposed sanctions on Iraq and took a series of measures that led ultimately to a war that was authorized by the United Nations. This action was seen as a model of how the United Nations was intended to work, although many outstanding and important issues remained to be resolved, particularly since Saddam Hussein remained in power.

Internal wars

Despite the war begun by Iraq, much of the conflict that took place in the 1990s occurred within rather than between states. The conflicts in Yugoslavia and Rwanda, for instance, were of an internal, ethnic character. These conflicts raised again a complex and controversial set of issues regarding 'humanitarian intervention'—the use of force by one state against another state in order, ostensibly, to prevent massive human rights violations in the latter state (see Chapter 10). Third World states had been especially suspicious of this idea because it was often used by Western states to justify the conquest of non-European societies. The international system faced an enormous challenge: how could it respond to genocide or threatened genocide, the ultimate atrocity? The United Nations proved especially inept and helpless to prevent the massacre of tens of thousands of people in Rwanda in 1994. In the case of Yugoslavia, the North Atlantic Treaty Organization began a bombing campaign to prevent further violence against the minority living in the Yugoslavian province of Kosovo, this despite the lack of an authorizing resolution from the Security Council. The NATO actions presented a complex moral dilemma for international lawyers. The NATO action was clearly illegal, but at the same time, it appeared that the situation demanded such action. As a result, the humanitarian intervention debate acquired prominence, once again, on the international agenda, and scholars attempted to conceptualize humanitarian intervention in a way that would allow intervention to prevent mass atrocities while preventing it from being used as an excuse for imperialism. While sovereign states were torn apart by civil war—Yugoslavia separated into a number of different states including Bosnia-Herzegovina and Croatia—in other cases, civil wars resulted in the collapse of authoritative, central governments that could control their territories and provide for the well being of their people. Countries such as Somalia were overwhelmed by warring factions competing for power. In all these cases, enormous human suffering was a consequence, and the international system responded as best it could by commencing peacekeeping operations which extended to actually controlling and governing the territories in question themselves. The atrocities committed in these regions inspired a further set of developments focusing on courts, such as the International Criminal Tribunal for the former Yugoslavia, based at the Hague, and established for the particular purpose of trying individuals responsible for major international crimes such as large scale murders, in the territories of the former Yugoslavia (see Chapter 12).

Globalization

The phenomenon of globalization, the intensifying interdependence of states as a result of commerce, migration, technology, and culture, another prominent feature of the 1990s, presents a further set of challenges to sovereignty. Trade, for instance, was becoming increasingly international; the economies of the vast majority of states became more dependent on exporting and importing goods in order to take advantage of the efficiencies of global markets. Trade had always been a concern of international law since its very beginnings. In 1994, however, the creation of the World Trade Organization (WTO) was a particularly important development and an outstanding example of how international law and institutions could coordinate the actions of states. The WTO establishes the basic rules that all member countries must observe in their trade relations with each other. What is remarkable about this institution, further, is that it compels all members to subject themselves to the dispute resolution mechanism of the WTO. Despite this fact, many powerful states, including the United States and China, have now submitted themselves to this process so in this case, it seems, states have been prepared to surrender their sovereignty to an international institution because of the perceived benefits they receive from membership of such an institution (see Chapter 15).

In addition to these developments, the sovereign state has been challenged by the emergence of a number of actors that play an increasingly prominent role in international affairs. Large corporations, operating transnationally, possess an enormous amount of economic power that often exceeds that wielded by sovereign states. On the one hand, they could play an important role in promoting economic development in poverty stricken countries. On the other, several such corporations operating in Africa and Asia have been accused of committing large scale human rights abuses—for example, by engaging in mining operations with no regard to the well-being of the local populations. Non-governmental organizations such as Amnesty International played an increasingly prominent role in promoting international law—in this case, international human rights law (see Chapter 7). The network of organizations constituting the International Campaign to Ban Landmines took the initiative to draft a treaty aimed at the elimination of landmines, and won a Nobel Peace Prize for its efforts. Non-governmental organizations such as these provided individuals with an accessible way to become involved in issues, such as the drafting of treaties, that had traditionally been the preserve of states.

The 'War on Terror'

The terrorist attacks on New York on 11 September 2001 and the subsequent United States response, most prominently the invasion of Iraq, presented a profound challenge to the international system and international law. The United States declared a 'war on terror' that consisted of several components, some of which were identified in its National Security Strategy of 2002. It asserted its right to engage in 'pre-emptive self-defence' in order to neutralize the new threats posed by international terrorists. The United Nations Charter, as traditionally interpreted, does not permit such a form of self-defence because it could encourage countries to begin wars against their rivals. Nevertheless, the United States argued that the new conditions warranted a change in the law. The United States also adopted a policy of democracy promotion based on the belief that terrorism flourished in non-democratic states. Many aspects of US thinking about the war on terror were made clearer by subsequent actions—most prominently, the invasion of Iraq, which took place without an explicit Security Council authorization and which was therefore widely regarded as illegal. What was especially disturbing was the alacrity and willingness with which the US declared that various fundamental norms of international humanitarian law and human rights law did not apply to individuals suspected of being terrorists—thus challenging the basic, foundational premise of international human rights law: that all human beings enjoy certain fundamental rights simply by virtue of being human. The massive and unprecedented disrepute that the United States has suffered as a result of the actions of the Bush administration has made it very likely that his successor, Barack Obama, will seek to pursue more traditional, multilateral approaches to international problems. Tellingly, furthermore, the collapse of the international financial system resulted in vehement calls for international cooperation and coordination to deal with a global crisis that had its roots in the United States. The emergence of China and the unmistakable shift of power—moral, intellectual, and economic—away from the West will likely result in an international system in which societies from East Asia to South America will demand various changes that cannot be ignored. But the question still remains as to whether these shifts will result in the betterment of the lives of the poorest people in the world, the billions who struggle to survive without the most elementary needs being satisfied.

The question of when and how international law affects state behaviour will be a subject of ongoing debate and analysis. Very often, as in the Congress of Vienna, the international system departs from the basic principle that 'all sovereign states are equal'; great powers establish the character of the system and, indeed, they are unwilling to participate in any international structure of government unless it provides them with a special role.

What is clear, from this brief examination of the history of international law, however, is the enduring resilience of international law and the flexibility and ingenuity that has been devoted, over the centuries, to making it work, and this despite numerous major failures. International law can be seen in at least two ways: first, as a set of rules that will be inevitably violated by powerful states intent on having their own way when the rules do not correspond with their interests. Or it may be seen as a mechanism by which states make arrangements among themselves precisely in order to further their own interests through cooperation. This includes creating a set of rules that ensures predictability and a stable environment in which expectations can be fulfilled.

Creating international regimes that meet the needs of all states is a difficult and challenging task. As debates about the character and content of human rights would suggest, it is far from easy to reach agreement about issues that profoundly affect both international and domestic society. States have their own views on how complex issues such as environmental degradation can be addressed. And yet, despite all this it is also true that little can be achieved without international cooperation when addressing the major problems of our time—massive poverty, the spread of diseases, environmental degradation, and human rights violations, to name but some of the challenges the international community faces. Furthermore, power is now dispersed in complex ways throughout the international system and as the recent experience of the Bush administration demonstrates, even the most powerful states cannot easily manage these challenging issues—of security, poverty, international finance—through unilateral action alone. For these reasons, international law remains relevant in international relations.

Table 3.1 Timeline

Time	Event	Development in IL
16th century	Colonialism	Legal scholars attempt to lay down first doctrines
1625	Grotius writes 'The Rights of War and Peace'	Law shifts from religion towards natural law
1648	Peace of Westphalia	Establishment of sovereignty doctrine
1815	Congress of Vienna	'Balance of power'
19th century	Further ascendance of the sovereign state	Positivism gradually replaces naturalist jurisprudence—IL based on state actions
1899 and 1907	The Hague Conferences	Development of laws of war (*ad bello* and *in bello*)
1919	League of Nations	First major international institution, creation of ILO, the Permanent Court of International Justice
1945–	United Nations	Universal Declaration of Human Rights in 1948, institutional structure to promote international peace and security; anticolonialism initiatives
1989–		Humanitarian intervention? Creation of WTO
1990s–	Rise of internal wars	
1994	Globalization	
		Challenge to IL?
2001–	'War on Terror'	

Conclusion

Sovereignty is the foundation of international law. International law can be defined primarily as the law that governs relations between states. The history of international law can be written in a number of different ways, and recent scholarship has attempted to depart from the traditional Eurocentric approach to the discipline. Both imperialism and wars have played a major role in the development of international law. The Peace of Westphalia in 1648 led to the emergence of the modern concept of sovereignty. The League of Nations, the world's first major international organization, was created after the catastrophic World War I. International human rights law, which has grown dramatically since its beginnings in 1948, presented a further major challenge to traditional ideas of sovereignty. The Cold War and the conflict between developed and developing countries profoundly shaped international relations in the years following the establishment of the United Nations. Since then, phenomena such as globalization and terrorism have led to increasing interdependence among states, and international law has expanded dramatically to address issues such as terrorism on one hand, and international economic relations on the other.

Questions

1. Why might it be important to study the history of international law?
2. What are the recent developments in the way in which the history of international law is studied?
3. How has imperialism shaped the history of international relations and international law?
4. What is the significance of Westphalia in understanding international law; in what ways have the Westphalian model of sovereignty been challenged over the years?
5. What is the significance of Grotius and Vattel for the development of international law?
6. What does the history of international law indicate about the major weaknesses and strengths of international law, including international institutions?
7. What impact have international institutions such as the League of Nations and United Nations had on international relations and law?
8. What are the central insights we receive from a historical perspective about the relationship between international law and international relations?
9. What would the international system be like if we completely abolished international institutions and international law?

Further reading

Alexandrowicz, C.H. (1973) *The European-African Confrontation: A Study in Treaty Making* (Leiden: A.W. Sijthoff). *A detailed study of the creation of legal relations between Europe and Africa that focuses on the nineteenth century.*

Anand, R.P. (1987) *International Law and the Developing Countries: Confrontation or Cooperation?* (The Hague: Kluwer Law International). *One of the pioneering books outlining the positions and views of developing* countries shortly after their acquisition of independence.

Grewe, W. (2000) *The Epochs of International Law* (Berlin: Walter de Gruyter). *A detailed and comprehensive history of the discipline of international law.*

Koskenniemi, M. (2000) *The Gentle Civilizer of Nations: The Rise and Fall of International Law 1870–1960* (Cambridge: Cambridge University Press). *A theoretically rich and insightful history of the period it covers, which traces the shift from formalist European international law to policy-oriented American international law.*

Nussbaum, A. (1954) *A Concise History of the Law of Nations* (New York: Macmillan). *A good basic introduction to the history of international law.*

Reus-Smit, C. (2004) (ed.) *The Politics of International Law* (Cambridge: Cambridge University Press). *A collection of essays, by international law and international relations scholars, that examines the relationship between law and politics by focusing on areas such as the use of force, the Kosovo bombing campaign, and climate change.*

Weeramantry, C. G. (2005) *Universalizing International Law* (The Hague: Martinus Nijhoff). *A recent and visionary attempt to expand the reach of international law.*

Websites

www.iilj.org/research/HistoryandTheoryofInternationalLaw.asp *The Institute for International Law and Justice at New York University brings together scholars working on the history of international law and publishes working papers on its website.*

http://avalon.law.yale.edu/20th_century/leagcov.asp

http://avalon.law.yale.edu/17th_century/westphal.asp *The Avalon Project at Yale Law School has compiled a wide range of historical documents and offers detailed information on crucial events in the history of international law—among others on the League of Nations and the Peace of Westphalia.*

http://www.un.org/aboutun/unhistory *This website gives a detailed account of the history of the United Nations.*

http://www.un.org/law/ilc *The International Law Commission has played an important role in the codification and development of international law over time—this website provides up-to-date information on its workings.*

Visit the Online Resource Centre that accompanies this book to access more learning resources www.oxfordtextbooks.co.uk/orc/cali/

Chapter endnote

1. For a comprehensive overview of the history and historiography of international law, see the various entries by Wolfgang Preiser and his colleagues in *The Encyclopedia of Public International Law*, Elsevier vol. 7, pp. 126273 (1984). These include essays by distinguished scholars from Asia and Africa.

Chapter 4

Perspectives on international relations in international law

Başak Çalı

CHAPTER CONTENTS

- Introduction
- What is international law?
- The purpose of international law
- The relevance of theories of international law in international relations
- Conclusion

CHAPTER OVERVIEW

This chapter surveys the theories of international law. It aims to identify the contribution each of these theories makes to the description, purpose, and relevance of international law in international relations. The chapter highlights the major sources of disagreement between different types and levels of theories of international law on the description and purposes of international law. It finally discusses the contribution of theories of international law to our understanding of international relations and shows how theories of international law respond to the persistent criticisms of the role and significance of international law in the *real world* of international relations.

Introduction

In the previous chapters, we have seen that theories of international relations assign different levels of explanatory power and importance to international law and historical analysis of international law focus on the relationship between state sovereignty, distribution of power amongst states, and the breadth and relevance of international law. In this chapter we will focus on theories of international law and how they approach the foundations of law in a world of sovereign states.

Theories of international law aim to set out a coherent understanding of international law by laying its foundations at a fairly abstract level. They respond to three basic theoretical problems: the problem of description, the problem of purpose, and the problem of relevance of international law. The problem of description corresponds to the question 'What is international law?' The problem of purpose corresponds to the question 'What is international law for?' The problem of relevance corresponds to the question 'Do states *really*, and if so why, comply with international law?' These three problems are interrelated and sometimes one theory may attempt to solve all three of these problems. Inadvertently or not, any theory that attempts to answer one of these questions will proffer a view on the other questions. Some theories of international law hold that an answer to one of these questions determines the answers to the other two.

Theories of international law are a dynamic collection of arguments that have been constantly revised in the light of international events and the problems of their time. They have a long history and cross theories of international relations. Different theories of international law compete in order to be seen as the *most convincing theory* to be used to respond to problems of international law. In different countries and at different historical points in time (see Chapter 3), a theory may be adopted from among those extant theories as the dominant international law position. Some theories become more popular and appealing at certain times because they capture the developments of their era better. In everyday practice, international lawyers, diplomats, and politicians may appeal to more than one theory in defending their positions on particular issues—and they may do so inconsistently. Of course, there is also scepticism about the utility of theories of international law. This scepticism is often portrayed through the image of a small circle of academics in their ivory towers discussing 'theory'—an isolated debate with little relevance to the real world. Theories of international law do, however, matter. They make up the backbone which supports and sustains the practice of international law. Theories, for any subject matter, provide a framework for guiding, understanding, and criticizing the practice. Theories of international law provide a structure with which to make sense of the international system and the legal significance and meaning of the actions of different actors in the system. Theories also allow us to imagine the future of international law and the ways in which the international law of the future could be different from the international law we know today. Different theories respond to different types of concerns and questions. It is important to keep in mind that theorists within a single approach may also have disagreements.

This chapter analyses the theories of international law by focusing on the three foundational problems we outlined at the start of this chapter, namely: description, purpose, and relevance. The problem of the *description* of international law enables us to identify the long-standing debate between positivism and naturalism in international law and contemporary contributions to this debate. The problem of the *purpose* of international law allows us to distinguish between framework theories and goal-oriented theories. The problem of *relevance* addresses the question of whether theories of international law have any real world relevance in understanding how states behave.

What is international law?

Theories of international law have classically attempted to tackle the question 'what is international law?'. As we have seen in Chapters 1 and 3, international law is generally defined as the law that regulates relations between states. This is, however, a *nominal definition*. It helps us to distinguish international law from domestic law and international politics, but it does not describe the underlying structure or the essence of international law.

Describing the essence of international law has been a major preoccupation of international law theorists since the famous negative claim by John Austin that 'international law is not really law, but it is positive morality' (Austin 1832). Given the thousands of international treaties, the existence of a global organization with almost universal membership (the United Nations) and an international criminal court this charge may at first seem outdated and irrelevant. The question of whether international law is law or not is nevertheless relevant as it shows us that however we define international law, it does not fit with the description of law put forward by Austin as the 'commands of the sovereign'.

John Austin (1750–1859) was a positivist theorist of law who defined the most important characteristic of law as being commands of a sovereign who could coerce its subjects to comply with law. As there is no sovereign power in international law, his conclusion about the definition of international law was straightforward and dismissive: that it simply was not law. Austin's negative description of international law was derived from his definition of law as such. Austin's conception of law has been challenged by many theories of international law. We can distinguish four broad schools that challenged his dismissive attitude towards international law as law: fellow positivists who did not share the command theory of law, naturalists, the process school of international law, and critical legal scholars.

Positivism about international law

Some theories are more popular and, therefore, accepted than others. International legal positivism is one such popular theory. Positivism is the name given to a group of theories about international law that share a common thread. The common thread is the agreement that law should be described as it is as opposed to what it should be. This means that any description of law should accurately reflect the social practices that make the law. Austin, as we have just seen, was a positivist who argued that an accurate description of law was the command of the sovereign backed up by sanctions. He, therefore, had serious doubts about whether international law was law at all. Positivists have disagreed with both components of this theory. Some positivists said international law was indeed about the command of the sovereigns, but without the threat of sanctions. Other positivists argued that command of the sovereign was not itself an adequate positivist theory (Hart 1961).

The idea that international law is the command of sovereign states is also known as the '**voluntarist**' or '**will**' theory of international law (Pellet 1992). Because positivism about international law has a number of branches that have developed through time, this view is also called '*classic legal positivism*' about international law. This theory describes international law as a system of rules created deliberately and explicitly by states. The voluntarist version of positivism responds to Austin's challenge of lack of sanctions by pointing that there is no need for sanctions in a system of rules where states have explicitly willed to be bound by the rules. This view finds its most stark expression in the 1927 judgment of the Permanent Court of International Justice in the *Lotus/Bozkurt Case*:

> International law governs relations between independent states. The rules of law binding upon States therefore emanate from their own free will as expressed in conventions or by usages generally accepted as expressing principles of law and established in order to regulate the relations between these co-existing independent communities or with a view to the achievement of common aims. Restrictions upon the independence of States therefore cannot be presumed. (*Lotus/Bozkurt Case* 1927)

The description of international law as law that each and every state has explicitly agreed to has important consequences for knowing what the substance of law is. Given that each state has to show its will to a rule that regulates its relations with other states, this could also mean that states can withdraw support at any time. International law then looks like an unstable *modus operandi* between states that can be subject to a state changing its will on any previous agreement. Under the classic scheme, international law is viewed as law, but it is also hard to know what the content of that law is, as nothing can be imposed on a sovereign state that it does not want to accept. The *classic positivist* position in this respect shares a common ground with *realist theories* of international relations. Even though classic positivists agree that international law is law, the impact of law on the behaviour of states is limited. States do not abide by the international laws they do not want to obey. Realist theories of international relations have also long claimed that international law is epiphenomenal to understanding international relations and state behaviour within it. The very reason for this is that the background conditions of the international system are **anarchic** (Waltz 1979). 'Anarchy' in this context is meant not as a condition of chaos, but one in which there is no sovereign body that governs nation states. International law is only relevant when it overlaps with the interests of states. In this respect the 'will of the state' in classic positivism and the 'interests of the state' in international relations realism overlap in their vision of international relations and the role of international law within it.

Classic legal positivism has been criticized by a number of positivists, who believe that the will of an individual state as the foundation of international law theory is not an accurate or sound description of international law as we know it. First, states act multilaterally on a wide range of international issues. The proposition that individual states are the sole arbiter of international law as it applies to them does not fit the practice of multilateralism through treaties in international law. If each state unilaterally defined international law, it would be impossible to have stable international organizations such as the United Nations, the International Telecommunications Union, or the World Trade Organization. A group of positivists, for these reasons, has moved from 'will' theories to theories based on 'consent' as a more sound description of international law. Under the positivist consent theories of international law, the description of international law is modified: international law is rules to which states have consented. Contrary to the will theory, the consent theory has a more stable outlook on international law, as consent is not something that a state can change whenever it pleases. Once a state has consented to a rule, there are further rules governing the bindingness of the law thus created—so consent implies more than will because it has a procedural element.

There are ways of giving consent to a rule of international law and consent can also be withdrawn by following a procedure (see Chapters 5 and 6). Consent theories, in this way, solve the problem of the constantly changing character of international law, but also remain respectful of the will of the states. There are significant parallels between the vision of the consent theories of international law and **institutional theories** of international relations. In both of these theories, the multiplicity of sovereign states as the description of the system is recognized, but there is a further emphasis on the *condition of cooperation* between sovereign states. Consent theories rely on this condition as well as theories that recognize the importance of institutions in managing interstate relations.

This version of positivism, however, also comes with problems. Once consent is viewed as the will of states expressed in certain ways, there is still the issue of defining the correct way to express consent. Sceptics of the consent theory will immediately point out that the theory does not solve the centrality of the will of the state in the description of international law: it merely formulates it in a different way. Unless one thinks that there was some 'imaginary original consent' to the consent theory and the procedures of expressing consent, the problem of the will of the state as the ultimate reference of international law is not solved. Most positivist theorizing accepts this caveat and argues that the consent theory still works because most states have accepted it as the norm and that there are good reasons to respect the consent of states, anyway. In a world of nation states with different interests, they argue, a consent-based positivist approach to international law is the best way to ensure coexistence or cooperation of states (Weil 1983, Kingsbury 2002).

From the preceding discussion we can see that consent theorists disagree with each other about what counts as consent. We can identify two broad approaches to the establishment of consent amongst positivists. First, there is the family of theories which focuses on the acts and deeds of individual states to identify which part of international law is binding amongst which combination of states. We can call these the *unitary state action-based* theories of consent. Under these theories, international law can be viewed and described as a pyramid. At the top of the pyramid, there are the rules that every state has consented to (or is assumed to have consented to); in the middle there are the rules that a large group of states has consented to; and at the very bottom, there are the rules that only apply to a very limited number of states.

Second, there is the family of theories which argues that we should not solely focus on the acts and deeds of individual states but also on other ways and fora through which states express their will. The practice of international courts and tribunals, the activities of the legislative organs of the United Nations (such as the General Assembly, the Peace-building Commission, the Human Rights Council) and the organs of regional organizations are examples of such fora. This is because, by delegating powers to international organizations and by accepting the jurisprudence of international courts and tribunals, states have implied that they consent to the activities of these organs. We can call these *collective state action-based* theories of consent (Simma and Paulus 1999). The description of international law under these theories is richer. It allows for a larger number of rules to be viewed as common to the society of states as a whole (see Chapter 6). There are parallels between this theory and the social constructivist theories of IR to the extent that state interests are viewed as being subject to modification and redefinition through socialization within the international system. The condition of the international system, therefore, is one of continuous interaction and socialization.

Natural law descriptions of international law

Natural law descriptions of international law are best understood in opposition to positivist theories of international law. As we have seen above, different versions of positivism agree that international law is based on the social practices of states alone. Natural law theories challenge this view as they regard it as neither a coherent nor a desirable description of international law. Natural law theorists hold that the law is not simply a function of social practices. It has a moral element at its very core. International law, therefore, cannot be described without reference to an account of these embedded moral rules.

For once, natural law theorists argue that positivism cannot account for the bindingness of international law, and for that purpose turn on the idea of 'original consent'. Positivists cannot explain why states should follow the principle of good faith in adhering to international treaties (known in Latin as *pacta sunt servanda*), which holds that all states shall be faithful to promises they make and honour treaties they sign. Natural law theorists point out that it is impossible to show that states have actually consented to this principle throughout history. They argue that it is implausible because the principle of good faith has a very good chance of coming into conflict with state interests at different times. It is, therefore, not in states' interests to blindly agree to the principle of good faith. As we nevertheless think that *pacta sunt servanda* is a central principle of international law, natural lawyers

Table 4.1 Positivist descriptions of international law

Voluntarism	Unitary consent	Collective consent
IL is what a state wills as IL	IL is what a state consents to through unilateral procedures as IL	IL is what states consent to through collective procedures as law
Close identification between state interests and IL	A small gap between state interests and IL as consent cannot be withdrawn at will	A larger gap between state interests and IL
Parallels with Realist Theories of IR	Parallels with Institutional and Liberal Theories of IR	Parallels with Social Constructivist Theories of IR

suggest that it makes more sense to treat the principle of good faith as a *moral* rule than as a rule accepted by social practices. The moral force of the rule, therefore, comes before and informs the social practice. The principle of good faith is a moral rule that is followed by most states most of the time because the common good of all states is served by having stable and predictable relationships with each other. Natural law theorists conclude that moral rules, such as these, are needed to complement and perfect the social dimension of law.

The undesirability of positivist descriptions of international law is the second issue natural law theories focus on. Natural lawyers refuse the positivist position that states can consent to any rule they please. Where states consent to immoral things, they argue, it should not be viewed as international law as such. This view highlights that too much from the character of law is lost when it loses its pull to justice. If an immoral rule, such as an interstate agreement to exterminate a people, is viewed as law, then law is nothing but a tool to legitimize any type of action committed by states, however brutal or devastating. Natural law theorists dispute that this is what law is. Law has to have an independent effect on its subjects and, therefore, it has to be more than what the subjects would like it to be.

Under natural law theories, the definition of international law, therefore, should make a reference to the moral point of law. In other words, international law has to be defined as a body of law composed of not only the actual will of states, but also of moral limits and goods which restrict what states can agree to make permissible and prohibitive. That natural law theorists disagree on the content of the common good that characterizes international law should, however, come as no surprise. Human rights, for example, is one of the contenders (Tesón 1998). These rights form the limits within which states would be free to fashion positive laws. International law is, in natural law theories, the body of rules that states agree to abide by in their relations with each other and which are compatible with the common good, however the 'common good' is defined.

Natural law theories of international law are at odds with international relations theories of realism. Natural law advocates that states ought to be compelled with moral reasons when abiding with international law. The latter does not. Natural law descriptions of international law fit more comfortably with social constructivist theories of international relations, because they share the common underlying assumption that norms have an independent effect on the behaviour of states. The condition of the international system, therefore, is one of an international society of states where states are capable of recognizing some moral point in their relations with each other.

International law as a process

The **process school** of international law has two further monikers. It is also known as the 'policy-orientated school' or 'New Haven School' because it was established at Yale Law school in the 1940s. This theory grows out of the dissatisfaction with the positivist and natural law descriptions of international law as rules either emanating from state will or from reason. The process school defines international law as an authoritative and controlling process of decision-making in which various actors in the world community participate (Ratner and Slaughter 1999). The process school does not see international law as a set of rules that have been made in the past, but as a process which takes into account past decisions, current international affairs, and the future. This theory holds that the relationship between law and policy is not only unavoidable, but also necessary for international law to be responsive to the emerging needs of international society. Describing international law as an ongoing process of authoritative decision-making enables international actors to deal with policy factors openly and systematically. This strengthens the effectiveness of international law and, in turn, states' obedience to it.

The process theory views international law primarily as a political process. This does not mean that all political decisions of international actors are synonymous with international law. Political decisions have to: (1) come from relevant and authorized actors; (2) they have to have prescriptive content; and (3) they have to be taken in accordance with criteria expected by the world community. International law is not made by states but by decision-makers with authorized powers. Such decision-makers include state officials, intergovernmental organizations, and non-state actors. The importance of the role played by an actor is determined by the specific international law question at stake.

The process school alters the description of law as a set of rules made by states by viewing it as a decision-making process undertaken by the relevant world actors. Similar to natural law approaches, the process school does not view international law simply as a platform where anything goes. It also states that international law has a purpose and a direction, which is to 'realize human dignity' (McDougal, Lasswell, and Reisman 1981: 550). We will discuss this direction further in the next section.

The description of international law as a constant interaction of policy, context, and authoritative past decisions assumes a great deal of common good faith on the part of the world's policy makers. The process theory of international law positions itself between positivism and naturalism by putting an emphasis both on the expression of state will and on principles that exist independently of that will. Sceptics of this theory are concerned that this middle position is not tenable and that states always try to manipulate the decision-making process to serve their own ends rather than pursuing a common aim that serves the world community as a whole. The process school, as a response, argues that it is still better that states openly show how their policy choices influence international law rather than them viewing international law as a set of rules that no state effectively obeys. The process school of international law sits better with students of politics because it is capable of crossing the disciplinary divide between international law and international relations jargon and is able to create a relevant space for international law in international politics. The process school of international law can be viewed as one type of social constructivist theory of international relations, where the legal and political processes are seen as mutually interdependent.

Critical legal studies and international law

Critical legal studies (CLS) theories are a family of approaches to international law which share a common point of dissatisfaction about how international law is defined by positivism, naturalism, and the process theories. These theories argue that a more accurate description of international law has to emphasize the contradictory and indeterminate character of international law. CLS shows that states, international organizations, and other international actors, such as NGOs, constantly draw contradictory conclusions from the same norms, and find contradictory norms embedded in the same texts or behaviours. For example, in the view of some interpreters, according to the long-standing debate on the lawfulness of humanitarian intervention, unilateral intervention by individual states is not prohibited by the United Nations Charter. Others argue that states can only use individual force in the case of self-defence and all other types of military force must be authorized by the United Nations Security Council (see Chapter 10). CLS scholars argue that even though the arguments put forward by international lawyers are predictable and highly formal, the outcome of such arguments is not determined by international law itself. International law, therefore, is more accurately defined as a set of arguments delivered in a particular format, but constructed for multiple purposes and from multiple perspectives by the decision-makers of the world community. What differentiates perceptions of international law from the perspective of the decision-makers, is politics (Koskenniemi 2000). CLS scholars do not advocate that international law is a pointless enterprise. They do, however, register caution about the objectivity of international law as an enterprise. They argue that international law arguments are shaped by the political preferences of actors and not the other way around. (Koskenniemi 1990).

We can already start to appreciate how this description of international law differs from the other three. The CLS description departs from positivism and naturalism as it does not view international law as an independent entity. At first glance, it has similarities with the process school, because it views international law as having a very close relationship with political views and the preferences of international actors. It does not, however, share the optimism of the process school about the process of international law yielding determinate outcomes about the content of international law. The reason for this is that CLS scholars think that international lawyers can achieve *any* substantive outcome for a legal problem as long as they apply the conventional argumentative patterns. The process school on the other hand thinks that past international legal agreements and decisions exert a stronger pull towards the right legal answers. CLS theories therefore, describe international law as an indeterminate language game.

CLS approaches to international law share an affinity with those critical international relations theories that are doubtful of attaining objective knowledge about international relations. This commonality allows both approaches to define their research agendas as questioning general theories about the international system and criticizing traditional views, positions, and concepts.

Table 4.2 Description of international law

Approach	Emphasis	Background assumptions about the international system	Parallels with IR approaches
Legal Positivist approaches	States as central law-makers	Anarchy	Realism Institutionalism
Natural Law approaches	The moral point in international law	Society of international states	Social constructivism
Process School	IL as an interactive process of world policy-makers	Society of international states as well as other international actors	Social constructivism
Critical Legal Studies	IL as a language	A collection of interacting actors historically brought together	Critical International Relations approaches

The purpose of international law

There is an important distinction we have to make when we talk about the purpose, or the purposes, of international law. This is the distinction between *outcome-oriented* theories and *framework* theories. Outcome-oriented theories of international law aim for desired results in international affairs through international law. They view international law as a *means to maximize* some sort of utility or value, such as human rights, human welfare, human dignity, or social justice. Framework theories, on the other hand, see international law in terms of facilitating relationships between entities. The reason for the existence of international law is to enable interactions, and not, as outcome-orientated theories would have it, to secure outcomes. Framework theories also pursue goals, such as the goal of peace, but the normative content of these goals are defined through their value for enabling interactions and not as an independent outcome.

In international law, natural law-oriented theories tend to be more outcome-orientated and positivist theories tend to be more framework-based. The process school of international law is also an outcome-oriented theory as it defines the aim of international law as the realization of human dignity. CLS scholars can be either outcome-orientated or framework-oriented in their definition of the purpose of international law.

Outcome-oriented theorizing about the purposes of international law has focused on human rights, human dignity, democracy, gender, and distributive justice as the desired results that international law should aim for. Some of these outcome-oriented theories assess the current state of international law in the light of these goals and identify the shortcomings of current international law and propose concrete changes. Outcome-oriented theories can identify such goals based on historical arguments, social theory, scientific developments (such

Table 4.3 Framework theories and outcome-oriented theories

Framework theories	Outcome-oriented theories
Aim to facilitate relationships between existing actors	Aim to bring about a desired state of affairs
Purpose is sensitive to how it enables interactions	Purpose sensitive to goals independently defined, e.g. justice, human rights

as environmental changes), social developments (such as poverty), political philosophy, or any combination of these.

Third World Approaches to International Law (TWAIL), for example, have viewed international law as a tool to remedy colonial wrongs and to redistribute wealth between those states that were colonized and the colonizers. In the 1970s, this approach informed and influenced General Assembly Resolutions at the United Nations. With the demise of the non-aligned movement and the collapse of the Soviet Union, TWAIL lost its political currency in international law-making circles. Similarly, **feminist** approaches to international law analyse international law from the perspective of gender and the gender inequalities embedded in the international legal system. They offer a critique of the consequences of a male-dominated practice of international law and propose guidelines for a more engendered practice of international law. Indeed the recognition of the act of rape as a basis of a war crime, a crime against humanity or, genocide charge (see Chapter 12) is an outcome of feminist critiques of international law. Other goal-oriented theorizing may simply critique the practice from the perspectives of the outcomes produced and question the desirability of such outcomes without proposing concrete changes. We can call these reflective outcome-oriented theories.

On the list of goals international law should aim for, human rights and global justice have received the most attention from the discipline of political philosophy because of the popularity and the strong moral appeal these ideas have in general. One leading theoretical discussion has concerned the possibility of practically applying the idea of human rights to the creation and recognition of new states in international law and using human rights as justification for humanitarian intervention (Buchanan 2004). In the case of global justice, the central questions are whether obligations of justice apply only within domestic political communities or whether they also apply internationally (see Chapter 16).

Outcome-oriented theorizing assigns goals to international law that are independent from the individual intentions of decision-makers. It further holds that these goals should compel decision-makers to act consistently to realize these goals. Because there are institutional constraints due to the nature of the international state system as to how much of a desired goal can be achieved in real-time international relations, outcome-oriented theories demand that decision-makers do as much as possible within their capacities. Such theories, therefore, focus on how we can reform the institutions that we have in order to maximize the goals aimed for. Outcome-oriented theories, therefore, can be both realistic and reform-focused. A realistic version of a human rights-based theory of international law, for example, may require that all international actors should respect human rights. Such a requirement would enable us to think about how international organizations such as the United Nations or the World Bank can respect human rights and how actors within these organizations should view their operations. Reform proposals consider what changes are necessary to current international institutions in order to better realize the goals of international law. Proposals for international taxation (for better distributive justice), a world court of human rights (for better protection of human rights), the reform of the United Nations to include a people's assembly (for more democracy in international law) are just a few examples of many such proposed reforms.

Because the very reality of the international system is that it is based on interstate agreement or consensus, outcome-oriented theories are often approaches to moral foreign policy. The process school of international law is the only theory that addresses both the foreign policy of states and the international system as a whole. That said, a great number of international treaties and international organizations, such as the United Convention on the Discrimination of All Kinds of Discrimination against Women and the United Nations High Commissioner for Human Rights, are concrete outcomes of outcome-oriented theorizing.

Framework theories of international law, on the other hand, are agnostic towards independent goals. This is not because they do not consider human rights or justice, for example, as valuable, but because they hold that international law exists for a different reason altogether. Its purpose is to create a framework to enable the relationship between international entities rather than the maximization of a pre-determined set of goals. Most framework theories concede that they regard states as the core international entities and international law is primarily concerned with facilitating interstate relations. International organizations, individuals, and non-state actors, such as armed groups, only enter into the framework as secondary international entities. They receive their significance from their indirect contribution to or their effects on the regulation of interstate relations.

Defining the purpose of international law in terms of relationships, primarily between states, is a common thread in positivist theorizing about international law. It involves making a number of assumptions. First, there is the assumption that there are a number of political entities with their own individual projects about goals they wish to pursue. Second, there is the assumption that none of these political entities exist in isolation from each other. They are inevitably related to each other and, furthermore, they need each other to realize their aims. Framework theories, therefore, start by saying that cooperation between political entities—each with its own individual trajectories and goals—is necessary for their peaceful coexistence. This is why international law exists. Concepts such as human rights or human development enter into framework theories as by-products or derivatives of cooperation or necessary elements for cooperation rather than as concepts with an independent purchase.

Framework theories do not specify what areas should be governed by international law because it is thought that this is largely determined by processes of historical development and the needs of cooperation. For example, for a very long period of time war (understood as armed conflict between two states) was permissible in international law. It was only after World War II that international law banned the use of force in international law except in cases of self-defence. This was because the consequences of war were viewed as too devastating for interstate relations. In a similar way, the international protection of human rights, international accountability for war criminals, protection of the environment, and international trade and the accountability of multinational corporations for complicity in international crimes are parts of the framework of international law. In the future, it is possible for this framework to include new issues and to establish international institutions that make international relations between states more heavily regulated by international law.

It is clear that there is a tension between *outcome-oriented* and *framework types* of theorizing about the purposes of international law. Outcome-oriented theories aim to bring international law closer to international justice. They demand that international law should strive to be as just a system as possible, even though they recognize the imperfections of the system and the injustices that exist within it. Framework theories, on the other hand, insist that it would be illegitimate to postulate substantive goals for international law without those goals being accepted as such by states. International law is essentially a framework of regulation and interaction between political entities with political lives of their own. By doing so, they also dispute the idea that international law is something that tries to reach a desired end rather than effectively facilitate interstate relations and cooperation. This means that international law would only promote a conception of the common good when states have collectively agreed to the promotion of that good as an aspect of their relationships.

The tension between these two types of theorizing perhaps looks less dramatic when we look at the actual practice of states in our contemporary world and the purposes of the United Nations. The United Nations Charter in its Article 1 sets out the four purposes for the United Nations:

1. to maintain international peace and security;

2. to develop friendly relations among nations based on respect for the principle of equal rights and self-determination of peoples;

3. to achieve international cooperation in solving international problems of an economic, social, cultural, and humanitarian character, and in promoting human rights; and

4. to be a centre for harmonizing actions in the attainment of these common ends.

These purposes suggest that the interstate system has moved away from a paradigm of detached coexistence or minimum cooperation. The protection of human rights and economic cooperation are parts of positive international law alongside international peace and security. This means that the gap between the framework for substantive cooperation and the goals international law should aim for may not be too wide, as it first seems.

The relevance of theories of international law in international relations

International law scholars often take for granted that international law as a discipline is crucial for understanding the conduct of international relations, its past, and its future. As discussions of theories of international relations show, however, not all international relations students agree with this assumption (see Chapter 2). Theories of international relations are not necessarily interested in the research questions international law asks. For the former, the driving question is why, *in the first place*, should we take international law seriously when studying international behaviour and the structure of the international system? What does international law tell us about the world we live in and how can we explain interactions and processes and predict the future of international relations? This difference in emphasis between *theories* of international relations and international law comes about because international relations has a pool of social, cultural, political, and historical explanatory factors that run alongside international law to understand and explain international relations as a system and the behaviour of individual states within the system. International relations theories, therefore, always assign *relative* importance to international law and its theories when studying international behaviour, international processes, and the international system.

International law theories constantly remind students of international relations about the legal aspects of their objects of inquiry. All of the theoretical schools of international law we discussed above agree that international law influences how the international system is constructed and how it operates. They provide perspectives to decision-makers to assess the current state of international law and its future. What is significant is that there are strong synergies and constructive dialogues between some theories of international relations and international law. As a general observation, we can say that the more international relations theories focus on non-material factors such as, norms and ideas, the more relevant the theories of international law become in international relations theory. Conversely, we can also observe that not all theories of international law are idealist. Positivist theories of international law, as we have seen, pay serious attention to accommodating state sovereignty as the basis of international law. The relevance of international law theories in international relations, in this respect, is a matter of degree about the overlaps and synergies between theoretical assumptions in both disciplines.

The empirical relevance of international law

The most important challenge international relations theory mounts towards international law theories is on the empirical relevance of international law in international relations. This challenge focuses on how state behaviour is explained and can be formulated as follows:

> International law is not important or relevant in the real world because state behaviour is not ultimately constrained by it (or states will always violate international law if it is in their interest to do so).

This challenge is the well-known *rationalist-realist* challenge to international law and it views compliance with international law as the most important element for defining what international law is. It further holds that international law is only relevant if it motivates State A to do X even if X is not in its interest. Furthermore, it argues that there is no overwhelming or significant evidence in the real world to support this proposition. If a state in fact acts in a way that is in accordance with international law the assumption is that this is merely a coincidence between a state's interests and international law. In other words, the challenge suggests that international law does not have a structural binding effect on states in the real world and that, therefore, its relevance as well as its law-like quality is to be suspected.

We can quickly see that this rationalist-realist challenge overlaps with Austin's rejection of international law based on his command theory. International law theory responds to the rationalist-realist challenge by highlighting the internal perspective of law and the need to be aware of the communicative nature of international law. From the perspective of international law, even where a state disobeys international law, the very fact that it is recognized as non-compliant by other states proves the significance of international law. In this sense, no international actor really stays outside the international legal framework. Positivist, natural law or critical legal studies scholars all agree with the fact that international law enables international events to be framed, discussed and evaluated in the form of a specific language shared by international actors.

All theories of international law further draw the distinction between the effectiveness of international law in certain places and at certain points in time and the overall function of international law in the international system. As much as effectiveness of international laws is an important issue both for international law and for international relations in general, it is an oversimplification to define only effective international law as relevant. Effectiveness is only one of the many complex aspects of international law and it is not clear why it should be seen as the most important one in identifying the importance of international law. This is all the more curious because we do not question the relevance of law in the domestic systems when it is ineffective. Ineffectiveness can be seen as a symptom of a legal culture, but it is not what makes law relevant to our everyday lives. This holds for international law as much as it holds for domestic law.

As much as international law may sometimes be ignored in international relations, it is still taken into account by states and other actors and it is used to *justify, explain,* and *evaluate* behaviour. It guides behaviour as it expresses expectations about how international actors wish to be treated in the future. In this respect, theories of international law caution students of international relations to empirical nuances. In the real world, there are multiple reasons for compliance and non-compliance with specific international laws. A state may comply with international law because: (1) of habit; (2) this is how it wishes to be treated by others; (3) it sees a particular behaviour in its long-term interest; (4) it believes this is the right thing to do; (5) it believes it enhances its reputation; (6) or all of the above; or (7) some of the above. The compliance reasons may change from one state to another as well as from topic to topic and from time to time. International law theories, therefore, make the empirical picture more complex than it may at first seem. They point to the fact that from the internal perspective of decision-makers there is a complex constellation of reasons to follow international law or to define themselves within the framework of international law.

The relevance of international law in the contemporary world

A more historically informed argument on the relevance of international law in contemporary international affairs needs only to look at the degree of interdependence and level of complexity in international law. No doubt states are involved in this as much as international organizations, international courts, tribunals, and non-governmental international law entrepreneurs. States are signing up to and ratifying an increasing number of multilateral treaties on issues ranging from the international environment, to prohibited weapons, human rights, individual criminal responsibility, and international trade and investment. They also set up international judicial, monitoring, and administrative institutions. Circumstances of international cooperation have effects on small and medium sized states as well as on major powers. International law has also become specialized into differentiated regimes—more akin to domestic law—under international human rights law, international criminal law, international humanitarian law, international environmental law, and international trade law. This makes it more difficult to talk about international law as a single unitary concept when assessing its relevance and calls for a more nuanced understanding of the different regimes of international law.

Conclusion

International law theorizing feeds both from politics and from moral-normative theories. It is located between the disciplines of law and international relations. It is rich with arguments and disagreements. But also, for these reasons, it is a frontier of both theoretical and practical thinking about international relations. We have seen that theoretical foundations of international law are under fire from at least two fronts. First, legal theorists have serious doubts as to whether international law is law in the first place and whether international law can ever be independent from international politics or the morality of powerful states. Second, we have seen that international relations scholars are suspicious about whether international law matters at all in controlling the behaviour of states. Theories of international law offer responses to such challenges and try to imagine the best principles that regulate the complex, diverse, and dynamic international society that we have. Theories of international law also serve as the constant reminder of the relevance of international law in enabling international relations and interstate cooperation.

Questions

1. What is international law?
2. In what ways do positivism and realism have similarities in describing international law?

3. What are the differences between natural law theories and positivist theories of international law?

4. What is the added value of describing international law as a process of decision-making?

5. What are the central claims of critical legal studies scholars about the value of law in international relations?

6. In what ways can we approach the purpose of international law?

7. What is the relevance of international law in international relations?

8. Is the relevance of international law empirically supported?

9. In what ways can we define international society?

10. What differences can you identify in the ways in which international law theories and international relations theories approach international law?

Further reading

Anghie, T., Chimni, P., and Mickelson, K. (2004) *The Third World and International Order: Law, Politics and Globalization* (The Hague: Kluwer Law). *A collection of essays focusing on the relationship between third world states and international law.*

Arendt, A. C. (1999) *Legal Rules and International Society* (Oxford: Oxford University Press). *An interdisciplinary analysis of the synergies between international law and international relations theories.*

Charlesworth, H. and Chinkin, C. (2000) *The Boundaries of International Law: Feminist Analysis* (Manchester: Manchester University Press). *A feminist analysis of the shortcomings of international law in accommodating a gender perspective.*

Higgins, R. (1994) *Problems and Process—International Law and How We Use It* (Oxford: Oxford University Press). *An excellent introduction to the process school of international law and how it is applied to international law problems.*

Koskenniemi, M. (2000) *From Apology to Utopia: The Structure of International Legal Argument*, 2nd edn. (Cambridge: Cambridge University Press) *A fulsome defence of the CLS argument in international law.*

Nardin, T. and Mapel, D. R. (2000) *International Society: Diverse Ethical Perspectives* (Princeton: Princeton University Press). *A comprehensive collection of essays on legal and moral theoretical perspectives on international law.*

Simma, B. and Paulus, A. L. (1999) 'The Responsibility of Individuals for Human Rights Abuses in Internal Conflicts: A Positivist View' *American Journal of International Law* 93: 302–16. *A modern interpretation of positivism in international law.*

Tesón, F. (1998) *A Philosophy of International Law* (Boulder: Westview Press). *A liberal and goal-oriented theory of international law.*

Websites

http://www.ejil.org *The European Journal of International Law publishes academic discussions on topics in international law theory.*

http://www.iilj.org/publications/HistoryandTheoryofInternationalLawSeries.asp *The Institute for International Law and Justice of NYU Law School features a range of interesting working papers in the area of international legal theory.*

http://www.opiniojuris.org *This website acts as a forum for discussion about international law and relations.*

http://www.asil.org *The American Society for International Law gives access to its publications and posts upcoming events in the area of international law.*

http://plato.stanford.edu/entries/legal-positivism/ *This Stanford Encyclopedia article on legal positivism gives a comprehensive overview of the history and influence of this theory beyond international law.*

Visit the Online Resource Centre that accompanies this book to access more learning resources www.oxfordtextbooks.co.uk/orc/cali/

PART II

IDENTIFYING INTERNATIONAL LAW

In this part of the book we introduce you to the ways in which specific international laws are identified in international relations. International lawyers say that in order for a statement to be law it has to come from a 'source' of international law. Sources of international law are procedures based in the collective consent of states to a particular rule, principle, or norm. When a rule or principle is identified as part of international law we say that it has *legal consequences* and it is *legally binding* as well as having political and/or moral consequences. For example, if a state commits genocide, we can call this not only a political catastrophe and a grave moral wrong, but also a violation of international law. There are different types of legal consequences that are attached to having international laws on a subject:

1. we establish that the rule, principle or norm has been recognized as law because it has been produced through a legal procedure;

2. we expect states (and other relevant actors) to behave in accordance with that international law as a matter of legal obligation;

3. a state can rightfully retaliate using peaceful means if another state is breaching its obligations against that state;

4. states (and other relevant actors) can bring claims before international courts for failing to obey international law; and

5. states (and other relevant actors) can legally demand the reversal of any law-violating behaviour, compensation for damages, and official apologies.

Knowing what international law says on a matter, of course, also has political consequences. For example:

1. we can criticize states for not following international law once we establish what that law is;

2. we can demand states (and other relevant actors) to follow international law; and

3. we can establish who follows and who violates international law.

In this respect there are important advantages to be gained from knowing what international law says on a particular subject matter both for states and other international actors on the international plane.

Sources of international law are invariably defined with respect to the famous Article 38 of the Status of the International Court of Justice:

The Court, whose function is to decide in accordance with international law such disputes as are submitted to it, shall apply:

(a)   international conventions, whether general or particular, establishing rules expressly recognized by the contesting states;

(b)   international custom, as evidence of a general practice accepted as law;

(c)   the general principles of law recognized by civilized nations;

(d)   subject to the provisions of Article 59, judicial decisions and the teachings of the most highly qualified publicists of the various nations, as subsidiary means for the determination of rules of law.

This Article exists in the Statute of the International Court of Justice, so that when states bring a dispute before the ICJ, the Court knows how to find out what international law says on a particular matter. Of these sources listed, *treaties and customary international law* are the *primary sources* of international law. *General principles of law* are there to help the Court to identify the law if treaties and custom are not clear. General principles of law mean that the principle identified by the Court has to be general enough to be commonly used by most states. *Teachings of publicists* are an auxiliary source and are there to help the judges clarify the precise meaning of a contested or unclear piece of treaty or custom.

The identification of international law has to primarily start from identifying what states collectively agreed to either by way of explicit agreement (*treaties*) or by way of looking at long-standing practices of states (*custom*). It is, however, recognized that there are certain limits to what states can bilaterally or collectively agree to. These limits are called *ius cogens* norms. There is a dispute as to what the list of such super-norms should contain. Universally accepted examples, however, include the prohibition of genocide and slavery. Two states, for instance, cannot make an agreement to enslave humans. Such an agreement would not have any legal validity and all other states would have a duty under international law not to recognize it.

Chapters 5 and 6 set out in greater detail how treaties are made, how customary international law is established, how these two primary sources of international law interact with each other, and what role is played by *ius cogens*.

It is very useful to approach the identification of international law as an *argumentative process*. There is no statute book to tell us what the international law on a specific issue is and it is more than likely that different states may have different views on what international law is at a given time. While some international laws bind all states (such as the prohibition of genocide or slavery), some laws only bind some states (such as regional treaties or regional custom) and some laws are only in force between two states (such as bilateral trade agreements). This is the fact of international law, which is based on an international system of states that does not have a central legislative body. How then do we go about identifying international law?

1. *State focus or issue focus*: The first step is to establish whether we are looking for an agreement between a group of states or an international law on an issue that binds all states.

2. *Treaty, custom, or both?* The next step is to identify whether the issue in question is governed by treaties, by custom, or by both. If a state is not party to a treaty, are there clear principles that we can establish as custom? If there are both treaties and customary principles, what is the relationship between the two?

3. *Is* ius cogens *relevant?* We can then think whether a *ius cogens* principle is relevant. If a particular international law is viewed as *ius cogens*, then it is a super-norm and states cannot make agreements contrary to it.

4. *Clarity?* Is the international law clear after having looked at treaties and custom, and, if necessary, the general principles of law?

It is important to note that once we consider these steps we may be able to say exactly what the international law is on a specific issue and which states it binds, or we may also say that international law is not clear, or there is no international law on a certain issue or that we found a rule, but it does not bind a specific state. Equally, if we do find a very clear international law on a specific matter, this does not mean that it could effectively be *enforced*. The latter question depends on whether there is any: a) strong conviction or pressure to follow international law, b) compulsory third party settlement, c) states willing to submit themselves to dispute settlement, or d) whether a state regards itself as a victim and decides to self-enforce international law against another state. We cannot, however, say that there is no international law because it cannot always be enforced. Rather, the identification processes of international law enable us to see which international laws are enforced, which are followed, and which are violated.

There are a wide range of *actors* in the domestic and international plane that play a role in the identification, creation, and enforcement of international laws. The primary actors for law-making are *states*. As institutionalist, constructivist, and liberal theories of international relations point out (see Chapter 2), however, the social fabric of international relations is not *solely* made up of states. Other actors range from international organizations, international courts, and tribunals to non-governmental organizations, religious groups, and multinational corporations—as well as some powerful individuals. These all come under the umbrella of non-state actors. Non-state actors cannot make international law as all law-making takes place through the formal sources of international law. They do, however, influence states by putting pressure on them, by influencing their preferences, and by framing issues.

Of all these actors, *international organizations* are themselves creations of international law and for this reason they play an important role in the identification of international laws that apply to them. Because their existence and activities depend on intergovernmental agreements they are also the single most important platforms for collective law-making, identification, and development. Through formalized meetings and conferences they facilitate the identification of emerging needs for regulation and cooperation and offer processes for drafting international treaties. The United Nations (UN) is the hub of the world's multilateral treaty making. It is also the repository of all international treaties. The *International Law Commission*, an expert commission set up by members of the UN, is where most international law is made in the literal sense. This Commission is a place where the ideas of important treaties are born and go through a long drafting process with the participation of all involved states. Regional organizations, such as the African Union, the Organization of American States, and the Council of Europe, fulfil similar regional roles. International organizations are also important for identifying state conduct that is relevant for the identification of customary international laws (see Chapter 6). Independent experts and the international secretariats of international organizations have to, by their nature, contribute to the elaboration and specification of international laws as their existence and functions are created by international law.

In Chapters 7 and 8 we turn to two other important actors in contemporary international relations that mark an important change from traditional and more state and intergovernmental organization focused international law to a more judicial and civil society focus: non-governmental organizations and international courts and tribunals. As we have seen in the discussion on the history of international law in Chapter 3 both of these are relatively new to the international plane, but their very existence affects the way we think about processes of law-making and identification. Both NGOs and International Courts and Tribunals are regarded as guardians of international law in a world where law is an output of intergovernmental processes. Chapter 7 on non-governmental organizations analyses an important puzzle in evaluating the engagement of civil society organizations in international law. Given that everyone accepts that states are the primary law-makers and enforcers in international law, why are non-governmental organizations increasingly interested in the making and enforcement of international law and participating in the work of international organizations? The discussion of non-governmental actors surveys the significance of NGOs and exposes the advocacy and campaigns background for treaty-making and discusses the distinction between legally binding and non-legally binding international instruments. Chapter 8 on international courts and tribunals provides a tour of the broad range of courts in international law and the very important role they play in the identification of international law. With more international courts and active non-governmental organizations in international relations, we see that states and intergovernmental organizations are not the only actors that identify and interpret what international law means in specific contexts. This means that even though the collective state authority is necessary to make international laws, the stage for the interpretation, specification, and application of international law is more diverse than it ever was and that identification of international law is a more complex and multi-authored process. More knowledge, understanding, and pronouncement of international law outside state and intergovernmental circles also have an effect on states' own approaches to understanding what the laws they make mean in practice.

Chapter 5

International treaties

Emmanuel Voyiakis

CHAPTER CONTENTS

- Introduction
- Why do states make treaties?
- The relationship between treaties, customary international law, and the concept of *ius cogens*
- The making of treaties
- Universality or integrity? Reservations to treaties
- Application, interpretation, and the position of third states
- Amending a treaty
- Ending international treaties
- Conclusion

CHAPTER OVERVIEW

In the absence of a world government, the standards that international agents are bound to observe in their relations are typically laid down in international agreements called 'treaties'. Treaties come in many varieties: some constitute international organizations, such as the United Nations. Others regulate particular areas of international law, such as the law of the sea. Others are purely commercial or 'synallagmatic', such as agreements about the sale of oil or about student exchanges between two states. The law of treaties is the body of international legal principles that regulate, at the most general level, questions about the conclusion, validity, interpretation, and practical application of all such agreements. The purpose of this chapter is to explain the basic concepts of the law of treaties and to highlight how their application may vary depending on the character of the treaty in question.

Introduction

A letter posted in Thailand reaches Greece. A flight from Frankfurt reaches Sydney via Singapore. Rita spends her first term as an exchange student in France. Ugandan authorities board a ship flying the Liberian flag on suspicion that the ship is carrying illegal weapons. Poland joins the European Union. The United Nations Security Council authorizes the use of force to liberate Kuwait from Iraqi invading forces. The European Court of Human Rights awards Eric compensation for injuries he suffered whilst in custody of the Hungarian police. These random examples are all practically possible because the states concerned have concluded treaties to facilitate them. There are thousands of international treaties concluded between states or international organizations. Identifying whether there is any treaty on an issue of international concern is the first step to identifying international law on a particular subject.

This chapter focuses on the reasons for and processes of treaty making in international law. This is arguably one of the most technical subject matters in international law. The law of international treaties employs a technical and specialized language in regulating international agreements. This is in contrast to the more general ways international relations scholars talk about international regimes (see Chapter 2). Understanding international law-making terminology and the way it is employed, however, is important for students of international relations for at least two reasons. First, most international political and legal work carried out by state officials as well as intergovernmental and non-governmental organizations involves treaty drafting, negotiations, and disputes over treaty interpretation. The knowledge of international treaty law is crucial for participating in these international processes. Second, the rules about rules, in this case rules about making, implementing, and terminating international treaties, increase the predictability of the process for all the participants concerned. It is for this reason that the international legal language is specialized in this field. This chapter will go through the process of treaty making by following the logical progression of an international treaty. It will start with rules for making them, follow this with interpreting treaties, and will conclude with changing the terms of the agreements or ending them.

> **Box 5.1 What is a 'treaty?'**
>
> Treaties are agreements governed by international law and concluded primarily between states. A treaty is legally binding and parties to an international treaty are able to hold each other accountable for breaches.

Treaties concluded between two states are called *bilateral treaties*. When treaties are concluded between more than two states, they are called *multilateral treaties*.

The title that an agreement has is not important for determining whether the agreement is a treaty. Agreements under international law can be called 'conventions', 'covenants', 'protocols', 'declarations', 'joint statements', or may carry no particular designation at all.

An international agreement does not always need to be in written form in order to be a treaty, although the existence of some form of record of the agreement is always useful for evidential purposes.

This definition excludes:

1. agreements between states and private individuals or corporations; and

2. agreements that states have decided that should not be governed by international law.

Why do states make treaties?

A generic answer to this would be that treaties facilitate international cooperation, which states have good reason to value. International trade is a typical example: without a net of bilateral and multilateral international agreements that set the terms for international trade in goods and services, interstate commerce would be practically impossible. Furthermore, treaties can help secure collective international goods like international peace and security, by allowing states to agree common standards of conduct, e.g. to refrain from using armed force in their international relations, and to set up international institutions, such as the United Nations (UN) or the World Trade Organization (WTO), and to equip them with the power to monitor and enforce those standards.

States use treaties for a wide range of objectives: to secure commercial bargains (sometimes called 'synallagmatic' treaties); to build international institutions; to set out common standards of conduct. Consider how these objectives are typically pursued within states: commercial bargains are the province of private contracts; institution-building can occur both at the private (e.g. corporations) and public (e.g. state organs) level; while the setting of general standards of conduct is almost the exclusive province of government. The contrast provides a further glimpse into the systemic importance of treaties in international society. They are the central pillars of regulating international relations. Given the lack of central governmental mechanisms that might create and impose certain international cooperative structures

Table 5.1 Types of international treaties

Type	Institution-building treaties	Treaties setting multilateral standards of conduct	Treaties that regulate reciprocal bilateral relations
Example	The United Nations Charter	International Covenant on Civil and Political Rights	Australia–Thailand Free Trade Agreement
	The Statute of the International Criminal Court	The Montreal Protocol on the Substances that Deplete the Ozone Layer	USA–Argentina Bilateral Treaty on Extradition
	Constitutive Act of the African Union		

'from above'—whether or not such mechanisms might be desirable—cooperation by international agreement is the most prevalent and efficient way for states to pursue most of their individual and collective aims.

Cooperation by agreement can involve different levels of commitment on the part of consenting states. States may find it politically expedient to declare that they will pursue a common aim without necessarily undertaking a duty to do so. More often than not, however, states will prefer that every party to an agreement should *also* be able to hold a party that breaches it *accountable* for that breach. For example, agreeing states may decide that a breach will entitle the victim to seek reparations; to terminate or suspend the agreement; or to submit disputes to the binding determination of a third party, e.g. an international court.

When international lawyers say that an international agreement is 'legally binding', they mean to denote agreements of the latter sort only, i.e. agreements the breach of which can make the breaching party accountable to the victim through available avenues of satisfaction and dispute settlement. The international law of treaties is concerned with such agreements. Its main objectives, and the standards which it must be judged against, are, first, to lay down *clear* and *fair* rules regarding the conclusion, validity, interpretation, and practical operation of treaties and, second, to be *flexible* enough to allow states to tailor the content and binding force of their agreements to their specific needs and interests.

Box 5.2 Where do we find the law of treaties?

The international law of treaties is, for the most part, contained in a treaty, the 1969 Vienna Convention on the Law of Treaties (VCLT). The VCLT is the 'treaty on treaties'.

The VCLT is a special treaty because:

1. even though only about half of the world's states have become parties to it, virtually all states recognize that its rules reflect generally binding customary international law.

2. even though many states have decided not to go through with the formal process of becoming parties to it, they follow the rules laid down in this treaty;

3. international lawyers, legal advisors, and negotiators rely on the VCLT without having to conduct laborious research on customary international law or check whether their negotiating partners are parties to the VCLT;

4. states are free to derogate from this treaty by agreement, but the vast majority of treaties are concluded and applied in accordance with VCLT;

5. VCLT rules can be applied even in respect of treaties that lie outside the VCLT's express scope;

6. even though Article 2(1)(a) VCLT specifies that the Vienna Convention applies only to treaties 'in written form', there is no doubt that the VCLT is also applicable to oral treaties as customary international law; and

7. although the VCLT has no retrospective effect, in the *Kasikili/Sedudu Island* case between Botswana and Namibia the International Court of Justice applied it in respect of a nineteenth century treaty!

The relationship between treaties, customary international law, and the concept of *ius cogens*

Is there a hierarchy of sources in international law?

International lawyers identify the sources of international law by reference to the Statute of the International Court of Justice (see Chapter 8). The three main sources of international law, stated in Article 38(1) of the Statute of the ICJ, are (1) treaties; (2) customary international law; and—when the other sources do not provide enough guidance—(3) general principles of law.

The fact that the Statute mentions treaties first may create the impression that treaties are hierarchically higher, i.e. that they would prevail over other sources in case of conflict, just as constitutional rules prevail over legislation in national legal systems. That impression is mistaken. The sources of international law are independent of each other and, as the ICJ confirmed in the *Nicaragua* case (*Military and Paramilitary Activities In and Against Nicaragua—Merits* 1986: paras 172–182) no source is hierarchically higher. Treaty rules tend to be either more *specific* or *newer* than rules of customary international law or general principles of law and, in that sense, will take precedence by virtue of the practical axiom that specific/newer rules have priority over general/older ones. By the same token, however, it is possible for a newer customary rule to have precedence over an older treaty rule. Treaties and customary international law can interact in two important ways. First, treaties can contribute to the development of customary law, both by codifying already existing custom and by providing an incentive for its future development. Second, customary international law is part of the background against which treaties are drafted, interpreted and applied. For example, states may conclude a treaty in order to give more legal precision to the content of a customary rule that they consider imprecise, or in order to avoid their relations being governed by customary norms. In either case, the proper interpretation of their treaty will require one to understand the treaty in the light of what customary international law requires or allows.

The concept of *ius cogens* in the Vienna Convention on the Law of the Treaties

It is often thought that, even if no *source* of international law is hierarchically higher than the others, certain substantive *rules* of international law enjoy such higher status. Article 52 Vienna Convention on the Law of the Treaties (VCLT) calls such rules 'peremptory norms of international law' or *ius cogens* norms and defines them as norms 'accepted and recognized by the international community of states as a whole as norms from which no derogation is permitted and which can be modified only by a subsequent norm of general international law having the same character'. Usually cited examples of such norms are the general prohibition of the use of force and the prohibition of genocide, torture and other crimes against humanity. Calling these norms *ius cogens* means that states are absolutely prohibited from derogating from those norms by agreement and that any agreement to derogate from those norms will be automatically null and void as a matter of international law.

There is no doubt that respect for the norms typically described as *ius cogens* is absolutely essential to the maintenance of any defensible system of international law. At the same time, perhaps calling these norms 'hierarchically higher' than the rest misses their true significance. There are no—and will probably never be any—examples of treaties endorsing the aggressive use of force or condoning genocide or torture. In that sense, the idea that any such treaties would be invalidated by the relevant *ius cogens* norms has only theoretical significance.

> **Box 5.3** *Pinochet* and the interpretive function of *ius cogens*
>
> The true function and significance of *ius cogens* norms is more nuanced. Consider the *Pinochet (No. 3)* case before the British Courts in 1999. The main issue there was whether a treaty, the 1984 Convention against Torture (CAT), had curtailed the personal immunities that Heads of State enjoyed under customary international law. This was controversial because, although the CAT allowed states to extend their jurisdiction over acts of torture carried out by foreign officials, it did not include any *express* provision restricting foreign Head-of-State immunities. What was the significance of this silence? One could plausibly argue that, if the drafters of the CAT wanted to restrict customary immunities, they ought to have said so. On the other hand, one could just as sensibly argue that allowing Heads of States to plead immunity against charges of torture would frustrate the aim of bringing alleged perpetrators of torture to justice. The majority of the UK House of Lords endorsed the latter view: it found that if one could interpret the CAT in two plausible but opposite ways, one ought to adopt the interpretation which is more consistent with any relevant *ius cogens* norms. Since the prohibition of torture is such a norm, it was held that the CAT should not be interpreted so as to allow perpetrators of acts of torture to escape justice and, therefore, that the CAT must be seen as having restricted the customary immunity of Heads of State in relation to acts of torture. In other words, the UK court did not use *ius cogens* norms to invalidate norms of state immunity, but to assist in their proper interpretation—we might therefore call this the *interpretive* function of *ius cogens* norms.

The making of treaties

Treaty-making is part of everyday diplomacy. Like most diplomatic work, it is a politically sensitive and highly technical process. The complexity of treaty-making depends on a variety of factors, such as the nature of the subject matter of the treaty (e.g. a treaty on a politically important or excessively technical issue may be harder to negotiate); the number of parties involved (bilateral treaties are typically easier to negotiate and conclude than multilateral ones); and the relationship between the proposed treaty and other international obligations of the negotiating parties (agreements amending existing treaties will usually be easier to negotiate). These factors often cut across each other: a treaty on a politically sensitive issue, such as the law of the sea, may often attract a high number of negotiating parties, while the high participation rate may in turn accentuate the political importance of the treaty and so on. It is not uncommon for a state that would not be inclined to support a multilateral treaty to actually take part in its negotiation, if that state estimates that standing by while most of the world proceeds with the proposed treaty carries significant political risk. The US attitude towards the creation of the International Criminal Court (ICC) is a case in point: although the US was initially opposed to the idea of such a court, it decided to join the negotiations leading up to the 1998 Treaty of Rome when it became clear that most states were in favour of creating the ICC. The advantage of this strategy is that it allows the state concerned to have some say on the drafting of the treaty, while still leaving it the option not to become party if the final product does not satisfy it fully.

We can distinguish between five stages in the making of a treaty: negotiation; adoption; authentication; expression of consent to be bound; and entry into force. A treaty only develops legal force when it has gone through all the stages. Although some of these stages may occasionally overlap, each can give rise to different problems.

Box 5.4 The stages of treaty making

1. Negotiation between states representatives in conferences, scheduled drafting sessions as well as in private meetings attended by diplomats, international legal teams, experts, as well members of international and non-governmental organizations.

2. Official representation by heads of state, heads of government, foreign ministers, or other representatives with 'full powers' to sign a treaty.

3. Adoption, authentication, and expression of consent to be bound in a public setting.

4. Entry into force of treaty by ratification of domestic parliaments.

Negotiation

International law does not prescribe a specific process for negotiating a treaty and states enjoy considerable freedom to use their bargaining power to achieve a desirable agreement. For example, international law does not bar a state from threatening to withdraw economic aid in order to convince recipient states to enter into an agreement with it. At the same time, this does not mean that states are absolutely free to wield their negotiating power. The use of threats of armed force or fraud in negotiation may make the treaty invalid and it is widely accepted that states have a general customary obligation to display good faith in their dealings with one another.

Representation and 'full powers'

A person is entitled to represent the state for the purposes of treaty-making if he produces 'full powers', i.e. an official document designating that person as a representative, or if it appears from the practice of the negotiating states that they intended to dispense with this formality. Certain officials are considered as representing their state without needing to produce full powers. These are: Heads of State or Government and Ministers of Foreign Affairs; heads of diplomatic missions; and representatives to international organizations and conferences. Acts performed without full powers or equivalent authority do not bind a state. However, they can acquire legal effect if the state involved subsequently affirms them.

Adoption, authentication, and expression of consent to be bound

Negotiation ends with the 'adoption' of the text of the treaty, when the content of the treaty is finalized and states can begin to consider their position towards it. But states do not actually become bound by a treaty until they express their consent to become parties to it. The VCLT lists several ways in which states can express their consent to be bound. These are signature; exchange of instruments constituting a treaty (e.g. an exchange of diplomatic letters); ratification, acceptance, or approval; accession (this term is used only when a state consents to become bound by an existing treaty); or any other agreed means.

Some means of expressing consent to be bound, such as signature, are simple and direct. Others, such as ratification, are more cumbersome. The choice of means usually depends on the political importance of the treaty in question. states typically agree that minor or technical treaties will become binding immediately on signature or by a simple exchange of instruments. Ratification, which involves the submission of the treaty for approval to the constitutionally competent branch of government (typically, but not always, the national Parliament), is usually reserved for treaties that contain substantial obligations, such as the creation of organizations, law-making treaties etc. The requirement of approval by national government allows for better democratic scrutiny of the treaty, but can also entail significant delays between the adoption of a treaty and the expression of states' consent to be bound.

Suppose that a state has signed a treaty setting up a free-trade area 'subject to ratification'. This means that although the state has 'adopted' the treaty text, it has not yet expressed its consent to be bound and so the treaty has not become binding on that state. Does it follow that the state in question is still free to increase tariffs on imports from its future treaty partners? Article 18 VCLT gives a negative answer.

It provides that states which have signed a treaty subject to ratification, or have consented to be bound by a treaty which has not yet entered into force (see next heading), have an obligation to refrain from acts that 'would defeat the object and purpose of the treaty', until they make clear their intention not to become parties to it or until the treaty enters into force. This obligation may be provisional in character, but it is not negligible, as it can limit the ability of signing states to shift their international policy. This was the reason why the United States found it necessary to state explicitly that, although it had signed the 1998 Treaty of Rome for the creation of the ICC, it had no intention to become bound by it.

Entry into force

The final stage in the making of any treaty is its 'entry into force'. Unless a treaty provides differently, treaties enter into force when all negotiating states have expressed their consent to be bound. Most treaties with limited participation—e.g. bilateral and regional treaties—adhere to this default rule. Multilateral treaties tend to have their own special provisions that allow the treaty to enter into force when a fair number of negotiating states—typically a quarter or a third of the total—have expressed their consent to be bound. The treaty's entry into force makes the treaty binding between states that have expressed such consent. States that express such consent after the treaty has entered into force become bound only from the date of their consent.

Universality or integrity? Reservations to treaties

Once the text of a treaty has been finalized and negotiating states consider whether to become a party to it, should they be able to choose to become bound by *part* of that treaty only? One would think not. The end of negotiations is supposed to produce a final balance of rights and obligations in the treaty; allowing states to pick and choose which parts of the treaty they want to be bound by seems to undermine that finality. Moreover, multilateral treaties often seek to establish a uniform set of standards for relations between states, e.g. a comprehensive code of the law of the sea or of the law on carriage of goods by air. Here too it would seem that the objective of uniformity can only be attained if the final treaty text is considered as a 'package deal' and individual states are not—as the law of the treaties puts it—allowed to compromise the 'integrity' of the treaty text.

However, under certain conditions the law of treaties *does* allow states to become parties to a treaty while avoiding being bound by some of its provisions. In the legal jargon, it allows states to enter 'reservations' when expressing their consent to be bound.

Box 5.5 What is a 'reservation'?

Article 2(1)(d) of the Vienna Convention on the Law of Treaties (VCLT) defines reservation as a:

> unilateral statement, however phrased or named, made by a State, when signing, ratifying, accepting, approving or acceding to a treaty, whereby it purports to exclude or to modify the legal effect of certain provisions of the treaty in their application to that State.

There are two reasons for this. First, when drafting a multilateral treaty with wide participation, getting all negotiating states to agree on every draft provision can prove difficult or practically unachievable. The possibility of entering reservations allows the process of treaty-making to continue, while giving states that are not fully content with the treaty to avoid being bound by certain provisions. Second, sometimes the political impact of a treaty will depend not so much on whether all parties to it subscribe to exactly the same package of rights and obligations, but on whether the treaty is acceptable to as many states as possible, i.e. sometimes achieving universality in participation may be worth the cost of fragmenting the integrity of the treaty text. Human rights treaties offer an illustration of this idea. Allowing reservations can sometimes be the only way of getting large numbers of states to agree to a human rights treaty, whereas insisting on the absolute integrity of the treaty text might risk putting states off the treaty altogether. At the same time, increasing participation by allowing states to tailor the treaty text to suit their individual policy preferences may risk undermining the practical effectiveness of the treaty in question. In general, there is no getting around the fact that deciding in favour of universality (i.e. allowing reservations) or integrity (i.e. prohibiting or limiting reservations) is a difficult political judgement and negotiating states may often disagree on the right strategy. A lot depends on the nature of the topic and the 'feel' of the negotiating process. When arriving at a set of common standards is very important and negotiators sense that agreement on a 'package deal' is within reach, states may decide to prohibit reservations and spend more time on the negotiating table. This is almost invariably the case in respect of treaties with few parties, but it can occur on the multilateral level as well.

> **Box 5.6** Convention on the Law of the Sea: high integrity versus low ratification
>
> The Third United Nations Conference on the Law of the Sea, attended by over 180 states, decided early on to prohibit reservations. Given the complexity of its subject matter, the final Convention on the Law of Sea was adopted in 1982 after almost ten years of negotiations (still a record duration), but the drafters' decision to ensure the integrity of the treaty has been vindicated in practice, since only a handful of states have decided not to ratify it.

What are reservations?

What sort of statements by states count as reservations? The VCLT defines a reservation as 'a unilateral statement, however phrased or named, made by a state when signing, ratifying, accepting, approving, or acceding to a treaty, whereby that state purports to *exclude or modify the legal effect* of certain provisions of the treaty in their application to that state'. Note that the name or the phrasing of the statement is not critical: what matters is whether the statement tries to achieve an excluding or modifying effect. In practice, this means that the 'interpretive declarations' that states sometimes append to their expressions of consent, and which contain those states' understanding of what the treaty requires or allows, may actually amount to reservations.

Basic rules on reservations

The most basic rule on reservations is that that states may formulate reservations to a treaty, except when (1) the treaty prohibits them; (2) the reservation is not amongst those allowed by the treaty and; (3) in all other cases, the reservation is incompatible with the 'object and purpose' of the treaty. The provision gives rise to three questions. First, who should have the competence to judge whether a reservation is incompatible with the object and purpose of a treaty? Second, if the reservation is incompatible with the object and purpose of a treaty, should a state entering the invalid reservation still be considered a party to the treaty, or should the invalidity of a reservation *also* entail the invalidity of that state's consent to be bound? Third, if a reservation is allowed by a treaty or is compatible with its object and purpose, are other parties required to accept the reservation and, if not, what are their practical options?

The VCLT does not answer the first question, but it is generally accepted that every other party to the treaty can judge whether a particular reservation is compatible with the treaty's object and purpose. In practice, this arrangement is favourable to reserving states, since it allows them to 'test the waters' by entering extensive reservations in the hope that other parties will not find them incompatible with the treaty's object and purpose. A more controversial issue is whether the institutions and monitoring organs set up by a treaty are *also* competent to determine whether a reservation is compatible with the treaty's object and purpose. In its decisions in *Belilos v. Switzerland* (1988) and *Loizidou v. Turkey* (1995), the European Court of Human Rights held that it was competent to decide that question with regard to the European Convention on Human Rights (ECHR). Similarly, the Human Rights Committee, which monitors the implementation of the 1966 International Covenant on Civil and Political Rights (ICCPR), has opined that it has competence to determine whether states' reservations are compatible with the object and purpose of the ICCPR.[1] The question is not conclusively settled in international practice: although the European decisions have been accepted by ECHR parties, some states have objected strongly to the views of the Human Rights Committee on the matter.[2]

The VCLT does not throw much light on the second question either. Here too, although there are some indications that the invalidity of a reservation does not generally entail the invalidity of the reserving state's consent to be bound, international practice is not settled. In its aforementioned decisions, the European Court of Human Rights held that the invalidity of Switzerland's and Turkey's reservations did not affect their status as parties to the ECHR; significantly, neither state proceeded to withdraw from that treaty.

The position of other states

When a reservation is allowed by the treaty, it is not necessary for other states to accept the reservation for the reserving state to become a party. By contrast, when the object and purpose of a treaty, or the limited number of negotiating states, suggests that preserving the integrity of the treaty is essential, the reserving state can only become party to that treaty if the reservation is accepted by all other parties. In all other cases, the VCLT lays down five rules. First, if a state accepts the reservation, the reserving state and the accepting state can consider each other as parties to the treaty, minus the provisions to which the reservation relates and on a basis of reciprocity (i.e. the reserving state too will not be able to invoke those provisions against the accepting state). Second, the fact that a state objects to the reservation does not entail that the reserving state and the objecting state cannot consider each other as parties to the treaty, unless the latter clearly states an intention to the contrary. Third, if an objecting state has not expressed a clear intention not to become a treaty partner with the reserving state, the provisions to which the reservation relates will not apply as between the objecting state and the reserving state. Fourth, a reservation and the expression of consent it is attached to become effective as soon as one other state has accepted the reservation. Fifth, states are deemed to have accepted a reservation if they do not raise an objection to it within twelve months from the date the reservation was notified to them.

Box 5.7 Point of discussion: assessing the VCLT regime on reservations

There is little doubt that the above rules put more value on achieving universality of participation in treaties than on preserving the integrity of the treaty text. The VCLT rules are favourable to reserving states, as they entail that a reserving state can count itself as a party to a treaty, as long as there is at least one other state that does not object to its reservations. Furthermore, under the VCLT rules, objecting states have no practical way of 'overcoming' or 'defeating' the reservation: they can either accept it or they can altogether refuse to become treaty partners with the reserving state. Having said that, states sometimes find political value in being able to register their general disapproval of another state's reservations. For example, in objecting to two US reservations to the ICCPR, the Danish Government stated that 'Denmark regards the said reservations incompatible with the object and purpose of the Covenant, and consequently Denmark objects to the reservations. These objections do not constitute an obstacle to the entry into force of the Covenant between Denmark and the United States.'

Despite its weaknesses, the VCLT regime on reservations has not created important problems in treaty practice. It is quite telling that a recent effort by the International Law Commission to elaborate on the VCLT provisions in respect of reservations to human rights treaties on the basis of developing international practice, based mostly on the examples discussed in this section, has not as yet come up with any significant improvements (International Law Commission, Reports on the Reservations to Treaties, 1993–2009). On the other hand, the ambiguities and gaps of the VCLT regime have worked as an incentive to negotiating states to adopt their own clear rules as to which reservations they want to make permissible. Modern practice shows that treaties tend either to prohibit reservations altogether or to specify a limited number of admissible reservations.

Application, interpretation, and the position of third states

Treaties must be observed in good faith, or, in the famous Latin expression, *pacta sunt servanda*. As a general matter, the fact that the treaty may be inconsistent with a party's domestic law is not a justification for failure to perform it. For example, when a state becomes party to a treaty prohibiting the imposition of the death penalty, it cannot invoke the fact that this form of punishment is allowed (or even required) under its Constitution as a justification for not performing its international obligations.

Third states

Treaties bind only parties to them. As Article 34 VCLT puts it, 'a treaty does not create either obligations or rights for a third state without its consent', except of course when the treaty provisions have developed into generally binding customary international law. For a third state to incur an obligation under a treaty, the third state must expressly agree to undertake it. The situation is more nuanced in practice, though. An economic alliance between states A and B may not create obligations for state C, but it may limit the market for that state's exports. Similarly, a boundary treaty between states D and E may not create duties for state F, but it may give rise to a situation that indirectly affects that state, e.g. by determining whether an illegal activity by organs of state F near that boundary makes F liable to state D or state E (or both). Creating rights for third states is simpler. Such rights arise as long as the treaty provides for them and the third state has not indicated any objection. Treaties regulating major international waterways, such as the Suez and Panama canals, contain provisions of this type.

Temporal and territorial application of treaties

Unless contrary provision is made, a treaty is not binding retroactively. It applies only to events and acts occurring after its entry into force. Moreover, unless an intention to the contrary is expressed, a treaty is binding on a state in respect of its entire territory. This rule has some practical importance, since it requires states with overseas territories (or, in older times, colonies) to make a declaration excluding those territories from the application of the treaty in question, if they so wish.

Practical problems can arise in the relationship between successive treaties on the same subject matter. This is especially so when not all parties to the earlier treaties are also parties to the later ones. Such discrepancies have the effect of fragmenting the applicable treaty rules. Conscious of this danger, negotiators typically try to include special provisions in their treaty governing its relationship with existing or future instruments. The most famous such example is Article 103 of the UN Charter, which provides: 'In the event of a conflict between the obligations of Members of the United Nations under the present Charter and their obligations under any other international agreement, their obligations under the present Charter shall prevail.' This radical stipulation is obviously justified in the light of the Charter's special status in the international system as the primary guardian of international peace and security. In less important instruments, one will typically find 'accommodation' provisions like that of Article 73(1) of the 1963 Vienna Convention on Consular

Relations: 'The provisions of the present Convention shall not affect other international agreements in force as between states parties to them.'

The interpretation of treaties

The VCLT provides two commonsense interpretive rules. Article 31(1) VCLT states the basic principle of interpretation, according to which 'A treaty shall be interpreted in good faith in accordance with the ordinary meaning to be given to the terms of the treaty in their context and in the light of its object and purpose.' In addition to the text of the treaty, the context of a treaty may include other instruments or agreements concluded in connection to the treaty, subsequent practice in the application of the treaty and any other relevant rule of international law that is applicable between the parties.

International case law illustrates the practical value of this basic principle. In the *Certain Expenses* Advisory Opinion,[3] the International Court had to determine whether UN members could be required to carry the cost of maintaining UN peacekeeping forces. Even though peacekeeping is not mentioned anywhere in the UN Charter, the Court found it to be perfectly consistent with the overall purpose of the UN to maintain international peace and security. Therefore, it was held that UN members could be required to pay for peacekeeping costs as part of their normal contributions to the UN budget.

Article 32 VCLT lays down a secondary principle of interpretation. It provides that interpreters may have recourse to the preparatory materials of a treaty (such as earlier drafts or records of negotiations) and the circumstances of its conclusion, when the application of the basic principle leaves the meaning of the treaty unclear or leads to a manifestly absurd or unreasonable result. Although this secondary principle sounds plain, it should be used with great circumspection. Records of negotiations do not always provide a sound guide to the meaning of the eventual treaty, since they often consist of partial statements that negotiating parties made in order to secure the best possible deal for themselves.

Amending a treaty

When drafting a treaty, the prudent diplomat should try to put in place a clear and reliable method for amending it, in order to ensure its effectiveness and adaptability to changing circumstances. This is especially important in respect of multilateral treaties, the vast majority of which are of unlimited duration.

The basic rule here that amending a treaty requires the consent of all parties. If not all original parties agree to a proposed amendment, the treaty is effectively fragmented in two: states consenting to the amendment are bound by the amended treaty in their mutual relations and by the original treaty in their relations with states who did not consent to the amendment.

Like the VCLT reservations regime, the regime governing treaty amendments has influenced treaty practice by serving as a reminder of the kind of complications that negotiators would do well to pre-empt. The 1929 Warsaw Convention on International Carriage by Air illustrates the difficult situation that can arise out of successive treaty amendments, each of which is consented to by a different proportion of the original parties. The Convention was amended six times and supplemented by a further treaty in 1961. Some of the parties to the Convention are not parties to any of the amendments. Many are parties to some amendments only and a few are parties to the supplementary treaty but not to the amendments. As a result, the Convention failed in its aim to create a unified regime for international carriage by air. The Warsaw Convention has now been replaced by the 1999 Montreal Convention on the Unification of Certain Rules of International Carriage by Air, but the amendments saga in this area of law is not over: the new Convention too contains no amendment provisions!

Most treaties contain their own amendment provisions to avoid the problems of fragmentation entailed by the VCLT rules. These provisions tend to adopt some version of what are often called 'automatic' amendments, i.e. rules that allow the amendment of a treaty *for all parties* once a specified number of states have consented. For example, Article 108 of the UN Charter provides: 'Amendments to the present Charter shall come into force ... when they have been adopted by a vote of two thirds of the members of the General Assembly and ratified in accordance with their respective constitutional processes by two thirds of the members of the United Nations, including all the permanent members of the Security Council.' The practical effect of Article 108 is that amendments can become binding even on states that voted *against* them or abstained.

Ending international treaties

International treaties may end for a variety of reasons. First, there may be good reasons not to recognize an international treaty having a valid status in the first place. This is called invalidity of treaties. Second, treaties may end because they have fulfilled their purpose or because states argue that they are unable to keep to the agreement. These issues are discussed under termination and suspension of international treaties. Finally, there could be disputes over treaty interpretation amongst states. This has led to the proliferation of diverse types of dispute settlement mechanisms (see Chapter 8).

Invalidity

Like all agreements, treaties can suffer from flaws that undermine their validity, e.g. a treaty may have been procured by coercion or it may involve the breach of a peremptory norm of international law (*ius cogens*). In such cases, and depending on the severity of the flaw, the only option for states may be to declare the treaty *invalid*, i.e. to declare that the treaty never created any legal duties for them.

The most basic principle of the law of treaties relating to invalidity is that only very severe defects in a treaty give states a right to declare their participation in it invalid. Furthermore, given that parties will often disagree as to whether a treaty is indeed invalid, they are required to follow certain procedural steps to invoke those grounds (these are discussed in the next section). Examples of invalid treaties are very rare in practice, but there is little doubt that the relevant VCLT provisions are a largely accurate statement of customary international law.

The VCLT provides that a state may declare its expression of consent to be bound by a treaty invalid, i.e. that the treaty *never* created any obligations for it, only in the following situations:

- when such consent was expressed in violation of its internal law regarding competence to conclude treaties, but only when the violation was manifest (i.e. objectively evident to any other state acting in good faith) and concerned a rule of internal law of fundamental importance, normally a constitutional rule;

- when that state's consent was based on an error relating to a fact or situation which was assumed by that state to exist at the time the treaty was concluded, except when that state contributed to its own error or the circumstances were such as to put it on notice of a possible error;

- when consent has been induced by the fraudulent conduct of another negotiating state, or by the corruption of a state's representative by another negotiating state;

- when consent has been induced by the coercion of that state or its representatives by another negotiating state; and

- when the treaty conflicts with a peremptory norm of international law (*ius cogens*). Existing treaties may become invalid once a contrary *ius cogens* norm emerges.

Termination and suspension

Under certain conditions, states may lawfully terminate or suspend a valid treaty. For a start, a treaty will terminate when it has achieved its objective, e.g. when goods have been delivered and payment made; when the treaty provides that certain events or dates will entail termination or suspension; or when all the parties agree to terminate or suspend it. However, if the treaty does not provide for a right to terminate or suspend, individual states cannot invoke such a right unless it is established that parties implicitly intended to allow it.

The most common ground states invoke to terminate or suspend a treaty is 'material breach' by another party, i.e. the repudiation of the treaty without adequate grounds, or a violation of a provision essential to the accomplishment of the object and purpose of the treaty. In this connection, it must be noted that the law of treaties is not concerned with explaining *why* a state may choose to breach its international obligations. Rather, it is concerned with determining the *rights* and *options* of the victim of the breach vis-à-vis the breaching state. This focus seems to reflect a genuine difference in the perspective of international lawyers compared to that of political scientists. Asking why states are tempted to breach their treaties is a question for the political scientist. It calls for research into the *motives* of state behaviour and, in particular, into how states weigh their various interests. By contrast, the task of international lawyers is to explain how a given defect in, or a breach of a treaty, changes the rights and duties between the parties to it. This task does not so much require one to know why a state has breached the treaty, but what the general practice of states *entitles* the victim of the breach to do in response.

When the treaty is multilateral, a breach by one party allows all other parties to terminate/suspend the whole treaty, or to terminate/suspend it only in relation to the breaching party. However, this provision does not apply in respect of treaties of a humanitarian character, i.e. state A cannot normally invoke the fact that state B has violated a human rights treaty in order to stop complying with the treaty itself. The reason for this exception is not hard to see: treaties of a humanitarian character do not reflect so much 'bargains' between states but rather shared commitments to standards of conduct towards individual persons. The fact that one state party has failed to observe those standards is not allowed to provide other states parties with the opportunity to renounce them.

The remaining grounds of termination/suspension are much less frequently found in practice. States may terminate a treaty when its performance has become impossible, e.g. where the treaty relates to an island that has since disappeared, or when there has been a 'fundamental change of circumstances', but only when those circumstances constituted an essential basis for the parties' consent, the effect of the change is radically to transform the extent of the obligations to be performed under the treaty, the treaty does not establish a boundary and the fundamental change of circumstances was not caused by a breach on the part of the party invoking it.

Unsurprisingly, international courts and tribunals hesitate to find that a treaty has either become impossible to perform or that there has been a 'fundamental change of circumstances'. The *Gabcikovo-Nagymaros* case between Hungary and Slovakia offers a useful illustration.[4] Hungary and Czechoslovakia had concluded a treaty to build a dam on the river Danube. After the dissolution of Czechoslovakia, Hungary claimed that Slovakia had failed to perform its part of the agreement. Slovakia argued that the collapse of the Eastern Bloc constituted a fundamental change of circumstances that allowed it to terminate the treaty. The ICJ was not convinced, holding that the political motivation behind the conclusion of the treaty was not an essential basis for the consent of the parties to it.

Settling disputes

Wherever a dispute arises as to the interpretation, application, and validity of a treaty, states have a variety of means at their disposal for resolving it. Unless the treaty in question prescribes a particular method of dispute settlement, such as resort to arbitration, states are free to choose, or *not* to choose, any available settlement means, or to employ more than one at the same time.

The main means of settling international disputes are negotiation; conciliation; mediation; arbitration; and adjudication. Of those, negotiation is the most useful and flexible. Practice suggests that most treaty disputes are indeed solved in that way. Negotiation may sometimes reveal that the dispute has resulted from inadequate communication or an incomplete knowledge of background facts. Often negotiations lead to the drafting of a new agreement to replace or supplement the existing one. When negotiations fail, states may resort to third parties in search of an amicable solution. Conciliation and mediation are processes of this kind. Conciliators and mediators are employed to hear the parties' respective claims and to make recommendations that facilitate the amicable settlement of their dispute. When this role is performed by officials of international organizations, such as the Secretary-General of the United Nations, it is referred to as 'good offices'. When means of amicable settlement fail, states may choose to resort to the more adversarial methods of arbitration and adjudication (see Chapter 8).

International law generally allows a state that has been the victim of a breach of a treaty to require the offending party to pay compensation or make some other form of reparation and to cease the offending conduct. If the other party fails to comply, states can resort to what international lawyers call 'countermeasures'. Countermeasures usually take the form of 'an eye for an eye': state A believes that state B's decision to expel one of its diplomats is wrongful and expels a diplomat of state B in response. But they can extend to the suspension of another treaty or customary law obligation, e.g. when state C freezes assets of the state D's central bank in order to induce the latter to cease the breach of a commercial treaty between them. Such countermeasures are lawful when they are necessary and proportionate. They are not lawful when undertaken as mere reprisals. In any event, countermeasures for the breach of a treaty may not include the threat or use of force against the territorial integrity and political independence of another state, or measures that violate fundamental human rights, the international laws of war in relation to reprisals, and peremptory norms of international law.

Conclusion

Treaties are part of everyday diplomacy and debate between international actors and this chapter has introduced their basic underlying concepts and explained how they apply in different circumstances. Treaties are the most prevalent and efficient way of securing international cooperation. Treaties play an important role in international relations not only because they enable states to act when there is mutual interest to do so. They also enable international institution building as the case of the World Trade Organization and the United Nations, and establish multilateral codes of international conduct, such as the law of the sea and human rights. The next chapters will show how treaties concluded in different areas help regulate these areas and how successful they are in setting out specific frameworks of appropriate conduct. As we have seen in this chapter the making of, interpretation, and termination of treaties themselves are subject to very detailed regulation in international law. The widespread acceptance of rules of treaty making shows that states regard these rules as fair and worth following. In this respect, the law regulating international treaties itself is a successful regime in international relations.

Questions

1. What is a treaty?
2. Where do we find the international law relating to treaties?
3. What functions do treaties perform in international relations?
4. How are international treaties made?
5. When does a treaty 'enter into force'?
6. When does a treaty become binding on a state? Is signature of a treaty enough to make a state bound?
7. What is *pacta sunt servanda*?
8. How are international treaties interpreted?
9. What are reservations to treaties? What purpose do they serve? Are they always allowed?
10. When is a treaty invalid? What are peremptory norms of international law (*ius cogens*)?
11. When may a treaty be lawfully terminated or suspended?
12. How are disputes about international treaties settled?

Further reading

Aust, A. (2007) *Modern Treaty Law and Practice*, 2nd edn. (Cambridge: Cambridge University Press). *A reliable survey of the law of treaties, with a very useful emphasis on its practical application and probably the most accessible account of the increasing use of agreements in the form of MOUs.*

Goodman, R. (2002) 'Human Rights Treaties, Invalid Reservations and State Consent' *American Journal of International Law* **96**: 531–60. *A very useful account of recent practice on reservations to human rights treaties, applying insights from compliance theories of international relations.*

McRae, D. (1978) 'The Legal Effects of Interpretative Declarations' *British Yearbook of International Law* 49: 155–98. *A classic discussion of the practice of entering reserva-*
tions 'by stealth' and a thorough discussion of the other potential effects of interpretive declarations.

Redgwell, C. (1993) 'Universality or Integrity? Some Reflections on Reservations to General Multilateral Treaties' *British Yearbook of International Law* 64: 245–82. *A thorough treatment of one of the most difficult questions in the theory and practice of treaties*

Reuter, P. (1995) *Introduction to the Law of Treaties*, 2nd edn. (Geneva: Presses Universitaires de France). *A concise, accessible, and interesting handbook on the law of treaties.*

Sinclair, I. (1994) *The Vienna Convention on the Law of Treaties*, 2nd edn. (Manchester: Manchester University Press). *An 'insider' account of the drafting of the VCLT and a reliable account of its provisions.*

Thirlway, H. (1989) 'The Law and Procedure of the International Court of Justice, 1960–1989 (Part One)' *British Yearbook of International Law* 60: 4–56. *A comprehensive survey and analysis of the International Court's more recent decisions relating to the law of treaties.*

Voyiakis, E. (2003) 'Access to Court v. state Immunity' *International & Comparative Law Quarterly* 52: 297–332. *A discussion of the function of ius cogens norms in the context of the relationship between the right of access to court for alleged acts of torture and state immunity under customary international law.*

Websites

http://treaties.un.org *This website compiles many of the most important treaties in international law in the areas of human rights, disarmament, commodities, refugees, the environment, and the law of the sea.*

http://untreaty.un.org/ilc/texts/instruments/english/conventions/1_1_1969.pdf *Here you can find the full text of the Vienna Convention on the Law of Treaties of 1969.*

http://fletcher.tufts.edu/multi/general.html *This site is another extensive source of international treaties.*

http://www.icj-cij.org/documents/index.php?p1=4&p2=2&p3=0 *This website contains the full text of the Statute of the International Court of Justice, which lays down the sources of international law in Article 38(1).*

http://www.un.org/Depts/los/index.htm *This UN website contains the Convention of the Law of the Sea and other related treaties.*

Visit the Online Resource Centre that accompanies this book to access more learning resources www.oxfordtextbooks.co.uk/orc/cali/

Chapter endnotes

1. General Comment No. 24 (52) of the UN Human Rights Committee, CCPR/C/21/Rev.1/Add.6, available through the online portal of the UN High Commissioner for Human Rights at <http://www2.ohchr.org/english/bodies/hrc/comments.htm>/.

2. For the observations by France, the United Kingdom, and the United States on the Committee's General Comment, see 4 *International Human Rights Reports* (1997) 6; 261; 265 respectively.

3. *Certain Expenses of the United Nations*, Advisory Opinion of the International Court of Justice, (1962) *ICJ Reports* 151.

4. *Case Concerning the Gabcikovo-Nagymaros Project* (Hungary v Slovakia), Judgment of the International Court of Justice, (1997) *ICJ Reports* 65ff.

Chapter 6

Customary international law

Jason Beckett

CHAPTER CONTENTS

- Introduction
- What rules govern the formation of CIL? The conduct-centred model
- The CIL approach to state behaviour: states as agents with legal motivations
- What are the material sources of CIL?
- Identifying particular rules of CIL: the tipping point
- (Why) do states comply with CIL?
- Conclusion

CHAPTER OVERVIEW

This chapter focuses on what customary international law (CIL) is and how we can identify it. CIL is an important source of international law as it is the only universally binding branch of public international law (PIL). It is also controversial because of this claim to universal application. This chapter first briefly maps the theories of CIL and then turns its attention to the dominant, conduct-centred model of CIL in international law. It then focuses on identification of particular CIL rules and how CIL evolves and changes. The chapter concludes with a discussion of how we can approach compliance with CIL.

Introduction

The common definition of custom is that it is accepted practice or that it is a practice of long-standing. Customary International Law (CIL), however, is a difficult sub-ject in international law, because there are many debates over just what counts as practice, accepted practice, or a long-standing practice, in sum, as CIL. This makes it all the harder to explain CIL to students of international relations and show its value and use. In particular, there is no clear list which tells us which international norms are customary, nor what the content of any given norm of CIL is exactly. Consequently, it is also complex to determine whether state conduct is in compliance with CIL or not. For example, there are perfectly clear arguments which—depending on the view of CIL adopted—support either (or both) the perfect legality and the blatant illegality of the 2003 invasion of Iraq.

Nonetheless, CIL must be studied because it is as authoritative a regime as international treaty law for describing what international laws there are and evaluating the legality of state action (see Chapter 5). The reason CIL constitutes a source of international law lies in the historical acceptance of certain long-standing practices by states as legally required and the recognition of this in Article 38 (1) of the Statute of the International Court of Justice (ICJ) as one of the primary sources of international law. Moreover, and unlike treaty law, CIL generates norms (permissive as well as prohibitive) which are binding upon all states. The mutual expectations CIL creates amongst states is as close as we can get to legislative activity for the international society of states. It is for this reason that CIL is vitally important in the analysis of state conduct.

Due in part to the lack of textual clarity in Article 38(1), and in part because it is such a far-reaching source of law, CIL is deeply contested both methodologically and politically. In a nutshell CIL is an attempt to create normative structures and rules to constrain and evaluate the conduct of states, but these structures and rules are, *themselves*, drawn from the conduct of states. This is often perceived as a problematic idea. The formation of CIL, in particular, is contrary to basic assumptions of realist and rationalist international relations scholarship. The over-arching objection is that CIL is just empty legal talk. It is merely a reflection of the tools strong states use to coerce weak states into doing what they want in international affairs. This objection is indeed part of a general realist view towards international law which holds that there is no difference between studying what strong states want and international law because the latter cannot independently affect the former.

The aim of this chapter is to show how international law analysis of CIL responds to this challenge in international relations. The chapter first outlines the areas of widespread agreement on CIL in international law. It then sketches the workings and effects of the dominant model of CIL which derives law from the actual conduct of states. This section should enable students consistently to identify the norms of CIL—both the universal prohibitions like the ban on torture, and new universal permissions like the claim of economic sovereignty in the exclusive economic zones (EEZ)—and to deploy these in analysis of the legality of state conduct.

> **Box 6.1** What makes CIL popular despite theoretical controversy?
>
> Universal application and dynamism
>
> Whilst treaties are binding only on those states which choose to sign and ratify them, norms of CIL are binding on all states from the moment they come into being. This is the great strength, the 'unique selling point' of CIL, and the feature which best accounts for its status as law, *despite* the difficulties inherent in its identification and application. It is through CIL that, for example, the prohibition on torture and other serious human rights violations are binding even on those states who are not parties to the relevant torture conventions. In this respect the CIL speaks to an important aspiration in international law by enabling equal application of international law to all states. Indeed, the principle of the bindingness of treaties (*pacta sund servanda*) is itself a norm of CIL.
>
> This, vital, universality of CIL is achieved through an equation of silence with acquiescence. More specifically, under the doctrine of tacit consent, failure to actively protest a norm during its evolution is deemed to be an endorsement of that norm. In this way, *both* the voluntary structure of PIL, and the universal normativity of CIL, are preserved.
>
> Arguments for the existence of CIL can rely on a wide range of practices, such as multilateral treaties and United Nations General Assembly Resolutions. The idea of CIL, therefore, enables one to make sense of the current complex practices of interstate activity. CIL is also important in order to codify existing practices. The analysis of CIL through studying complex interstate practices is a key task of the International Law Commission, the United Nations body responsible for codifying international law.

What rules govern the formation of CIL? The conduct-centred model

In this section we focus on the general question of what counts as CIL. Because law has no corporeal reality (it is not a physical 'thing' like a table or an island) there is some dispute as to what, exactly, *counts as* a legal norm. The answer to this question is all the more complex in a horizontal legal system because there is a constant need to differentiate legal norms from moral and political ones. This dispute is *ontological* in nature,[1] and must not be confused or elided with interpretive disputes which are concerned with what particular CIL norms say or mean. The debates over what counts as law (what counts as a legal norm) must be resolved *before* CIL can be accurately perceived or described.

There have, over the years, been many competing theories of CIL. Some based in moral analyses, others in political processes. The former start the analysis of CIL by looking at the content of norms and the latter by looking at the process within which norms are created. None can be dismissed out of hand, but a few points of general (though not universal) consensus can be discerned.

There is general agreement that CIL is a system of rules, and that it is derived from the observable practice of states. However, it is also generally agreed that it contains a 'subjective element'. The two constituent elements of CIL are called: state practice and *opinio iuris* (or *juris*). The classic judicial statement on the emergence of custom comes from the *North Sea Continental Shelf Cases* which concerned a dispute between Germany v Netherlands and Denmark before the International Court of Justice:

> Not only must the acts concerned amount to a settled practice, but they must also be such, or be carried out in such a way, as to be evidence of a belief that this practice is rendered obligatory by the existence of a rule of law requiring it.[2]

Although somewhat opaque, both the Statute and the ICJ clearly refer to there being two elements which must coincide to create CIL. Moreover, it is only with a two-element theory that any degree of consistency, objectivity, or neutrality can be brought to CIL. If we only look at the bare practice of states, we simply observe what states do. We need to have an account of why states do what they do in order to understand CIL. If we only look at what states should accept as law we impose CIL on states. We have to show that there is a common understanding amongst states about the belief of the legality of specific conduct. Finally, there is widespread agreement that the generation or evolution of norms of CIL does not require the individual and explicit consent of each state. This means that no state alone controls the law-making and law changing process under CIL: It is an aggregation of state practice with intent that creates CIL. This principle of aggregated conduct responds to the criticism that CIL is simply what strong states do. It may be descriptively correct that strong states often set examples to other states and that their actions are more likely to be mimicked or followed. This does not, however, mean that CIL is in principle what strong states want. Indeed, in contested areas, such as anticipatory self-defence or humanitarian intervention (see Chapter 10), the preferences of strong states are contested under CIL.

The CIL approach to state behaviour: states as agents with legal motivations

States engage in a diversity of practices, be they political, courteous, or legal, in everyday international politics. No legal rules can be distilled directly from

the mere practice of states; there must be some form of differentiation, or discrimination between normatively relevant, and normatively irrelevant conduct. In
theories of CIL the concept of *opinio iuris* plays precisely this differentiating role.
Put succinctly, one simply cannot treat all state conduct as 'practice', state conduct
must be judged against the rules of CIL. However, certain forms of conduct might
be intended to, or have the effect of, changing those very rules. Meanwhile, other
forms of conduct may be in pursuance or breach of those same rules. CIL, therefore, not only looks at what states do, it also asks what kind of legal motivation,
if any, is attached to the conduct of states. We can think of four generic forms of
state conduct:

1. conduct in compliance with existing law;

2. conduct at variance with existing law, but not intended to create law;

3. conduct in breach of old law, but not intended to create new law; and

4. conduct in breach of old law, but intended to create new law:

   a. which fails; or

   b. which succeeds.

In the light of this, *state practice* is what states actually do; but also, and more precisely, state practice is some of what states do. More precisely again, state practice
is that portion of state conduct which manifests and indicates *opinio iuris*: conduct
intended by states to create new law, or reform existing law.

The subjective element '*opinio iuris sive necessitatis*' literally translates from Latin
as 'belief of law or necessity'. It is the subjective element in the formation of CIL
because *opinio* is some form of belief imputed to states. Consequently, it is a way of
making sense of (or classifying) both the actions of states and the responses of their
peers. As a result, *opinio iuris* is a community concept; it is an attitude (a mindset,
belief, or expression of consent) which must not only be held by the acting states,
but also reflected by their peers.

Norms of CIL can evolve *only* from the consistent conduct and belief of states
(i.e. from state *practice*). This is, indeed, the unifying core, the touchstone, of CIL
as a whole: CIL is a manifestation of the will of states drawn *directly and exclusively* from the observed practice of the international community of states *viewed
as a whole*. CIL, therefore, provides a conceptual lens to evaluate state behaviour
as well as motivations for action, support, and dissent. It is for this reason that
international law and relations theories that do not have any room for motivations of states in driving their behaviour have important difficulties to engage
with CIL.

Case Study 6.1 Nuclear weapons through a CIL lens

Are there any CIL principles regulating the use of nuclear weapons?

Nuclear weapons are possessed by a small group of states, but they have not been used since the end of World War II. What does this mean in terms of CIL?

Some nuclear weapon possessing states may believe that they only possess nuclear weapons as a deterrent, so possession of weapons may reflect a desire to prohibit them.

Some other nuclear weapon possessing states may believe that they have a right to use these weapons to protect themselves from attacks of a similar kind as a matter of CIL. It is simply that such circumstances have not arisen.

Some states who do not possess nuclear weapons may aim to possess them and think there is a right to use them.

Some states who do not possess nuclear weapons may believe that these weapons are unlawful to use as a matter of CIL.

What effect might these types of conduct and lack of conduct with diverse motivations have on the formation, evolution, or alteration of CIL in this area?

Consider Judge Shahabudeen's dissenting opinion in the **Nuclear Weapons Advisory Case**:

> In view of the position taken by the ... proponents of legality ... over the past five decades, it will be difficult to argue that the necessary *opinio juris* later crystallized if none existed earlier.

> [T]he position taken by the proponents of illegality would bar the development of the *opinio juris* necessary for the subsequent emergence of any such permissory rule.

> [It] is reasonably clear that the opposition shown by the proponents of legality would have prevented the development of a prohibitory rule if none previously existed, and that the opposition shown by the proponents of illegality would have prevented the development of a rescinding rule if a prohibitory rule previously existed.[1]

---

[1] *Nuclear Weapons Advisory Opinion* (1996) ICJ Reports 226, at 379.

Even if we treat states as agents with legal motivations, it is not possible to determine what the CIL rules are conclusively by analysing these motivations. In some cases the practice of states may be inconsistent, and thus reflect an inconsistent *opinio iuris*. This is one way of approaching the use of nuclear weapons in international law, for example. In such cases CIL is unable to evolve *despite* the intentions of both supporters and dissenters.

We can contrast the case of nuclear weapons with those of prohibition of torture and the emergence of the Exclusive Economic Zone (EEZ) respectively. In the nuclear weapons example, we *appear* to have both practice and *opinio*, but in fact we have neither because of the split in community expectations, beliefs, and actions. In the case of torture, the 'practice' is (tragically) considerably more uniform. According to Amnesty International, some 135 states routinely use torture (perhaps others are also complicit in this, sending their suspects on so-called 'black flights' to the torturing states). There seems to be depressingly little official *state* protest at these activities. This would appear to amount to a great deal of state practice.

However, no state in international law has ever claimed a general *right* to torture. States either deny that they torture, offer spurious excuses as to why (their particular variant of) 'torture-lite' is permissible, or put the torture down to the acts of 'rogue elements'. In other words, no state expresses an *opinio iuris* favouring torture, and the international community thus has no cause to respond to such a claim. Torture then offers a paradigm example of state *conduct*, which is not CIL because it reflects no *opinio iuris*; it is not even intended as constitutive of new legal norms.

The advent of the EEZ reflects an opposite to each of the previous examples: here the conduct was intended as norm creating, and was accepted as such: a new norm of CIL *was* created. Under both the 1958 Geneva Convention on the Territorial Sea, and the then applicable CIL, states could claim a territorial sea and a contiguous zone of twelve nautical miles from the baselines. Beyond this was the 'high seas' an area of maritime freedom, with particularly entrenched freedoms of fishing and resource exploitation.

During the negotiations for the 1982 Convention on the Law of the Sea (UNCLOS) certain states put forward the idea of a 200-nautical mile Exclusive Economic Zone; which would significantly reduce both the scope and the freedoms of the High Seas. Several states supported this idea, many were quiet, and a few objected vociferously. Those in favour began claiming such zones. They sought to enforce their claims by prohibiting ships from other nations from fishing (or otherwise exploiting resources) there. Initially, there was some protest, which was met by a claim of emerging legal right. But gradually, the conduct of those claiming the EEZ was endorsed and emulated. After just a few years almost every coastal state in the world had declared an EEZ, and the protest had been abandoned.

In this case we see all the ingredients of a successful evolution of CIL. We have a clear and consistent conduct. This is supported by an *opinio iuris* on the part of those acting; and thus becomes state practice. This practice is then acquiesced in, endorsed, and emulated; this fulfils the community aspect of *opinio*. As a result, a new norm of CIL is formed. Unfortunately, few examples of CIL are quite so universally accepted, nor quite so clear cut.

What are the material sources of CIL?

Many practitioners and academics distinguish between the so-called 'material' and 'formal' sources of law. Essentially a formal source is what makes a certain norm law; inclusion of CIL in Article 38 of the ICJ Statute, for example. A material source is what gives that norm *content*; i.e. what actually occurs to create the norm. Thus Article 38(1) is the *formal* source of CIL; what states actually do (with the requisite *opinio*) is the *material* source. There are several material sources of CIL, namely, unilateral state actions, resolutions of major international organizations, significantly the United Nations General Assembly Resolutions, treaties, and other texts.

State actions

CIL derives from what states actually do. However, states, unlike human beings, are not 'real' actors. States can act only through human beings, and even then, only through certain human beings (state officials) acting in certain ways (i.e. in their official capacity). A president can act on behalf of his state, but his decisions over what to have for breakfast—no matter how consistent, well reasoned, or regimented—do not count as state actions or conduct, let alone as the basis of state practice. As Shaw has put it:

> A state is not a living entity, but consists of governmental departments and thousands of officials, and state activity is spread throughout a whole range of national organs. There are the state's legal officers, legislative institutions, courts, diplomatic agents and political leaders. Each of these engages in activity which relates to the international field and therefore one has to examine all such material sources . . . in order to discover evidence of what states do. (Shaw 2008: 78)

Probably the most important repository of state practice is the national archive of each state. Also of immediate relevance are national legislative acts incorporating, or defying, proposed rules of CIL, or judicial findings which support, rely on, or dismiss arguments of CIL (like the *Pinochet* case, establishing the UK position on the customary status of the prohibition on torture). Formal statements of intent, protest, or support are also forms of practice; and more so any practical implementation of these—e.g. sending troops, offering logistic support, withdrawing, or downgrading consular relations, etc.

Finally, several states also keep a 'digest' of developments in CIL and state conduct over the preceding year. In the United Kingdom, for example, this is termed

UK Materials in International Law (UKMIL), and can be found in the *BYBIL* annually. However, the digest is probably the least reliable (though obviously the most accessible) record of state practice; as it has a necessary editorial bias, and a certain degree of retrospective reconstruction.

United Nations General Assembly Resolutions

The role of the United Nations General Assembly (UNGA) resolutions in general PIL is contested. Viewed functionally, the General Assembly resembles a national legislature; however, according to its own Charter, UNGA resolutions are no more than recommendations. Indeed, an early suggestion that the Assembly be granted law-making powers was defeated with only a solitary supporting vote. Nonetheless, certain UNGA Resolutions *do* have normative, indeed *legal*, force and effect because of the wide and consistent support they attract from a large number of states. The best way to make sense of this is by perceiving those resolutions as part of the *corpus* of CIL, but as *material* sources of PIL.

That is General Assembly Resolutions are not law *as* resolutions, but rather *qua* CIL. It is the *content* of the resolutions, and the responses of states to them, which give them legal effect. This distinction is important, as it rules out the argument that a resolution adopted unanimously or by consensus is *automatically* part of CIL, or *therefore* reflects CIL. It should also undermine the argument that resolutions automatically enter CIL.

Instead, the crucial factor—the formal source—remains CIL: state practice and *opinio iuris*. The key is to continue to look at what states actually do. Thus, even *if* voting in the UNGA could be considered as an example of state practice, what would it amount to? Surely, it could amount to no more than a contribution to a rule that states must vote in certain ways in the UNGA, or that state representatives must raise their hands at particular times rather than others. No truly *material* practice has taken place. UNGA resolutions that are adopted unanimously or by consensus are not, therefore, *automatically* part of CIL and an assessment of states' intentions is necessary in adopting and supporting them.

A possible alternative is to perceive UNGA resolutions not as practice, but as evidence of *opinio*. In this vein, the ICJ, in the *Nuclear Weapons Advisory Opinion*, stated:

> General Assembly resolutions, even if they are not binding, may sometimes have a normative value. They can in certain circumstances provide evidence important to establishing the existence of a rule or the emergence of an *opinio juris*. To establish whether this is true of a given General Assembly resolution, it is necessary to look

at its content and the conditions of its adoption; it is also necessary to see whether an *opinio juris* exists as to its normative character. Or a series of resolutions may show the gradual evolution of the *opinio juris* required for the establishment of a new rule.[3]

However, this statement seems incomplete, even evasive. *How* might one discover 'whether an *opinio juris* exists as to its normative character', except by looking outside the resolution to the *actual* practice of states? The question then remains identical: have states acted in a consistent manner, such that evidences *opinio iuris*, and on a scale which leads to the generation of a new norm of CIL? This has, undoubtedly, happened. Perhaps the best example is the *Declaration on the Granting of Independence to Colonial Territories and Peoples*, (GA Res. 1514) (1960), which went on to form the basis of the CIL—and quite possibly *ius cogens*—right to self-determination.

Treaties and other texts

Treaties can become custom, and customary rules can be codified into treaties, and indeed a single rule can have force as simultaneously both treaty and customary law. Perhaps the most famous, and important, instance of a treaty rule becoming accepted as CIL is the definition of State laid out in Article 1 of the *Montevideo Convention on the Rights and Duties of States*. This norm is particularly important because it defines the direct subject of PIL, the state. It is interesting, and famous, because it never actually achieved the status of conventional (i.e. treaty) law due to a lack of ratifications.

Nonetheless, the formula laid out—that to be a state, an entity must possess: a defined territory; a permanent population; an effective government; and independence ('the capacity to enter into relations with other states')—has formed and focused the basic understanding of statehood (and indeed of the structure of PIL, viz. effectiveness over legitimacy) for many years (see Chapter 9). Paradoxically then, it was the very success of the definition which precluded the convention from coming into force: it was simply unnecessary as conventional law. However, it should be emphasized that it was not the *content* of the convention which made the definition of statehood part of CIL. Rather, it was the *reaction of states* to that content which ensured its entry into CIL. Sufficient quantity and generality of state support is again key to the emergence of CIL.

Some treaties have the specific aim of codifying CIL. Here groups of states, or learned societies of international lawyers, or UN bodies like the Sixth Committee or the ILC undertake to codify *already existing* rules of CIL. This is an area of PIL which courts controversy, and for a simple reason: if the rules of CIL really were so clear as to be uncontroversially codified, then there would be no need to codify them. Consequently, codification always tends toward a 'tidying up', indeed a 'progressive development'—passed off as a 'clarification'—of the often nascent, putative, indeterminate, or contested rules of CIL. There is no normative hierarchy between conventional and customary law, the two can coexist, intertwine, and even modify one another. Thus when the parties to a treaty—and non-party states—act in a manner consistently at odds with the treaty's provisions, their conduct may give rise to a customary rule modifying, or even revoking, the treaty in question. Likewise, the parties to a new treaty almost invariably wish to alter—or opt out of—the pre-existing law, and thus ratify the treaty precisely to modify CIL, at least between the parties.

There are two basic conflict-resolving rules of general international law: that later law supersedes earlier, and that more precise rules apply in preference to more general ones. Thus the twin questions are: which is the more up-to-date law, treaty, or custom? And, which rule is most precisely applicable to the question at hand?

As a result, one cannot simply take at face value any convention's claim to be a codification; but *neither* can one dismiss a claim of customary status simply on the grounds of underwhelming ratification or conventional support. An absence of ratification could precisely signal support and success: if the convention codifies already existing CIL, then there is no need to support it as conventional law as well. Once again then, one must look not only at the text of the treaty, but at the reactions, the conduct and practice, of states.

Identifying particular rules of CIL: the tipping point

State practice is that conduct of states which manifests, or implies, *opinio iuris*, but this leaves us with four (or, perhaps five) types of practice, and an open question: how much practice is required to create a rule of CIL? We can posit a simple topography of types of conduct:

1. practice intended as rule creative;

2. practice in support of a putative new rule;

3. practice in partial support (modification) of an evolving rule:

   a. intended to qualify that rule; or

   b. intended to extend that rule; and

4. practice in rejection of a putative or evolving rule.

To return to the example of the EEZ; when such zones were initially claimed by some states, there was a clear normative intent: to alter the legal regime regulating the High Seas (1). What became vital then was the response of other states, and especially maritime states. Many simply emulated the claims (2) or agreed to respect the zones claimed (2). However, others sought to modify the rule, even as it crystallized. Certain Latin American States, for example, sought to claim a 200-mile territorial sea, thus radically extending the scope of the proposed rule (3(b)). This extension was not widely endorsed.

Consequently, the conduct of these states, although motivated by *opinio*, and thus classifiable as practice, had, in reality, little or no normative effect. Such states would be legally entitled to retain their claims to a 200-mile territorial sea, as a standing invitation to normative change (1). However, they would *not* gain the corollary entitlement to enforce their claims against third states. Thus they could *claim* a territorial sea of 200 miles, but would be in breach of CIL if they should attempt to prevent third states from exercising the freedoms of the high seas, as modified *only* by the EEZ regime, in the area between 12 and 200 nautical miles from the shore.

A few states—noticeably the USA and Japan—rejected the idea of the EEZ, maintaining a commitment to the classic freedoms of the high seas. As a result, they specifically sent their fleets to fish in areas (outside of the established territorial seas) where other states had claimed EEZs. This is a clear example of practice in rejection (4). However, this practice was itself widely protested, and that protest is an odd amalgam of type 2 and type 4 conduct: conduct in support of the new rule, and rejection of its proposed qualification or rejection. In the end, even the US dropped its objections and claimed its own EEZ.

The overall result of all of this state practice—which was generally uniform, though not universal—was the creation of the EEZ regime in CIL. But this, again, begs rather than answers the question of how much practice is needed to generate a new rule, or modify an existing one. There is no clear answer to this question, certainly no numerical threshold. There have been several attempts to offer a quantified or formulaic solution, but my favoured answer is colloquial: it takes a heap of state practice (which necessarily includes a heap of *opinio*) to generate normative evolution.

I owe the following to Stephen Fry:

The great thinker Zeno once sat a pupil of his down at a table and put a bean in front of him. 'Is this a heap?' he asked the pupil. 'No' said the pupil, who was very smart. 'Of course it isn't, it's a bean.' Zeno then placed another bean beside the first. 'Is this a heap then?' 'No.' Zeno added beans, one at a time until the student said 'Yup, guess you could call that a heap.' 'Ah,' said Zeno. 'So a heap is twenty-seven, is

that right? You are telling me that the word "heap" actually means twenty-seven?'
At which point the pupil got uncomfortable and bopped Zeno on the head with
a discus.

A heap is indefinable, yet contextually recognizable; though the importance of
context—or the question of which factors are relevant to context—has not been
definitively settled. Some factors, however, can be identified: there is no minimum
length of time over which a practice must take place, *however*, the less time which
passes, the more 'uniform and consistent' the practice must be. The more practice
there is, the less uniform it needs to be; conversely, sparse practice must be virtually
uniform. Certain writers maintain that the more 'reasonable', or 'consonant with
World Order Values', a proposed rule, the less practice is required.

Box 6.2 CIL and consent: the question of persistent objector

The persistent objector theory claims that states have an 'opt-out' option as regards nascent rules of CIL. In essence, the claim is that an individual state which objects to a rule,
persistently, and from the very beginning, will not be bound by that rule, even *if* it becomes
part of CIL, and therefore binding on all *other* states minus the objector. There is a very
limited degree of doctrinal support for the persistent objector theory.

Conceptually, this theory relies on the idea that CIL emerges if and only if an individual
state consents to that rule. This, however, goes against the collective assessment of state
practice and *opinio iuris* underlying CIL formation.

CIL in the real world

As we have seen from the examples discussed uncovering, and identifying, the rules
of CIL is not only controversial, but also an onerous task. State practice is widely
dispersed, often awkward to identify, hard to weigh, and generally not uniform.
Added to this, states' international legal officers are often busy and under pressure.
There is thus a temptation, if not to take shortcuts, then at least to take the path
of least resistance. This leads to a phenomenon identified as 'bureaucratic inertia',
which gives an added force to the customary claims of both treaties and certain
UNGA resolutions. Put very simply, under pressures of time, it is *easier* to consult
a written source, and to take that as definitive. A treaty which claims to lay down the
rules of CIL offers clarity and ease. *Therefore*, it is incorporated into legal advice.
The effect, of course, is that the treaty is then acted upon—treated as CIL—and that

very action, and the normative belief/intent it implies, becomes state practice, and thus (partially) constitutive of the norm's status as a norm of CIL. This (virtuous or vicious) circle then reinforces the treaty's claims to customary status. Other states build upon this.

The compatibility of CIL with *ius cogens* norms

Ius cogens norms are higher-order, non-derogable, norms; which fit awkwardly into the conduct-based structure of CIL. *Ius cogens* norms are intended to place constraints on all of IL as they have the power to annul international laws that are contrary to *ius cogens* norms. Neither international treaty law nor CIL, however, give a further indication of how such super norms might be identified. The importance of the content of norms and not the process which creates them is at the forefront for identifying *ius cogens* norms (Weil 1983: 425). This definition has a strong natural law tint to it as it is concerned with laws all states ought to follow (see Chapter 4).

The *ius cogens* debate gives rise to the idea of 'relative normativity'. That is, the idea that some norms are, for whatever reason, more important, more normative than others; and on to the idea of 'super norms' embodying a necessary moral content of law, or imposing necessary moral limitations on law. The hegemonic aspect of this claim is often overlooked, but ought to be emphasized. The key question is a simple one: *if* there is a necessary link between law and morality then how do we decide which moral principles to impose on the conduct of states, or what the correct division of labour is between moral principles and principles based on state conduct? A common criticism in this regard is the dominance of Western (Northern) liberal states and their preferences being presented as universal moral principles. This leads to the true crux of the question: what are IL or CIL *for*? The classic image of P/CIL in a pluralistic society of states revolves around the search for consensus, common ground, common interest, and agreed universals; even if these prove hard to find. This consensus building differentiates CIL from moral preferences of powerful states.

Box 6.3 Discussion point: morality and CIL

Is there a necessary relationship between any *particular* morality and CIL?

One argument would suggest that some moral precepts and axioms are *automatically* incorporated into the *corpus* of CIL; or that some principles are accepted into the body of

CIL on a lower level of evidence (of general support) than are other (normal) rules. This would mean, for example, that rules prohibiting, e.g. genocide or torture are treated differently from those pertaining to Maritime Delimitation or Diplomatic Immunities.

Another argument would suggest that there is no need to give preferential treatment to morality of any kind as a matter of principle. Members of the international community are engaged in a joint enterprise seeking the realization of cooperation and peaceful existence. This would mean that law should reflect solely the observable aims of the international community.

(Why) do states comply with CIL?

Compliance studies form another inherently controversial aspect and study of CIL. This is so for several reasons: firstly, the content of many international obligations appears indeterminate, this makes it awkward to distinguish compliance from breach; second, states are not always entirely honest (let alone transparent) about their actions, this is a particular complicating factor in the deinstitutionalized realm of CIL; third, even where compliance or non-compliance can be observed with some certainty, the factors motivating state conduct tend to be opaque at best. Furthermore, the value of CIL extends beyond whether states comply with CIL norms or not. CIL has a strong communicative element and its key function in international relations is to analyse legal motivations and assess the legality of state action.

Factors contributing to compliance with CIL: state identity and systemic benefits

There are two ways of looking at the factors that contribute to compliance. First, we can analyse compliance from the perspective of an individual state and second, from the perceptive of the benefits all states receive from compliance.

As liberal international relations scholars and social constructivists also point out (see Chapter 2) a state's identity as far as it defines an attitude towards international law is an important factor in compliance. It has been suggested for example that 'domestic regime type' (i.e. liberal democracies, democratizing states, authoritarian states) or the self-perception of the size of the state (i.e. small states, big states) may be an important factor in determining attitudes towards international law. A further argument extrapolating the work of Immanuel Kant on peace among republican states; liberal international relations scholars argue that democratic, or liberal, states have an inbuilt propensity towards respecting the demands of legality. This view has also received attention in international law research. Scobbie, has noted that:

> At the very least, if a (democratic) State departed from [Customary] Rules, it may be faced with the necessity of justifying its actions to domestic political audiences, or even to the judiciary in those States where customary international law is automatically incorporated into domestic law. (Scobbie 2007: 21)

This view adds further complexity to compliance with CIL in countries with strong rule of law traditions applying CIL principles in domestic courts. Empirically, however, there are also counter examples where neither democratic structures nor independent domestic courts play a role in compliance with CIL rules. The US torture practices in Guantanamo Bay Camp is a case in point. For non-democratic states, different domestic constraints and international pressures apply in their attitude towards particular CILs. Weak or 'rogue' states face a very real possibility of sanctions or enforcement actions in the event of breach. Even strong non-democratic states may face trade sanctions, or at least the adverse effects of international disapproval.

The second perspective is to approach CIL compliance in terms of systemic benefits to all states in complying. CIL allows for the management of mutual expectations, thus states obey because they are expected to obey, but also because they expect others to obey. Rules, in short, bring predictability to conduct. This predictability is reinforced by peer pressure amongst states, states' concerns for their own reputations (as 'good' or 'law abiding'), a belief in the fairness of particular norms or the system of IL as a whole, perhaps a sense of moral obligation, and finally a wariness of the potential costs of non-compliance.

Beyond, but also bolstering, this desire for predictability and stability there are three primary incentives for obeying CIL: clarity, interest, and moral exculpation. The clearer and more determinate a legal rule is, the greater its 'compliance pull'. In other words, states have a propensity to obey the law, as this depoliticizes decision-making, leaving the right thing to do as the lawful thing to do. Similarly, as CIL reflects the 'morality' or confluence of interests of the international community *of states* as a whole, then, generally speaking, obedience should, in any given instance be in any given state's best (long-term) interests.

Finally, and drawing once more on Kant, obedience to the law provides moral exculpation for both the initiation *and the outcome* of a political choice, or course of action. Lawful action is beyond moral reproach. Even the most mediated approach is deflected: the law may be criticized, but those who act in accordance with it may not be. The inverse also applies: those who choose to breach the law must justify not only their conduct, but *also* the outcomes (the side effects) of that conduct. They bear a full *moral* responsibility for all of the effects of their unlawful conduct.

Conclusion

CIL is generally defined as a collective practice of long-standing. In this chapter we have attempted to elucidate the meaning, and explain the value, of CIL as a source of international law. CIL has importance, as it is the only universally binding branch of IL. What counts as CIL is a subject of theoretical controversy, but understanding CIL is indispensable to the identification of international laws. CIL rules are also part of many domestic judicial systems. This means that they have relevance not only in international politics, but also in domestic courts. The CIL rules in international law have a strong communicative aspect. They signal mutual expectations of states. They also contribute to the stability and predictability of interstate behaviour. CIL is also a good indicator for identifying the demands for, and resistance to, changes of international laws. This chapter has shown that the conduct-centred model emphasizes that CIL is a collective law-making process in international relations. It accommodates the legal motivations of supporters as well as dissenters in arguments for the existence, change or modification of CIL's rules.

Questions

1. What is customary international law?

2. What makes customary international law important?

3. Who is bound by customary international law?

4. What is state practice? What are the sources of state practice?

5. What is *opinio iuris*? How does it relate to state practice?

6. How much state practice is needed to create a new rule of CIL? Does this depend on the content of the rule?

7. In what way can we approach the relationship between customary international law and morality?

8. How can we tell whether states comply with CIL or not?

9. What reasons are there for states to comply with CIL?

10. How do we distinguish breaches of CIL simpliciter from breaches intended to create new rules?

11. What are the possible effects of the responses of other states to a putative breach of CIL?

Further reading

Akehurst, M. (1974–75) 'Custom as a Source of International Law' *British Yearbook of International Law* 47: 1–53. *The classic text on the orthodox British understanding of CIL.*

Beckett, J. (2006) 'Rebel Without a Cause? Martti Koskenniemi and the Critical Legal Project' *German Law Journal* 7/12: 1045–88. *For a more political, and critical, exploration of the role of public international law in international life.*

Falk, R. (1966) 'On the Quasi-Legislative Competence of the General Assembly' *American Journal of International Law* 60: 782–91. *A wider understanding of the sources, and effects, of public international law.*

Franck, T. (1995) *Fairness in International Law and Institutions* (Oxford: Oxford University Press). *The classic liberal text on the instrumental value of law to world affairs.*

Koskenniemi, M. (2007) 'The Fate of Public International Law: Between Technique and Politics' *Modern Law Review* 70: 1–30. *For a normative defence of the value of public international law, and lawyers, as political actors.*

Schachter, O. (1989) 'Entangled Treaty and Custom' in Y. Dinstein (ed.) *International Law at a Time of Perplexity: Essays in Honour of Shabtai Rosenne* (Dordrecht: Martinus Nijhoff), 717–38. *A comprehensive study of the interplay of the two principle branches of IL.*

Scobbie, I. (1997) 'The Theorist as Judge: Hersch Lauterpacht's Concept of the International Judicial Function' *European Journal of International Law* 8/2: 264–98. *A clear theoretical exposition of the role of theory in legal decision-making at the international level.*

Tasioulas, J. (1996) 'In Defence of Relative Normativity: Communitarian Values and the *Nicaragua* Case' *Oxford Journal of Legal Studies* 16: 84–128. *An articulate defence of the liberal-moralist approach to CIL.*

Weil, P. (1983) 'Towards Relative Normativity in International Law?' *American Journal of International Law* 77: 413–42. *The classic defence of the positivist understanding of CIL.*

Websites

http://www.nyulawglobal.org/globalex/Customary_International_Law.htm *This website is a useful tool set up by New York University Law School to help students research customary international law.*

http://www.un.org/law/ilc/ *The International Law Commission plays an important role in the progressive development and codification of international law and this website provides up-to-date information on its work.*

http://www.icj-cij.org/docket/index.php?p1=3&p2=4&k=e1&p3=4&case=95 *The International Court of Justice's website gives access to its materials, among others relating to the legality of the threat of use of nuclear weapons.*

http://www.un.org/documents/resga.htm *All the resolutions taken by the UN General Assembly are published on this website.*

http://www.un.org/ga/sixth/ *The United Nations Sixth Committee, along with the ILC, undertakes to codify already existing rules of CIL.*

Visit the Online Resource Centre that accompanies this book to access more learning resources **www.oxfordtextbooks.co.uk/orc/cali/**

Chapter endnotes

1. Ontology is the study of what exists.
2. (1969) *ICJ Reports* 4, at para. 77.
3. (1996) *ICJ Reports* 226, at para.70.

Chapter 7

Non-governmental organizations and international law

Meghna Abraham

CHAPTER CONTENTS

- Introduction: non-governmental organizations in a terrain occupied by states
- Motivations for NGO involvement in international law
- NGOs and sources of international law
- NGO participation in intergovernmental organizations and processes
- The role of NGOs in the development of international law
- The role of NGOs in the enforcement of international law
- Evaluating NGO involvement in the development of international law
- Conclusion

CHAPTER OVERVIEW

International law is traditionally understood as a domain which is created by states and which concerns interstate relations. This chapter focuses on the role of one type of non-state actor, non-governmental organizations (NGOs) in the development of international law in expanding and transforming the interstate paradigm of international law. NGOs do not have a formal standing in international law but have for close on two centuries now influenced and shaped its development. This is particularly the case for specialist areas of international law such as international environmental law, human rights law, humanitarian law, criminal law, and labour law.

Introduction: non-governmental organizations in a terrain occupied by states

Earlier chapters have discussed how states create various forms of international law from treaties to customary international law. It is largely undisputed that only states can *create* international law and that the formal sources of international law are state-centric. Although states are the ultimate repository of law-making power in the international law system, other actors play a role in exerting influence over the development and enforcement of international law. These include national liberation movements such as the Palestinian Liberation Organization (PLO), international organizations such as the United Nations, businesses, religious groups, and non-governmental organizations, and even certain powerful individuals. All of these actors are broadly categorized as 'non-state actors' because they do not officially represent a state. They are admittedly very different from each other in terms of their capacities and the degree and ways of influence they have over international law-making. In this chapter we look at non-governmental organizations (NGOs), which stand out as a significant non-state actor for the identification of international law. NGOs are the only non-state actors that aim for the identification, progressive development, and enforcement of international law and they have been recognized to play this role through establishment of formal representation at international law-making fora and international organizations.

In this chapter we will define NGOs as organizations which do not operate for profit and which have been created with the purpose of actively advancing a political or social agenda. There are particular areas of international law where NGOs play a more important role. These are areas such as human rights, humanitarianism, protection of the environment, fighting impunity for international crimes, social justice, and indigenous peoples' rights that are mostly associated with progressive causes that cross borders. For this reason, international relations literature also calls NGOs international 'norm entrepreneurs' and views them as playing an important part in transforming the landscape of state-focused international relations (Finnemore and Sikkink 1998). The main point of international NGO activity is to influence the behaviour of states and often to motivate them to pursue specific ends through international law.

This chapter will outline motivations for NGO involvement in international law-making. We will discuss how NGOs approach the sources of international law and consider reasons for NGOs to support non-binding legal instruments (called 'soft' law) as well as treaties. We will then examine how NGOs have increased their access to intergovernmental organizations and international negotiations and what role NGOs play in the development and enforcement of international law. We conclude by considering some of the ways in which we can evaluate NGO involvement in international law-making.

Box 7.1 Definitions of NGOs

There are various definitions of non-governmental organizations. Broadly speaking, any organization which is *not* a governmental body could be considered a non-governmental organization. This can cover a wide range of organizations and entities from charities, corporations operating for profit, terrorist groups to religious groupings. In addition to groups set up with the goal of advancing a public or social cause, the term can also include groups set up to promote the interests of their members such as trade unions and associations which represent business interests. These organizations may operate within a country, a region, or internationally.

In the narrow sense, however, the term NGO is used to refer to *not for profit organizations*, which have social and political agendas that aim the advancement of a public good.

Motivations for NGO involvement in international law

A common characteristic of the NGOs which utilize international law is that they want to influence the behaviour of states towards people, natural resources, or species located within and outside the states' territories. In order to do this NGOs rely on the socializing effects of international law and institutions on the actions of political actors domestically and internationally. Human rights or environmental NGOs typically devote considerable resources, for example, in trying to influence governments to adopt standards and regulations on specific issues. NGOs have a strong interest in the process of making international law as it offers a route to not only develop but also implement international standards.

Box 7.2 The earliest NGO attempts to shape international law

The earliest attempts by an NGO to shape international law include the campaign of the British Anti-Slavery and Aborigines Protection Society (the predecessor of Anti-Slavery International) for an international ban on slavery including the adoption of the Slavery Convention in 1926. NGOs have since then devoted considerable resources to the development of international law.

Involvement in the international law-making process may seem inefficient, considering the amount of time taken to adopt an international instrument, the state-centric nature of international law, the difficulties of getting agreement across a majority if not all states, and the weak enforcement mechanisms found in international law in general. Nevertheless, NGOs, like states, turn to international law-making when seeking to resolve issues which require collective action and collective recognition. The international ban on slavery presented such a dilemma as states were reluctant to unilaterally give up their economic advantages linked to slavery if other states did not follow suit. A modern day equivalent of this dilemma is limiting greenhouse gas emissions linked to climate change. Similarly, NGOs may also try to develop international law on issues which require cooperation between two or more states. Conservation of endangered species may require cooperation between several states: the state where the species is located, states through which the species are traded and states in which consumers of endangered species are located.

A significant part of NGO activity concerns campaigning for recognition and implementation of norms of appropriate behaviour, such as standards on the treatment of prisoners and the rights of women. In such cases, NGOs turn to international law, international NGO coalitions, and advocacy because of the relative gains of international law in comparison to establishing such standards domestically. We can identify six types of reasons for this: overcoming domestic politics and barriers, economies of scale, better forum for negotiations, opportunities to increase commitment, enhancing NGO legitimacy, and creation of international enforcement mechanisms.

Overcoming domestic politics or barriers

A domestic NGO often turns to standard-setting at the international level to try and circumvent barriers in domestic politics. So for instance, it may be easier to push certain countries to accept standards on non-discrimination against minorities in an international forum where they could face embarrassment if they were seen to be opposed to such a standard. A further reason to prefer an international over a domestic standard is that an international standard may be longer lasting. A commitment by a state under international law offers a degree of protection if there is a dramatic and negative political turn in domestic politics. Withdrawing from an international commitment can be more difficult politically for a state than merely amending its domestic law.

Economies of scale

For an international NGO trying to get various states to agree to prohibiting torture or to allow trade unions to form and operate, it may be easier to push for an international agreement on these matters rather than convince each state individually to accept this as a standard. If NGOs are able to convince a critical mass of states for a particular standard, it is more likely for other states to follow the same standard (Keck and Finnemore 1998).

Better forum for negotiations

NGOs may choose international law-making processes because this enables them to target countries (through lobbying and campaigning) which they are otherwise unable to operate in and therefore cannot influence through domestic political channels. In authoritarian or semi-authoritarian states domestic NGOs may face repression from political authorities and international NGOs can be more effective in campaigning for the domestic causes (Risse et al. 1998).

Opportunities to gradually increase the scope or level of the commitment

The perceived weakness of international law that it often has vague standards and is difficult to enforce may be an asset in terms of getting a larger number of states to agree to it and to make a commitment to implementation. So the same state which refuses to recognize economic, social, and cultural rights in its domestic law may become a party to an international treaty requiring it to guarantee these rights. It may do so because it believes the wording of the treaty is broad enough not to change its domestic arrangements and/or the enforcement mechanism is too weak if it did not. Once the state becomes a party, NGOs can then use a variety of means to strengthen the interpretation of treaty provisions (i.e. increase the scope of the commitment made by the state) and apply pressure on a concerned government for implementation.

Enhancing the legitimacy of NGOs

The recognition of states' responsibilities for issues or groups that NGOs are campaigning for in one or more countries may also have the knock-on effect of increasing the recognition for and acceptability of the work of these NGOs. A high profile example is the International Campaign to Ban Landmines, which was awarded the Nobel Prize in 1997 jointly with its then coordinator Jody Williams for taking the idea of a ban 'from a vision to a feasible reality'. By participating in international negotiations and conferences, NGOs may also gain recognition which may be useful for fundraising or, in some contexts, even offer a degree of protection (from being shut down or the staff being targeted) to the NGOs activities.

Mechanisms for international enforcement

International law creates not only standards but also enforcement or monitoring mechanisms (See Chapters 13 and 14). Though these mechanisms may be of varying strengths, each may offer a NGO with opportunities for applying pressure on the state to comply with the obligations it has undertaken. In addition to the formal mechanisms that exist for monitoring the implementation of a particular set of standards, NGOs use public opinion and the media to persuade states to adhere to their commitments under international law. They also use advocacy, litigation, or political lobbying within the concerned state as a means of encouraging or securing compliance. In the most extreme scenarios, NGOs may seek international sanctions or direct military intervention in a state to bring about change.

NGOs and sources of international law

NGO perspectives on the sources of international law may differ from those of some international lawyers and jurists because they approach international law as a means to influence state behaviour in a sustainable way. NGOs, therefore, are interested in the wider question of how international norms can be created and effectively internalized by state actors rather than the jurisprudential questions of the status of legal texts in international law. In this context, NGOs are supportive of international treaty making as well as other non-conventional forms of international cooperation.

It is within this context we can analyse the proliferation of soft law instruments in international law and the NGO support in their creation and utilization. Soft law is a term used to describe a variety of instruments used in the domain of international law, which (in contrast to rules of customary international law and obligations under treaties) are generally considered to be non-binding on states. The term soft law is used to contrast it with hard law, and the latter indicates commitment to be legally bound by a rule by states. Despite this lack of legal qualification, states have been engaged in creating soft law documents in diverse areas ranging from the environment to the protection of human rights and development. States may establish 'soft' law agreements because of their flexibility (they can be replaced or amended more easily than treaties) or precisely because it may be easier to get agreement on the content when the form of the instrument is not legally binding. Individual states may have different motivations for supporting or voting for soft law documents. These can range from genuine commitment to follow the rules set to gaining or maintaining diplomatic reputation.

Box 7.3 Soft law instruments

Soft law instruments are a diverse range of documents created by states, organs of international organizations, or treaty bodies. They include:

- resolutions or declarations adopted by the General Assembly and other intergovernmental bodies such as the Human Rights Council. Some examples of this type of instrument are the Universal Declaration on Human Rights, 1948, and the Declaration on the Right to Development, 1986 (both adopted by the General Assembly), and resolutions on the human rights situation in countries such as Sudan, Myanmar, and North Korea adopted by the Human Rights Council;

- declarations or other documents setting out broad commitments adopted at interstate conferences. Some examples are the Rio Declaration on Environment and Development (adopted at the UN Conference on Environment and Development in 1992), and the Vienna Declaration and Programme of Action (adopted at the World Conference on Human Rights in 1993);

- interpretative guidance provided by UN human rights treaty-monitoring bodies and other autonomous intergovernmental institutions; interpretative guidance or principles developed by UN independent experts; and codes of conduct, guidelines, and recommendations of international organizations. An example is the Guiding Principles on Internal Displacement, which were developed by the Special Representative of the UN Secretary-General on Internally Displaced Persons (IDPs) and identified the rights and guarantees relevant to IDPs in all phases of displacement. Another is General Comment Number 15 adopted by the UN Committee on Economic, Social and Cultural Rights in which it interpreted the right to an adequate standard of living to include the right to water.

Some academics and practitioners dismiss the entire category of soft law because they believe it does not constitute 'law' and does not have any value (Weil 1983: 413–17). The central problem with soft law from this perspective is that no state accepts to be legally bound by it. Therefore, it has no legal authority. We could compare this position to realist international relations theories given that the latter does not see any value in international law, whether hard law or soft law. When looking at international norms however, which is the primary focus of NGOs, it is hard to draw watertight distinctions between 'binding' and 'non-binding' norms. Some treaty provisions may, in practice, be 'soft law' because they are worded so generally that they do not identify any specific commitment on part of the state. Similarly, a soft law instrument such as the Universal Declaration on Human Rights (UDHR) may over time increasingly acquire an authority quite at odds with its status as a non-building declaration an authority quite at odds with its status as a non-binding declaration of the General Assembly. Many of the articles of the UDHR have arguably now become statements of customary international law (International Council for Human Rights Policy 2006: 16).

Given the weak formal enforcement mechanisms in international law the practical difference between a treaty and an appropriately worded soft law declaration can also be fairly limited. Though soft law agreements may represent a weaker form of commitment by a state, it is still a commitment. Guzman has suggested that rather than viewing treaties and soft law as distinct legal structures, one should view them as different points on a spectrum of commitment (Guzman 2008: 144). Based on the context, a commitment made under a soft law instrument may be taken as seriously by a state as a treaty obligation. For example states may strictly adhere to their commitments regarding export of nuclear materials contained in the guidelines adopted by the Nuclear Suppliers Group of countries.

For NGOs in particular, there may be little practical difference between so-called 'hard' and 'soft law' when seeking to establish standards for the behaviour of states. A soft law instrument, such as the General Assembly Declaration on Human Rights Defenders, setting out standards of behaviour for the treatment of 'human rights defenders' can still be relied upon by NGOs as a commitment that the state has to respect. NGOs also argue in this and similar cases that as the Declaration draws on standards contained in treaties, even if the form of the instrument is non-binding, the provisions are a restatement of treaty provisions and hence are indirectly binding. In contexts where the instrument offers interpretative guidance, such as those developed by UN human rights treaty bodies, many NGOs can and do argue that as these bodies have been delegated this function under the treaty they offer an 'authoritative' interpretation.

NGOs may also seek to strengthen the enforcement mechanism for soft law commitments by advocating setting up a mechanism to monitor implementation. NGOs lobbied the former Commission on Human Rights to set up the mandate of the Special Representative of the Secretary-General on the Situation of Human Rights Defenders. The mandate's activities included 'report[ing] on the situation of human rights defenders in all parts of the world and on possible means to enhance their protection in full compliance with the Declaration; . . . To establish cooperation and conduct dialogue with Governments and other interested actors on the promotion and effective implementation of the Declaration.'[1] NGOs have subsequently used this mandate extensively both to seek protection for human rights defenders under threat and to promote and strengthen the norms in the Declaration itself.

We now turn to the question of how NGOs obtain access to the intergovernmental fora where international law is created.

NGO participation in intergovernmental organizations and processes

NGOs have greatly increased their participation in intergovernmental organizations and in law-making processes over the last three decades. This has involved both an expansion in the rules and practices facilitating NGO participation as well as an increase in the numbers and types of NGOs who participate.

The main entry point for NGOs into the UN system has been Article 71 of the UN Charter which provides that the Economic and Social Council (ECOSOC) may 'make suitable arrangements for consultation with non-governmental organizations which are concerned with matters within its competence'. ECOSOC operationalized this provision by setting up a system to grant 'consultative status' to NGOs.[2] The purpose of arrangements for consultation with NGOs is identified as securing expert information or advice from NGOs having special competence, or to 'enable international, regional, subregional and national organizations that represent important elements of public opinion to express their views' (ECOSOC Resolution 1996/31, para. 20).

To qualify for consultative status, NGOs must be of a 'recognized standing within the particular field of its competence or of a representative character'. Other requirements include that it have an established headquarters with an executive officer, a democratically adopted constitution, an authority to speak for members, representative structure and accountability mechanisms to members, and be funded primarily by national affiliates/components or individual members. Any funding or support received from governments has to be declared to the ECOSOC Committee. NGOs may operate at the national, regional, or international levels. In 1946, forty-one NGOs were granted consultative status by ECOSOC. Today the number of NGOs with consultative status has increased to 3,172.

While the rules for NGO participation are still governed by the Resolution, NGOs have gradually increased the level of their participation through 'practices', which have been built up slowly and institutionalized. NGOs cannot vote or sponsor proposals but, in some UN bodies, participate in parts of negotiations which were once considered the exclusive province of states. For example, NGOs are now able to participate in informal negotiations along with states on resolutions at the Human Rights Council while this was not the case in earlier years. Another significant innovation is the increasing acceptance of participation of NGOs without consultative status with the UN, at conferences and preparatory meetings for drafting international instruments.

The greater interaction between NGOs and intergovernmental organizations has also enabled NGOs to shape the agenda of these organizations and feed into international law-making processes through submission of information and support in terms of expertise.

Despite all the innovations and the increasing number of NGOs that attend international conferences and meetings of intergovernmental organizations, there are still a number of practical constraints on the participation of NGOs. Though many NGOs have found creative ways to overcome some of these constraints, they play a role in determining which NGOs are able to participate and their level of engagement.

The process to determine which NGOs can obtain consultative status with ECOSOC can be politicized (a committee of nineteen states[3] considers the applications), is time-consuming and may be administratively cumbersome. States are able to ensure that some NGOs who monitor and publicize human rights situations in their countries are never approved or to ask for their status to be suspended (for some examples see Lindblom 2005: 383–5). Some NGOs who do not have consultative status are able to overcome this hurdle by relying on partners with the necessary status to accredit them as part of their delegations.

Most negotiations on international law instruments and meetings of key intergovernmental bodies are held in New York, Geneva, or Vienna and the negotiations span a number of years. The ability to invest resources in terms of staff time and to bear the logistical costs therefore play a significant role in determining which NGOs are able to participate. Most international NGOs that engage substantially with the system have offices in or close by these locations. This also places them at an advantage in negotiating processes as their UN staff tend to have personal relationships with delegations, which is an asset while lobbying and exchanging information, and also a more in-depth knowledge of the procedures and practices of the concerned body (which can be opaque and difficult to understand for a newcomer).

NGOs have tried to overcome these constraints by forming informal or formal coalitions, which enable them to share information and resources and facilitate the participation and draw on the strengths of a more diverse group of NGOs. For instance, the Coalition for the International Criminal Court brought together nearly 500 NGO member participants (the largest delegation) at the Rome Diplomatic conference on the International Criminal Court in 1998.[4] The Coalition started with 25 NGOs but now has over 2000 members from 150 countries in the world and is notable for the effective coordination between its wide and diverse membership.

The internet has also enabled NGOs to share information more widely and quickly, to coordinate positions and advocacy and has also led to greater transparency in the proceedings of UN bodies.

Given these constraints, international NGOs or well resourced regional and national NGOs are in a better position to influence the agenda of intergovernmental bodies. This can be because of their knowledge of the system, their role as 'experts' and/or their ability to invest the resources necessary for a longer-term engagement.

For an NGO which is able to succeed in part or most of its objectives domestically, the international route may only be rational to the extent that it offers support to its domestic advocacy. For many NGOs it may be logical therefore to consider 'going international' as a small component of their overall advocacy strategy. NGOs from countries where there may be little prospect of getting change in the human rights situation domestically, however, may often be forced to invest resources in advocacy at international fora and to join forces with other NGOs to try and bring international pressure to bear. For instance, Colombia has been the subject of advocacy by both national and international NGOs for a number of years.

The role of NGOs in the development of international law

NGOs may be involved in all stages of the making of treaties or of other international instruments, from negotiations, drafting, to the adoption of the instrument. NGOs are also closely involved in efforts to enforce and implement international law. Indeed, if we examine a specialist domain of international law such as international human rights law, NGOs have influenced the development of most, if not all, of the instruments that exist today. From the adoption of the first major international human rights instrument, the Universal Declaration of Human Rights (UDHR), 1948 to the most recently adopted—the Optional Protocol to the International Covenant on Economic, Social and Cultural Rights, most of these instruments originated because of NGO advocacy.

Initiating new standards

NGOs have influenced the development of new international standards in a variety of ways. These include researching and campaigning for adoption of issue-specific standards either in the form of soft law or international treaties, or optional protocols to treaties that creates monitoring mechanisms.

Case Study 7.1 Standard setting: Amnesty International and the Convention against Torture (Korey 2001: 170–80).

The Convention against Torture originated in a public campaign by Amnesty International (AI) for the abolition of torture in 1972. AI carried out detailed research, published a world-wide survey highlighting the practice of torture in over sixty countries, and organized petitions in various countries which over a million people signed on to by the end of 1973. AI also organized an international conference on torture bringing together government representatives, UN staff, and NGOs. AI chose 10 December, the anniversary of the adoption of the UDHR, for its symbolic value as the date for both the launch of the campaign in 1972 and the conference. Several government representatives then highlighted their concerns about the practice of torture at the General Assembly which responded by adopting a resolution condemning torture and other cruel, inhuman, or degrading treatment or punishment and by resolving to keep this issue on its agenda.

AI continued to campaign on the issue, highlighted the human rights violations perpetrated by the Pinochet regime after the military coup in Chile, and began to call on its network of members and volunteers to send letters to various authorities in response to 'urgent action' appeals on behalf of victims of torture. This led to an increase in the number of governments expressing concern about the issue at the General Assembly; not only Western governments but also significantly the USSR and Bulgaria. From this point, the process evolved through a UN Congress for the Prevention of Crime and the Treatment of Offenders to the General Assembly's adoption of a declaration which included for the first time a definition of 'torture'. In 1984, the General Assembly adopted a treaty, the Convention against Torture and Other Cruel, Inhuman or Degrading Treatment or Punishment (Convention against Torture).

The AI's campaign for the Convention against Torture is also a good example of how soft law instruments can help build support for standards before drafting a treaty. There are a number of later treaties including the Convention on the Rights of the Child, the Optional Protocol to the Convention against Torture, the Optional Protocol to the Convention on the Elimination of All Forms of Discrimination against Women, and the International Convention for the Protection of All Persons from Enforced Disappearances, which also owe their conception to NGO advocacy.

Many of the methods which were pioneered in the 1970s by AI in the areas of research, networking, intergovernmental, and media campaigning have been used by others subsequently. NGOs publicize human rights concerns and gaps in protection within the international system to place the need for new international standards on the agenda of states and IGOs. The monitoring and documentation undertaken by NGOs as well as submissions to international bodies helps set the ground for this but NGOs also use the media and various forms of public campaigning. Similarly, in the environmental domain, NGOs have shaped public consciousness of issues such as climate change, nuclear proliferation, genetically modified food, etc. This helps keep an issue or a country in the spotlight, generate international concern about the situation, and build momentum towards the need for international action.

NGOs also target particular governments, through their own lobbying at international fora or through domestic NGOs and actors, to champion international legal initiatives on a particular theme or country.

Once a state decides to sponsor or support an initiative, the alliance with NGOs can help to strengthen its advocacy efforts because of the additional resources in terms of lobbying and information gathering brought in by the NGOs. NGOs may have varying degrees of collaboration for specific initiatives. In the case of the Optional Protocol to the Convention against Torture for instance, NGOs supporting the process held regular meetings with 'friendly' states to discuss strategies, forming a true coalition. NGOs are also less constrained by the formal protocols of negotiations between states and can be more flexible and innovative in their diplomacy. So while a state would not normally attempt to shame another state publicly for its opposition to an initiative, an NGO can do this.

In the last three decades, NGO have increasingly used international expert bodies to initiate standard setting on human rights. This route is particularly useful in order to build basic acceptance of states. NGOs have carried out advocacy with the former Commission on Human Rights or its subsidiary body Sub-Commission on the Promotion and Protection of Human Rights, lobbied to appoint independent experts to study particular areas, identified gaps in protection and made recommendations for future action. NGOs have also contributed to any study or consultative process set up to examine situations or draft an instrument. Two such examples where NGOs helped to set standards are the International Convention for the Protection of All Persons from Enforced Disappearances and the UN Declaration on the Rights of Indigenous Peoples, which both originated from the former Sub-Commission on the Promotion and Protection of Human Rights.

NGOs may also jump on the bandwagon when states or international bodies suggest the development of a new international law instrument to support such a call, to shift focus, or to block such an initiative when they consider it unproductive. An example of the former is the Rome Statute for the International Criminal Court and of the latter is the Multilateral Agreement on Investment (MAI) which was being negotiated within the Organization for Economic Cooperation and Development. NGOs galvanized opposition to the MAI through a successful global campaign, run largely on the internet, in which they highlighted their opposition to 'secret' negotiations over a treaty which they perceived as protecting the rights of foreign investors at the expense of governments ability to legislate in the public interest (Boyle and Chinkin 2007: 76).

NGO participation in negotiations, drafting, and entry into force of treaties

Once a law-making process is initiated, NGOs remain involved in the negotiations and drafting process to try and influence its content. NGOs continue advocacy at domestic and international levels to build the support base for the initiative and for the substantive content that they are lobbying to include in the instrument. Coalitions which bring together diverse groups of NGOs, such as the one formed for the International Criminal Court, are particularly effective as they may allow pressure to be brought from varying constituencies such as faith-based groups, women's organizations, etc. At this stage of the process, NGOs also gain greater influence by acting as sources of expertise or assisting states and IGOs in carrying out the preparatory work for the instrument.

NGOs undertake a large, or a strategic, portion of the preparatory work for the development of the instrument. They may prepare initial drafts of the instrument itself, generally with a group of experts (who may be from academic backgrounds, UN or regional mechanisms, or from NGOs). An example of this is the draft of the Optional Protocol to the Convention against Torture, which was developed by the International Commission of Jurists and the Swiss Committee against Torture (now the Association for the Prevention of Torture) in 1990 and submitted by the Costa Rican Government as its proposal in 1991.[5] NGOs may also prepare commentaries on drafts, background documents, analyses of particular issues, highlight positive examples or practice from regional or national systems.

Box 7.4 NGOs as communicators of complex legal issues

During the negotiations on the Rome Statute for the International Criminal Court, Amnesty International produced a series of fact sheets on key issues which presented complex legal issues in an accessible manner and made it possible for non-experts to understand what was at stake. This kind of information is valuable not just for other NGOs in their advocacy but also for government delegations, particularly smaller delegations which may be overstretched and lack the staffing and resources to engage in their own analysis of the issues. In contrast, larger NGOs or coalitions of NGOs may devote considerable resources to undertaking this kind of work and have staff members who are experts on thematic issues or the ability to draw on a network of expertise. This kind of preparatory work is also helpful for the secretariats of international bodies supporting international law-making processes. These bodies may lack the resources and the expertise to undertake detailed preparatory work themselves or find it easier to rely on NGOs to carry out these functions.

Many states also rely on the expertise, information-gathering and 'naming and shaming abilities' of NGOs through the negotiating and drafting process. NGOs disseminate information, make oral statements, and lobby for the participation of experts including from regional systems. Through bilateral exchanges with delegations, they try and clarify issues of concern to governments. In between formal meetings as well, NGOs may convene or join meetings with states and experts to gather support for a particular draft/approach or resolve deadlocks on controversial issues in a less politically charged atmosphere.

NGOs who have representatives at international organizations or others who follow the process for a long period also build relationships with individual diplomats. These relationships encourage sharing of information and open up opportunities to persuade the delegate to change his/her views. As a channel of influence, it may be particularly effective when the diplomat has not been given instructions from capital and may have the discretion to shape his/her country's position. NGOs may also need to rely on this channel of advocacy for countries where they do not have domestic partners or where partners lack the ability to lobby the government.

NGOs use the threat of negative publicity to pressurize a government to either modify its position or to refrain from blocking or sabotaging the initiative. NGOs also carefully monitor, compile, and report on state positions in order to judge the level of support on certain issues. This information is communicated to partners based in the country for follow-up lobbying but can also be used in the domestic and/or international media.

Another route that has been used is the participation of NGOs as part of the state delegation or supporting smaller delegations to participate (sometimes in an attempt to neutralize powerful states who may be opposed through the weight of numbers). A striking example of this is the establishment of the Association of Small Island States by Greenpeace and the Center for International Environmental Law (now the Foundation for International Environmental Law and Development) in 1989. The two NGOs then coordinated the policy positions of thirty-seven states, who were members of the association, in the climate change negotiations (Spiro 2006: 21).

As discussed in the Chapter 5 on treaties, the final steps of the international law-making process for treaties is for states to become parties to it. The treaty also specifies a minimum number of states which have to become parties for the treaty to become operational. NGOs play a major role in encouraging states to become parties and also take other steps to promote the effective use of the instrument (such as lobbying for the implementing body to be allocated sufficient resources). The locus of lobbying shifts even more to political bodies, such as parliamentary bodies, within countries and NGOs may try and develop resources to boost the capacity of a larger group of domestic NGOs to engage with the ratification campaign.

Typically, states that have supported the initiative are high on the list of targets with NGOs asking states to follow through on their support by taking on the commitment. In addition to lobbying, mobilization of public opinion, embarrassment using comparisons with other states' ratification records, NGOs may also rely on state to state lobbying. Once a supportive state becomes a party, NGO lobbying may shift to trying to persuade it to invest efforts in convincing other states to become parties. States that have invested a lot of efforts in the initiative may be more responsive to taking on such a role. Ratification campaigns can also open up strategic opportunities for NGOs based in the country to open up a wider discussion within the country on measures that a state should take to bring its domestic laws and policies in conformity with the instrument.[6] This process may be useful in promoting greater awareness of the rights and standards in question and may achieve some of the goals set by NGOs domestically in terms of extending protection/strengthening enforcement mechanisms even if the state does not ratify the instrument.

How can we explain NGOs' ability to influence the process?

A state taking up an issue in response to lobbying by domestically based NGOs is relatively straightforward to understand. Domestic NGOs use various forms of political leverage and bureaucratic influence to influence the state's policy on an international initiative as they do on domestic policies (Spiro 2006: 9). What is more complicated to assess is why a state takes up an issue because of lobbying by an international NGO or an international coalition of NGOs. Do states only act when there is a coincidence between their interests and the interests of the NGOs or do NGOs independently shape the incentives of states? The answers are speculative and contested both in theories of international relations and international law.

Unlike other areas of international law such as trade law or environmental law, states do not have a clear motivation to 'prefer that other states treat their own nationals, in a right-respecting fashion' (Spiro 2009: 3). It is difficult therefore to explain state sponsorship of international human rights standard setting initiatives, in response to lobbying by NGOs, purely in terms of a coincidence between the state's interests and the interests of NGOs. There are some situations in which the two do come together or where NGOs may try and convince states of this fact. For instance, Anderson considers that some states extended support to the International Campaign to Ban Landmines because they viewed it as 'an important counterweight to the hegemony of the United States' (2000: 107). This, however, can not be said to be a comprehensive explanation.

Another explanation could lie in the way in which NGOs have shaped reputational incentives to encourage states to identify and prove themselves in terms of their promotion of human rights. On the flip side, they may threaten negative reputational consequences for states which oppose initiatives to expand protection for human rights. This may be significant both for the state's own self-identity but also in its relationship with other states. The reputational incentive may be most effective when the state in question also considers that it already complies, or wants to, with the standard it is promoting so it does not bear a high risk or cost in terms of compliance. Many states have also built a reputation as the champions of certain human rights issues and traditionally sponsor thematic resolutions and other initiatives linked to these themes. They may wish to build on this reputation by being the architects of a treaty or hard law instrument. States are also not monolithic and sometimes an individual ambassador or minister who is committed to a particular issue can play a significant role in ensuring that the state takes on a leadership role in pushing forward a law-making initiative.

In some cases, being identified internationally as supporters of a particular human rights concern may help deflect attention from the state's handling of this issue domestically. By taking on a role as an international champion the state may be signalling to its domestic and/or an international constituency that it is committed to this issue and this may help defuse criticism it could otherwise come into.

The role of NGOs in the enforcement of international law

The primary objective of NGO involvement in the development of international law is to develop standards, which they can then ask the state to comply with. NGOs use a variety of tactics and strategies to encourage or 'shame' the state into complying with its commitments or use all possible domestic and international political and legal mechanisms to ensure accountability for a failure to comply. It is not possible to do justice to this vast area of NGO activity so we will therefore briefly discuss these under the overarching themes below.

Publicize non-compliance

The entire model of interstate enforcement of international treaties has limited value in the area of international human rights law as states may not have an incentive to monitor how another state treats its nationals or react to instances of non-compliance. For instance, the interstate complaint mechanisms (to complain about alleged violations of the treaty by another state) found in many international human rights treaties have never been used by any state.[7]

NGOs therefore fill this gap by generating and disseminating information about non-compliance. This information may be published by the NGO, reported in the media, and submitted to domestic bodies, IGOs, and human rights monitoring bodies. Guzman considers this to be an important variable in the way the work of some human rights NGOs, such as Amnesty International, can affect state behaviour. 'Credible reports that shed light on the conduct of states reduce uncertainty regarding their compliance and, therefore, increase the reputational consequences of a violation' (Guzman 2008: 99). To ensure that this information is considered credible, NGOs need to demonstrate their non-partisan nature. Organizations that are open to well-founded challenges in terms of bias and inaccuracy can lose the ability to affect the reputation of states.

Clarification of what is non-compliance

A major challenge in relation to some areas of international human rights law is to clarify and establish when a violation or non-compliance has occurred. This can be the case when the treaty provision is broad or vague, where there is no agreement that a rule of customary international law exists or when dealing with a non-binding instrument. NGOs contribute to the process of clarification by advancing their own legal analysis of provisions. They also support expert monitoring bodies in developing interpretative guidance on provisions. These can take the form of new soft law documents, by which NGOs then try to hold states to account. There can be a tension here for NGOs between their interest in expanding the scope of application of a rule and their interest in being taken seriously when making assertions of non-compliance.

Lobby for action in response to non-compliance

NGOs may not stop at merely providing information but typically try and use all possible avenues to ensure accountability for non-compliance. These avenues include litigation, advocacy, and public campaigning.

NGOs may file complaints before domestic, regional, or international judicial or quasi-judicial mechanisms to get judicial pronouncements requiring the state to modify its conduct. They may also demand prosecutions of perpetrators and reparations for victims.

Advocacy activities may take the form of persuasion within states or reliance on expert or political bodies to apply pressure on the state to alter its conduct. These bodies may include National Human Rights Institutions, Parliamentary bodies, and other monitoring bodies at the domestic level. Internationally these may include any of the enforcement mechanisms ranging from the UN Security Council to a statement by an individual UN appointed expert. In the most extreme cases, NGOs may call for sanctions, withdrawal of aid, or other coercive measures to force a state to comply.

Evaluating NGO involvement in the development of international law

In the preceding sections of this chapter, we have examined some of the ways in which NGOs influence the development of international law. In this section we will consider some of the possible ways in which we can evaluate the involvement and influence of NGOs in this area.

Redressing a democratic deficit?

NGO participation is sometimes justified on the basis that it allows for representation of voices at the international level which would otherwise go unheard. It is argued that NGOs lend legitimacy to the international law-making process. However, the contrary argument is that NGOs distort the process.

One of the main discussions revolves around the legitimacy of 'unelected' NGOs exerting influences over processes which are the domain of sovereign governments who are, at least in theory, meant to represent the interests of their populations. John Bolton has argued that within the (democratic) nation-state, political interests compete for governmental power in order to receive legitimacy to implement their preferred policies domestically, and to negotiate on behalf of the nation internationally. Civil society, in this context, provides an opportunity for opposition groups—who were defeated at the ballot box—to put forward their positions. The troubling aspect for democratic theory here is whether or not the 'interests' defeated during the election should have a say alongside popularly elected governments, or whether this undermines the legitimacy of the system (Bolton 2000: 217–18).

The claim that NGO participation contributes to a democratization of international law-making processes and that NGOs constitute a channel for conveying 'world opinion' (Anderson 2000: 91–120, Boyle and Chinkin 2007: 57–62) has also been challenged from those who point out that only a few well-resourced NGOs and coalitions of NGOs influence and initiate international standard-setting and shape the content of these standards. This concern is strengthened by the fact that international NGOs are typically small, highly professional, 'elite' organizations funded by western donors and are not very representative of the people whose concerns they are advocating (Anderson 2000: 117–18).

On the other hand, NGO influence may be exaggerated by such critics—ultimately, international instruments have to obtain state consent (and thus domestic political endorsement) before they bind a state.

Moreover, other factors may also undermine the democratic quality of the international law-making process. Not all states participating in international negotiations are democratic, and even if they are, their negotiating positions may not be representative of the aspirations of its citizens and represent the views of special interests within the country. Many issues that form part of international negotiations may not be democratically deliberated within a country.

In any case, not all international standards should depend on their acceptance by the democratic majority. Just as we acknowledge the need for constitutional protection of fundamental rights domestically, even if this constrains majority rule, minority rights, prohibitions against racial discrimination or even torture in international law should not depend on endorsement from political polls or election platforms.

The value of NGO participation and influence may not be said to be rooted in facilitating greater involvement of citizens in international law-making, and thus 'democratizing' international law-making—as argued above, most NGOs are not representative in character or created to serve such a function. But NGOs may add democratic value through their monitoring and publicizing of states' positions, which may lead to greater transparency of otherwise opaque and distant international negotiations. By broadening the agenda of international law-making NGOs also increase the responsiveness and relevance of international law.

How do we gauge how effective NGOs have been?

The extent to which we consider NGOs effective in international law-making depends on our criterion for effectiveness. If we measure NGO success by the degree to which they have influenced the development of new standards in specialist areas such as human rights, NGOs have been extremely successful. Almost the entire body of international human rights law bears the imprints of NGO influence. They have also successfully shaped the reputational incentives of states so that support for or opposition to the development of international human rights may affect a state's reputation.

It gets more complicated if we try and gauge how effective NGOs have been in using international law to change the behaviour of states. A part of this requires us to assess the complex empirical question of how international law constrains the behaviour of states. In the human rights field, recent empirical studies have suggested that there is only a limited correlation between ratification of human rights treaties and adherence to human rights standards (Hathaway 2002)—although others have challenged these findings (Goodman and Jinks 2003).

There is no doubt that NGOs use international law, in a variety of ways, to apply pressure on states to change their behaviour. NGOs can point to success in a number of cases (releases of prisoners or stopping forced evictions), changes in policies and laws within countries, international action on a country such as humanitarian intervention. What may be difficult though is to establish a tight causal relationship between NGO advocacy, their reliance on international law, and changes in state behaviour as there may be a number of other explanatory variables which others could point to.

Conclusion

The analysis in this chapter indicates that it is not possible to ignore NGOs as actors in the areas of international law and relations. It would also be advisable to see them as having influence only where their interests coincide with states instead, NGOs act independently, in collaboration with, or in opposition to states. Modern law-making, particularly in specialist areas of international law, would be impossible to conceive of without the involvement of NGOs.

NGOs have been the catalyst for the development of international law in a variety of ways. They shape the incentives of states in initiating, supporting, adopting, or becoming parties to international law instruments. They are also important agents for enforcement; they provide information on compliance; and lobby for action in situations of non-compliance. In summary, NGOs have used international law to shape international and domestic politics and the behaviour of political actors and are likely to do so for the foreseeable future.

Questions

1. Why are NGOs interested in international law-making?

2. How have NGOs increased their participation in international law-making?

3. Which NGOs are able to participate and what are some of the constraints on NGO participation?

4. How do NGOs influence and contribute to international law-making?

5. What channels of influence do NGOs use to influence states?

6. Why do NGOs invest effort in 'soft law'? What is its significance in international law and organizations? What is its relevance for students of international relations?

7. What is the difference between binding and non-binding norms? How much of a difference does this make in practice?

8. In what ways can we evaluate the involvement of NGOs in international law-making?

9. What are some of the concerns around NGO participation in terms of diversity and representativeness of NGOs?

10. How effective do you think NGOs have been in influencing the development of international law?

Further reading

Boyle, A. and Chinkin, C. (2007) *The Making of International Law* (Oxford: Oxford University Press). *This book provides a clear and comprehensive account of international law-making and the role of NGOs as participants in these processes.*

Charnovitz, S. (2006) 'Nongovernmental Organizations and International Law' *American Journal of International Law* 100: 348. *This article maps out some of the main issues about NGOs and international law.*

International Council for Human Rights Policy, International Commission of Jurists, and Inter-national Service for Human Rights (2006) *Human Rights Standards: Learning from Experience* (Geneva: International Council for Human Rights Policy). *This report describes international human rights standard-setting processes.*

Lindblom, A. (2005) *Non-Governmental Organisations in International Law* (Cambridge: Cambridge University Press). *This book examines the legal status of NGOs in international law and the different avenues for NGOs to cooperate with, participate in the proceedings of, and submit cases to intergov-*

ernmental organizations, international, and regional judicial bodies.

Martens, K. (2006) *NGOs and the United Nations: Institutionalization, Professionalization and Adaptation* (New York: Palgrave). *This book describes the interaction between NGOs and the United Nations in policy initiating, developing, and implementing processes, using leading international NGOs as case studies.*

Risse, T., Ropp, S., and Sikkink, K. (1998) *The Power of Human Rights: International Norms and Domestic Change* (Cambridge: Cambridge University Press). *Through case studies, this book examines how NGOs use international norms and institutions for influencing state behaviour.*

Spiro, P. (2009 forthcoming) 'NGOs and Human Rights: Channels of Power' in *Research Handbook on Human Rights* (Cheltenham: Edward Elgar). *This chapter examines the different pathways used by human rights NGOs in order to assess the role of NGOs in global decision-making.*

Websites

http://www.amnesty.org.uk/ *Amnesty International is a worldwide movement of people who campaign for internationally recognized human rights for all.*

http://www.hrw.org/ *Human Rights Watch is a leading independent NGO in the area of human rights dedicated to defending and protecting human rights.*

http://www.un.org/dpi/ngosection/index.asp *The Department of Public Information of the United Nations acts as liaison between NGOs and the UN and provides information on how this interaction works.*

http://www.icbl.org/ *The International Campaign to ban landmines is a network of more than 1,400 NGOs in ninety countries and informs about its activities as well as the Mine Ban Treaty and related topics.*

http://www.antislavery.org/ *Antislavery International is one of the world's oldest international human rights organizations which has, since 1893, sought to influence international policy and law-making against slavery and related abuses.*

Visit the Online Resource Centre that accompanies this book to access more learning resources www.oxfordtextbooks.co.uk/orc/cali/

Chapter endnotes

1. UN Commission on Human Rights resolution 2000/61, para. 3.

2. ECOSOC Resolution 1996/31, paras 22–24.

3. The current members are Angola, Burundi, China, Colombia, Cuba, Dominica, Egypt, Guinea, India, Israel, Pakistan, Peru, Qatar, Romania, Russian Federation, Sudan, Turkey, United Kingdom, and United States of America.

4. See the 'Our History' section on the website of the Coalition for the International Criminal Court, available at http://www.iccnow.org/?mod=cicchistory (last visited 4 May 2009).

5. The NGOs based the draft on an original draft prepared and submitted by the Costa Rican government in 1980 but updated the text based on the experience of the European Committee for the Prevention of Torture as well as input from a series of regional consultations. For more information see, Inter-American Institute for Human Rights (IIHR) and Association for the Prevention of Torture (APT) (2005), Optional Protocol to the UN Convention against Torture and Other Cruel, Inhuman or Degrading Treatment or Punishment: A Manual For Prevention, (IIHR and APT), 42, available at http://www.apt.ch/component/option,com_docman/task,cat_view/gid,45/Itemid,99999999/lang,en/ (last visited 19 April 2009).

6. See as an example, International Women's Rights Action Watch Asia Pacific (2008), Our Rights Are Not Optional! Advocating for the implementation of the Convention on the Elimination of All Forms of Discrimination against Women (CEDAW) through its Optional Protocol: A Resource Guide, (Kuala Lumpur: International Women's Rights Action Watch Asia Pacific). The resource guide provides information and arguments that NGOs can use in their advocacy with governments but also provides tips on using this process strategically in the context of developing a multi-pronged approach towards realizing women's human rights.

7. Office of the High Commissioner for Human Rights website, section on human rights bodies—complaint procedures, available at http://www2.ohchr.org/english/bodies/petitions/index.htm#interstate (last visited 5 May 2009).

Chapter 8

International courts and tribunals

Juan M. Amaya-Castro

CHAPTER CONTENTS

- Introduction: international courts in contemporary life
- What are international courts?
- What are the functions of international courts?
- When are international courts successful?
- The future of international court and tribunals
- Conclusion

CHAPTER OVERVIEW

This chapter introduces a type of institution that is increasingly important in the field of international law: international courts. The last few decades have seen an enormous rise in the number and importance of such courts, not just for states but for all (international) actors. Increasingly, what international courts do catches the headlines; and increasingly, states and others have to include international courts in their policy-making and strategic calculations. First, the chapter will describe what international courts are, what they do, and how they do it. The chapter will then look at the wider functional and systemic context: How do international courts contribute to and affect international relations? Finally, the chapter will explore ways of assessing the value of international courts.

Introduction: international courts in contemporary life

At the turn of the twentieth century there were no international courts or tribunals. One hundred years later, some thirty international courts produce thousands of judgments every year. States devote more and more money and resources to defending their positions in legal fora. More and more, ordinary citizens are starting to feel the growing importance of courts in international life.

The emergence and growth of international courts has brought about significant changes in some of the most essential features of international law. First, international courts, by way of interpreting treaties, customary international law, and general principles of law have significantly contributed to identification of international laws and their precise meaning. States who submit themselves to the authority of international courts find it increasingly difficult to challenge the findings of such courts. Second, the existence of international courts has been an important conduit through which international law, once the law to which only states had recourse, has become accessible to non-state actors. Actors other than states—such as international organizations (IOs), non-governmental organizations (NGOs), corporations, and individuals—now have access to international courts in various ways, sometimes even as equal parties to states in international proceedings. Non-state actors are now able to legally compel states to comply with certain international obligations (see Chapter 7). International courts have also contributed to the growing importance of international organizations (IOs), of which they sometimes form a part. This expansion in the influence of IOs has to a large degree changed the way we think about state sovereignty.

These and other dimensions of the role of international courts and tribunals will be examined in this chapter. To begin with, though, it is important to understand what international courts actually are, and what they do. This will help to assess their role in the overall context in which they operate, and contribute to a better understanding of the overall system of international law and international relations.

What are international courts?

International courts are many different things. In the most basic sense, they are groups of men and women who have been given the legal authority and responsibility to decide legal disputes. In this sense they are like national courts. International courts play multiple roles: they are dispute settlement bodies, they are important elements in a system of legal enforcement, and they participate in the identification, development, and creation of international law. In all of these functions international courts must rely on international legal sources—primarily treaties, customary international law, and general principles of law—in order to reach a judgment: in other words, they interpret and apply international rules. Most importantly, their decisions are legally binding upon those who come before them.

Types of international courts

There are various types of international courts, as well as various ways of organizing international courts into types.

Global courts

Generally speaking, when people refer to global courts they mean courts that deal mainly with interstate conflicts and have a global reach. The quintessential example here is the International Court of Justice (ICJ), which is an organ of the United Nations (UN) but is also open to non-member states of the UN.

Regional courts

There are also a number of regional courts that operate only in particular geographical areas, such as the oldest court of all, the Central American Court of Justice (CACJ). There are several of these courts in the Americas (4), Europe (4), and especially in Africa, which has seen a virtual explosion of regional courts, and now counts eleven of them. There are no regional courts in Asia, although there has been discussion about creating an international court in the context of the Association of South East Asian Nations (ASEAN). Regional courts are often organs of regional integration organizations, such as the European Union, the Andean Community, and the East African Community.

Thematic courts

In addition to global and regional courts, there are also several thematic groupings of courts, like the three existing human rights courts. Even though they are all regional courts—one in the Americas, one in Europe, and one in Africa—they can be considered as a separate type because they deal mostly with individual complaints against states and focus on a particular issue. Similarly, even though the International Criminal Court (ICC) is a court with global reach and could be said to be a 'global' court, it is considered to belong to the group of international criminal courts (see Chapter 12). This group also includes the *ad hoc* tribunals

(tribunals created for specific conflicts), such as the Yugoslavia Tribunal (ICTY) and the Rwanda Tribunal (ICTR), and the hybrid international criminal courts (which are partly international and partly national courts).

Such hybrid courts have increasingly been established in the aftermath of war and humanitarian crises. Hybrid courts are strictly speaking national courts, but they come about through an agreement between the state and the United Nations and often incorporate international elements such as procedural rules and foreign judges. They generally operate on the territory of the states in question and will apply national law unless otherwise agreed. In the wake of the Yugoslavia Tribunal it has become evident that the prosecution of those who perpetuate atrocities has a wider role in the overall transition to a post-war society. This role can be more effectively performed when the tribunal is situated in the country itself, rather than far away, and thus the hybrid approach is taken to increase the involvement of the people and institutions in the country where the atrocities occurred. Finally, hybrid courts are significantly cheaper than international courts.

Aside from these courts, there are a number of entities that offer 'arbitration' as a service. These are distinct entities in a number of ways and are often not seen as international courts, but as 'quasi-judicial bodies' even though they share many of the same functions and features.

Box 8.1 International courts and tribunals

Global courts

International Court of Justice (ICJ): The Hague, The Netherlands (1945)
International Tribunal for the Law of the Sea (ITLOS): Hamburg, Germany (1988)
World Trade Organization Dispute Settlement Body (WTO DSB): Geneva, Switzerland (1994)

Regional courts

Europe:
Court of Justice of the European Communities (ECJ): Luxemburg, Luxemburg (1952)
Benelux Court of Justice: Brussels, Belgium (1965)
European Free Trade Area (EFTA) Court: Luxemburg, Luxemburg (1992)
European Court of Human Rights (ECtHR): Strasbourg, France (1950)
Americas:
Inter-American Court of Human Rights (IACtHR): San José, Costa Rica (1969)
The Court of Justice of the Andean Community (TJAC): Quito, Ecuador (1979)
Caribbean Court of Justice (CCJ): Port of Spain, Trinidad & Tobago (2001)
Central American Court of Justice (CACJ): Managua, Nicaragua (1907)

Africa:

African Union Court of Human and People's Rights (ACHPR): Arusha, Tanzania (1998)

African Court of Justice (ACJ): Arusha, Tanzania (2003)

Arab Maghreb Union Judicial Authority (AMUIJ): Nouakchott, Mauritania (1999)

Court of Justice of the Common Market of Eastern and Southern African (COMESA): Khartoum, Sudan (1994)

Court of Justice of the East African Community (EACJ): Arusha, Tanzania (1999)

Court of Justice of the Economic Community of Central African States (ECCAS): not yet determined (1984)

Court of Justice of the Economic and Monetary Community of Central Africa (CEMAC): N'Djamena, Chad (1999)

Court of Justice of the Economic Community of West African States (ECOWAS CCJ): Lagos, Nigeria (1975)

Court of Justice of the Organization for the Harmonization of African Business Law (OHADA): Abidjan, Ivory Coast (1995)

Tribunal of the Southern African Development Community (SADC): Windhoek, Namibia (1992)

Court of Justice of the West African Economic and Monetary Union (WAEMU): Ouagadougou, Burkina Faso (1994)

International Criminal Courts

International Criminal Tribunal for the Former Yugoslavia (ICTY): The Hague (1993)

International Criminal Tribunal for Rwanda (ICTR): Arusha, Tanzania (1994)

International Criminal Court (ICC): The Hague (1998)

Hybrid courts

Extraordinary Chambers in the Courts of Cambodia (ECCC) (2001)

Programme of International Judges in Kosovo (2004)

Special Court for Sierra Leone (SCSL) (1996)

Special Panels for Serious Crimes in East Timor (2000)

Special Court for Lebanon (2007)

Finally, there are a number of other entities that are neither courts nor arbitral bodies, but that perform similar functions. Various human rights treaties have created 'committees'—such as the Human Rights Committee, or the Committee on the Elimination of Discrimination Against Women (CEDAW Committee)—that receive and pronounce themselves on complaints in ways similar to courts, but with the important difference that their decisions are not legally binding. The fact that a report by one of these committees is not legally binding does not mean that it is without effect. In fact, many states will tend to accept and implement decisions, as if they were legally binding. In this

Box 8.2 Arbitration

Arbitration was the nineteenth-century precursor to modern international courts. In fact, the first big international court, established in 1899, was the Permanent Court of Arbitration (PCA), which still exists and is quite active. In addition to the PCA, a special arbitral tribunal was created for dealing with the ramifications of the conflict between Iran and the US in the 1970s and 1980s, the Iran–US Claims Tribunal. Bilateral Investment Treaties (BITs) and Free Trade Agreements (FTAs) like the North American Free Trade Agreement (NAFTA), which have grown exponentially in numbers since the 1990s and now amount to more than 2,700, contain arbitration provisions that allow foreign investors to bring cases against states, frequently through the International Centre for Settlement of Investment Disputes (ICSID). Mercosur, the regional organization for the Latin American cone (Argentina, Brazil, Paraguay, and Uruguay) started originally with a mechanism based on arbitration but is increasingly moving towards the establishment of an international court. And the World Trade Organization's Dispute Settlement Body (DSB) has a two-tier system, with a 'panel' stage which is more like arbitration (parties choose the panellists), and an 'appellate' stage which, with its limited number of appellate body members who serve in rotation, is considered to be more like a court.

Arbitration differs from adjudication in several ways. Whereas courts are permanent, arbitral panels (as they are often called) are *ad hoc*, or created for a particular case. While courts have a permanent composition and a fixed procedure, arbitration procedures and the composition of panels are determined by the parties for each case. This gives arbitration a lot of flexibility in relation to a court. In addition, courts are usually concerned with developing international law in a more or less consistent and coherent way, whereas arbitration panels are more focused on settling specific disputes. Because of this, courts have a bigger systemic impact than arbitration. Because of the flexibility and relative informality of arbitration, there has been a growing reliance on arbitration proceedings in the context of international economic disputes, and many people expect this type of mechanism to become increasingly more significant and important. Arbitration panels are created in the same way in which international courts are created: by treaty and either specifically (*ad hoc*) for a particular situation, or in advance, as a mechanism by which future disputes can be addressed.

sense, one can argue that the reports are politically or even morally binding. Similarly, the World Bank Inspection Panel can review complaints and issue non-binding opinions about the environmental impact of loans provided by the World Bank. Because their reports are also not legally binding, these bodies are often omitted from lists of international courts, even though they can be important and influential in the development of international law. Additionally, some international entities have been set up to deal with the awarding of financial claims on a massive scale. The United Nations Claims Commission, for instance, awarded hundreds of thousands of claims brought by people and companies who had suffered as a result of the Iraqi occupation of Kuwait. Though the claims commission follows court-like procedures, it is dealing with a very narrow range of issues in an almost bureaucratic way, and is therefore not regarded as a court.

How international courts are formed

International courts are created by states. This can happen directly, when states negotiate and sign a treaty to establish a court, such as in the case of the International Criminal Court (ICC), which was created by a treaty called the Rome Statute of 1998. It can also happen indirectly, when an international organization empowered by states to act on their behalf directs that a court be established, such as in the case of the international criminal tribunals for Yugoslavia and Rwanda, which were created by the United Nations Security Council.

International courts can also be created as part of an international organization. So, for instance, the International Court of Justice (ICJ) is an organ of the United Nations (UN), the Andean Court of Justice is an organ of the Community of Andean Nations, and the European Court of Justice is an organ of the European Union. These international organizations are themselves created by treaties, one part of which creates an international tribunal to deal with the settlement of legal disputes within that organization.

The treaties or decisions by which international courts are created are important documents for the functioning of these courts because they specify how much each particular court can do, which cases it can hear, who can bring a claim against whom, and which legal sources the court can apply in each case, topics we will turn to in the following sections. Since there are many differences between the various international courts, lawyers will always first consult these treaties before bringing a case to them.

Who can bring a case to an international court?

There are several different types of international court proceedings. First, there are proceedings between states—provided for by practically all international courts.

Second, there are proceedings between individuals and states. Here individuals (or companies, or NGOs) can bring a case against a state if they feel that they have been wronged by its actions or laws. Such proceedings are most commonly dealt with by human rights courts, but also occur in the area of international investment treaties or regional integration organizations, such as the Court of Justice of the East African Community.

Third, individuals and other non-state actors can bring cases against international organizations. So far, this type of proceeding is available exclusively in regional integration organizations, such as the Court of Justice of the European Union, and in labour disputes, such as when employees of international organizations settle administrative disputes with their employers in the Administrative Tribunal of the UN.

Fourth, international criminal tribunals can bring cases against individuals. This is a very recent development that only began in the 1990s with the creation of special international criminal tribunals that dealt with crimes committed in Rwanda and the former Yugoslavia, and which culminated in the creation of the International Criminal Court (ICC). In these proceedings, the international criminal tribunals have their own prosecutors who bring cases against individuals suspected of having committed genocide, war crimes, or crimes against humanity.

Finally, a national court can request a preliminary ruling or clarification of the law from an international court (see below Box 8.7 on the ECJ). This type of proceeding is typical of organizations that pursue regional integration. Under this proceeding, a national judge can ask the international court to pronounce itself on the correct interpretation or the legality of a rule or act of the regional organization. After receiving a preliminary ruling from the international court, the national court uses this information to make its own judgments.

The access of non-state actors to international courts has impacted on how we conceive of international relations. This development means that states may have to answer to individuals or non-governmental organizations for their conduct (see Chapter 13). It also means that individuals can be answerable for their actions carried out as state officials (see Chapter 12). These new international legal relationships add new layers of complexity to international relations simply as interstate relations.

Box 8.3 Jurisdiction and admissibility

In order to initiate any proceedings before an international court, the case must meet certain jurisdictional and admissibility requirements. A case before an international court generally proceeds through a preliminary phase and a merits phase. In the preliminary phase, the court establishes whether it has jurisdiction and whether the case is admissible. Then, if the case is taken up by the court, it will proceed by looking at the facts and making a ruling on the merits of the case.

Jurisdiction

For a court to have jurisdiction over a dispute means that the court has the competence, authority, or power to look into the case. Jurisdiction is granted by the states that created the court, and the rules for jurisdiction are set out in the treaty or decision that established it. Sometimes an international court will have 'obligatory' or 'compulsory' jurisdiction. This means that the states granted it the authority to hear a certain type of case once and for all. Often, though, courts only have jurisdiction on a per-case basis, which means that states must consent to jurisdiction in each case separately. In many cases, jurisdiction can be also be revoked by the state after it has been accepted.

The best example of this is the International Court of Justice. States can recognize its jurisdiction in various ways. They can do it unilaterally, officially declaring that they accept the jurisdiction of the ICJ. They can do it collectively, including a provision into a treaty stating that any future conflict about the implementation or interpretation of that treaty should be brought to the ICJ. States can also agree to voluntarily submit a particular legal dispute to the ICJ. In any of these situations, however, states can choose to limit the topics or issues that the ICJ can deal with. Other courts, like the Inter-American Court of Human Rights, require that states explicitly recognize its jurisdiction without imposing these limits. States and individuals often overlook the important question of jurisdiction, and bring cases that cannot be addressed by the court (or 'exceed its jurisdiction'). Such cases are dismissed by international courts at the preliminary stage.

Admissibility

Another part of the preliminary phase is the question of admissibility. For a case or complaint to be admissible it needs to fulfil a number of criteria which are either specified in the treaty establishing the court or flow from general rules of customary international law. For example, many international tribunals require the 'exhaustion of domestic remedies'. This means that all available national procedures need to be tried out before a case is brought to an international tribunal. The idea behind this rule is to allow states a chance to resolve the matter themselves, before they are exposed to international scrutiny. This rule is very important in the context of human rights tribunals. Cases are frequently dismissed as inadmissible. For example, in the European Court of Human Rights as many as 80% of cases are declared inadmissible and end at this stage.

Merits

Once a court has established that it has jurisdiction and that the case is admissible, it can move on to look at the substance of the case. During this 'merits phase', the court listens to arguments presented by the parties to the case. Occasionally, it will hear arguments from other parties as well. Depending on the type of proceeding, it may listen to experts or hear witnesses, and in some cases it can carry out an investigation to inform itself directly of the facts. Most proceedings have a written part, in which there is an exchange of arguments in writing, and an oral part, in which the court listens and poses questions to the parties and their lawyers. Once they have heard all sides, the judges retreat and deliberate, and finally they produce a judgment.

All in all, international court proceedings can last anywhere from six months to six years, although in many cases this depends on how fast the parties want to see a judgment. Sometimes they are not really in a hurry. Other times the case never reaches a conclusion because the parties decide to settle out of court. For example, a case brought to the ICJ by Libya against the United States and the United Kingdom in 1992 produced a decision on the preliminary phase in 1998 and was finally removed from the Court's list 'at the request of all the parties' in 2003.

Provisional measures

Sometimes one of the parties will ask a court to pronounce itself before the case has been concluded, or, as the expression goes, 'to order provisional measures'. Usually this involves a request to suspend a particular action while the case is pending. Provisional measures are frequently requested in the field of human rights, when an international court can for instance ask a state to suspend an extradition, while

---

Box 8.4 Reforming the European Court of Human Rights

In an attempt to deal with an ever growing case load, the Council of Europe is trying to reform the way the European Court of Human Rights handles cases. At the end of 2007, over 100,000 cases were pending before the Court, and its forty-five judges were not able to keep up. Some estimate that its case load will double in the next three to four years, as more and more people find their way to the Court. Though a lot has been done to streamline the procedure and strengthen the supporting legal staff, it has not been enough to stem the flow. In 2004 the Council of Europe adopted Protocol 14, which amends some key features of the way that the Court handles applications. The main purpose of the reforms is to make it easier for a case to be declared inadmissible. In particular, the Court will now be able to declare cases inadmissible if the applicant has not suffered a 'significant disadvantage'. Human rights NGOs have voiced their concerns about these changes because they will make it more difficult for individuals to access the Court.

it looks into the case. A famous example of a provisional measure is the request submitted by Serbia and Montenegro in 1999, asking the ICJ to order members of NATO to halt their bombing campaign. The ICJ declined to issue the ruling because it determined that it did not have jurisdiction. Even in these provisional procedures, questions of jurisdiction and admissibility matter.

Judgments

Judgments are binding on the parties, and an appeal or review is possible only in very few instances. Depending on the type of proceeding, a judgment can mean different things. If the dispute was between two states, the court will establish which state was in breach of its international legal obligation; which is a different way of saying that the state violated international law. If the case is brought by a non-state actor against a state, the court will establish whether the state breached its obligations under international law. If the case was brought against an individual accused of committing war crimes, the court will establish the criminal responsibility of the individual. We will go into the effect of these decisions below.

Advisory Opinion

There is one type of procedure that is different from all the others. Sometimes a court can be asked to give a so-called 'Advisory Opinion'. A request to do so can come from an organ of an international organization, such as in the case of the UN General Assembly, which can ask the ICJ to render an Advisory Opinion, or it can come from individual states, as is the case with the Inter-American Court of Human Rights. Advisory Opinions are, as their name indicates, not legally binding and express an international court's authoritative views on a particular issue. Both legal scholars and states will generally take these Opinions seriously because of their persuasive authority. Individual states, however, may refrain from strictly implementing the Court's findings if they disagree with them.

Box 8.5 What rules do international courts apply?

Generally speaking, international courts apply rules of international law. However, this does not mean that they can apply *all* rules of international law. Their legal scope is determined in a number of ways. The treaty that establishes the court in question usually stipulates which law can be applied. Some courts, like the ICJ, can apply a wide scope of international law. Others have a very narrow frame: the WTO Dispute Settlement Body, for instance, can only apply WTO law, and the European Court of Human Rights can only apply the European Convention on Human Rights.

For the ICJ, the question of which law to apply is linked to the question of jurisdiction. A recent example of this is related to the war that broke out between Russia and Georgia in the fall of 2008. Though this conflict had many legal dimensions, there was only one relevant basis on which Georgia could initiate proceedings against Russia. It just so happened that Russia (and Georgia) were both parties to the Convention on the Elimination of All Forms of Racial Discrimination (CERD), which allows states to bring cases related to racial discrimination to the ICJ. Of all the various multilateral and bilateral treaties to which both countries were a party, this happened to be the only one that Georgia could invoke in order to involve the ICJ's jurisdiction in this case. So, though the case could have involved various topics, the ICJ could only apply CERD, and no other international rules, when deciding the case.

What is the effect of international judicial decisions?

Legal effect

Judgments of international tribunals are legally binding. This means that states have a legal obligation to abide by them, to implement them, and to enforce them. Sometimes a court indicates to the state how it should do this. It may instruct the state to abolish a particular policy, order it to pay compensation, or order that the states negotiate a settlement. In the context of human rights courts, one can see diverse approaches. In some cases, the European Court of Human Rights has considered that the fact that a violation has been found was in itself sufficient compensation. In other cases, that court has ordered significant financial reparations. The Inter-American Court of Human Rights has done the same, but has gone further and has ordered in some cases that the state perform a number of symbolic acts of apology and repentance as a form of reparation for gross human rights violations.

Even where a court indicates specifically how a state should abide by its obligations, it remains up to the state and its national authorities to enforce the judgment. In other words, judgments of international courts do not automatically enter into effect, but need to be put into effect by the state in question. Unlike in domestic affairs, where a national judge can order the release of a prisoner, the release of information, or the release of assets, and this order has value with jailers, public authorities, banks, etc., this is not the same with international judgments. International judgments are legally binding declarations that a state has breached (or not) international law. But they cannot be directly enforced at the national level. One notable exception here is the Inter-American Court of Human Rights. Its judgments can be enforced by national judges, without intervention by the national government or legislature. This can sometimes lead to confusion and to problems of enforcement, and it can also lead to problems not going away. An example of this is the large number of Italian cases that keep coming to the European Court of Human Rights. These relate to the problem that the judicial system in Italy is very slow. Cases can be pending for up to twenty years. In the past, the European Court has found this to be a breach of the European Convention of Human Rights, which in Article 6 stipulates that judicial proceedings have to take place within a 'reasonable period' in order for these proceedings to be fair. For decades though, the Italian state has been unable to do anything about it. It takes a lot of time and a lot of resources to change a state of affairs that is so complex and deeply rooted in the legal culture of a country. This meant that Italians keep going to the European Court of Human Rights and that this court keeps finding breaches of international law, with little else changing.

Enforcement

The absence of an 'international enforcement agency' often figures in criticisms of international law, and seems to buttress realist approaches to international relations. However, as a matter of fact, most international judgments are complied with. Mutual or collective agreement to comply with court judgments is an important compliance factor. Different tribunals also have different enforcement mechanisms, depending on what their constitutive treaty stipulates. So the Statute of the ICJ allows states to call on the UN Security Council for support if the other party in the case does not comply with a judgment. This is not necessarily an effective mechanism, especially when it concerns trying to pressure a permanent member of the Security Council itself. A well known example concerns a case brought by Nicaragua against the US, related to covert military operations that the US had carried out against Nicaragua. The US disagreed that the court had jurisdiction and refused to participate in the merits of the case. The final judgment was in favour of Nicaragua, but the US refused to accept this on the basis that the ICJ should never have had jurisdiction in the first place. Naturally, any action by the Security Council was effectively vetoed by the US. As a gesture of goodwill to the US, and in an attempt to obtain the release of large amounts of financial assistance, Nicaragua agreed to drop the matter. Though Nicaragua was bullied by the US into doing this, one can argue that Nicaragua was better off with the ICJ judgment because it gave Nicaragua some bargaining power that it would otherwise not have had. Even so, the Nicaragua case remains an exception, and most judgments are duly complied with.

In other instances where international courts are part of the institutional structure of an international organization back-up mechanisms operate to supervise compliance with international tribunals. For instance, the European Court of Human Rights falls under the Council of Europe. Its main executive body is the Committee of Ministers. This entity has the task of reviewing compliance with the Court's judgments. It can put significant political pressure on states to comply, but has as its only real instrument the possibility of expulsion from the organization. This is a very blunt weapon, and it can be counterproductive, since it would cut off access to the Court for the inhabitants of the country involved.

The issues of compliance and enforcement indicate that what is at stake is the degree to which states are truly integrated into some sort of strong political relationship and the role of international courts in processes of political interrelation. In the case of the European Court of Justice, for example, the value at stake is European integration. For an EU member it would require too much political capital to openly defy the ECJ, just like it cannot defy the other organs of the EU itself. This degree of political interrelation or integration does not exist in other regional contexts and this is a factor affecting compliance. However, many continue to see international courts as important catalysts in processes of political integration.

What are the functions of international courts?

Dispute settlement

International courts are part of the larger 'system' of public international law. Within this system, they perform a number of functions. One of these is the function of settling disputes—at least to the extent that they can be translated into legal disputes. For instance, the border dispute between Ethiopia and Eritrea was 'settled' by an arbitral tribunal set up under the auspices of the Permanent Court of Arbitration in 2002. This tribunal decided exactly where the contested boundary ran and which towns, villages, roads, and rivers belonged to which country. The tribunal was set up as part of a ceasefire arrangement between the two countries who had just fought a war over the issue. However, in 2008 tension rose again between the two countries and it became clear that the roots of the conflict were much more complex and that it would take more than a legally binding judgment for it to be resolved. This illustrates the point made above that international courts are part of the larger *political* 'system' of international relations. The role that they can play in processes of dispute settlement is related to the political context in which they operate, but in doing their work, international courts and tribunals can at times contribute to the resolution of disputes.

Enforcing international law

International courts are changing the way in which international law is enforced. States used to rely on a system of self-help to enforce compliance with international law. This meant that they could retaliate or take countermeasures in view of breaches by other states. So, if one state seized assets of the nationals of another country, without justification, the other country might do the same back, as a countermeasure, to force the first country to change its ways. It is clear that as a system of enforcement, this one is very prone to escalation and extremely sensitive to power asymmetries. International courts are a move away from that system and a move towards a system in which courts, by stating clearly and unambiguously who was in the legal wrong, could improve the system of enforcement. This particular function made a quantum leap when international human rights tribunals and regional integration courts were allowed to hear cases brought by individuals. Whereas states have not been so eager to bring cases against another state, preferring instead to use familiar and more controllable diplomatic channels, individuals (and other non-state actors) have been eager to challenge states on the international plane. In this way, individuals can now trigger enforcement mechanisms and enforcement has become much more decentralized. And because individuals need to first challenge the state at the level of national courts, national judges have also become a part of the enforcement system.

Box 8.6 Judicial review of Security Council actions

As the activities of the Security Council have increased, so too have concerns about the legal limits of Security Council action. Can the Security Council violate international law? If so, who can review its actions? For many, this is a role to be played by the International Court of Justice (ICJ), the principal judicial body of the United Nations and arguably the world's most prestigious court. Others vehemently deny that the ICJ has such a function, and argue that its Statute does not provide for such authority. So far, very few cases that have come before the Court have raised questions that could lead it to pronounce itself on this matter, and many consider it unlikely that the ICJ would risk confronting the Security Council in this way. Another international court, the ECtHR, has considered that it cannot pronounce itself on the actions of the UN. However, the ECJ recently annulled the EU's implementation of the Security Council's asset-freezing resolutions on the ground that they violated EU norms of fair procedure and property protection. Though this does not directly review the Security Council's resolutions, it does pronounce itself on their accordance with international standards. It is to be expected that these types of tensions and conflicts will increase in the future.

Identifying and developing international law

International courts have become an intrinsic part of the law-making processes of public international law. Though it is the states who are the most important law-making actors, international courts play a very significant role in this process by interpreting the very content of international laws in concrete situations in which states disagree. In this role, international courts have clarified the general meaning of many important international law doctrines. This will be readily apparent when reading any international law book which will contain numerous references to judgments by international courts. Judgments of courts are not legally binding on other states in most cases, even if these states have also accepted that court's jurisdiction. However, an international court's interpretation of a particular treaty or its recognition of the existence of a rule of customary law will often carry significant authority amongst both states and their lawyers. Besides, international courts will generally be faithful to their own judgments and judgments of other courts, and states will be mindful of this.

In the course of doing their work, international courts often advance ground-breaking and foundational interpretations of the legal rules that they are applying. Take for instance the ruling by the ICTR, in which Jean-Paul Akayesu was found guilty of the crime of genocide. In this ruling, the Rwanda Tribunal found that mass and systematic rape could constitute a part of the crime of genocide. This was not based on a particular rule which stated that rape could be an instrument of geno-cide, but rather on an analysis by the Tribunal in light of the systematic mass rape that occurred in Rwanda and had previously occurred in the former Yugoslavia. The example makes clear how international tribunals can be useful contributors to the development of international rules. Whereas it would take years to reach the necessary agreement to draft a treaty, and even more years for there to be practice sufficient to constitute customary law, international courts, in their dealing with concrete situations, can be much more responsive to changing conceptions and to new developments. As such, they add a degree of flexibility to the process of making and developing international law.

This function of international courts is exemplified by the procedure that allows them to render Advisory Opinions on questions submitted to them. Though Advisory Opinions are not binding, many of them are subsequently used as authoritative state-ments of the law. Moreover, they often grab the headlines. The International Court of Justice's Advisory Opinion that the wall built by Israel in the Occupied Territories was illegal did not result in Israel's removal of the wall, but it has made world news and has given activists and politicians a blunt argument to use against Israeli policies.

Furthermore, international courts and tribunals can sometimes change the very nature of the political processes in a particular context. As such, they perform a role in the systemic context that they help create through their existence. This is most clearly visible in the case of international organizations pursuing regional integration. The European Court of Justice has often been called 'the engine of European integration', because many of its decisions were instrumental in breaking both political and legal, resistance to removing barriers between EU member states. States and other international or transnational actors adapt their strategies according to legal processes offered by international courts. They do so more at some times than at others, more in regional integration contexts than with the ICJ. But, for example, even before the International Criminal Court had started its first case, many states and other actors were already taking its existence into account and were adapting their policies in light of the ICC's arrival on the scene. This does not always happen in the most desirable ways. Sometimes, what seemed to be a political solution to a problem can be complicated by the presence of legal institutions. For instance, ongoing Ugandan peace talks between the government and the rebels stalled because of the ICC Prosecutor's investigation of the rebel leader. At the moment of writing, it seems that the Ugandan rebel leaders are not interested in peaceful settlement as long as the ICC is committed to bringing them to criminal prosecution.

Summing up, international courts perform multiple functions, and have in many ways changed the rules governing international relations. They play a role in processes of dispute settlement, in the enforcement of international law, and in the interpretation, development, and even making of new international rules. They have opened up the playing field to individuals, to non-state actors, and to national judges, profoundly changing the political architecture of many countries and regions. But they are also limited by their own design and require a friendly political context to perform these roles.

Box 8.7 The European Court of Justice and the uniformity of EU law

Though the ECJ has greatly contributed to the development of EU law, it also keeps that development in check. Since national judges have to interpret and apply EU rules, it was considered essential for these interpretations not to diverge from each other, and national judges are supposed to consult the ECJ before applying EU law. Upon receiving a request for interpretation, the ECJ hands out a special type of judgment, called 'preliminary ruling'. The growth of the EU, both in terms of the number of countries (and national judges) and in terms of the scope of its rules and regulations, has made uniformity in interpretation both more desirable and more difficult to achieve. Like its human rights counterpart (the ECtHR) the ECJ is struggling to keep up with an ever growing number of cases.

When are international courts successful?

Success for international courts is difficult to measure. The European Court of Human Rights has been called a 'victim of its own success', referring to the fact that it has been swamped with cases and cannot deal with the waves of new applications reaching it every day. One way in which a court's success can be measured is by the number of cases brought to it. The ICJ had a big drop in cases brought to it during the late 1960s and only started to pick up again in the 1980s. A common explanation for this was that in the 1950s and 1960s it decided some cases in ways that were perceived too 'conservative', for the political mood of the time, and in particular against the massive processes of decolonization which were changing the way international politics and international law was perceived. This bad reputation was so damaging that the Convention on the Law of the Sea, adopted in 1982, created a new tribunal, the International Tribunal of the Law of the Sea, which was supposed to be more representative of the new times and more 'modern' than the ICJ. However, in the same decade, the case load picked up again for the ICJ. More 'progressive' references to human rights in the 1980s were said to have restored confidence in that court.

Whether a particular judgment was 'successful' will often only show over time. Agents of governments often argue during the oral proceedings of cases that taking a particular decision will be 'bad for the court's credibility'. A court's credibility, however, is not necessarily the same as its popularity, which can be fickle and capricious. Ultimately, what may matter more is whether the judgments a court produces are good ones. Are they sufficiently based on the wealth of legal precedents? Are they carefully argued and persuasive? Will they be used as a reference by lawyers and judges in the years to come? Sometimes judgments are quickly forgotten, and sometimes they are memorable and lasting. Sometimes a dissenting opinion by a judge in the minority of the court will be more memorable than the judgment itself.

For some people, including judges, an international court needs to stand above the political interests of states and other actors. It should not care about being popular and even if states and others walk away and forget its judgments, the court needs to stick to its role as a strict interpreter of the rules. For other people, including judges too, an international court needs to be in touch with the world of states and other actors, with the mood of the times, it needs to be responsive, pragmatic, and realistic. Ultimately, they would argue, international law is better off with international courts than without them, so interpretation of international laws by courts should be flexible to increase their political acceptance. For this last group of people, politically acceptable judgments allow international courts to remain relevant for international relations.

Whether or not courts will prove successful in terms of cases brought to it is hard to predict—the Central American Court of Justice is the oldest international court in the world, but for no obvious reasons Central American countries have brought most of their cases to the ICJ.

The ECJ can be seen to be extremely successful. Its judgments are respected, and the EU donates lavish resources to help do its work as well as possible. Over the last fifty years the ECJ's powers have increasingly been expanded. More and more cases are brought to it by more and more actors (states or national judges) and every year, thousands of law students from all over Europe visit its building in Luxemburg as 'the place where the action is'. Its Andean sibling, the Andean Court of Justice, cannot be said to be successful in this way. Many law students in the Andean region hardly know about this court, and they do not think that anything important happens at all there. States in the region have been stingy with resources. Even so, the Andean judgments are very similar to those of the ECJ and have even been inspired by the European judgments (another token of the ECJ's success). This may partly be explained by the political context. In the Andean region there is too much political instability for a serious and sustainable political commitment with integration to emerge. It may be a chicken-and-egg situation. The European Court of Human Rights is often credited to have been pivotal for the endurance of European democracies and rule of law. But, it may be the other way around: the endurance of European democracies and rule of law may have been the primary condition for the success of the Court.

The future of international courts and tribunals

The steep increase in the number of international courts and tribunals has received both support and scepticism. Many people see it as a sign that the international legal edifice is strengthening and welcome international law playing an increasingly prominent role both in international relations as well as in domestic affairs. For the supporters of this development, more international courts mean more international rule of law. It means more states and other actors will be able to bring each other to court. It also means that international law will develop faster, since courts play an important role in that respect. For these supporters, this will mean that important international rules related to areas such as human rights, humanitarian law, environmental law, etc. will be better implemented and enforced. More international courts will also mean that the better courts can prevail even if the weaker courts don't. This phenomenon is also known as 'forum shopping' and it means that people, when given the choice, will choose the court that offers best results. This type of competition will also yield, according to the enthusiasts, 'cross-fertilization', a metaphor used to describe the way in which different courts will influence each other in ways that will strengthen the fabric of international law.

Others, however, worry about the proliferation of international courts. They fear that it will lead to a 'fragmentation' of international law. With so many courts, there are bound to be contradictions in their pronouncements, which will lead to confusion and disarray, and even to injustices. They are less optimistic about the 'forum shopping' phenomenon, since they believe that courts are not supposed to work according to such 'free market' logic. Rather, they fear that international law will be undermined in its authority by divergence and contradiction. If different courts cannot agree on the correct interpretation and application of a rule, then how will states be supposed to agree? Both sides may have a point in their projections, but it remains to be seen how the phenomenon of more and more prominent international courts will impact on the world they govern, and on the various actors, big and small, that use them.

Conclusion

This chapter has looked at the various types of courts that exist in contemporary international life. It has looked at the differences between them but has focused on the significant features that are characteristic to all international courts. In particular, it has described the processes by which international courts can come about. It has looked at the various ways in which international courts can become the site of a legal dispute: who can bring a case to a court and against whom? It has also looked at how international courts operate, the rules that they apply and what the effect is of an international court's judgment. Finally, some attention has been devoted to the question of when a court is successful and what the future holds for international courts in the international system.

Questions

1. Name some of the ways in which an international court can be formed.
2. What is the role of 'jurisdiction' in the functioning of an international court?
3. What are the phases in which an international court deals with a case?
4. Who can bring a case to an international court?
5. Are international judicial decisions binding?
6. How are international judgments enforced?
7. How do international courts participate in the identification, development, and creation of international law?
8. What are the challenges faced by some of the European international courts?
9. What are the most important functions of international courts in international relations?
10. What makes an international court successful?

Further reading

Amerasinghe, C. F. (2009) *Jurisdiction of Specific International Tribunals* (Leiden: Nijhoff Publishers). *An exhaustive analysis of the jurisdictional dimension of the work of international courts.*

de Búrca, G. and Weiler, J. H. H. (2001) *Collected Courses of the Academy of European Academy of Law, 10–1* (Oxford: Oxford University Press). *A comprehensive analysis of the European Court of Justice.*

Janis, M. W. (ed.) (1992) *International Courts for the Twenty-first Century* (Dordrecht: Nijhoff Publishers). *Though a bit out of date on some topics, this book provides an excellent overview by reputable authors of the past and of the various visions of the future.*

O'Connell, M. E. (2006) *International Dispute Resolution: Cases and Materials* (Durham, N.C.: Carolina Academic Press). *This book allows students to see international adjudication from the perspective of the broader field of international dispute settlement.*

Romano, Cesare (1999) 'The Proliferation of International Judicial Bodies: The Pieces of the Puzzle' *New York University Journal of International Law and Politics* 31/4: 709–51. *A special issue devoted to the question of proliferation, provides an overview of the various arguments and their various perspectives.*

Wildhaber, L. (2006) *The European Court of Human Rights, 1998–2006: History, Achievements, Reform* (Kehl: Engel). *A comprehensive analysis of the European Court of Human Rights.*

Websites

www.icj-cij.org *The website of the International Court of Justice, the principal judicial organ of the United Nations gives access to cases, advisory opinions, and information on current activities.*

http://www.itlos.org/ *This is the homepage of the International Tribunal for the Law of the Sea which provides materials relating to the Tribunal's activities.*

http://www.ccj.org/ *This website informs on the activities and cases of the Central-American Court of Justice.*

http://www.pict-pcti.org/ *The Project on International Courts and Tribunals is an initiative by academics from universities in different countries and conducts and publishes research on the more than twenty international courts and tribunals that now exist internationally.*

http://www.aict-ctia.org/ *The project on African International Courts and Tribunals is an essential resource to research Africa's regional and sub-regional courts.*

http://curia.europe.eu *The website of the European Court of Justice offers information on its cases and activities in all official languages of the European Union.*

http://www.tribunalandino.org.ec/ *The Andean Tribunal of Justice offers information about past and present cases.*

Visit the Online Resource Centre that accompanies this book to access more learning resources www.oxfordtextbooks.co.uk/orc/cali/

PART III

TOPICS IN INTERNATIONAL LAW

In this part of the book we set out a selection of major topics of contemporary international law and relations in greater detail—namely statehood, the use of force, the conduct of armed conflicts, international crimes, human rights, the environment, trade, and global justice. The aim of each chapter is to expose what the body of international law in any given area is *really* about and in what ways the discussion of these central themes in international relations, such as human rights, trade, or environment, seen through the lens of international law, affects how we approach the subject matter. The chapters further identify the major institutional developments in these issue areas and set out how international politics and the international system have shaped international law and how international law in turn shapes political analysis and international relations. These discussions by experts in each topic thus expose students to the distinct international law perspective on the issue.

We can make some general observations about approaching the relationship between international law and international relations through a topical lens. First, each topic has its own special characteristics depending on the subject it aims to regulate. In some topics, the law is very closely related to the fundamental interests of states, as in the areas of creation of new states and the use of force. Some topics are in constant need of reassessment and re-evaluation due to changing circumstances, such as the protection of the environment. Other topics are very hard to regulate due to difficulties in identifying a common ground for all states and other relevant stakeholders. These characteristics play an important role in determining how clear international laws and principles are on each topic.

In all the topics discussed in this book the first thing to note is that international law fulfils a number of important functions. In some areas, international law primarily aims to limit the options states have with which to achieve their policy objectives (e.g. the use of force, protection of the environment, or human rights). In other areas, international law sets a framework through which all states can realize common benefits (e.g. trade). International law can also aim to deter individuals from using the powers they have as either state actors or powerful non-state actors unduly (international crimes). It may further aim to provide guidance for political decisions (the recognition of states). Finally, in many areas, international law creates institutions that provide the development and application of international laws. In most topics, international law undertakes more than one of these functions.

Topics and functions of international law

Use of force	Limiting policy options, creating international institutions
Trade	Framework for common benefits, creating international institutions, limiting policy options
International crimes	Deterring individuals, creating international institutions
Self-determination, recognition, secession	Providing guidance for political decisions, limiting policy options
Human rights	Limiting policy options, creating international institutions, providing a framework for cooperation
Environment	Limiting policy options, setting a framework

The regulation of topics by international law is a dynamic process and there is a constant revision of the rules and norms in each topic. It is, therefore, important to follow the creation of new treaties and soft law instruments, and reflect on the position of customary international law for each topic. In some topics, the scope of regulation is expanding. This is seen, for example, in the case of the large number of treaties signed to protect the human rights of vulnerable groups. In other topics, circumstances constantly require new regulation or flexible interpretation as in the case of emerging environmental threats. In other areas, customary international law has an important effect on treaty law, as in the case of the use of force.

The regulation of topics in international law is not even in its robustness and comprehensiveness. This is the outcome of the interaction between the difficulties inherent to the subject matter, the diversity of conflicting state interests and the preferences and presence of historical circumstances acting as an impetus for international regulation. We can observe, in particular, that in some topics; (a) it is not clear what the specific international laws are that bind all states (environment); (b) it is not clear whether there could be any international laws without a change of the international system itself (global justice); (c) international law and international

	Complexity inherent in the subject	Diversity of state interests and preferences	Historical impetus
Use of force	Low	High	World War II
Creation of states	Low	High	–
Environment	High	High	–
Human rights	Medium	High	World War II
Humanitarian law	High	Low	Hague Peace Conventions of 1899 and 1904, World War II
Trade	Medium	Medium	World War II
Global justice	High	High	–

politics are closely intertwined and rules look more like guidelines for good action rather than robust laws (recognition of states); (d) there is a larger list of objectively established principles often together with dispute settlement mechanisms and interpretive monitoring bodies (trade, human rights, international crimes).

It is useful to think of this uneven breadth of regulation in the light of theories of international relations. Realist and institutionalist rational approaches to international law make an important claim that it is more likely that states will commit to international laws that coincide with their own interests. In other words, regulatory options that require minimum changes to a states' foreign and domestic policy interests are more likely to be successful. A detailed analysis of topics, however, will show that when international law not only regulates, but also creates institutions for monitoring of international commitments, this may not be the case. The creation of institutions inserts a degree of unpredictability into the identification of international laws. This could mean that: (a) states may be unwilling to create international institutions or that (b) they may disrespect the decisions of such bodies that do not coincide with their own interests. In the case of the protection of the environment, we observe that states have been unable to create institutions. In the case of trade, however, there are not only international institutions, but also compliance by major powers with unpopular decisions against them delivered by these institutions. In the case of human rights, on the other hand, we see a large number of institutions, a mixed record of membership to such institutions, and a mixed record of compliance with unpopular human rights decisions. Liberal and constructivist international theories are able to explain adherence to unpopular international laws by way of domestic pressure or by states being socialized to accept those decisions. Marxist approaches, on the other hand, contrast the successes of trade regimes with the lack of progress made in creating a more just international order that takes the needs of the poor into account.

In the light of the differences in state behaviour across different topics of international law, we can say that theories of international relations have varying explanatory currency depending on the topic international law regulates. States react and behave differently in different areas of international law due to a combination of factors, such as domestic make-up, socialization, strategic calculation of interests, or geographic location. It is, however, apparent that the clearer an international law is on a specific topic, the more difficult it becomes to ignore that law in justifying state behaviour. International law in different topics, therefore, is both sensitive to political factors and is able to affect how political factors themselves are viewed.

CHAPTER 9

States and international law: the problems of self-determination, secession, and recognition

Christopher J. Borgen

CHAPTER CONTENTS

- Introduction
- International law and statehood
- International law of self-determination
- The problem of secession in international law and international relations
- Conclusion

CHAPTER OVERVIEW

States are the main actors of international relations and the primary subjects of international law. Yet, statehood itself is not easy to define. States themselves disagree as to what is or is not a state. This chapter will examine not only statehood as a legal construct but also the relationship between state sovereignty and the self-determination of peoples. To do this, this chapter will focus on the problem of secession. The chapter will start with a discussion of how we describe the characteristics of 'statehood'. Related to this, it will consider the international law concerning the recognition of states. The chapter then turns to the international law of self-determination and outlines how this political ideal has become a legal concept and how it relates to the territorial integrity of states. Drawing these various strands together, the chapter will then consider how international law approaches the problem of secession. It highlights the majority view that international law does not recognize a right to secession and that it addresses secession as a factual event that may have complex legal consequences. The chapter will close with two case studies: the declaration of independence by Kosovo and the conflict between Georgia and Russia over South Ossetia.

Introduction

Is there any role for international law in the creation or recognition of states? Are there objectively defined criteria for statehood? In the world today there are micro-states recognized by all and other entities with large populations barely recognized by any. Compare Nauru and Taiwan. Nauru, a small island in the South Pacific with just over 14,000 citizens and a land area of 13 square miles, is widely recognized as a state and is a member of the United Nations. By contrast, Taiwan, a prosperous political entity with a population of more than 22 million, is recognized by only about twenty states and is not a member of the UN.

These two examples show that there can be disagreement as to what is a state and, consequently, as to the total number of states in the world. For example, the United States recognizes 194 states, but that number includes Kosovo and does not include either South Ossetia or Abkhazia. Russia, for its part, does not recognize Kosovo, but it does recognize both South Ossetia and Abkhazia. In any case, a useful baseline is the number of UN member states: 192 (at the time of writing). However, it is also important to keep in mind that UN membership is not a prerequisite for statehood and that there have been widely recognized states that were not UN members, such as Switzerland, which only became a UN member in 2002.

This chapter considers the complex interplay of international law and international relations in the birth, modification, and demise of the main actors of the international systems: states. In order to do this, it will introduce and discuss three concepts related to the creation of new states and the dismembering of existing ones in contemporary international relations: self-determination, secession, and the recognition of states.

This chapter will first examine whether there is a tension between the sovereignty of states and the self-determination of peoples. While many readers may come to this chapter with at least a basic understanding of what is—or is not—a state, the definition of self-determination has been the source of some confusion. Even though self-determination is a political ideal with deep roots in Western philosophy, as a legal concept its history is relatively short and its exact outline is ill-defined. Political leaders and jurists have noted a possible tension between a right of self-determination and the protection of territorial integrity itself, another cornerstone of the modern international system. In part, the clash seems to arise from one right (self-determination) favouring 'peoples' over states and the other (territorial integrity) favouring existing states over peoples. Secession is the point in which the contrast between self-determination and territorial integrity is at its sharpest. When should a people be able to dismember a state? As such, the topic of secession also relates to sovereignty and the very stability of the international system.

How international law does—or does not—attempt to regulate secession will be the central question of this chapter. As a means of approaching this complex issue, we will consider the practical problem of the recognition of states. In other words, when there seems to be a successful secession, what is the proper response? May an existing state recognize a new state? Must it? Conversely, is it prohibited from giving such recognition? Can international law even regulate such diplomatic activity?

As we shall see in this chapter, because of the high political stakes involved in dismantling existing states and the danger this poses to international peace and security, the debate still rages over the proper role of international law. Many, if not most international lawyers believe that international law does not include a right of secession. Others argue that, under extreme circumstances, an oppressed people have a right of secession as a remedy under international law. The goal of this chapter is to explain the political ramifications of these two views and to set out the legal justifications for each.

International law and statehood

Statehood and sovereignty

States are the main actor in global politics and are the focus of classic international law. While international law since World War II has increasingly addressed issues related to non-state actors such as individuals, international organizations, and, as we shall see in this chapter, 'peoples', this has been in addition to, not instead of, its role regulating state behaviour. Consequently, before considering the law and politics of how states are born (and, to a certain extent, one way in which they can die), we should consider what a state is, both juridically and practically.

Sovereignty is the core attribute of statehood. Key elements of sovereignty include independence, territorial authority, and territorial integrity.

The modern conception of sovereignty is traced to the Treaty of Westphalia, signed in 1648. Sovereignty included full and exclusive authority over the territory in question. Each state was the supreme authority within its territory and had no right of action within another's territory. Westphalia thus codified the doctrine in the European state system that no entity—emperor, pope, or other decision-maker—is above the level of the state. The state became the main actor in the international system (see Chapter 3). Although this concept has been modified somewhat, particularly in the defence of human rights, the basic idea that there is a 'zone of privacy' within a state's domestic system still exists.

Another important aspect of sovereignty is international 'personhood,' also called international 'personality' (see Chapter 1). International personality means that, among other things, an entity is able to enter into treaties and make legal claims before international and domestic courts. Personality signifies that an entity has certain rights and (potentially) responsibilities. International personality is crucial in order to be able to undertake the modern breadth of diplomatic activities such as becoming a member of the UN and other interstate organizations, accessing certain international tribunals, and making legally-enforceable agreements including contracts and treaties. (It is important to note that while all sovereigns have some form of international personality, not all entities with some form of international personality are sovereign.)

As the state became the pinnacle of the international system in the wake of Westphalia, so the goal of many national movements became achieving statehood. Although there is no single text that explains what is required to be a state, the 1933 Convention on the Rights and Duties of States, better known as the Montevideo Convention, sets forth a series of benchmarks that are generally accepted in the international community. An entity that claims to be a state should possess the following qualifications:

1. a permanent population;

2. a defined territory;

3. government; and

4. capacity to enter relations with other states.

Each of these terms potentially presents its own set of problems. For example, what does it mean for a territory to be 'defined'? What if the borders of an entity are in dispute, such as the boundary between Niger and Benin in Africa? Does that mean that neither Niger nor Benin are states for not having a defined territory? Or what of the disputes over Israel's borders?

While questions such as these can be the fodder of much political debate and rhetoric, international lawyers try to discern principles from state practice. For example, while many states may have border disputes, a border dispute is not the same as questioning whether or not an entity has any territory. A rule stating otherwise would throw the international system into turmoil as the status of many states would be put into question. The legal interpretation of these terms is linked to a pragmatic appreciation of what is or is not workable. At the same time, legal principles affect international relations by acting as a litmus test for which entities are or are not states.

Professor Martti Koskenniemi, an international lawyer and former diplomat, contrasts what he calls the 'legal approach' to sovereignty—in which law exists prior to, and thus regulates, state sovereignty—with the 'pure fact approach'—in which sovereignty is external to law and thus law must bend to sovereign will, not vice versa. Realist and rational approaches in international relations, in this respect, are akin to 'pure fact approach' as they do not make any space for international law in this field because they regard that the question of becoming a state is determined by material conditions and pre-calculated responses of other states in the international system. Under the legal approach, law does play a role in defining the criteria for the emergence and dissolution of states. Many UN instruments and documents use the rhetoric of the legal approach. Koskenniemi, however, argues that sovereignty doctrine is based on neither one nor the other solely, but rather oscillates between the two. For example, the pure fact of occupying a certain territory does not in itself create a state if other states do not accept that this act meets the criteria for statehood (Koskenniemi 2005: 228–31).

This leads us to the question of recognition of statehood and its role in international relations.

What is the recognition of statehood?

If an entity meets the criteria listed in the Montevideo Convention, is it a state? The answer to this question is not clear, neither in theory nor in practice. Entities claiming statehood also seek formal 'recognition' of their statehood by other states. The recognition of a state is the decision by one state to accept that another state has come into existence, such as, for example, the recognition by France of the establishment of Bangladesh as a state. The general view is that recognition is not a formal requirement of statehood. Rather, recognition merely accepts a factual occurrence.

Box 9.1 Recognition of governments

The recognition of a state should not be confused with the recognition of a government, which refers to the formal recognition that there has been a change of government—perhaps under difficult circumstances such as a coup or a revolution—within an existing state. The 1979 Iranian revolution leading to the establishment of the Islamic Republic as the new government of the continuously existing state of Iran is an example of a situation that brings into question whether or not to recognize a government.

This is sometimes called the 'declaratory' view of recognition. By contrast, the 'constitutive' view is that recognition is a requirement for juridical statehood.

Although recognition is not a formal requirement of statehood, it is very important nonetheless. The extent to which a new state is able to participate in the international community is, in practice, largely determined by the extent of its relationships with other states. Such bilateral relationships are based upon mutual recognition. However, although under the declaratory view recognition is supposedly apolitical and merely the acceptance of a factual occurrence, no state is required to recognize an entity claiming statehood. The giving or withholding of recognition is an act with significant political ramifications.

By recognizing an entity as a state, the recognizing state gives its opinion that the entity meets the requirements under international law for statehood. But when an entity is not generally recognized, its position in the international system is put into question. It will have difficulty joining international organizations, such as the WTO, or receiving assistance from international financial institutions, such as the World Bank or the International Monetary Fund. Entities with a contested status may be prevented from joining the UN. Similarly, any country that does not recognize a putative state will not accord that entity sovereign immunity. Thus, although recognition is not a formal requirement of statehood, the lack of recognition—especially by politically powerful states such as the US, Russia, or EU member states—can significantly narrow the future prospects of an entity claiming statehood.

Whether or not one state chooses to recognize another state is, as a matter practice, largely a question of politics. While international law provides guidelines for when a state should or should not recognize another state, there is little risk of formal sanctions if those guidelines are transgressed. States do face two other risks, though. The first is the reputational harm that may be associated with a questionable recognition or non-recognition. For example, a state that recognizes a separatist entity that does not really have the characteristics of statehood may be viewed as supporting unlawful behaviour and it may find its own moral authority damaged in diplomatic negotiations on related or unrelated issues. Second, any arguments that a state makes in regards to recognition or non-recognition may come back to haunt

---

Box 9.2 Secession versus succession

The state system is not static. In 1960, there were about one hundred states. Today there are over 190. States appear and disappear through decolonization, merger into new states, absorption of one state into another, secession, and dissolution, among other possible actions. The rules of state succession govern the transfer of rights and obligations from one state to another when one of these evolutionary processes takes place. Secession is thus a method by which a new state can be formed while the rules of succession pertain to apportionment of rights and duties in any instance of state formation.

it in regards to other entities. For example, some have said that Russia's arguments for recognition of South Ossetia (discussed in Case Study 9.2) could cause it problems in regards to Chechen separatists. Legal arguments are double-edged swords.

However, although an entity may not be a recognized state, and thus may not enjoy (as a practical matter) all the fruits of statehood, it is important to note that being unrecognized does not *excuse* an entity from various norms of international law. For example, entities with effective control of territory will be considered responsible for the protection of human rights within that territory.

With the rise of the Westphalian system, states became the most important entities in global political relations. Non-state actors defined primarily by ethnicity, religion, or geography were comparatively marginalized. At times such groups, in seeking the fruits the Westphalian system had to offer, sought to become states. In the next section, we will consider the evolving concept of self-determination and how it relates to statehood. We will then turn to the most difficult of political dilemmas in this regards: the problem of secession.

International law of self-determination

Self-determination is a concept that sits uneasily within the state-centric Westphalian system. On the one hand, arguments based on self-determination have been used to try to form new states. This use of self-determination exemplifies that statehood is the 'gold standard' of the international system. However, groups seeking statehood also use the principle of self-determination to justify why they should be able to separate part of the territory from an existing state and use that for the territory of a new state. These justifications implicitly (and sometimes explicitly) claim that there are times in which the prerogatives of statehood itself can be trumped by claims of self-determination such that a state will lose sovereignty over part of its territory. This is the problem of secession.

Before turning to this difficult question, though, we need to consider the law and the political rhetoric of self-determination.

Self-determination: from political rhetoric to legal right

While the roots of the concept of self-determination include the American Declaration of Independence (1776) and the French Revolution (1789), the concept became emphasized in modern international politics via various speeches (including the Fourteen Points and the Four Principles speeches) made by US President Woodrow Wilson in the closing days of World War I (1918). However, the use of the term led to more confusion than clarity at Versailles:

> 'When the President [Woodrow Wilson] talks of "self-determination" what unit has he in mind? Does he mean a race, a territorial area, or a community?' It was a calamity, [Secretary of State Robert] Lansing thought, that Wilson ever hit on the phrase. 'It will raise hopes which can never be realized. It will, I fear, cost thousands of lives. In the end it is bound to be discredited, to be called the dream of an idealist who failed to realize the danger until it was too late to check those who attempt to put the principle into force.' (Macmillan 2002)

As exemplified in this quote, Woodrow Wilson's Secretary of State, Robert Lansing, was prescient in his framing of the issues that would spin forth from the principle of self-determination. Who has a right to self-determination? Who does not? As a matter of right, to what lengths can one go in seeking self-determination? Secession? War? These questions plagued the American negotiators after World War I, and would continue to be at issue, to varying degrees, into the twenty-first century.

While Woodrow Wilson's Fourteen Points highlighted the ideal of self-determination, the United Nations Charter re-emphasized the term. In Article 1, para. 2 it states that one of the purposes of the UN is:

> To develop friendly relations among nations based on respect for the principle of equal rights and self-determination of peoples, and to take other appropriate measures to strengthen universal peace . . .

While self-determination was an important political principle pertaining to the founding of the UN, it was not clear that it was a legal right that could be used by individuals or groups to make claims.

However, the concept of self-determination was subsequently included in Article 1 of both the International Covenant of Civil and Political Rights (ICCPR) and the International Covenant of Economic, Social, and Cultural Rights (ICESCR), the cornerstone treaties of international human rights law. Article 1 of these treaties, both of which were concluded in 1966, states:

> All peoples have the right of self-determination. By virtue of that right they freely determine their political status and freely pursue their economic, social and cultural development.

This 'legalized' the concept of self-determination, taking it out of the realm of mere aspiration or rhetoric. However, there was still the question of what the scope of this right would be—who can claim a right to self-determination and what does that right entail?

Applying self-determination to international relations: who or what has a right of self-determination?

Various experts have argued that self-determination was understood in the 1960s as simply another term for decolonization. Thus, the phrase '*all peoples* have the right of self-determination' should be understood to mean that *all colonies* have the right to be independent. While this interpretation was useful for a time, as the era of decolonization ended, the question of how one should define 'peoples' became more contentious.

As the Canadian Supreme Court put it in an opinion concerning the legal ramifications of a possible secession of Quebec, the meaning of 'peoples' is 'somewhat uncertain'.[1] That is an understatement. At various points in international legal history, the term 'people' has been used to signify, among others, citizens of a nation state, the inhabitants in a specific territory being decolonized by a foreign power, or an ethnic group.

Modern interpretation has shied away from a purely ethnographic definition of 'peoples' as it would not take into account, for example, whether the citizens of a multi-ethnic state are a 'people'. Others have argued that ethnicity-based definitions could lead to inter-communal strife. Various commentators have attempted to reframe the analysis by defining the idea of 'the self-determination of peoples' on non-ethnographic terms. For example, Professor James Crawford of Oxford argues that groups with a right to self-determination include:

1. colonies;

2. states;

3. distinct political-geographical areas within existing states, whose inhabitants are arbitrarily excluded from any share in the government such that these territories are essentially non-self-governing; and

4. any other territories or situations where the parties have agreed to apply the concept. (Crawford 2006: 127).

Therefore, all the citizens of a multi-ethnic state would, by category (2), be one people. But, even if we accept this dynamic definition of 'people', we still need to assess *what the right of self-determination would actually entail*. In other words, does self-determination include a right to secede from an existing state?

Applying self-determination to international relations: the territorial integrity of states

The territorial integrity of states is ensured in Article 2(4) of the UN Charter which states:

> All Members shall refrain in their international relations from the threat or use of force against the territorial integrity or political independence of any state, or in any other manner inconsistent with the Purposes of the United Nations.

Similarly, the Helsinki Final Act also provided for inviolability of borders, although it does allow for border changes if through peaceful means and based on an agreement among the parties involved.

Related to this is the legal principle *uti possidetis juris*. Originally used in the decolonization of Latin America in the nineteenth century, *uti possidetis* meant that former colonies that achieved independence would have the same borders as the boundaries it had as a colony. This principle was subsequently applied in the decolonizations of the twentieth century, and, with greater controversy, to the newly independent states after the end of the Cold War. In this last case, the pre-existing boundaries used were not colonial borders, but the administrative boundaries used within the USSR or Yugoslavia.

While the ICJ has noted that *uti possidetis* is a relevant principle in interpreting the application of self-determination, others argue that it is of little consequence. These jurists explain that *uti possidetis* defines the borders of a state at the time of independence. It has no bearing as to whether or not an entity may secede from an existing state. All states, regardless as to whether they were formed by decolonization or by other means, have a right to territorial integrity; the concept of *uti possidetis* does not add anything to this, according to these jurists.

Between the prohibition of the use of force to change borders in the UN Charter and, possibly, the rule of *uti possidetis,* has secession effectively been declared illegal under international law?

The problem of secession in international law and international relations

Secession is the separation of part of the territory of an existing state so that that territory may itself become a new state. The pre-existing state continues on, minus the territory that has seceded.

> **Box 9.3 Secession versus dissolution**
>
> Secession from a state is not the same as the dissolution of a state. Dissolution is when a state ceases to exist. Its territory may be reorganized as one or more new states, but the prior state no longer exists.
>
> During the Yugoslav War, the European Community established the Arbitration Commission of the Peace Conference on Yugoslavia, better known as the 'Badinter Commission', to resolve questions of international law that arose from the conflict. According to the Commission's findings, the Socialist Federal Republic of Yugoslavia was already in the process of dissolution at the time fighting began. As such, Croatia and Bosnia had not attempted to secede, they merely proclaimed their sovereignty during a time of the dissolution of Yugoslavia. The USSR's transformation into the newly independent states is another example of dissolution. By contrast, the conflicts over South Ossetia and Abkhazia (in Georgia), Northern Cyprus, and Transnistria (in Moldova) are considered attempted secessions, as the parent state still exists in each case.

The majority view: no right of secession

In 1970, the UN General Assembly passed General Assembly Resolution 2625, the Declaration on Principles of International Law Concerning Friendly Relations and Co-operation among States in Accordance with the Charter of the United Nations, better known as the Friendly Relations Declaration.[2] This special resolution was passed at the twenty-fifth anniversary of the founding of the United Nations to restate the basic principles of the organization. After defining self-determination in language similar to the ICCPR and the ICESCR, it then goes on to state:

> Nothing in the foregoing paragraphs shall be construed as authorizing or encouraging any action which would dismember or impair, totally or in part, the territorial integrity or political unity of sovereign and independent States conducting themselves in compliance with the principle of equal rights and self-determination of peoples as described above and thus possessed of a government representing the whole people belonging to the territory without distinction as to race, creed or colour.

From the birth of the United Nations, diplomats and jurists emphasized that a right of self-determination was not a 'right of secession'. The drafting committee for the UN Charter noted that 'the principle [of self-determination] conformed to the purposes of the UN Charter only insofar as it implied the right of self-government of peoples and not the right of secession' (Cassese 1995: 40).

By this interpretation, self-determination is a right of 'internal self-determination': meaningful participation in the political, economic, and cultural life within one's state. This is contrasted with 'external self-determination', or the ability to separate and start a new state. Among the various self-determination units described above, only colonies have a right to external self-determination. And, of course, a section of a state may separate from and leave a pre-existing state with the consent of that state.

A Commission of Experts convened by Quebec's National Assembly to assess the legal issues related to a hypothesized secession of the province concluded:

> For colonial peoples, this choice [over one's destiny] includes the possibility of independence; for others, that possibility is precluded, but at the same time it implies the right to one's own identity, the right to choose and the right to participate: 'It also, at least for now, stopped being a principle of exclusion (secession) and became one of inclusion: the right to participate. The right now entitles peoples in all states to free, fair and open participation in the democratic process of governance freely chosen by each State'. Identity and democracy are its two essential components, but not independence except—according to certain authors who express this view with caution—in the case of an extremely serious and continued denial of the right so defined.[3]

The concern of many experts is that if there was a right to secession, it would cause a downward spiral in the state system. Aggrieved groups within existing states would make realistic (or unrealistic) claims of a right to secession assuming some of those claims were successful, aggrieved groups within newly formed states may then make their own realistic (or unrealistic) claims that they have a right to secession, and so on. Rather than the roughly 190 states that exist today, we would have a world of hundreds, if not thousands, of microstates. The coordination problems would be immense.

Nonetheless, one cannot say that international law makes secession illegal. While secession does not operate as a right (according to the majority view), it is not prohibited by international law. Rather, attempted secessions are, first and foremost, considered internal matters that are regulated by domestic law.

International law, by contrast, is largely silent regarding secession. However, under certain circumstances a secessionist dispute may implicate international law:

- when a new entity seeks recognition as a sovereign state (in which case there are rules for recognition or non-recognition);

- the establishment of an armed insurgency (in which case there are the laws of armed conflict);

- if there is a threat to international peace and security (which would thus likely become an issue for the UN Security Council);

- if another state intervenes militarily to aid the separatists (which would likely be a violation of the UN Charter); or

- if the secessionist group becomes a *de facto* regime (discussed below).

There are also ongoing obligations under international law regarding the monitoring and enforcement of human rights norms. But, according to the mainstream view, outside of decolonization there is no right to be able to secede from an existing state.

The reply: the 'extreme cases' argument

While the dominant view is that there is no right to secession, some jurists contend that in certain circumstances a people do have a right to 'remedial' secession, which is sometimes referred to as 'external self-determination'. The argument that self-determination gives a remedy of secession outside the colonial context is highly controversial.

Proponents of remedial secession often refer to the Friendly Relations Resolution of the UN General Assembly, described above. As mentioned earlier, the resolution excludes secession as a means of forming a sovereign state *when the existing state respects equal rights and the self-determination of peoples*. Rather than emphasizing the ban on secession, as the mainstream jurists do, those supporting remedial secession emphasize the caveat that secession is not a remedy only when the existing state respects internal self-determination. This is viewed as implying that when the state does not respect internal self-determination, external self-determination may be an option. This caveat of the Friendly Relations Resolution has been reiterated in the 1993 Declaration of the UN World Conference on Human Rights and the General Assembly Declaration on the Occasion of the Fiftieth Anniversary of the UN in 1995 (Tomuschat 2006a: 34–5).

This interpretation may have found its way into state practice in *re Secession of Quebec*, the advisory opinion issued by the Supreme Court of Canada on the issue of secession. The Canadian court found that '[a] right to external self-determination (which in this case potentially takes the form of the assertion of a right to unilateral secession) arises only in the most extreme cases and, even then, under carefully defined circumstances . . .'[4]

While the form of what a rule of external self-determination would look like is a bit hazy, any attempt to claim a situation where secession trumps territorial integrity must *at least* show that:

1. the secessionists are a 'people' (as defined in a manner recognized by the international community);

2. the state from which they are seceding seriously violated their human rights; and

3. there are no other effective remedies under either domestic law or international law.

Some may also argue that the entity seceding must be a contiguous territory with definable borders.

Those arguing in favour of secession as a remedy admit that state practice is thin but claim support from the case of Bangladesh and possibly from the case of Kosovo.

Secession and state practice

Besides the legal issues, as a matter of practice secession is disfavoured by the international community. Aside from instances of decolonization, the only clear case since World War II of a secession contested by a pre-existing state that was both successful 'on the ground' and was accepted and recognized by a significant portion of the international community is Bangladesh. (Eritrea may also be considered a successful secession, although some would say that (1) it was only part of Ethiopia due to a UN programme, thus placing it in a different category from separatist projects that well up within the domestic sphere of an established state and (2) the Ethiopian government ultimately accepted the separation, albeit after a protracted conflict.) We will consider the cases of Kosovo and South Ossetia at the end of this chapter.

Some unsuccessful attempted secessions, such as Northern Cyprus, have nonetheless resulted in territories being separated from their pre-existing states for decades. Yet, they are considered unsuccessful to the extent that they are not welcomed by the international community as sovereign states. Diplomatic practice shows us that military success 'in the field' does not necessarily lead to political legitimacy and the recognition of statehood. This observation can both support that states have been socialized to be suspicious of secession, as constructivist international relations would suggest, or that this is a self-protecting behaviour in order not to encourage secession against oneself as rationalist international relations scholars would suggest. Regardless of the approach one pursues, we can say that there is a strong overlap between the international law on secession and state behaviour.

In the next section we will consider the legal and political implications in state recognition.

> **Box 9.4** Unsuccessful attempted secessions since 1945 (a partial list)
>
> - Nagorno-Karabakh (Azerbaijan)
> - Republika Srpska (Bosnia Herzegovina)
> - The Karen and Shan states (Burma)
> - Tibet (China)
> - Katanga (Congo)
> - Turkish Federal Republic of Northern Cyprus (Cyprus)
> - Abkhazia (Georgia)
> - East Punjab (India)
> - Kashmir (India)
> - Kurdistan (Iraq/Turkey)
> - Anjouan (Islamic Republic of the Comoros)
> - Gagauzia (Moldova)
> - Transnistria (Moldova)
> - Biafra (Nigeria)
> - Bougainville (Papua New Guinea)
> - Chechnya (Russian Federation)
> - Somaliland (Somalia)
> - Tamil Elam (Sri Lanka)
> - South Sudan (Sudan)
> - Democratic Republic of Yemen (Yemen)
>
> List adapted (with adjustments) from Crawford (2006).

Recognition and secession

In arguments over attempted secessions, the issue of legality often shifts from the question of the legality of the secession itself, to the issue of whether or not to recognize the seceding entity as a new state. A frequent reason for not recognizing an entity as a new state is if it originated from an act contrary to international law. Territorial changes caused by the use of force are generally seen as unlawful and will not be recognized.

An example of this could be the reaction of the international community to Turkey's invasion of Cyprus in 1974 that led to the proclamation of the Turkish Federated State of Cyprus (TFSC). While the Security Council did not call for non-recognition of the TFSC, in Security Council Resolution 367 (1975) it did note its regret over the proclamations of the TFSC and did say that no action should be taken by any member state of the UN that would divide the island. The situation further devolved with the November 1983 proclamation by what had been the TFSC that the now newly named Turkish Republic of Northern Cyprus ('TRNC') was an independent state. Security Council Resolution 541 (1983) called upon states not to recognize any Cypriot state other than the Republic of Cyprus. Only Turkey has recognized the TRNC and the Security Council called the proclamation 'invalid'.

A second reason for not recognizing an entity as a state is its lack of independence in relation to another state. For example, but for Russian assistance, including military assistance, energy subsidies, and diplomatic cover, the so-called Transnistrian Moldovan Republic (or 'TMR'), the group seeking to secede from Moldova, would probably not be able to survive as a separate entity. The TMR is not recognized by any other UN member state.

Beyond the issue as to whether a state finds it prudent to recognize a new entity as a state, there is the question of whether recognition of a secessionist entity can itself be an illegal act. While some jurists argue that granting recognition of a new state that was formed by an illegal act (usually due to an illegal invasion or occupation) would perpetuate and actually reward that illegal activity, state practice has been mixed in this regard, especially if the illegal act seems irreversible.

The question that remains is: what is the legal status of an entity that controls territory but remains largely unrecognized?

De facto regimes

Entities that have taken control of territory but have not been recognized as states are called *de facto* regimes. They possess some, but not all the attributes of statehood. Their unique status does give rise to certain rights and responsibilities.

A *de facto* regime may undertake normal acts required for the support of its population and it may conclude agreements that are held at a status below treaties. However, while the *de facto* regime has certain rights and responsibilities, acts by *de facto* regimes have uncertain legal effectiveness (unlike the acts of actual states). As they are not recognized states, it is harder to enforce the decisions of *de facto* regimes through the courts of established states. Moreover, if the *de facto* regime (that is, the partially seceded entity) becomes reintegrated with the state from which it was seeking separation, any agreement or contract of the *de facto* regime becomes invalid. The only exception is that the reintegrated state may be held liable for the acts of the *de facto* regime that were 'part of the normal administration of the territory concerned' on the assumption that such acts were neutral (Frowein 1992: 966–98).

If, on the other hand, the *de facto* regime becomes a state, then its acts will be binding on the new state.

Conclusion

Since the Treaty of Westphalia, states have been at the centre of the international system and of classic international law. The concepts of sovereignty and territorial integrity capture important aspects of the characteristics of statehood. Based on the Montevideo Convention, a state must have a permanent population, a defined territory, a government, and the ability to enter into international relations.

States note the arrival of new states through a process of recognition. The declaratory view of recognition holds that recognition is not required for statehood. If an entity is not recognized, it has little ability to have diplomatic relations, join international organizations, and undertake many activities that are common for states.

Self-determination has evolved from being political rhetoric to an international legal right. The right of self-determination may be claimed by a 'people', a term which has different meanings in different circumstances. Self-determination allows a people to participate meaningfully in their political system and freely pursue their economic, social, and cultural development. Applying the right of self-determination itself can lead to different results in different contexts. Self-determination for colonized peoples allows for the ability to separate the colony from the colonial state so that the colony may gain independence and become a sovereign state. For a state as a whole, self-determination means the right to be free from external interference in its pursuit of its political, economic, and social goals. For communities that are not colonies and within existing states, self-determination means 'internal self-determination', the pursuit of minority rights within the existing state. Some argue that in non-colonial cases, self-determination may also allow for secession under 'extreme cases' and 'carefully defined circumstances'. This is highly contested.

Thus, self-determination is not a general right of secession. However, secession is not prohibited by international law; it is simply treated as a fact that may or may not have occurred. This chapter has aimed to provide an overview of the most relevant debates relating to these complex issues.

Case Study 9.1 Kosovo

On 17 February 2008, the Parliament of Kosovo declared Kosovo's independence from Serbia. Kosovo had been a majority Albanian province (with a Serb minority) within Serbia and its predecessor states. Kosovo became an autonomous province in 1963 and remained as such until autonomy was rescinded in 1989. Throughout the 1990s,

Kosovar Albanians sought either a restoration of autonomy or independence. In 1998, the Serb Government initiated police and military actions in the province, resulting in widespread atrocities. In March 1999, the North Atlantic Treaty Organization ('NATO') launched a controversial air campaign to force the Serb Government to withdraw the police and military. In the aftermath of NATO's intervention, the UN Security Council passed Resolution 1244, which authorized the UN's administration of Kosovo and set out a general framework for resolving the final political and legal status of Kosovo. While Security Council Resolution 1244 had language relating to resolving the ongoing conflict over Kosovo and that, pending determination of Kosovo's final status, Kosovo should have substantial autonomy within Serbia, the resolution did not use the term 'self-determination'. For the next nine years, the UN participated in the administration of Kosovo, while political negotiations over the final status of the territory were large-ly inconclusive. In December 2007, the mediators announced the process had ended in an impasse. On 17 February 2008 the Assembly of Kosovo declared Kosovo's inde-pendence. While the US, Great Britain, France, Germany, and a host of other countries formally recognized Kosovo as a sovereign state, Serbia, Russia, Romania, Moldova, Cyprus, and other states have argued that Kosovo's secession and/or the recogni-tion of that secession would be a breach of international law. The day after Kosovo's Parliament declared independence, Secretary of State Condoleezza Rice announced that the US recognized Kosovo as an independent state and further explained:

> The unusual combination of factors found in the Kosovo situation—including the context of Yugoslavia's breakup, the history of ethnic cleansing and crimes against civilians in Kosovo, and the extended period of UN administration—are not found elsewhere and therefore make Kosovo a special case. Kosovo cannot be seen as prec-edent for any other situation in the world today. [1]

Even prior to the declaration of independence, Russian Foreign Minister Sergei Lavrov called a potential Kosovar secession a 'subversion of all the foundations of international law, . . .'[2] The majority of states have positions somewhere in between these two poles. As of the time of this writing, sixty-two states have recognized Kosovo's independence.

At the moment, it is too early to tell what the long-term impact of Kosovo's independ-ence and the widespread recognition of Kosovo's independence will be. The legal question has come to the forefront as on 8 October 2008, at the request of Serbia, the UN General Assembly by a vote of 77 for, 6 against, and 74 abstaining, asked the International Court of Justice to provide it with an advisory opinion on the question: 'Is the unilateral declaration of independence by the Provisional Institutions of Self-Government of Kosovo in accordance with international law?'

---

[1]United States Recognizes Kosovo as Independent State, Statement of Secretary of State Condoleezza Rice, Washington DC (18 February 2008) available online at <http://www.america.gov/st/texttrans-english/2008/February/20080218150254bpuh5.512637e-02.html> (visited 7 March 2009).
[2]Paul Reynolds, *Legal Furore over Kosovo Recognition* (BBC News 16 February 2008), available online at <http://news.bbc.co.uk/2/hi/europe/7244538.stm> (visited 13 April 2009).

Case Study 9.2 South Ossetia

In the months leading up to Kosovo's declaration, South Ossetia and Abkhazia, two separatist enclaves within the former Soviet Republic of Georgia, became more vociferous in their own calls for independence. South Ossetians are ethnically distinct from Georgians and have comprised a semi-autonomous community within Georgia for 700 years. In the Soviet era, they were an 'autonomous region', a status that granted certain limited autonomy within Georgia, which was a hierarchically superior 'Union Republic' with greater rights of sovereignty.

In the aftermath of the break-up of the Soviet Union, Georgia was recognized internationally as a sovereign state with the same borders that it had as a Union Republic within the USSR. Tensions between the South Ossetian community and the Government of Georgia, which had flared at times under the Soviet Union, rose to a new high after independence. A civil war erupted and Russia intervened, assisting South Ossetia. Since 1992, South Ossetia has been effectively separated from the rest of Georgia, and Russia has maintained a military presence there. At no point until 2008 did any UN member state recognize South Ossetia as a sovereign state.

Over the course of the spring and summer of 2008, tensions once again increased between the Government of Georgia and South Ossetia. There is much controversy over different versions of the events. Russia contends that in the first week of August, Georgia began unprovoked shelling of cities in South Ossetia. Georgia, for its part, maintains that throughout that summer there had been numerous provocations from the South Ossetians, including the use of deadly roadside bombs and other attacks. Russia claimed that the Georgian shelling targeted, among other things, Russian peacekeepers in the region. The Georgian leadership responded that Russian troops were not targeted but notes that the Russian troops often actively supported South Ossetian forces.

What is clear is that on 8 August 2008, the Russian military crossed out of South Ossetia in force and began a military campaign that ranged through much of Georgia, attacking major ports and cities and coming within kilometres of Tbilisi, the Georgian capital. After a brokered ceasefire, Russian forces returned to their bases in South Ossetia. On 26 August 2008, Russia officially recognized both South Ossetia and Abkhazia (another separatist entity in Georgia) as sovereign states. In September it signed Treaties of Friendship, Cooperation and Mutual Assistance with each. Nicaragua has also recognized the statehood of these territories. As of this writing Nicaragua and Russia are the only two states to recognize South Ossetia or Abkhazia.

Russian President Dmitri Medvedev explained Russia's actions by stating that '"sovereignty is based on the will of the people" and "territorial integrity can be demonstrated by the actual facts on the ground".' He further explained that Russia was not denying the principle of territorial integrity as one of the fundamental principles of international law, it was just recognizing the 'specific situation' that it is unlikely that the South Ossetians can live in a single state with the Georgians.

Foreign Minister Lavrov also stated, regarding Russia's recognition of South Ossetia, that (as paraphrased in press reports) 'Georgia's territorial integrity was destroyed by Georgian President Mikhail Saakashvili himself when he decided to order a bombardment of a peaceful town in South Ossetia last summer'.[1]

If we accept the international borders of Georgia at the time of the dissolution of the USSR, then the relevant self-determination unit would be the state of Georgia and the 'people' are all the people of Georgia (including South Ossetia and the rest of Georgia). Even if we were to define the inhabitants of South Ossetia as a separate people, inasmuch as South Ossetia is recognized as part of Georgia, then the traditional view is that self-determination only allows for minority rights within the existing state, not secession from that state. Thus, for Medvedev's implied argument to be correct, even if South Ossetians are a people for the purpose of the law of self-determination, one would also have to agree that 'external self-determination' or secession can be a remedy in cases besides decolonization. In such a case, the South Ossetians would need to show that they suffer extreme and persistent abuses by the Government in Tbilisi and that there is no other option for resolving this crisis.

---

[1]*Russia Steadfast on Kosovo*, B92 Online (17 February 2009), available online at <http://www.b92.net/eng/news/politics-article.php?yyyy=2009&mm=02&dd=17&nav_id=57224> (visited 25 February 2009).

Questions

1. How does international law define states? Does this legal definition adequately capture political reality?

2. What is the difference between the recognition of statehood and the recognition of a government?

3. Can international law regulate the recognition of states? Can it regulate the recognition of governments? Why or why not?

4. How do self-determination, secession, minority rights, and sovereignty relate to each other?

5. What does it mean to say that self-determination is no longer a political ideal but a legal right? What purposes may be served by 'legalizing' self-determination?

6. What may be some of the political or diplomatic consequences of using the various definitions of 'people' for the purposes of self-determination?

7. How can self-determination be defined today?

8. Are secession or any issues related to secession regulated by international law? If such regulation exists, is it effective?

9. Assess the arguments, both legal and political, for and against the concept of 'remedial' secession.

10. Does Kosovo meet the legal requirements of statehood? Does Taiwan?

11. What are the strongest arguments in favour of the illegality of the recognition of Kosovar independence? What, by contrast, are the best arguments in favour of the claim that recognition of Kosovo's independence is legal?

12. How strong or weak are Medvedev's and Lavrov's arguments justifying Russian recognition of South Ossetia?

13. Can a state make a legal argument for the recognition of Kosovo but the non-recognition of South Ossetia? Vice versa?

Further reading

Cassese, A. (1995) *Self-Determination of Peoples: A Legal Reappraisal* (Cambridge: Cambridge University Press). *An influential text; Cassese subsequently became a judge on the International Court of Justice.*

Crawford, J. (2006) *The Creation of States in International Law*, 2nd edn. (Oxford: Oxford University Press). *A comprehensive examination not only of how states are created, but of sovereignty and statehood itself.*

Grant, T. D. (1999) *The Recognition of States: Law and Practice in Debate and Evolution* (Santa Barbara, CA: Praeger Publishers). *A comprehensive analysis of recognition as a matter of political practice and law.*

Hannum, H. (1996) *Autonomy, Sovereignty, and Self-Determination: The Accommodation of Conflicting Rights* (Philadelphia, Pennsylvania: University of Pennsylvania Press). *A good set of historical case studies.*

Kohen, M. G. (ed.) (2006) *Secession: International Law Perspectives* (Cambridge: Cambridge University Press). *An excellent collection of essays from a variety of viewpoints on issues of secession and self-determination.*

Lalonde, S. (2002) *Determining Boundaries on a Conflicted World: the Role of Uti Possidetis* (Montreal: McGill-Queen's University Press). *Historical overview of the concept of uti possidetis and issues in its current application.*

Lynch, D. (2004) *Engaging Eurasia's Separatist States: Unresolved Conflicts and De Facto States* (Washington, DC: United States Institute of Peace Press). *Discusses the concept of de facto regimes in the context of the separatist conflicts in Georgia, Moldova, and Azerbaijan.*

Summers, J. (2007) *Peoples and International Law: How Nationalism and Self-Determination Shape a Contemporary Law of Nations* (Leiden: Martinus Nijhoff). *A comprehensive history of the evolution of the concept of self-determination.*

Weller, M. and Metzger, B. (eds.) (2008) *Settling Self-Determination Disputes: Complex Power-Sharing in Theory and Practice* (Leiden: Martinus Nijhoff). *Presents a variety of case studies in self-determination conflicts with a particular emphasis on power sharing as a conflict resolution mechanism.*

Wilde, R. (2008) *International Territorial Administration: How Trusteeship and the Civilizing Mission Never Went Away* (Oxford: Oxford University Press). *Looks at the role of trusteeship and international territorial administration in relation to post-conflict societies, self-determination, and issues of sovereignty.*

Websites

http://www.eisil.org/index.php?sid=438841738&cat=188&t=sub_pages *Electronic Information System for International Law (EISIL) page on 'Self-Determination'. Includes links to primary sources, websites, and research resources.*

http://www.eisil.org/index.php?sid=438841738&cat=14&t=sub_pages *Electronic Information System for International Law (EISIL) page on 'States and Groups of States'. Includes links to subheadings, each of which includes primary sources, websites, and research resources.*

http://www.unhchr.ch/html/menu2/i2intslf.htm *The Office of the High Commissioner for Human Rights provides a compilation of documents and news relating to self-determination.*

http://www.unmikonline.org/ *This site provides information on the mandate and activities of the United Nations Interim Administration Mission in Kosovo, which was established after the 1999 NATO campaign.*

http://avalon.law.yale.edu/20th_century/wilson14.asp *The Avalon Project of Yale University webpage for the Woodrow Wilson Fourteen Points speech.*

http://avalon.law.yale.edu/20th_century/intam03.asp *The Avalon Project webpage for the 1933 Convention on the Rights and Duties of States, also known as the Montevideo Convention.*

http://www.un.org/en/members/index.shtml *UN webpage listing all member states.*

Visit the Online Resource Centre that accompanies this book to access more learning resources www.oxfordtextbooks.co.uk/orc/cali/

Chapter endnotes

1. *re Secession of Quebec* [1998] 2 SCR 217 (Canada) at ¶ 123 (1998).

2. Declaration on Principles of International Law Concerning Friendly Relations and Co-operation among States in Accordance with the Charter of the United Nations, GA Res. 2625 (XXV).

3. Thomas M. Franck et al. (2000) 'The Territorial Integrity of Quebec in the Event of the Attainment of Sovereignty', in Anne F. Bayefsky, ed., *Self-Determination in International Law: Quebec and Lessons Learned* 241, at Sec. 3.08 (Kluwer).

4. Secession of Quebec at ¶ 123.

Chapter 10

Use of force in international law

Nigel Rodley and Başak Çalı

CHAPTER CONTENTS

- Introduction
- The general framework on the use of force in international law
- Self-defence
- The use of force, self-defence, and non-state actors
- Unilateral humanitarian intervention?
- The collective security system under the United Nations Charter
- The power of international law on the use of force: rhetoric or controlling?
- Conclusion

CHAPTER OVERVIEW

This chapter is about the normative grounding of the use of force in international law and the operation and limits of international law in international relations in this area. The chapter first provides an overview of the unilateral and multilateral legal bases for using force in international law. It covers the use of force in self-defence, the use of force against non-state actors and unilateral humanitarian intervention. It then discusses the basis for using force under the auspices of the United Nations. The chapter concludes by discussing the success of international law on the use of force in restraining state behaviour since 1945.

Introduction

Use of force is one of the central topics in international law and international relations. In any society we think of law as the means of preventing conflict, especially violent conflict, among its members, and so the use of force in interstate relations goes to the heart of what we expect the key function of international law to be: namely, to enable states to coexist in peace and to avoid violent conflict that claims human life. Historically, too, the use of force has been a central preoccupation of thinkers. The conditions under which states may wage war and, once war starts, how states should conduct that war have been tackled by the classical international law theorists ranging from Vitoria (1557) to Gentili (1598); from Suarez (1610) to Grotius (1625) and from Pufendorf (1688) to Vattel (1758.) All of these classical theorists are also part of the just war tradition, the tradition that sets out moral limits to waging war. There are a lot of overlaps between modern international law and the just war tradition on the use of force. There are also a lot of differences. International law on the use of force can be described as a long-standing effort to develop prescriptive norms on the use of deadly force by states which are capable of guiding state conduct. International law in this area, therefore, aims to be both action-guiding and effective.

In as much as use of force is a historically important topic in international law, it is also a topic burdened with disagreements about what the precise rules are. Furthermore, there are serious doubts about whether international laws on the use of military force can successfully constrain state behaviour at all. The decisions by states to use force are so fundamentally intertwined with their perceptions of protecting primarily their fundamental interests that few states may wholeheartedly commit to unconditional compliance with predetermined rules on their conduct. On the other hand, states do not want a system of complete chaos where it is hard to determine from where the next military attack may come. This has two important consequences. First, there have always been efforts to regulate the use of force through international law because states prefer a system that manages mutual expectations. Second, states also prefer to have room to manoeuvre and have, therefore, developed their own interpretations of the rules and on many occasions have demanded—not necessarily successfully—that the rules be reinterpreted or changed in the light of new circumstances. The right to collective self-defence during the Cold War, humanitarian intervention during the 1990s, and international terrorism post 2001 are examples of such circumstances. Historically, therefore, the use of force in international law developed as an area where states have both demanded rules and have fought to keep their autonomy when deciding to use force themselves. Some people would say this makes for bad international law as international law risks being no more than what each state thinks it is. We shall later return to this discussion.

This chapter first considers the general international law framework for the use of force by providing a brief summary of the law governing the use of force prior to the drafting of the UN Charter and the contemporary international law in force since 1945. It will then discuss the legal bases for the use of force; self-defence, humanitarian intervention, and multilateral use of force under the collective security mechanism of the United Nations, and the different interpretations of what the rules are. The chapter will conclude by assessing how best we can understand the effectiveness of international law governing the use of force.

The general framework on the use of force in international law

The most important characteristic of post-World War II international law is the ban on the use of force in international relations by the United Nations Charter. Article 2(4) of the United Nations Charter, probably the most famous Article of the Charter, states: 'All Members shall refrain in their international relations from the threat or use of force against the territorial integrity or political independence of any state, or in any other manner inconsistent with the Purposes of the United Nations'. This ban had its historical roots in the Kellogg-Briand Pact of Paris in 1928 which renounced waging war as an instrument of national policy. Before World War II, sixty-three states signed the Pact. The Kellogg-Briand Pact was unsuccessful in constraining state behaviour, but it laid the normative framework for convictions at Nuremberg and Tokyo Military Tribunals for waging aggressive wars and the United Nations Charter. The fact that there is a universal

Table 10.1 The use of force framework in the United Nations Charter

Use of force by states	Use of force by the UN Security Council
Reason: self-defence Article 51	Reason: collective security Article 39
Nothing in the present Charter shall impair the inherent right of individual or collective self-defence if an armed attack occurs against a member of the United Nations, until the Security Council has taken measures necessary to maintain international peace and security. Measures taken by members in the exercise of this right of self-defence shall be immediately reported to the Security Council and shall not in any way affect the authority and responsibility of the Security Council under the present Charter to take at any time such action as it deems necessary in order to maintain or restore international peace and security.	The Security Council shall determine the existence of any threat to the peace, breach of the peace, or act of aggression and shall make recommendations, or decide what measures shall be taken, in accordance with Articles 41 and 42, to maintain or restore international peace and security.

ban on the use of aggressive force by the Charter is a significant historical development. Prior to 1945, states held the ultimate authority over deciding to restrain from aggression and it was recognized under customary international law that states could wage war for reasons of self-help, self-defence, and, possibly, humanitarian intervention.

The United Nations Charter was a fundamental shift because it limited the reasons that all states can use for going to war for self-defence. It also gave the United Nations Security Council the power to legitimize the use of force in international relations. This innovative thinking which took the decisions to use force as far away as possible from individual states was a result of the devastating consequences of World War I and I and the rise of international pacifism as a political ideal. The United Nations Charter created an international authority, the Security Council, to act on behalf of the member states when international peace and security in the world was threatened. This was called the 'collective security mechanism'.

Box 10.1 How many times has the ban on the use of force been violated?

The United Nations Charter tells us that if a state is not using force in self-defence, it is in violation of international law. Timely questions to ask at this stage would be how many times has the ban on the use of force been violated and which states have done this? These questions are difficult to answer. Because of the decentralized system of international law we only have allegations and claims in diplomatic fora and assessments by international legal writings that states have violated the ban on the use of force.

A further difficulty in this area is the relationship between treaty law and customary international law on the use of force. Because the UN Charter is open to interpretations, a state which uses force internationally could make three types of arguments:

1. according to a correct interpretation of the Charter, the use of force was lawful;

2. the use of force is lawful under customary international law and the UN Charter should be interpreted in the light of this;

3. the use of force may be a violation of the UN Charter, but it is aimed at modifying customary international law and the interpretation of the Charter.

To date, there have only been two interstate cases before the International Court of Justice:

- in the case of *Nicaragua v the United States* (1986), the US was found in violation of international law; and

- in the case of *Congo v Uganda* (2003), Uganda was found in violation of international law.

Self-defence, on the other hand, was viewed as a reasonable, logical extension of the idea of self-preservation in the face of an imminent attack.

The United Nations Charter's balancing vision of unilateral self-defence and the 'collective security mechanism' also needs to be seen in the light of the institutional shortcomings of the post-World War II world. With the world having two 'superpowers' during the Cold War and one after, the Security Council was not furnished with the resources and capabilities to become the world's police force. The Charter's vision was the creation of an independent military staff committee that would carry out assessments of international peace and security and react promptly. This never materialized. The United Nations Security Council is a coordinating body of major power interests in responding to collective security threats rather than an independent and impartial mechanism transcending the interests of states.

The United Nations Charter has an important effect on the development of customary international law on the use of force. Because virtually all states in the international system are parties to the Charter, customary international law on the ban on use of force runs parallel to treaty law. States, who fight for exceptions to the ban on the use of force, however, frequently turn to customary international law to modify dominant interpretations of the UN Charter.

Self-defence

Self-defence is the only uncontestedly legitimate reason to use force unilaterally that survived World War II. The United Nations Charter sets out the right to self-defence in Article 51 of the United Nations Charter (see above Table 10.1). This Article points to an important tension in the mindset of the drafters of the UN Charter about the meaning of self-defence. First, Article 51 stipulates that the right to self-defence is an inherent right of states. This means that the right to self-defence existed prior to the UN Charter and that a state's right to defend itself is not dependent on a treaty agreement between states. The recognition of self-defence as an inherent right also suggests that there exist rules governing the right to self-defence under customary international law. Article 51 further recognizes that this right can be exercised individually and collectively. This means that a collection of states can use force collectively against an aggressor state, and that this is legitimized by the United Nations Charter. Second, the United Nations Charter requires states to inform the Security Council immediately of the measures they have taken to defend themselves. This part of the Article 51 suggests that the right to self-defence should not be viewed as an alternative to the UN collective security system. In other words, even though states have an inherent right to protect themselves from armed attacks, they should not wage a prolonged war under the guise of self-defence.

The necessity to recognize a state's individual and collective right to self-defence and the need to promote the logic of collective security for all states are sound objectives, but they do not sit comfortably together when assessing what happens in practice. Firstly, there is the problem that states do not want to delegate control over a military operation, which they believe protects their vital interests, to the Security Council. Indeed, since 1945, no military operation carried out in the name of self-defence has been handed over to the Security Council by a sovereign state. This is explained by states not being willing to lose authority and control over military decisions of a defensive nature. Second, it is difficult to get the Security Council, a political body made up of fifteen UN member states, five of which (China, France, Russia, the United Kingdom, and the United States) are permanent, to act consistently when a state attacks another state. In practice, the result has been that the Security Council has not taken a central role in individual or collective self-defence operations—with one exception. This was the Security Council action after the invasion of Kuwait by Iraq in 1990. In contemporary international law the downplaying of the role of the Security Council in cases of individual or collective self-defence is regarded as a reasonable compromise.

When can states resort to the right of self-defence?

This is one of the most controversial questions in the field of use of force. It raises two interrelated problems. First, who decides when is the right time to use self-defence? Second, what objective standards are there to decide when self-defence can be used? Because the UN Charter recognizes an inherent right to self-defence it is generally viewed that the state that has been attacked has the right to decide. If the Security Council is able to act promptly, it can also signal whether a state is entitled to use the right to self-defence under particular circumstances, as it did with Security Council Resolution 1368 recognizing the right to self-defence of the US against Afghanistan after the September 11 attacks of 2001. When a state is part of a security alliance, a larger number of states are involved in the decision-making process even if they have not themselves been attacked. The problem here is that if a number of states can determine when it is right to invoke the right to self-defence this may lead to wars of aggression. It is, therefore, important to have objective standards to establish when states can *really* use their right to self-defence. This later question is a part of ongoing controversy as the answers depend on an assessment of factual questions as well as what the standards mean. The controversy on the standards focus on two central issues:

1. what kinds of circumstances trigger the need to self-defence by using military force? and

2. in what manner should states use their right to self-defence?

What circumstances justify self-defence?

The timing of the right to self-defence depends on interpreting the wording of the UN Charter. This recognizes the right to self-defence 'if an armed attack occurs'. Three possible readings of this clause have been proposed. The first is what may be termed as the 'strict' interpretation. For a state to be able to use the right to self-defence, an armed attack must actually occur. In other words when the first bomb hits the ground, any state has the indisputable right to self-defence. Only in this way, it is argued, can the weak system of international law avoid states resorting to aggression in the name of self-defence. This strict interpretation has been challenged by some decision-makers and legal experts as being unrealistic. They typically point to the case of having knowledge that the attack is imminent. If state A knows that in two hours a bomb will fall in one of its cities, what justifies waiting for this to happen before using the right to self-defence? Given that the purpose of the right to self-defence is to protect the political and territorial integrity of a state, a degree of anticipatory or pre-emptive self-defence seems to be both necessary and acceptable in international relations. The question then becomes how to avoid the notion of such pre-emptive self-defence being stretched and so blurring the distinction between aggression and defence. The second reading of self-defence incorporates this concern and is based on an understanding of imminent armed attack. An armed attack may not have occurred, but all the evidence shows that it will occur and waiting for it to occur would be too costly. The third reading of self-defence extends the notion of pre-emptive self-defence beyond the point of imminence and argues that states may defend themselves against potential threats before they actually become real threats. Many international lawyers dismiss this last point for two main reasons. First, it is very difficult to distinguish self-defence and aggression when states operate with potential threats rather than imminent attacks. Second, there is an even greater danger than with the second reading that self-defence is no longer an exception to the ban on the use of force, but a routine justification for the use of force by strong states in international relations. In other words, self-defence by deadly force must be a necessity in the light of circumstances and not one of a number of policy options. The first and second readings both have numerous and influential adherents. The first reading, with the apparent support of the International Court of Justice, accepts the practical problem raised by 'realists', but says that the rule must be construed strictly. Thus, as with mitigating circumstances in national law, the response of the international community to a genuine (non-abusive) act of anticipatory self-defence (a real attack was indeed about to occur) would be one that refrains from imposing any sanction in response to the action. In both readings, therefore, international law may be understood as supporting a self-defence doctrine which is flexible enough to address imminent and dangerous attacks, but also robust enough to set an objective standard to assess state action in the face of necessity.

The conduct question

The conduct of a state facing an armed attack is important because it raises the question of whether states have a free hand when responding in self-defence. This question was particularly prominent during the Cold War when there was a nuclear race between the western and the eastern blocs. Could a state wipe out another nation in exercising its right to self-defence? This is a disturbing, but also a difficult question to answer because the answer is dependent on the actual circumstances of the armed attack. The International Court of Justice in its Advisory Opinion on the Legality of Nuclear Weapons in 1996 recognized the possibility that if the life of a nation is at stake, it may use nuclear weapons to defend itself. This means, however, that the attack from the aggressor has to be of a particularly catastrophic kind, probably involving nuclear weapons or similar. International lawyers use the language of 'proportionality' of self-defence to address this point. Here, proportionality means that the response to the attack must be adequate to the nature and the scope of the attack itself. If a state responds to the destruction of one of its sea vessels by destroying a village, for example, it is hard to appreciate the proportionality of the response. In actual situations, examples are a lot more fine-tuned and more detailed assessments of facts are required to understand whether a state has used its right to self-defence responsibly. Given the lack of an institutional body that could make such assessments, it is mostly left to individual states and United Nations organs (in particular the Security Council and the General Assembly) to judge the overall conduct of states exercising their right of self-defence.

The use of force, self-defence, and non-state actors

A central bias of the international relations system is its statist character in framing, assessing, and evaluating problems of international legal life. The use of force framework for states is not immune from this. The United Nations Charter bans the use of force or threat of use of force by states against states. The right to self-defence is also defined as a right of a state against another state. A necessary element of an armed attack is that such an attack must be attributable to a state. Non-state actors do not figure in this international framework because the regulation and the consequences of their activities are viewed primarily as domestic. When a criminal gang uses violence against civilians, the state defends the victims by prosecuting the criminals under domestic laws of murder. There have been, however, circumstances when the state-state paradigm of the use of force is challenged by violent non-state actors located in so-called failed or weak states. These are particular types of non-state actors. They are armed groups with access to military resources, a recognizable structure and hierarchy and, at times, also controlling territory. For international law a significant question with respect to violent non-state armed groups is whether they are supported by a state actor in their activities. There are two possible scenarios in this regard:

1. *affiliated non-state actors*: they are armed groups supported by the government of the territory they are based in which attack another state (e.g. USA, Taliban, and Al Qaeda in Afghanistan); and
2. *non-affiliated non-state actors*: they are armed groups located in a failed state or a weak state and, independently of the state in which they are located, attack another state. (e.g. armed groups in the territory of the Democratic Republic of Congo/Uganda).

The two categories defined above are not rigid. For example, a state may not be actively supporting an armed group, but showing a degree of acceptance of its activities (Hezbollah in Lebanon) or a state may be indifferent to the activities of an armed group in its territory or too weak to stop it (PKK in Iraq). From the perspective of international law, if a state supports the violent activities of a non-state actor, it is clear that the victim state has a right to self-defence against the supporting state. In cases where the link between the non-state actor and the host state is weak or non-existent on the other hand, the international legal position is not as clear-cut. The reason for this goes back to the discussion of the necessity and proportionality requirements of the right to self-defence in international law. As a first option a state that is attacked

> **Box 10.2 Self-defence, terrorist attacks, and armed attacks**
>
> After the 11 September 2001 attacks on the World Trade Center in New York and the Pentagon, the United States' Government argued that it had the right to fight a 'war on terror'. This political rhetoric did not have a corresponding legal category in international law. International law defines war as taking place between two states and self-defence as a response to an actual or imminent armed attack. It is possible for a state to use its right to self-defence against another state, which supports a non-state armed group. This means that those who carried out the attacks become legitimate military targets. UN Security Council Resolution 1368 confirmed this view. If, on the other hand, there is no state to attribute with non-state actor violence, it is more appropriate to see an attack as a law enforcement matter, i.e. violations of domestic laws and matters of international crimes, such as aircraft hijacking, aircraft sabotage and possibly as crimes against humanity.

by a non-state armed group needs to seek the cooperation of the host state in arresting and prosecuting the members of that armed group. It is only when the attack is disastrous or the host state is unwilling or unable to cooperate that the self-defence paradigm is relevant. Of course, in such a situation the host state may be understood as supporting the armed group in a way that brings it closer to the first option.

Unilateral humanitarian intervention?

Unilateral humanitarian intervention refers to situations when a state or a group of states claim to use force to save the lives of citizens of another state. A key feature of this definition is the intention that informs the use of force decision. This intention is defined as 'saving lives' in cases where there is an imminent threat to considerable numbers of people living elsewhere. Humanitarian intervention is an important part of the just war tradition that is informed by a moral imperative to protect the innocent. Throughout history, civilians have suffered at the hands of their own states or at the hands of warlords in failed states. Several examples since 1990 illustrate why the need to save individuals from widespread and systematic killing is a real problem in current international relations. For instance, the 1994 Rwanda genocide which saw twenty per cent of the Tutsi population murdered by the Hutus, or the Srebrenica massacre of 1995 in the former Yugoslavia which claimed 8,000 Bosnian lives in one day.

International lawyers have long discussed the question of whether humanitarian intervention was part of customary international law pre-1945; if it were custom, whether it has survived 1945 and if neither is the case, whether the state practice in contemporary international relations supports a customary right to humanitarian intervention (Rodley and Çalı 2007).

The political reality of humanitarian intervention has compelled some authors to argue that it is or should be allowed in post-UN Charter international law. Here, the argument focuses on the fact that a unilateral humanitarian intervention is not *really* an intervention against the territorial integrity or the political independence of a state. The aim of such a military intervention is precisely humanitarian and if the intervening state pulls out as soon as the humanitarian mission is fulfilled it does not in fact interfere with the domestic activities of a state.

In fact, international law and international politics have long been sceptical of a legal right to unilateral humanitarian intervention because of the danger of abuse of this right by states. For international lawyers, significantly, recognizing a right to unilateral humanitarian intervention has always been a question of bad policy. This means that no one really denies that there could be circumstances where innocent lives can only be saved by outside intervention. The central problem is that states do not act with a single motivation when they decide to use force and real-time interventions with mixed motivations are prone to cause more suffering than they

Table 10.2 Proponents and opponents of humanitarian intervention

Proponents of unilateral humanitarian intervention in international law	Opponents of unilateral humanitarian intervention in international law
The purpose is humanitarian.	Self-defence is the only basis of unilateral use of force in international law.
It is not directed against territorial integrity or political independence.	Humanitarian intervention is precisely against the territorial integrity and political independence of the state whose sovereignty is thereby violated.
It does not violate the principle of non-intervention.	Recognizing unilateral humanitarian intervention upsets the stability of the international system.
If no other option is possible, states have a duty to save lives.	Humanitarian intervention is subject to abuse and selectivity.
	Collective security mechanisms should be used and improved.

> **Box 10.3** Kosovo: unilateral humanitarian intervention and the mitigating circumstances argument
>
> The military intervention by NATO in Kosovo in 1999 sparked a new round of debate on unilateral humanitarian intervention in international law and international relations. NATO member states argued that they intervened in (then) Serbia and Montenegro to save the lives of the Albanian majority in the region of Kosovo from the oppressive Serbian Government. This intervention was successful in defeating the Serbian forces in Kosovo. It also set in motion the *de facto* separation of Kosovo from the rest of Serbia and the subsequent declaration of independence by Kosovo. A central argument of NATO member states was that the United Nations Security Council was unable to act because of Russia's threat to veto any collective action and this necessitated acting unilaterally. Political and legal commentators were divided on the question of whether NATO had no choice but to intervene unilaterally and whether the threshold of necessity was met in this case. Politicians and international lawyers were divided along the same four lines. One group argued that the intervention was unlawful; another group argued that it was indeed lawful given the circumstances; a third group argued that it was unlawful, but legitimate politically and morally; and a final group argued that the Kosovo case was a sign of legal change in itself. In the midst of this controversy, however, an international lawyer (Franck 2003) offered a fifth approach to this controversy. He suggested that international politics was too messy to be governed by international law at all times and extreme circumstances may require states to step out of international law temporarily to deal with the exigencies of a situation. This means that the constraining power of the law is untouched by state behaviour, but that the states stepping out of the law are not punished for their actions. This is what may be called the mitigating circumstances argument for humanitarian intervention.

may end, and set in motion bigger armed conflicts. It is for these policy reasons that international law favours humanitarian interventions to take place under the collective security mechanism of the United Nations rather than unilaterally.

The collective security system under the United Nations Charter

As stated earlier in this chapter, the collective security system established under the United Nations Charter was an institutional and legal innovation of the post-World War II world. The central ideas behind this system are spelt out in Chapter VII of the United Nations Charter entitled 'action with respect to threats to the peace, breaches of peace and acts of aggression'. This chapter recognizes that it is the task of the UN Security Council to determine when there is a threat to international peace and security (Article 39) and that the Security Council can take the measures that it deems necessary (Articles 40, 41), including the use of armed force (Article 42) in order to maintain and restore international peace and security. Article 25 of the UN Charter further states that all members of the UN agree to comply with the decisions of the Security Council. These powers are unique in the history of international organizations as no international body has been given the powers to authorize the use of force in the name of the international community before.

The purpose of the collective security system has been to break the monopoly of states over the use of force. When we study the activities of the Security Council since 1945, however, we find that the legal and political evolution of the collective security system has led to a plurality of forms of legitimization for the use of force by the United Nations collective security system. Significantly, during the Cold War, the collective security mechanism did not operate because of the threat of veto from one of the permanent members of the Security Council. The United Nations, therefore, was unable to collectively interfere, for example, in conflicts of self-determination, decolonization, and the proxy and regime-change wars between the Soviet Union and the USA in Asia, Africa, and Central America.

In the meantime, however, the United Nations developed the practice of using peace-keeping forces in countries where parties consented to the UN blue berets overseeing a ceasefire or peace agreement. Because the United Nations never received agreement from member states to establish a stand-alone military force, the United Nations peacekeeping forces emerged as a patchwork of multinational troops from volunteer-ing states. These forces rest on the doctrine of mutual consent from all parties involved, impartiality towards the parties, and use of force only in self-defence. The General Assembly of the UN and the Security Council were both involved in establishing these peacekeeping forces. As a result, the UN was not able to oversee conflicts before they erupted, but it could after hostilities paused in places such as Kashmir (India–Pakistan), the Golan Heights (Israel–Egypt), and Cyprus (Cyprus–Turkey). The UN was prepared to use force to contain the civil war that broke out in the Congo in 1960 after Belgium left. But United Nations casualties, including the death of the then Secretary-General, and the lack of commitment from member states to fight the war led to the serious failure of the collective security system (McCoubrey and White 1996).

The end of the Cold War saw the United Nations collective security system enter a new phase. This is better described as a proliferation of collective security systems rather than the revival of the Security Council from the Cold War divisions. Since the 1990s, the Security Council has increased its peacekeeping activities considerably and has more frequently authorized the use of force. It has not, however, emerged as the sole and undisputed centre of collective use of force decisions in international relations. The increased willingness of regional organizations such as NATO, the European Union, the African Union, and ECOWAS to intervene in the world's internal conflicts has meant that the United Nations collective security mechanism has taken on the role of legitimizing as well as authorizing state action. In particular, the more risky, dangerous, and short term a military operation is, the more frequent it has become for the UN Security Council to 'contract-out' the action to a group of states or endorse their actions. When an operation incorporates the long-term goals of state and institution building in the aftermath of a civil conflict, it is more common to have UN-led multi-dimensional peacekeeping operations.

International relations developments point to the regionalization and, possibly, privatization of collective security arrangements. This asks the question as to whether private security companies will become a regular part of future collective security mechanisms. It is not clear what this means for the future of the collective security mechanism from an international law perspective. International law primarily concerns itself with the legitimation of decisions to use force through applying correct procedures. It also frowns on mercenarism which is not easily distinguished from using private entities to deploy armed force. Even though the Security Council is itself not a representative body of the world's states and peoples, it has assumed the role of being the only legitimate institution when it comes to authorizing the use of force. The strong compliance rate with the decisions of the Security Council in this area also points to the fact that states have widely accepted the role of a UN-mandated political body to take collective decisions or to endorse the decisions of regional actors. The plurality of actors involved in collective security and the lack of hierarchical relationships between the UN Security Council and regional organizations, however, also raise the problem of an accountability gap in the legal regulation of the use of force. This is a question closer to the home of international lawyers because it raises the problem of accountability, that is, regulation and blame when an operation endorsed by the Security Council, but carried out by a state or a regional organization, goes wrong.

The Security Council through its resolutions has also affected how the use of force is interpreted in international law. The most important trend in Security Council resolutions since the 1990s has been the expansion of the interpretation of 'a threat to international peace and security'. The Security Council has moved away from a strictly statist understanding of such a threat towards a more human security focused understanding. This has meant that the Security Council has become more willing and able to authorize the use of force in order to protect civilians, women, and children caught

Table 10.3 The UN Charter and the proliferation of the collective security system

Type	Examples
Use of peacekeepers recommended by the General Assembly and carried out by a UN peacekeeping force	United Nations Emergency Force (UNEF 1) (1956)
Use of peacekeepers authorized by the Security Council and carried out by a UN peacekeeping force	United Nations Operation in Burundi (ONUB) 2004
Use of force authorized by the Security Council and carried out by a regional organization	Operation Artemis—European Union in Democratic Republic of Congo Operation (2003)
Use of force endorsed by the Security Council and authorized and carried out by a regional organization	ECOWAS intervention in Liberia (1990)
Use of force authorized by the Security Council and carried out by an individual state	Operation Turquoise—France in Rwanda (1994)
Operation Palliser—United Kingdom in Sierra Leone (2000)	
Use of force carried out by collective agreement of a regional organization in relation to a member state of that organization	African Union Mission in Sudan (2004)
Use of force for collective self-defence recognized by Security Council	Operation Enduring Freedom, US and allies in Afghanistan (2001)
Use of force in the territory of a state with the consent of that state	International Security Assistance Force of NATO in Afghanistan (2003)

up in civil conflict or domestic oppression. From one perspective, we can see this as the revival of the idea of collective humanitarian intervention. Security Council Resolution 1674 in this respect is significant. Not only does it recognize that 'peace, security and human rights are interlinked and mutually enforcing', it also reaffirms that the United Nations has a 'responsibility to protect populations from genocide, war crimes, ethnic cleansing and crimes against humanity'.[1] This resolution signals that permanent members of the Security Council are willing to recognize any major threat to human life, be these threats part of domestic or interstate problems, as a legitimate basis for the authorization of the use of force under the United Nations Charter.

Despite inconsistencies in responding to humanitarian crises around the world and continuing disagreements amongst its permanent members, the Security Council has lost neither legal nor political centrality in the collective security mechanism. States turn to the Security Council to legitimize their decisions to use force and

Box 10.4 Responsibility to protect

The term 'responsibility to protect' was first presented in the report of the International Commission on Intervention and State Sovereignty in 2001 as a new approach to face the challenge of protecting the lives of civilians who are caught in large-scale violence because their states are collapsed, or unable or unwilling to protect them.

'Responsibility to protect' doctrine says that the central principle of international law—state sovereignty—must yield to the grave violations of human rights and humanitarian law, including genocide, ethnic cleansing, and crimes against humanity.

In the 2005 World Summit, all members of the United Nations embraced this doctrine. The World Summit Outcome Document stated that:

- it is primarily the responsibility of each and every state to protect the lives of its citizens from ethnic cleansing, genocide, and crimes against humanity;
- the international community should assist states in every way to this end; and
- if a state 'manifestly fails' in its responsibility, the international community must take stronger measures, including the use of force, through the Security Council.

There is an ongoing discussion on the legal status of the responsibility to protect doctrine in international law as some states argue that responsibility to protect was not agreed on as a 'norm' at the World Summit. Some argue that the Security Council is the ultimate authority on the use of force and the primary determinant for action is the agreement of its members rather than the situations on the ground.

peacekeeping or enforcement missions authorized by the Security Council are likely to receive political acceptance in the international community. This is not, however, to suggest that the Security Council is an efficient mechanism that takes impartial and timely decisions at all times. The very idea of a collective security mechanism has taken root in international practice and the attitudes of states, civil society, and the public towards the Security Council is an excellent example of international law in action within a highly politicized and divisive international political context.

The power of international law on the use of force: rhetoric or controlling?

The previous sections have indicated the dynamics of interpreting the international law rules on use of force within the framework of international politics. It should be clear by now that one of the important lessons of this chapter is that international law does not exist in a vacuum. On the contrary, there is a very close relationship between the interpretation of international law and the international political context. This is especially the case in one of the most important legal and political questions of international life: the external use of deadly force sanctioned by a political process. Some international commentators appreciate the proximity of international law to politics; some, of course, take an opposing stance. Proponents of these views can come from anywhere on the spectrum that ranges from realism to constructivism (see Chapter 2). Those international relations observers who take a strong realist position, however, believe international law is insignificant in driving state action with regard to the use of force. This is because realists explain conflict as an outcome of material conditions and power relations.

When the role of international law in regulating the use of force is viewed as an overall positive development in international relations one can first think of the function of international law as a way of managing mutual expectations amongst states. The international law on the use of force serves precisely this purpose. The UN Charter framework sends a number of messages both to strong and small states and non-state actors intending to use force domestically and internationally. First, if an armed group targets a civilian population it is likely that the Security Council would authorize the use of force to stop this from happening. This, however, does not tell us anything about whether such an intervention would be timely or effective.

Second, the fact that states and regional organizations turn to the Security Council for recognition and legitimation means that the collective legitimation of the use of force through international law matters in international relations. States do take into account the possible costs of not receiving legitimation from the Security Council in deciding the course of their military behaviour. Thirdly, in the case of strong states, such as the US and Russia, we do not observe them rejecting the United Nations Charter outright, or turning away from the Security Council on a regular and consistent basis. This means that the international law on the use of force figures in the long-term benefit calculations of strong states as well as of smaller states. Many states, weak or strong, do contest the meaning of the provisions of the United Nations Charter when interests vital to their political standing are at stake. Even in these cases, however, a major power challenging international law has not caused international law to change and correspond to such preferences. As we have seen within the context of the discussion of the meaning of self-defence in international law and the emergence of non-state armed groups, there is room for expanding the interpretations of concepts so that they better capture the realities of international life. So change in international law is not necessarily a dangerous development in itself. The pre-emptive self-defence doctrine developed by the United States between

2003 and 2009 was rejected by many states. The tendency, therefore, for strong states to disregard international law is not a sufficient reason to regard international law as irrelevant in the sphere of the use of force. It should be recognized, though, that international law on the use of force is an international norm that faces violation in international life.

Thirdly, in the case of peaceful and small and medium size states (the majority of the United Nations), the United Nations is an important channel and sometimes the only way to contribute to the maintenance of international peace and security. This means that the international law on the use of force has socialized most of the states in the international system to make sense of wars, allegations of self-defence, and calls for the deployment of peacekeeping troops within the language and the framework of international law. In this respect, international law on the use of force plays a constitutive role of interstate conduct in international relations.

Those who view the proximity of international law to politics as negative, point to the fact that states have, most of the time since 1945, acted based on their own preferences and calculations of their own state interests. The instances when these states have adhered to the UN Charter can better be explained by the 'low cost' of compliance rather than state-internalization of international law. In other words, when important interests *really* are at stake, states pay no attention to international law on the use of force nor are they concerned with any possible long-term damaging effects of their behaviour. Instead, they manipulate existing rules by offering alternative interpretations that merely serve the purpose of tailoring international law to fit their real interests. A clear example of this is the US-led invasion of Iraq in 2003 that was justified by the protagonists through the potential threat of Iraq holding 'weapons of mass destruction'. The key point in this argument is that states only interact with international law on the use of force *selectively*. They turn to international law when it suits their own private assessment of a particular situation. When the fit is not there, they offer an alternative interpretation of what the rules are.

Regardless of where one falls on the negative/positive spectrum, a number of general observations can be made about how international law scores in political debate. First, international law provides a structure for making arguments in the area of use of force whether this is rhetoric, action-guiding principles, or standards of evaluation. International law serves to limit the range of arguments politicians, diplomats, and legal experts use on political and legal platforms. Second, international law offers a framework for evaluating state conduct that is embedded in both the collective practice of states and in principles that makes sense of this practice. This evaluative role of the international law framework on the use of force is all the more significant in an era where international governmental and non-governmental organizations monitoring and evaluating state conduct and international law are on the rise. Such an evaluative framework further enables political shaming and the mobilization of public opinion. In some cases, it also legally demands liability for actions. The strength of the international law framework in this respect comes from the collective recognition of principles for the regulation of the use of force by a diverse range of policy-makers in world politics.

Conclusion

This chapter has set out the international law framework for the use of force in international relations. International law on the use of force is both a creation of the United Nations Charter and subsequent practices of states since 1945 in the international arena. The chapter shows that because of the high-politics aspect of the use of force, international law has faced two important challenges. First, politicians and international lawyers have constantly contested the scope of what international law says. This is both because of novel developments in international politics, such as the rise of internal armed conflicts and non-state armed groups, and states protecting their monopoly over decisions to use force in international relations. Second, the importance of the subject matter has led to heated discussions about the relevance of international law on use of force decisions and created committed sceptics and supporters in both international law and international relations.

Questions

1. What is the importance of the United Nations Charter for the use of force in international relations?
2. Which Articles of the United Nations Charter regulate the use of force in international law?
3. What is the scope of the right to self-defence?
4. What are the arguments for and against anticipatory or pre-emptive self-defence?
5. Can states invoke a right to self-defence against non-state armed groups?
6. What are the policy arguments for and against unilateral humanitarian intervention?
7. What is the collective security mechanism and how has it developed since 1945?
8. Is it important that the UN Security Council authorizes or endorses use of force decisions by regional organizations? If so, why?

9. What are the arguments in favour of the relevance of international law for state behaviour in the area of use of force?
10. What are the arguments against the relevance of international law for state behaviour in the area of use of force?

Further reading

Art, L. J and Waltz, K. (2008) *The Use of Force: Military Power and International Politics*, 7th edn. (Lanham, MD: Rowman and Littlefield Publishers). *A realist assessment of the use of force in international relations.*

Dinstein, Y. (2005) *War, Aggression and Self-Defence* (Cambridge: Cambridge University Press). *A detailed analysis of the bases of unilateral use of force in international law, including the legality of use of force by states against non-state actors.*

Finnemore, M. (2004) *The Purpose of Intervention: Changing Beliefs about the Use of Force* (Ithaca, NY: Cornell University Press). *A social-constructivist analysis of what kinds of arguments states have historically mobilized for intervening in the internal affairs of other states and how historical arguments compare to our contemporary conceptions of humanitarian intervention.*

Franck, T. M. (2003) *Recourse to Force: State Action against Threats and Armed Attacks* (Cambridge: Cambridge University Press). *A comprehensive discussion of the evolution of international law on the use of force and its competing interpretations.*

Franck, T.M. and Rodley, N. (1973) 'After Bangladesh: The Law of Humanitarian Intervention by Military Force' *American Journal of International Law* 67/2: 275–305. *A classic analysis of the lawfulness of humanitarian intervention in international law.*

Gray, C. (2008) *International Law and the Use of Force* (Oxford: Oxford University Press). *A comprehensive introduction to the international legal framework on the use of force since 1945.*

Holzgrefe, J. L. (2003) *Humanitarian Intervention: Ethical, Legal and Political Dilemmas* (Cambridge: Cambridge University Press). *A multidisciplinary analysis of humanitarian intervention as a moral, legal, and political issue in international relations from leading contributors in three disciplines.*

McCoubrey, N. and White, H. (1996) *The Blue Helmets: Legal Regulation of United Nations Military Operations* (Sudbury, MA: Dartmouth). *A comprehensive legal analysis of how the United Nations peacekeeping operations have evolved and the international legal basis for their establishment and status.*

McQueen, N. (2006) *Peacekeeping and the International System* (Oxford: Routledge). *A political analysis of the evolution of peacekeeping using detailed historical and contemporary case study analysis.*

Rodley, N. and Cali, B. (2007) 'Revisiting Kosovo: Humanitarian Intervention on the Fault-lines of International Law' *Human Rights Law Review* 7/2: 275–97. *A comprehensive analysis of the humanitarian intervention debate and its implications for international law methodology.*

Walzer, M. (2006) *Just and Unjust Wars: A Moral Argument with Historical Illustrations* (New York: Basic Books). *A modern interpretation of the just war tradition discussing moral arguments in favour of using force in international relations.*

Websites

http://www.un.org/Docs/sc/ *The UN Security Council informs on all its activities and provides access to reports and resolutions.*

http://www.iciss.ca/report-en.asp *Here you can find the full text of the Report of the International Commission on Intervention and State Sovereignty.*

http://www.crimesofwar.org/ *The Crimes of War Project is a collaboration of journalists, lawyers, and scholars dedicated to raising public awareness of the laws of war and their application to situations of conflict.*

http://www.un.org/Depts/dpko/dpko/ *This website contains all the relevant information on the activities of the United Nations Department of Peacekeeping Operations.*

http://www.asil.org/insights.cfm *The American Society of International Law regularly publishes on current topics in international law, and often discusses the legality of international activities.*

Visit the Online Resource Centre that accompanies this book to access more learning resources www.oxfordtextbooks.co.uk/orc/cali/

Chapter endnote

1. Security Council Res. 1674 of 28 April 2006.

Chapter 11

International humanitarian law

Elizabeth Griffin and Başak Çalı

CHAPTER CONTENTS

- Introduction
- What is international humanitarian law and how is it made?
- The nature of international humanitarian law
- Purposes of international humanitarian law and its basic principles
- Compliance with international humanitarian law
- Non-state actors and compliance with international humanitarian law
- Conclusion

CHAPTER OVERVIEW

This chapter examines international humanitarian law (IHL), the body of international law that contributes to our understanding of the regulation of violence in international relations. The chapter commences with an examination of the roots of international humanitarian law—that is, the institutional history of IHL and the sources of IHL. It then explores the purpose of IHL which is to regulate the use of deadly force by each and every party to an armed conflict. The chapter particularly focuses on the basic principles of IHL, which aim to strike a balance between military necessity and the principle of humanity during times of armed conflict. The chapter concludes by discussing what reasons states have to comply with IHL and indicators of compliance.

Introduction

International humanitarian law (IHL) is the branch of international law that provides rules that regulate the conduct of armed conflict. The very idea that international law can play a role in regulating the most violent form of organized human conduct—war—is problematic and has often been challenged. One simply needs to open a newspaper or watch the news to see the horrific consequences of war on every continent. When we see the death, suffering, and destruction caused by war we might well be tempted to say 'law is simply irrelevant during war'. However, the idea that armed conflict should be regulated by a set of international rules is extremely forceful; it has moral weight and it is important in international relations. The human misery and destruction that occurs as a result of war demands that the international community seek ways to regulate violence and minimize the horrific consequences of war. Indeed, since ancient times the international community has sought ways to regulate the horrors of war. The history and development of IHL provide evidence that states see the value of agreed codes of conduct to regulate conflict and as the nature of conflict has changed so too the international community has attempted to respond to new horrors by expanding and adapting the rules of IHL.

IHL is the body of law that regulates the conduct of hostilities by all parties to a conflict once an armed conflict has commenced. IHL (also called *ius in bello*) should be distinguished from the law governing the use of force (also called *ius ad bellum*—see Chapter 10) which concerns the legality of decisions about going to war. IHL concerns the regulation of violence *once a conflict has commenced*. It provides detailed rules that regulate the means and methods of warfare and which aim to protect those persons that are not taking part in a conflict, including civilians and soldiers that are out of action (also called *hors de combat*). Even though states have failed to abolish wars altogether in international relations, there is now a solid corpus of IHL which provides guidance to soldiers, commanders, politicians, non-state armed groups, war reporters, and civil society about how to behave in times of conflict. IHL helps us to make sense of tactical and strategic decisions taken by the military, orders of politicians, and the behaviour of civilians in times of armed conflict.

This chapter provides an overview of the nature and basic principles of IHL and it discusses the effectiveness of this unique body of international law. The chapter commences with an examination of what IHL is and how it is made and how it has developed over time. We then explore *how* IHL regulates armed conflict through a number of basic principles. The rules of IHL are extensive and wide-ranging and the chapter does not attempt to cover every aspect of IHL. Rather we focus on some key foundational principles that underpin IHL and we discuss some of the debates and difficulties that arise in interpreting these principles particularly within the context of contemporary conflicts. The final part of this chapter addresses the important question of compliance with IHL and reasons and incentives for state and non-state actors to comply with IHL.

> **Box 11.1 War and armed conflict: what is in a name?**
>
> The international legal definition of armed conflict has changed over time:
>
> - initially, the existence of armed conflict was recognized only when two states officially declared war against each other. War in this legal sense can only take place between two states;
> - after 1949, it was accepted that an armed conflict exists even if one of the states does not recognize it. From 1949 onwards, any use of armed force by one state against the territory, ships, or air force of another state was said to trigger an armed conflict;
> - any armed conflict between two or more states is known as an 'international armed conflict';
> - the 1949 Geneva Conventions recognize that there can be armed conflicts within a single state. The Geneva Conventions refer to a conflict that occurs within one state as a 'non-international armed conflict'.

What is international humanitarian law and how is it made?

IHL is one of the oldest branches of international law and its roots pre-date modern international law and its state system. Attempts to regulate armed conflict date back to ancient times and are evident across many diverse cultures throughout history (Meron 1998). Modern IHL is made up of a large number of diverse international treaties concluded in the past 200 years and customary international law.

Historically, the development of IHL has been prompted by a combination of a destructive war, appeal to humanitarian considerations, and the logic of the need for reciprocity-building in relation to these considerations. The 1864 Geneva Convention, for example, concerns the amelioration of the condition of the wounded in the battlefield. This treaty shows that all parties recognize the strong moral appeal of not killing or abandoning a wounded soldier and the lack of military necessity in targeting the wounded. This mutual understanding creates the conditions for cooperation and fair play on the battlefield. The historical background, however, also plays a decisive role. The 1864 treaty was a direct response to 45,000 soldiers left behind in the battle of Solferino of 1859.

The historical progression of IHL further shows that the subject matter of IHL has gradually expanded to address advancements in weapons technologies and the consequences of war for civilians. Until 1949, for example, a large body of rules was developed concerning the means and methods of warfare and the treatment of soldiers who were captured by enemy forces (prisoners of war), but there were no rules regarding the protection of civilians. During World War II, the aviation and aerial bombing technology made it possible to bombard territories over thousands of square kilometres. This was the first time when the number of victims was higher among civilians than among soldiers. This and the horrors of the Nazi run concentration camps, where civilians were tortured, murdered, and subjected to various cruel forms of medical experimentation, promoted the drafting of the most well-known of IHL treaties, the 1949 Four Geneva Conventions. These Conventions, amongst other things, set out explicit rules for civilian protection during war. More recently, the nature of conflict has changed and there has been a rise in bloody civil wars. The international community has responded to the changing nature of conflict, albeit not swiftly enough for many, by attempting to formulate rules that govern civil wars (referred to by international lawyers as internal armed conflicts). As warfare changes and adapts the international community continues to be confronted with new forms of violence that require the development of IHL. One contemporary challenge for IHL is the regulation of the use of computers and robotic technology in armed conflict and attacks carried out by computers (also called computer network attacks).

Box 11.2 What does IHL regulate?

Modern IHL is concerned with six central topics:

1. permissible use of weapons and military tactics;
2. protection of those who can no longer fight (wounded, sick and shipwrecked troops, prisoners of war);
3. the duties and rights of neutral parties to a conflict;
4. rules regulating occupation;
5. the protection of people who do not take part in the fighting (e.g. civilians, medics, and aid-workers);
6. the protection of cultural, religious sites, and the environment.

The order of these six topics reflects the historical progression of IHL, which is coined as the 'humanization' of IHL (Meron 2000).

The humanization of IHL, that is the increasing focus on the humanitarian protection function of IHL, is reflected both in the changes in the name of the topic and the development of its substance. IHL was traditionally referred to as the 'laws of war' or 'the international law of armed conflict'. The emphasis on international 'humanitarian' law in the title of this chapter reflects the development of this body of law as also being very much concerned with the protection of those not directly involved in hostilities and minimizing the suffering and restoring the dignity of all those who find themselves in the line of fire. Modern IHL requires parties to an armed conflict to also take into account the sustainability of the environment and the infrastructure necessary for the survival of the civilian population and culture.

IHL treaties

Of all the IHL treaties, the Hague Regulations, the four Geneva Conventions, and two Additional Protocols of 1977 together stand out. The international treaties signed in the Hague in 1899 and 1907 after two Peace Conventions are together known as the 'Hague Regulations'. For the main part, the Hague Regulations create rules that relate to weapons and targeting during war. The four Geneva Conventions of 1949 and their two Additional Protocols of 1977 focus more on protection of civilians and those who are no longer able to fight (sometimes called *hors de combat*). Since 1977 IHL has attempted to respond to developments in the field of modern weaponry and certain weapons have been outlawed (e.g. cluster bombs, chemical and biological weapons, and anti-personnel landmines). There is not, however, a treaty that bans the use of nuclear weapons. The legality of the proliferation and use of nuclear weapons has been subject to controversial proceedings before the International Court of Justice (see Chapter 6).

International treaty-making in IHL has always been multilateral and a large number of states have ratified IHL treaties. For example, the 1949 Geneva Conventions has 194 state parties and its 1977 Additional Protocol on Protection of Civilians in Times of International Armed Conflicts has 168. The near universal numbers of parties to these treaties provide evidence that these treaties now have the status of customary international law. The high ratification rate also demonstrates that states recognize the need for an internationally agreed framework for the regulation of armed conflicts.

Box 11.3 Major IHL treaties

1856 Declaration Respecting Maritime Law
1868 St. Petersburg Declaration Renouncing the Use, in Time of War, of Explosive Projectiles Under 400 Grams Weight
1899 Declaration Concerning Asphyxiating Gases
1899 Declaration Concerning Expanding Bullets
1907 Hague Conventions Respecting Laws and Customs of War on Land
1907 Hague Conventions

1925 Geneva Gas Protocol

1949 Geneva Conventions

1954 Hague Convention on Protection of Cultural Property in the Event of Armed Conflict

1972 Biological Weapons Convention

1977 II Additional Protocols to Geneva Conventions of 1949

1980 Convention on Certain Weapons

1993 Chemical Weapons Convention

1997 Ottowa Convention on the Prohibition of Anti-Personnel Landmines

2005 III Additional Protocol to Geneva Conventions of 1949

Customary IHL

Customary IHL is important because it establishes which rules apply to all states regardless of their ratification status of the myriad of IHL treaties. The proliferation of international courts and tribunals interpreting IHL rules and increased monitoring of state commitments by non-governmental organizations (see Chapters 7, 8, and 13) also give further utility to customary IHL in the application of IHL to specific armed conflicts.

In the field of IHL, treaties play a significant role in the formation of customary international law with respect to non-treaty parties. Treaties both attract support for treaty norms from non-ratifying treaties and point to divergent practices between parties to an IHL treaty and others. A large body of customary IHL is evident in the field of protection of civilians and soldiers who are no longer able to fight. A 2005 International Committee of the Red Cross (ICRC) study of customary IHL found that most customary rules mirror those of treaty provisions and most states think similar rules for treatment of civilians should apply in the context of international as well as internal conflicts (Henckaerts 2005). Indeed, deliberate targeting of civilians is a strong candidate for a *ius cogens* prohibition in international law.

The area of choice of weapons points to a different relationship between treaty law and custom. Treaties that prohibit certain weapons are widely ratified by states, but there is also contrary state practice by states that oppose the ban of a weapon, and/or actively produce, use, and sell it. The Ottawa Convention of 1997 on the Prohibition of Anti-Personnel Landmines, which has attracted 150 signatures, is a case in point. Despite a significant number of states committed to no longer produce, stockpile, and transfer anti-personnel landmines, a small number of states remain outside the treaty system and are opposed to an immediate ban of landmines. This international dynamic creates difficulties for solidifying customary international law. Given that customary international law is a dynamic process (see Chapter 6), the position of landmine-producing states needs to be continually observed before we can say that near universal ratification of the Ottawa treaty shows signs of emerging as custom.

The nature of international humanitarian law

The nature of IHL as a body of international law is unique due to a number of its institutional features. These are, the actor-centric nature of IHL; the existence of two sets of rules for international and internal conflicts; and the incorporation of a non-state actors, and the International Review of the Red Cross, in its implementation.

IHL and actor-centricism

IHL challenges international relations and law approaches that view states as unitary actors and international law as only regulating relationships between states. IHL regulates the conduct of *all* actors that are involved an armed conflict: these actors may be states (be it as fighting parties or neutral observers), but they may also be any individual or group of individuals of any nationality that are involved in an armed conflict—e.g. rebel groups, soldiers, medical officers, civilians, or non-governmental humanitarian organizations.

In this respect, IHL approaches international law not as an interstate phenomenon, but as an actor-based phenomenon. It is the involvement with an armed conflict that triggers the applicability of IHL to various actors. Even though IHL is made in the same way as other branches of international law in that it is made by states, the obligations, duties, privileges, immunities, and prohibitions of IHL are applicable not only to states but also to individuals, armed non-state groups, neutral parties, and even non-governmental organizations. The very nature of IHL means that it is not possible to fully understand or analyse this branch of international law through a state-centric lens and it is necessary to disaggregate the actors involved in an armed conflict. As we will see in Chapter 12, IHL does not only incur state responsibility. In addition, individuals can be held criminally responsible before domestic and international courts for violating rules of IHL (called 'grave breaches' in the 1949 Geneva Conventions on war crimes). States also have a duty to repress breaches of IHL regardless of who commits it (civilians or combatants) and not only an individual soldier, but also soldiers within a chain of command can be responsible for the same violation of IHL. The fact that IHL creates obligations not only for states, but also for individuals is a key design factor that must be borne in mind when examining the purposes and effectiveness of IHL.

International and internal armed conflicts

Historically, the regulation of civil wars (referred to by international lawyers as non-international armed conflicts or internal conflicts) was not seen as being an appropriate topic to be addressed in international relations. This can be explained by the reluctance of states to give away a part of their sovereignty in dealing with internal dissidents and secessionist movements and the understanding that state armed forces and non-state armed forces are not equal parties in a conflict. Due to the resistance to regulate internal conflicts, IHL has different rules that are applicable in international and non-international (internal) armed conflicts. In particular, states regard dissidents as criminals rather than combatants. It is for this reason that no prisoner of war status exists in internal armed conflicts.

In 1949, states controversially accepted that minimum considerations of humanity should apply in internal armed conflicts. In 1977 the Second Additional Protocol to the 1949 Geneva Conventions in its first article further defined a non-international armed conflict as taking place between a state party to the Protocol and dissident armed forces or other organized armed groups which have a command structure and control part of a territory and codified fifteen further rules about how parties should conduct themselves in such conflicts. This Protocol received support due to decolonization and secessionist movements around the world at the time, but also attracted resistance as 'giving rights to terrorists'. Since 1977 the increasing humanization of IHL coupled with the strengthening of the human rights movement and more international focus on the need to respond to non-international armed conflicts has generated more concern and, in turn, rules that regulate civil wars. Despite this, the rules that govern non-international conflicts are less developed and weaker than those applicable to international armed conflicts.

> ### Box 11.4 Primary rules applicable in international and non-international armed conflicts
>
> The rules applicable in international and non-international armed conflicts are different. When attempting to determine which specific rules are applicable to a particular conflict one must first classify the conflict as either international or non-international. The following are the most important rules that are applicable to different types of conflict.
>
> Rules applicable in international armed conflicts.
>
> - Hague Conventions
> - Geneva Convention I relating to the *wounded and sick* members of armed forces *in the field*

- Geneva Convention II relating to the *wounded, sick, and shipwrecked* members of armed forces *at sea*
- Geneva Convention III relating to the *Treatment of Prisoners of War*
- Geneva Convention IV relating to the *Protection of Civilians*
- Protocol I relating to the protection of the *victims of international* armed conflict
- Customary international law

Rules applicable in non-international armed conflicts:

- Common Article 3 to the four Geneva Conventions of 1949 (this is one provision on non-international conflicts which is placed in all four Geneva Conventions)
- Protocol II of the Geneva Conventions relating to the *protection of victims of non-international* armed conflict
- Customary international law

In reality, classifying a specific conflict is often not a straightforward matter. This is the case, for example, where states interfere in non-international armed conflicts. In such situations what appears to be a non-international armed conflict becomes what is known as an 'internationalized non-international armed conflict'. Such conflicts give rise to considerable debate about the classification of the conflict and whether the rules governing international or non-international conflict bind some or all of the various actors engaged in the conflict.

IHL and the International Committee of the Red Cross (ICRC)

Another unique element of IHL is that it is the only body of international law that provides a special status and role to an international humanitarian organization. The 1949 Geneva Conventions task the International Committee of the Red Cross (ICRC) to play a major role in encouraging compliance with IHL and it is recognized in treaty law as having the authority to visit prisoners, organize relief operations, reunite separated families, and carry out other humanitarian activities during armed conflicts. Many states recognize the international legal personality of the ICRC and accord it privileges and immunities under their domestic laws.

Purposes of international humanitarian law and its basic principles

The most basic purpose of IHL is to manage armed conflicts. IHL provides rules which regulate how parties can lawfully conduct armed hostilities in a manner that limits human suffering and minimizes damage (e.g. to the environment, infrastructure, and cultural and religious objects). IHL recognizes that parties to a conflict are entitled to do whatever is necessary to win the war (the principle of military necessity) but it creates rules that aim to ensure that the damage that results from armed conflict is minimized and that unnecessary suffering is not inflicted upon any person. IHL does not prohibit all forms of killing or violence during armed conflict. Indeed, one of the purposes of IHL is to provide clear rules as to when it is lawful to kill during armed conflict. However, IHL requires that parties to a conflict only do whatever is necessary to win the war. The only legitimate aim of a war is to weaken the military force of the other side. It is not therefore legitimate for parties to a conflict to pursue other aims, e.g. deliberately killing innocent civilians, instil fear in the civilian population by using sexual violence as a weapon of war, or to attempt to exterminate or displace an entire ethnic group out of a particular location (sometimes referred to as 'ethnic cleansing'). IHL essentially seeks to limit human suffering and ensure that any conflict is strictly regulated and carried out on the basis of legal rules. In this section we discuss a number of foundational principles of international law. While these principles might seem straightforward when they are read in a textbook, the practical application of these principles is hugely problematic and it gives rise to lengthy legal and political debates.

Box 11.5 IHL basic principles: military necessity

- Parties to a conflict are allowed to do whatever is necessary to win the war (in line with IHL).
- The only legitimate object of war is to weaken the military force of the enemy.
- Military necessity cannot be invoked as a reason for violating IHL.
- There must be a balance struck between humanity and military necessity.

Underpinning IHL is the idea that human beings should be treated in ways that recognize their moral worth and dignity. One of the central purposes and features of IHL is to limit human suffering and protect innocent victims of conflict and out-of-action fighters (*hors de combat*). Thus, parties to a conflict are not allowed to randomly kill, torture, starve, or lay siege to innocent civilians and they must respect the dignity of all *hors de combat*. Every person must be treated with dignity and humanity and IHL provides many extensive rules that set out how particular groups should be protected in both international and non-international armed conflicts. Different rules govern the protection of civilians, medical personnel, *hors de combat*, prisoners of war, journalists, humanitarian workers, religious personnel, and other categories of people.

> **Box 11.6** IHL basic principles: protection of humanity and the prohibition of superfluous injury and unnecessary suffering
>
> - All human beings must be treated with humanity and parties must respect human dignity. The principle of humanity means that parties to a conflict are not, for example, able to kill and maim at random, ethnically cleanse populations, forcibly displace civilians, burn down religious monuments, torture, use sexual violence as a weapon of war, or use cruel, inhumane, or degrading treatment of any kind against any human being.
> - Although the killing of combatants is allowed, IHL prohibits inhumane and painful ways of killing (e.g. drowning and torture).
> - Some weapons have been outlawed as they cause superfluous injury and unnecessary suffering (e.g. chemical, biological, and poisonous weapons, expanding and exploding bullets, and weapons primarily causing injury by non-detectable fragments).

Common Article 3 of the Geneva Conventions sets out the minimum standards for armed conflicts and calls for humane treatment of those not directly taking part in hostilities. The principle of humane treatment is also the basis of treatment of prisoners of war, the duty to allow access for humanitarian relief and medical personnel, treatment of civilians, respect for the dead, and a duty to inform families about the fate of missing persons. All of these sub areas of IHL, therefore, include positive duties or prohibitive actions to fulfil the aim of respect for the moral worth of humans. The killing of innocent civilians, torture, sexual violence, mutilation of dead, bodies and medical experimentation are prohibited and respect for humanitarian relief personnel, and protection of medical personnel are required. Implicit in the appeal to values common to all humanity is also the idea that there is nothing to gain from not fulfilling these duties and observing these prohibitions and that the IHL rules that stem from the principle for respect should be seen as separate from maximizing military gain during a conflict. The principle of reciprocity also does not apply to such rules. For example, the fact that one party to a conflict tortures prisoners of war does not give the other party the right to torture the prisoners of war from the other side. If both parties torture prisoners of war, both are regarded as having acting unlawfully and they may be prosecuted for violating IHL.

The principle of humanity also relates to the protection of fighters as well as civilians. While IHL recognizes the legitimacy of killing combatants in certain circumstances (where this is justified by military necessity) it also places restrictions upon the killing of combatants and prohibits superfluous injury and unnecessary suffering.

Box 11.7 Common Article 3 to the four Geneva Conventions

Common Article 3 to the four Geneva Conventions:

- applies to any armed conflict not of an international character occurring in any state;
- provides the basic minimum guarantees of humanity and it is accepted as customary international law; and
- binds all parties to the conflict including state military forces and non-state groups, including rebels.

Common Article 3 prohibits:

- violence to life and person, in particular murder of all kinds, mutilation, cruel treatment, and torture;
- discrimination of any kind (e.g. based on race, colour, religion or faith, sex, birth, wealth, or any other similar criteria);
- hostage taking;
- outrages upon personal dignity, in particular humiliating and degrading treatment;
- passing of sentences and the carrying out of executions without previous judgment pronounced by a regularly constituted court, affording all the judicial guarantees which are recognized as indispensable by civilized peoples.

Common Article 3 also sets out that the wounded and sick shall be collected and cared for and sets out that an impartial humanitarian body, such as the International Committee of the Red Cross, may offer its services to the parties to the conflict.

IHL requires all parties to a conflict to balance military necessity inherent in armed conflicts with humanitarian principles that aim to protect the basic human interest in freedom from suffering. Balancing military necessity and humanity requires parties to an armed conflict to ensure that they respect the principle of distinction and to ensure that any action carried out is proportional to its aim. Achieving the correct balance between military necessity and humanity is not a straightforward or an easy matter. While IHL provides rules and principles it does not provide textbook answers or any easy solutions. Parties to armed conflicts are required to make quick decisions about actions that may have devastating impacts upon human lives or the environment. The decisions that they make will never be ideal and will be subject to long-term legal and political scrutiny and criticism.

The **principle of distinction** determines who is a legitimate target during the conduct of hostilities. This principle states that combatants and civilians, military objectives and civilian objects must be distinguished at all times and attacks can only be directed against combatants and military objectives. Civilians cannot be deliberately targeted so long as they do not take direct part in hostilities. Following on from the principle of distinction, attacks that cannot discriminate between combatants and civilians are prohibited. It is important to note that this has been made lawful only after World War II. Techniques such as carpet bombing used in Germany and Japan by the UK and the USA were regarded as efficient ways to end the conflict. The ban in indiscriminate attacks in the 1949 Geneva Conventions has influenced the course of technology and carpet bombing has largely fallen away to precision bombing in current modern warfare, as we have seen during the first Gulf War of 1990.

Box 11.8 IHL basic principles: the principle of distinction and proportionality

- In order to protect humanity armed forces are required to distinguish between military and civilian targets and they are only allowed to direct their operations against military objectives.

- IHL prohibits the direct targeting of civilians and civilian targets such as schools, religious buildings, patrimonial sites, and hospitals.

- A party to the conflict may only target a civilian object in exceptional circumstances where there is clear evidence that a civilian object is being used for military purposes and where it can justify an attack on the basis of military necessity. Any such attack must be proportionate to the aim.

- In modern non-international conflicts, civilians and military targets are often not easy to distinguish, for example, where fighting is carried out by rebels that operate out of densely populated civilian areas.

- IHL obliges all parties to a conflict to ensure that their actions are proportional to the military aim.

- A disproportionate attack is 'an attack which may be expected to cause incidental loss of civilian life, injury to civilians, damage to civilian objects, or a combination thereof, which would be excessive in relation to the concrete and direct military advantage anticipated' (Protocol 1 Article 51).

During any armed conflict all parties to a conflict are required to ask a number of important questions before carrying out an attack. Commanders must make decisions about what they can target, which weapons they can use, and what kind of impact a specific military action will have on people and the environment.

In essence, IHL sets out rules that determine *who* can and cannot be attacked; *what* can and cannot be attacked and *how* the attackable can be attacked.

The **principle of proportionality** requires the weighing of the concrete and direct military advantage and the incidental loss to civilians, and damage to civilian objects for each attack and other strategic decisions. If the latter is anticipated to be excessive in relation to the former, that attack is prohibited under IHL. The principle of proportionality is a cornerstone of targeting decisions during armed conflicts where military objectives are located in civilian areas or the conflict is fought in densely populated areas. This principle does not apply to the conflict as a whole, rather, it is a guiding principle for each and every strategic decision taken by the commanders. IHL does not provide a list of the number of injuries or deaths that would be acceptable when pursuing a particular military aim. This means that every situation must be analysed on the basis of the information available at the time in good faith—an extremely complex and controversial task.

IHL prohibits both indiscriminate attacks (e.g. carpet bombing) and disproportionate attacks. A disproportionate attack is one that leads to excessive civilian damage and/or casualties. While IHL does prohibit both indiscriminate and disproportionate attacks, this does not mean that all civilian deaths and injuries that result during war are unlawful. Parties to an armed conflict and in particular commanders are required to take all feasible precautions to ensure that any attack complies with the basic principles of IHL that we have discussed.

The **principle of precaution** goes hand in hand with proportionality and it demands that constant care is taken to spare the civilian population; civilians and civilian objects. The precautions need to be feasible and should be aimed at minimizing incidental loss and injury. The precaution principle applies to both decisions of targeting and choice of weapons. It requires parties to have made an assessment prior to any attack and to cancel any attack which becomes apparent to be disproportionate. Parties should also give advance warning prior to attacks. This principle also applies to the party receiving the attacks and it requires states or other groups to protect the civilian population against the effects of attacks. Parties to a conflict also have a duty to avoid locating military objectives in densely populated areas and to remove civilians from the vicinity of military objectives.

Box 11.9 Collateral damage

IHL prohibits the direct targeting of civilians and civilian objects and provides that any attacks carried out must be proportionate to the military aim. When planning an attack, parties to a conflict, in particular commanders, are obliged on the basis of the information that they have available to them to ask themselves the following questions:

- Is there a military purpose to the planned action? If so what is it?
- Is what I want to attack a military objective? Does the attack properly distinguish between civilians and military personnel and objectives?
- What means and methods can I use to ensure that the attack is not indiscriminate or disproportionate? What weapons can I lawfully use?
- Will this attack lead to any unnecessary suffering?

Taking precautions prior to attack is an obligation under IHL. However, as there is no outright prohibition of killing under IHL it may be that an attack that leads to the loss of civilian life or civilian injury may be deemed to be lawful if it can be demonstrated that commanders took all necessary precautions and carried out their attack in line with the rules of IHL. In such a situation any loss of civilian life or injury to civilians may not be viewed as unlawful. Where civilians are killed or injured as a result of an attack carried out according to the rules of IHL it is sometimes referred to as 'collateral damage'. This is a colloquial term often used in international relations to describe incidental loss of life, injury to persons, or damage to property and the environment. Attacks that do lead to incidental loss of life but are lawful raise a number of ethical, moral, and political questions.

Sceptics of IHL might argue that minimizing the effects of killing is a slippery slope and it is difficult to constrain the logic that sits at the core of armed conflict: to destroy the enemy. It is inconceivable for armed conflicts to be sterile, especially when conflicts are fought in densely civilian-populated areas or when it is difficult to draw a distinction between a fighter and a civilian. The difficulty of minimizing the actual suffering of armed conflict, however, does not mean that there cannot be any principles or rules that guide the decisions of those employing military power. IHL does not challenge the fact that some types of killing are lawful within the context of armed conflicts. Combatants have a licence to kill other combatants and destroy military targets. IHL also recognizes that a combatant in an international armed conflict cannot be prosecuted for taking part in hostilities and has immunities as a prisoner of war. This is the starting point of IHL: it aims to establish which forms of violence are legitimate and which ones are not during armed conflicts. However, the prohibition of superfluous injury or unnecessary suffering and the principles of distinction—proportionality taken together with the obligation to take precautions—have proved to be powerful tools that have emerged and which go some way to minimize the effects of conflict.

Compliance with international humanitarian law

The assessment of the theoretical and empirical conditions of compliance with IHL is a complex enterprise as it requires making some assumptions about the motivations of states agreeing to IHL norms in the first place, the indicators for compliance and the relationship between non-compliance and accountability. There are also further questions about the assessment of the compliance of non-state actors with IHL. We will discuss these issues in turn.

Motivations of states and IHL: why do states agree to rules that govern armed conflict?

The central discussion about motivations of states concerning IHL takes place between those who think that states are agents that can act out of humanitarian compassion and for norm-driven reasons and those who think that a state's reason for agreeing to IHL are self-interested and instrumental reasons with the view of maximizing its own interests and preferences. Posner categorizes these camps as optimists and pessimists about the basis for agreement on IHL rules (Posner 2002). These camps also correspond with constructivists and realist rationalists in international theory (see Chapter 2). Constructivists emphasize the power of IHL norms to provide a framework for engaging in armed conflict and the way in which IHL provides the very vocabulary and constitutive rules to make sense of armed conflict. IHL enables the international community to evaluate the conduct of wars and the attribution of blame to states and individuals for their action in the light of rules agreed by the international community. The principle of distinction between civilians and combatants, for example, is a central concept to assess attribution of blame. Many IHL rules are also action-guiding for a diverse number of actors during conflicts and they enable these actors to have expectations about the conduct of civilians, combatants, the medical and humanitarian personnel. An empirical factor on the side of the constructivists is the existence of a wide corpus of IHL agreed by a large number of states. IHL, therefore, can be regarded as a field of international law where socialization is high and persuasion with the content of norms is an important aspect of compliance.

Realist-rationalists, on the other hand, emphasize that states, especially in times of armed conflict, primarily seek to ensure their security and material power. This very condition makes states instrumental agents in deciding which rules it will confirm and which it will not and humanitarianism has to be seen in terms of instrumental value in deciding whether it will pull towards compliance. Rationalists also emphasize that the logic of reciprocity is central to understanding IHL and that the erosion of trust between parties to observe the IHL rules is a powerful factor for an actor to put humanitarian considerations aside, however appealing they may be from a legal or moral perspective. This view, therefore, holds that actors do not follow IHL because they are moved by considerations of humanity, but because following rules offers them a comparative advantage compared to not following the rules. Once a state decides that the comparative advantage is no longer there, it will flout the rules. IHL compliance is successful as long as a state thinks that it advances its own security or its interests. Realist-rationalist arguments find empirical support in the behaviour of major powers towards IHL. For example, it is significant to note that China, India, Russia, and the United States are not parties to the 1997 Ottawa Convention on Anti-Personnel Landmines. United States and India are not parties to the 1977 Additional Protocols to the Geneva Conventions. In the case of landmines, we can see that these states still see an additional utility in using landmines in conflicts. In the case of the Second Additional Protocol to the Geneva Conventions on the Protection of Civilians in non-international armed conflicts, the realist-rational argument that this Protocol gives undue protection to insurgents is prominent.

It seems that it is not fruitful to approach this debate as an either/or scenario. It is true that IHL is the language of the conduct of armed conflicts and all state actors debate the terms of their or others' behaviour within the boundaries of this language. Even in the case of the US argument that the terrorists they fight do not meet the prisoner-of-war status laid down in laws of war (Paust 2007), the point is the challenge of the settled norms of IHL rather than refusing the laws of war altogether. It is, however, also true that adhering to a language does not in itself point to respect for the law. There may be reputational benefits to be seen to be adhering to the language of laws of war, with not much cost against it.

There is, however, also evidence that IHL is not just language. IHL is diffused into practices of all armed forces: this is a requirement of the 1949 Geneva Conventions. Every state trains its armed forces based on IHL rules, and Hague and Geneva regulations in particular. It is also true, however, that reciprocity is the basis of IHL-compliant behaviour and IHL defines the terms of such reciprocity. The rules of IHL also respond to giving due recognition to the interests of states. The interests of states in securing military objectives and avoiding loss and injury of their own civilian population and civilian objects, is recognized by IHL. In this respect, IHL states that in order for a state to secure its own interests of military advancement and security of its own people it has to agree to rules that also protect the security of the enemy civilians. This logic also applies at the level of the individual in the battlefield. In order to be treated humanely as a prisoner of war, it is in the interest of a soldier to treat another prisoner of war humanely. IHL, therefore, operates by persuading actors about the reasons to comply with the IHL and some states are more socialized into IHL principles than others. There is, further, an argumentative dimension to IHL, especially encouraged by the proportionality and precautionary principles. Because both of these principles are heavily fact sensitive, they require discussions and debates in good faith in order to establish whether they have been respected or not.

Indicators of compliance

IHL includes hundreds of specific rules, prohibitions, and duties that are codified in over fifty treaties and by customary international law. When we study specific instances of compliance in specific conflicts, whether the conflict is international or non-international internal, and whether the treaties are ratified by the parties to the conflict, make a significant difference in assessing compliance. We can approach indicators for compliance by focusing on central topics within the IHL regime.

Box 11.10 Indicators for compliance with IHL

1. Compliance with prohibited acts during armed conflict (i.e. torture, hostage taking).
2. Compliance with positive obligations during armed conflict (i.e. duty to inform the families of missing persons).
3. Compliance with proportionality and precautionary principles in the planning of a military operation.
4. Compliance with duty to train military on IHL rules and principles.
5. Compliance with prosecuting individuals for breaches of IHL (see also Chapter 12).

These different areas or indicators of compliance correspond to different types of obligations that states agree to undertake in IHL. The fifth area on the list is particularly important as states have a duty to prosecute and punish individuals who fail to observe the rules of IHL. As will be discussed in Chapter 12, violations of IHL has a special form of jurisdiction under international law: universal jurisdiction. When we take this multidimensional view of compliance, we find, for example, that an army is complying with prohibitive acts or the proportionality principle but that it does not prosecute its soldiers who violate IHL. Conversely, we may find cases where IHL training is low, but prosecution rates are high. Different types of indicators for IHL, therefore, can show different types of compliance behaviour of a single state.

Non-compliance and accountability

Unlike the developments in other areas of international law, such as international human rights law (see Chapter 13), there are no international courts or bodies that are specifically charged with assessing compliance with IHL. The Geneva Conventions of 1949 leave this primarily to states themselves and as we discussed earlier, states are under a duty to try individuals alleged to have committed war crimes and punish those individuals in the light of the facts and the IHL rules. This institutional design is thought to be flawed by some as it enables the states to be the judges of their own performances in times of armed conflict. Violations of IHL that stem from failure to observe principles of proportionality and precaution are especially suspect to this charge as these principles require implementation at the highest ranks of the military responsible for overall strategy of a war. Considering the close relationship between high military ranks and politicians, it is clear to see that there is not a strong incentive structure to prosecute violations of IHL involving high-ranking commanders and political orders. A particular response to this problem has been to criminalize some gravely heinous acts, such as the intention to destroy a people or 'ethnic cleansing', internationally—Chapter 12 discusses these in greater detail. It is, however, important to note that even though IHL is unique in that is creates individual duties under international law, the statist nature of enforcing such duties presents an obstacle for gaining compliance by high-level political and military leaders. From a more sociological perspective, states tend to become more protective of their political leaders and armies in times of conflict. This also has an effect on lack of prosecutions of leaders for violations of IHL.

There are a number of international institutional avenues that can be triggered to hold persons that do not comply with IHL to account. In the case of international armed conflicts, one of the state parties can bring a case to the International Court of Justice if both parties accept the voluntary jurisdiction of this court (see Chapter 8). A case can also be brought against an individual before the International Criminal Court if the state where the suspected war crime is committed is a party to the International Criminal Court Statute or where the state of the person committing the war crime is a party (see Chapter 12). Both of these avenues, however, depend on the consent of the states to be called into account or allow their national to be tried before international courts. The accountability mechanisms for violations of IHL in times of internal conflicts are, on the other hand, much fewer. Members of rebel forces, when captured by state forces are subject to criminal prosecution under the domestic laws of that country. Members of state forces, however, escape accountability in most cases, as either the state does not recognize that IHL is applicable or the state does not prosecute members of its own armed forces for their conduct in defending their own territories. The internal conflicts in South America and Europe have been an exception to this defensive principle as civilians were able to bring cases against security forces before regional human rights courts in places such as Colombia, Peru, the United Kingdom, Turkey, and Russia (see Chapter 13).

Non-state actors and compliance with international humanitarian law

IHL rules assume that if an armed force with an identifiable command structure is involved in an armed conflict, be it international or non-international, it is bound by the rules of IHL. Members of such forces have the same obligations that states have to respect the rules of IHL. The criterion to trigger IHL duties for a non-state armed group is its capacity to behave as an army. The logic of reciprocity also applies to conflicts between two non-state armed groups or between a state and a non-state armed group. The IHL requirements can be conceived as a measure to protect a group's own security and secure humane treatment of its armed forces. There are also examples of observance of IHL by non-state actors by committing themselves to commitments, declarations, or codes of conduct (Clapham 2006). Secessionist non-state actors have a further incentive to follow IHL rules in order to receive acceptance and recognition as an insurgency movement internationally. In this respect, compliance with IHL can also be seen through an instrumental lens as a way of contributing to the future status and reputation of a non-state actor group.

There are also, however, a significant number of civil conflicts where such incentive structures do not exist. This may be due to the lack of interest amongst fighting parties to receive international legitimacy or recognition, collapse of mutual trust between the parties and escalation of violence, the lack of checks and balances within a non-state armed group, the inability of the armed group to discipline its individual members, the lack of international pressure and monitoring, or the existence of a very unequal power relationship between parties to the conflict.

The latter scenario has especially devastating effects on IHL observance. When a party to a conflict has a significant military disadvantage, it tends to fight the conflict in dense civilian areas, to use civilians as human shields, or encourage its combatants not to respect rules of openly carrying arms and wearing distinctive signs in order to indicate their combatant status. All of these acts themselves constitute violations of IHL.

There is, however, the further problem of how the stronger party conducts its actions in the face of such behaviour. For example, IHL suggests that the principle of distinction should be respected in all targeting decisions. This principle does not, however, specifically deal with the use of voluntary and forced human shields. While some argue that a voluntary human shield is someone who loses his or her protection as a civilian and becomes a legitimate target, others disagree and argue the principle of proportionality and precaution requires the attacker to consider all other ways before targeting a civilian. It is also a matter of debate as to whether a forced human shield can be a military target. Non-state actor non-compliance with IHL, therefore, puts into danger the compliance of the other parties to the conflict, be it state and non-state actor.

The increase in the privatization of armed conflicts creates a further challenge for compliance of non-state actors with IHL. The involvement of private military companies (PMCs) (employed by both states and non-state actors) gives rise to a new set of complex questions of how to ensure PMCs follow IHL and are held responsible for IHL violations. Abuses of IHL by PMCs, such as the involvement of members of PMCs in the torture and inhuman interrogation techniques in the Abu Ghraib prison in Iraq (Singer 2007) demonstrate the importance of this issue.

The contracting out of military activities to private companies is often used by governments as a way of avoiding soldier fatalities and avoiding public criticism at home and abroad. Like individual members of armed groups, individuals working for PMCs are responsible for IHL violations. However, IHL also assumes that individuals participate in hostilities under clear command structures and that there is an institutional framework to train, discipline, and prosecute a soldier under domestic law. Because PMCs are private companies or corporations, their employees do not have the same kind of relationship to the state that a soldier has. This different kind of relationship between the state and the private company and the company and the privately employed soldier creates a structural barrier that prevents systematic respect for IHL by PMCs. This structural problem is part of a wider policy debate about how PMCs should be regulated and who should regulate them to ensure that they do not violate principles of IHL.

Conclusion

In this chapter we provided an overview of the basic principles of the body of international law that regulates armed conflicts: international humanitarian law. We highlighted that IHL is a unique body of international law that creates direct duties not only for states, but also for armed groups and individuals under international law.

This challenges the interstate outlook on international law. We first set out where this body of law can be found and which topics and relationships it regulates and we outlined some unique features of this body of law. We then explored the purposes of IHL and the conceptual tools and principles it employs in order to reach these purposes. We highlighted that compliance with IHL is a good prism to evaluate the debate between constructivism and realist-institutionalism in international relations as reaching military objectives and defending one's own nation and people and rules that regulate conflicts have a complex relationship conceding points to each side of the debate. We finally discussed the complexities around compliance and non-state actors and the reasons of incentive and motivation structures for non-state armed groups and private military companies in complying with IHL rules.

Case Study 11.1 Internal conflicts and international responses

Arcadia is a state made up of two ethnic groups: the Arcadians (80%) and the Utopians (20%).

The Government of Arcadia is comprised entirely of Arcadians. Over the past ten years, the Arcadian Government has systematically discriminated against Utopians in Arcadia. The Arcadian Government has banned Utopians from attending university, working in the government, and accessing the social welfare and health systems. Thousands of Utopians have been detained without trial for 'crimes against the Arcadian state' and many thousands have simply 'disappeared'.

Five years ago, frustrated with the denial of their rights, a group of Utopians formed the Utopian Liberation Front (ULF). Since that time, ULF has been fighting against the Arcadian Government. The fighting is confined to the north of Arcadia around the city of Oxford which is populated by Utopians.

Two years ago, the Arcadian Government commenced 'Operation Anti-Terror', a military campaign aimed at eradicating the ULF. The Arcadian Government has stated that 'Operation Anti-Terror' is a necessary and legitimate response to the terrorist threat posed by the ULF in Arcadia.

On the 20 May, the Arcadian military received credible information that ULF fighters have established a strategic base in the city of Oxford. The city of Oxford is under ULF control. The commander of the Arcadian military believes that ULF is storing weapons in a Utopian mosque and has established an important communications centre in a hospital. Both the mosque and the hospital are in the centre of Oxford and both are being used by the civilian population. There are around 400 patients in the hospital and 60 people pray at the mosque each day. The commander of the Arcadian military is planning to deploy fighter jets equipped with the latest precision targeting systems over Oxford to attack the mosque and the hospital from the air.

Discuss the lawfulness of the planned attacks on the mosque and hospital. What specific issues would the Commander of the Arcadian forces need to take into consideration when planning this attack to ensure that it complies with IHL? What additional information, if any, would the Commander need to know in advance of the attack?

On the 22 May, the commander of the Arcadian armed forces authorizes his forces to carry out the air attacks on the mosque and the hospital. The attack takes place at 16.00 hrs. The attack on the hospital leads to the death of all 400 patients and 100 medical and other staff. The attack on the mosque leaves 5 dead and 59 injured.

The world media, the United Nations, and the international diplomatic community are extremely concerned about the loss of civilian life and injuries that resulted from the attack carried out by Arcadian forces on the hospital and mosque. You are a diplomat working for the Draconian Government, the current president of the UN Security Council and you have been asked to prepare a brief on the attacks and possible courses of action. How would you structure your brief?

Questions

1. What is armed conflict and how is it defined in IHL?
2. How is IHL different from other types of international law?
3. What is the relationship between IHL, international history, and the advancement of technology?
4. What are the central topics covered by IHL?
5. What does the 'humanization' of IHL mean and how could we assess this?
6. What are the central purposes of IHL? How does the body of rules of IHL achieve such purposes? (We recommend reading through the treaties in order to answer this question.)
7. What are the basic principles of IHL?
8. What motivates states to be bound by IHL?
9. Should states disregard IHL when they are fighting with non-state actors with no regard to IHL?
10. What challenges do private military companies bring to IHL?
11. Is there a need to rethink the basic principle and rules of IHL?

Further reading

Detter, I. (2000) *Law of War* (Cambridge: Cambridge University Press). *A comprehensive discussion of the contemporary challenges to international humanitarian law and changing legal context of modern warfare.*

Dinstein, Y. (2005) *War, Aggression and Self-Defence* (Cambridge: Cambridge University Press). *A comprehensive analysis of international humanitarian rules and how rules apply in real-time situations, such as the conflicts in Iraq and Afghanistan.*

Henckaerts, J. M and Doswald-Beck, L. (2005) *Customary International Law*. Vol. 1: The Rules (Cambridge: Cambridge University Press). *A compilation and analysis of customary international humanitarian law that applies during international and internal armed conflicts in the light of the developments in state practice.*

Meron, T. (2000) 'The Humanization of Humanitarian Law' *American Journal of International Law* 94: 67–121. *A comprehensive account of how principles of humanity and respect have permeated into the corpus of international humanitarian law.*

Posner, E. (2002) *A Theory on the Laws of War* (Chicago: Chicago Law Papers). *A realist-rationalist analysis of the reasons states have for making and complying with international humanitarian law.*

Roberts, A. (2008) 'The Equal Application of the Laws of War: A Principle Under Pressure' *International Review of the Red Cross* 90/872: 931–62. *A thorough analysis of whether international humanitarian law should apply differently to those involved in fighting depending on the worth of their causes for fighting.*

Singer, P. W. (2007) *Corporate Warriors: The Rise of the Privatised Military Industry*, 2nd rev. edn. (Ithaca: Cornell University Press). *A comprehensive discussion of the history of the privatization of the military and the problems the privatization poses for regulation.*

Websites

http://www.icrc.org *Website of the International Committee of the Red Cross containing all the relevant legal documents on IHL, a database of national implementation, and access to the leading journal, The International Review of the Red Cross.*

http://www.icrc.org/Web/eng/siteeng0.nsf/html/party_main_treaties *This specific link belongs to the International Committee of the Red Cross and it provides a list of all states parties to main international humanitarian law treaties.*

http://www.icrc.org/ihl *Database providing the texts of over 100 international humanitarian law treaties and commentaries on the meanings of articles on some of the core treaties.*

http://www.crimesofwar.org *This is an excellent introduction to the main principles of IHL, including comments on application of IHL to ongoing conflicts by experts.*

http://www.crisisgroup.org *This is an excellent website to get information about recent conflicts around the world providing factual information as well as political analysis.*

http://www.icrc.org/web/eng/siteeng0.nsf/htmlall/montreux-document-170908 *The full text and commentary on the Montreux Document on Private Military and Security Companies.*

Visit the Online Resource Centre that accompanies this book to access more learning resources www.oxfordtextbooks.co.uk/orc/cali/

Chapter 12

International criminal law

Paola Gaeta

CHAPTER CONTENTS

- Introduction
- The birth and evolution of international criminal law
- The core crimes and the rationale behind their international criminalization
- The enforcement of international criminal law at the international level
- The relationship between international criminal courts and national courts: primacy versus complementarity
- Conclusion

CHAPTER OVERVIEW

This chapter explains what international criminal law is and why and when it has asserted itself as a branch of international law. The first part of the chapter outlines the birth and evolution of international criminal law, focusing on the main three phases of this process. Next, it explains the reasons behind the international criminalization of conducts amounting to the so-called 'core crimes' (war crimes, crimes against humanity, and genocide). Finally, it examines the main features of the most well-known international criminal courts and tribunals, the merits and demerits of international criminal proceedings in comparison to domestic proceedings, and the coordination between the judicial activities of international criminal courts and national courts in the repression of international crimes.

Introduction

International criminal law is a branch of international law made up by rules on the personal criminal accountability of individuals for conducts amounting to international crimes. International criminal law directly attaches criminal account-ability only with respect to international crimes proper, which comprise the so-called 'core crimes': war crimes, crimes against humanity, and genocide. All these crimes express what can be called 'state criminality', for they are crimes usually perpetrated by state officials in their official capacity, often with the tolerance, acquiescence or direct support of the apparatus of the state. Their direct criminalization under inter-national law is now undisputable. It has its roots in the gradual emergence of a set of 'supra-national' values, proper to the international community as a whole, that must be safeguarded against those states that—through their individual organs or their whole apparatus—disregard them.

The assertion of international criminal law as a branch of international law is a recent phenomenon that occurred around the early 1990s, with the establishment of international criminal courts. Until that time, the criminalization and repres-sion of international crimes was entirely left to national courts, and international law merely confined itself to enjoin individual states to punish those crimes, and to enhance their judicial cooperation (in the field of extradition and collection of evidence abroad) to ensure their repression.

The international law approach to international crimes aims to specify what kinds of obligations states have in punishing individuals who commit international crimes and what institutional arrangements need to be in place for the effectiveness of international criminal law. Theories of international relations, on the other hand, adopt varying degrees of a scepticism or optimism towards international criminal law. Sceptic positions highlight that international criminal law will be abused by states and states will only cooperate with international courts or organizations if they are coerced or if it is in their interests to do so. Scepticism towards international law is further supported by the fact that most powerful states in the world are not parties to the International Criminal Court, but they unilaterally declare situations in the world as international crimes. Realist theories of international law, in particu-lar, explain this scepticism by suggesting that the anarchical nature of the society makes it impossible for the altruistic application of international criminal law. The more optimistic accounts on the other hand, emphasize the transformative nature of international criminal law and how the institutionalization of international crimes can shape the interests of state actors. The mobilization of non-governmental actors and domestic courts by international criminal law may also shape the attitudes and preferences of state actors towards international criminal law.

This chapter aims to trace the development of the normative framework of inter-national criminal law and its institutions. It identifies two significant contribu-tions of international criminal law to understanding international relations. First, international criminal law modifies the state sovereignty doctrine in the area of criminal justice by creating the category of international crimes. Most international relations theories grapple with the idea that over a hundred states in the world have accepted that international and domestic political decisions have criminal components that can be prosecuted domestically or internationally. The normative force of this idea, rather than narrowly defined self-interests of states, does most of the work in explaining the widespread commitment to international criminal law. Second, the institutional framework of international criminal law (the International Criminal Court) is based on the diffusion of principles of international criminal law in domestic states, especially amongst the domestic judiciary. This sets in motion the empowerment of domestic judges as important actors of international law in the areas of international crimes.

Box 12.1 International crimes versus transnational crimes

International crimes must not be confused with another class of crimes, which are sometimes also described as 'international' crimes on account of their strong transnational dimension, but that are committed by private individuals for private purposes (think, for instance, of piracy, money laundering, counterfeiting of currency, drug trafficking, corruption, trafficking in human beings, and so on). International criminal law does not deal with this class of crimes, that can better be termed 'transnational crimes'. The role of international law in respect to this class of crimes is simply to provide the appropriate framework to allow states to better organize the joint repression of such crimes, in particular by way of treaties on judicial cooperation. The idea is that states usually have a strong interest in repressing those crimes that are transnational in nature and jeopardize their common interests. Therefore, there is no need for international law to directly deal with them, to avoid impunity, as instead is the case with international crimes proper.

The birth and evolution of international criminal law

The first phase: the Nuremberg and Tokyo Tribunals

It was with the establishment of the International Military Tribunal at Nuremberg (IMT or Nuremberg Tribunal) and the International Military Tribunal for the Far East (Tokyo Tribunal) that, for the first time in history, the principle according to which individuals acting on behalf and with the protection of their state can be held personally accountable for crimes committed in violation of international law was asserted. This was a landmark event. Until then, subject to limited exceptions, foreign national courts were not allowed to sit in judgment over individuals who had acted as state representatives, for the international rules and principles on state immunity shielded them from criminal accountability. The predominant doctrine was that state officials could only be judged by their own courts, to ensure that foreign states did not interfere, through their judicial systems, in the exercise of the sovereign authority of other states. In practice, the doctrine of state immunity guaranteed impunity for crimes committed by state officials under the colour of law, since it was highly implausible that the national courts of those officials would have sat in judgment over crimes expressing 'state criminality'. At the international level, the only available remedy when those crimes were committed was to claim the international responsibility of the state as such, and require the states to provide reparation for the illegal conduct of its state officials. In a well known dictum, the Nuremberg Tribunal wiped out this doctrine and asserted the following principle: 'Crimes against international law are committed by men, not by abstract entities, and only by punishing individuals who commit such crimes can the provisions of international law be enforced.' Since then, the notion of individual criminal accountability of individuals responsible for international crimes has become firmly embedded in international law.

Box 12.2 The Nuremberg and the Tokyo Military Tribunals and trials

The Charter of the International Military Tribunal at Nuremberg (the London Charter) was signed on 6 August 1945 by France, the UK, the US, and the USSR after very difficult negotiations relating to the list and definition of the crimes to be subject to its jurisdiction, as well as the rules of procedure and evidence that the Nuremberg Tribunal had to follow. The London Charter conferred the Nuremberg Tribunal jurisdiction over three classes of crimes: crimes against peace, war crimes, and crimes against humanity. Article 8 ruled out the possibility for the defendants to successfully rely upon having acted *qua* state officials or in obedience to superior orders to escape criminal responsibility. The London Charter provided that each of the signatory states had to appoint one chief prosecutor, one lead judge, and one alternate judge. The prosecution charged twenty-four individuals (Hitler and many others closest to him committed suicide and did not face trial at Nuremberg), the best known among them being Hermann Goering. The Tribunal rendered its final judgment on 30 September and 1 October 1946 (the trial had started one year before, with the receipt of the indictment by the defendants, on 10 October 1945). It acquitted three people on all counts, and found the others guilty on at least one count. One of the most challenging tasks of the Tribunal, from a strictly legal point of view, was to demonstrate that the prosecution of crimes against peace (namely, having waged a war of aggression) did not violate the principle of legality in criminal matters; in other words, that the Tribunal was not exercising criminal jurisdiction over a conduct that, at the moment it was carried out, was not considered as a criminal act. In this regard the Tribunal pointed out that various international treaties, such as the 1928 Kellogg-Briand Pact and the 1924 Protocol for the Pacific Settlement of International Disputes, banned resort to wars of aggression. As regards the unavailability of the defence of having acted *qua* state officials or in obedience to superior orders, the Nuremberg Tribunal asserted that 'individuals have international duties which transcend the national obligations of obedience imposed by the individual state' and that 'the principle of international law, which under certain circumstances protects the representatives of a state cannot be applied to acts which are condemned as criminal by international law'.

The Tokyo Tribunal was established in January 1946, by virtue of a Decree issued by the US General D. MacArthur to implement Article 10 of the Potsdam Declaration (which provided that 'stern justice' was to be done for war criminals). Its Statute was very similar to that of the Nuremberg Tribunal, and conferred on the Tribunal jurisdiction over crimes against peace, war crimes, and crimes against humanity; again, the Statute of the Tokyo Tribunal ruled out the defence of having acted in an official capacity or in obedience to superior orders. All the signatories of the instrument of surrender of Japan (Australia, Canada, China, France, the Netherlands, New Zealand, the UK, the US, and the USSR), plus India and the Philippines, appointed a judge of the Tribunal. Unlike the Nuremberg Tribunal, there was a sole Chief Prosecutor, a US national (Joseph Keenan). The Presiding Judge was an Australian, Sir William Webb. The trial started on 29 April 1946 and the majority judgment was given in November 1948. The Prosecution had charged twenty-eight people, all of them high level military and political leaders of Japan. All defendants were found guilty on at least one count. (In the meantime, however, one defendant had died and another one was declared unfit to stand trial; in total, therefore, the Tribunal convicted 26 people.) Some judges issued dissenting judgments. In particular, the Dutch Judge B. Roling argued that aggressive war was not a crime entailing personal criminal responsibility under international law.

The second phase: the adoption of treaties for the repression of international crimes by states

After the remarkable experiment made with the establishment of the Nuremberg and Tokyo trials, states decided to cope with international crimes by following the approach that was normally used for the repression of transnational crimes (i.e. crimes committed by private individuals, usually for private ends, but having a strong transnational component—such as drug trafficking, money laundering, and so on: see Box 12.1 above). While debating the establishment of a permanent international criminal court, they drafted treaties or treaty provisions for the prosecution and punishment of crimes such as genocide and war crimes (and also torture and apartheid). These treaties 'simply' enjoined contracting states (1) to criminalize those conducts within their own legal orders and (2) to punish the responsible persons or, for war crimes amounting to grave breaches of the 1949 Geneva Conventions (see Box 12.3), to extradite them to another contracting state. In other words, with regard to crimes perpetrated within the context of state criminality or state violence, the international community reacted by resorting to the traditional institutional framework of adopting specific treaties or treaty rules aimed at imposing on states the duty to criminalize the prohibited conducts, and of organizing judicial cooperation for their repression. International law was simply a tool for the coordination of the exercise of criminal jurisdiction by states, instead of directly criminalizing and punishing conducts amounting to international crimes.

Unfortunately, this traditional institutional framework was not well suited for the prosecution and repression of international crimes, and consequently was seldom employed by contracting states: some of them even failed to pass the necessary implementing national criminal legislation; or, when they possessed all the necessary legal requirements for the exercise of their criminal jurisdiction, they simply failed to make use of such jurisdiction. For a long time the scheme with which national criminal jurisdictions had to deal with forms of state criminality, committed either at home or abroad, simply proved unworkable (and to some extent it still is today). This should come as no surprise: when crimes are committed abroad by state officials on behalf or with the support of their state, third states tend not to interfere with the conduct of such officials, although—faced with mass-scale crimes—international law allows (and in some cases even obliges) them to act. When crimes are committed domestically, various reasons can stand in the way of prosecution: if the crimes are perpetrated under an authoritarian regime, prosecutors and judges have to wait for its toppling; however, when this occurs, amnesty laws are normally passed 'for the sake of' national reconciliation, or immunities, or the statute of limitation are urged by the culprits, or other political and legal hurdles are relied upon.

The turning point: the establishment of international criminal courts

The establishment in the early 1990s of the International Criminal Tribunal for the former Yugoslavia (ICTY) and for Rwanda (ICTR) opened a new era: for the first time in history truly international criminal tribunals were set up to prosecute and punish genocide, crimes against humanity, and war crimes, i.e. the so-called 'core crimes'. Their creation paved the way to the establishment of the International Criminal Court (ICC) in 1998 and of a group of mixed criminal tribunals, some of them with a strong international component as is the case with the Special Court for Sierra Leone. All these international or mixed criminal tribunals exercise their jurisdiction over individuals who may be indicted on account of *criminal rules of a truly international nature*. Those rules are provided for in their constitutive instruments: they describe the prohibited conducts and indicate what criteria must be applied for sentencing; in addition, they are normally supplemented by other international rules, chiefly customary rules, and by general principles of law common to national legal orders. These international and mixed criminal tribunals, in particular the ICTY and the ICTR, have spawned a copious case law, thus contributing to the emergence of new international customary rules supplementing those which already existed. Finally, and more importantly, their functioning, although not flawless, has contributed to disseminating the idea that there are criminal conducts that may not go unpunished, and that individuals responsible for them must be brought to justice.

The international community has therefore begun to enforce its criminal prohibitions through international or quasi-international courts and tribunals that apply international criminal rules directly. In a nutshell, with regard to the core crimes the *ius puniendi* (i.e. the right to punish) has ceased to be an exclusive state prerogative; furthermore, it is exercised at the international level on behalf of the international community as a whole. Plainly, states can still prosecute and punish individuals who engage in those criminal conducts. However, the current exercise of national criminal jurisdiction in this field can better be described as a judicial activity performed for the international community as such, rather than as a modality of exercise of a sovereign power. One could go so far to say that, with respect to the core crimes, the new approach has reversed the traditional one briefly described above: now it is national criminal law and national criminal jurisdictions that constitute the instrument enabling the international community to repress such crimes. These are crimes directly criminalized at the international level. As few international mechanisms have been set up to prosecute and punish the responsible individuals, national judges, if and when they step in and exercise their criminal jurisdiction over those crimes, also act as judicial organs of the international community thereby accomplishing a sort of *dédoublement fonctionnel* (role splitting), a phenomenon well known to international lawyers and of which some national courts seemed to have been fully aware.[1] It is as though the international community, still an imperfect community, availed itself of national criminal courts to enforce its criminal prohibitions.

Be that as it may, we can however conclude that in the field of core crimes there now exists a branch of international law comprising a truly *international* criminal law.

The core crimes and the rationale behind their international criminalization

International crimes, as noted above, encompass war crimes, crimes against humanity, and genocide. The international criminalization of each of these crimes has its own rationale and has followed its own path.

War crimes

War crimes comprise serious violations of international rules regulating the conduct of the belligerent parties during an armed conflict (so-called 'international humanitarian law' or the 'laws of war/armed conflicts') (see Chapter 11). The rationale behind the assertion of individual criminal liability under international law for war crimes can be traced back to the eighteenth century, when national criminal codes and military manuals started providing for the right of a belligerent to prosecute and punish his own soldiers for violations of the laws of war. As for war crimes committed by enemy personnel or civilians, it would seem that the power of a belligerent to exercise his criminal jurisdiction was initially limited to the time of the armed conflict and, in any case, only within occupied territories. However, armistice or peace treaties could contain a clause whereby the victorious belligerent imposed upon the defeated states the obligation to surrender alleged war criminals for trial. World War I abruptly launched the discourse on war crimes in the international arena. Article 228 of the Peace Treaty of Versailles constitutes the first clear international recognition of the right of a belligerent party to bring to justice persons belonging to the other belligerents for violations of the laws and customs of war after the end of hostilities.[2] The path towards criminalization of war crimes developed through: (1) the establishment of the Nuremberg and Tokyo Tribunals; (2) the adoption of specific provisions in the four 1949 Geneva Conventions on the protection of the victims of war and the 1977 Additional Protocol (namely the provisions on the so-called 'grave breaches'); and (3) a set of criminal provisions contained in few other treaties of international humanitarian law. This process culminated in the 1990s, with the creation by the UN Security Council of the ICTY and the ICTR, and with the establishment of the ICC and other international criminal courts and tribunals. The rationale behind the international criminalization of conducts involving serious violations of the rules of international humanitarian law is clear. It lies in the need to ensure—also by way of a threat of criminal sanctions—that some elementary principles and considerations of humanity are respected in warlike situations, so as to reduce the suffering and misery caused by war as much as possible.

Box 12.3 Definition and classes of war crimes

War crimes are serious violations of the laws of armed conflict entailing individual criminal accountability under international law. The laws of armed conflict can be split into two main groups: the rules regulating the *conduct of hostilities* (i.e. the method and means of war), codified at the Hague Peace Conference in 1899 and 1907 (the so-called Hague law) and those regulating the protection of persons who do not, or no longer, take part in the hostilities (i.e. *the victims of war*), codified in Geneva by the four 1949 Conventions (the so-called Geneva law). Those rules, however, only apply to international armed conflicts, namely to conflicts between states. Non-international armed conflicts are scarcely regulated by international law. States tend to consider those conflicts as a matter pertaining to their domestic affairs, and therefore are regulated by national law only, for they relate to situations where a group of individuals (rebels or insurgents) takes arms against another group or against the state, thereby illegally resorting to *private* armed violence. Until the 1977 II Additional Protocol to the 1949 Geneva Conventions (which deals with high intensity non-international armed conflicts), the only provision applicable to non-international armed conflicts was the one contained in the four 1949 Geneva Conventions: common Article 3. This provision spells out basic humanitarian principles to be respected in conflicts of non-international character, and requires that all persons except those engaging in fighting must be protected in all circumstances and be spared from violence to life and limb (such as murder, mutilation, torture, cruel treatment). In addition, common Article 3 prohibits other conduct, such as the taking of hostages, and the passing of sentences and the execution of penalties without judgment by a regular constituted court and fair trial. The 1977 II Additional Protocol has expanded and supplemented the protection afforded by common Article 3, and contains a few rudimentary provisions on the regulation of the conduct of hostilities in non-international armed conflicts.

Against this background, one can easily understand why, to establish whether a war crime has been committed, one has first to classify the conflict as international or non-international in nature (since a different set of rules apply to these two kinds of conflicts). Once having classified the armed conflict, a war crime may consist either in the serious violation of a rule on the conduct of hostilities, or a rule protecting the victims of war. Therefore, there are four different classes of war crimes.

In international armed conflicts, war crimes consist of: (1) serious violations of the Hague law (such as attacking an undefended village, directly attacking the civilian population or individual civilians, using weapons causing unnecessary sufferings); (2) serious violations of the Geneva law, in particular those listed by the 1949 Geneva Conventions as 'grave breaches' (murder, torture, inhumane treatment, and other prohibited acts against persons protected by the Conventions, namely sick, wounded, prisoners of war, and civilians in internment camp or in occupied territories).

In non-international armed conflicts, war crimes consists of: (1) serious violations of the laws on the conduct of hostilities applicable to non-international armed conflicts (some of them are codified in Additional Protocol II); (2) serious violations of common Article 3 of the Geneva Conventions.

Crimes against humanity and genocide

As for serious violations of human rights amounting to crimes against humanity and genocide, the case is slightly different. The path towards their international criminalization is not rooted in national criminal legal systems, as is the case with war crimes, but started at the international level with the adoption of the Statute of the IMT and the Nuremberg trial. The story is well known: the Allies had to find a way to come to terms with odious crimes committed by the Nazis against Germans, or against the civilian population of the Allies of the Third Reich. These crimes did not fall under the notion of war crimes (that can be committed only against an enemy population, or enemy combatants). Moreover, under traditional international law the treatment by a state of its own citizens or those of Allied countries was a matter pertaining to the 'internal and external affairs' of states, and no interference from other states was envisaged or allowed. Crimes against humanity were therefore conceived of as a sort of 'umbrella' notion, to be applied if necessary to fill the lacunae left by the notion of war crimes, subject however to an important limitation: these crimes had to be linked to the perpetration of war crimes or crimes against peace, i.e. they had to be connected with war. However, after these truly international first steps, the notion of crimes against humanity remained 'dormant' for a long time, and the process of its international criminalization never went through the adoption of specific treaty provisions, as was the case in war crimes such as grave breaches of the 1949 Geneva Conventions. On the contrary: the notion of crimes against humanity was by some national courts conceived of as strictly connected to World War II and the punishment of German and Japanese criminals, as if there was no international rule prohibiting crimes against humanity except for the one that had evolved from the Nuremberg Charter.[3]

> **Box 12.4 Definition of crimes against humanity**
>
> Crimes against humanity were first defined by the London Charter establishing the Nuremberg Tribunal as 'murder, extermination, enslavement, deportation, and other inhumane acts committed against any civilian population, before or during the war, or persecutions on political, racial or religious grounds in execution of or in connection with any crime within the jurisdiction of the IMT, whether or not in violation of the domestic law of the country where perpetrated'. As is clear from this definition, crimes against humanity could be punished only if they were linked or connected to the commission of the other two crimes under the jurisdiction of the Nuremberg Tribunal, namely war crimes and crimes against peace. In practice, it required a link with the war. Therefore, the Tribunal decided that this link certainly existed for acts committed after 1 September 1939, which was when World War II started, and did not take into consideration acts committed before that date.
>
> The definition of crimes against humanity was the object of intense negotiations at the Rome Conference for the establishment of the ICC, since there were numerous delegations who wished to retain the requirement of the link with an armed conflict. This position was eventually defeated, and Article 7 of the ICC Statute provides that crimes against humanity consist of some conducts (expressly enumerated by the Article itself, such as murder, rape, torture, and so on) when committed as part of widespread or systematic attack against a civilian population, with the knowledge of the attack, without requiring a nexus with an armed conflict.

Genocide, which was punished at Nuremberg as part of the wider notion of crimes against humanity in the form of persecution or extermination, took a different route. Its international prohibition was solemnly incorporated in the 1948 Convention for the Prevention and Punishment of Genocide. On the one hand, this Convention requests contracting states to criminalize genocide within their legal orders and obliges the territorial state to punish persons responsible for genocide; on the other hand it went so far as to envisage the future establishment of an international criminal court endowed with jurisdiction over acts of genocide. The Genocide Convention was rapidly ratified by a large number of states, and the general revulsion against this crime quickly gave rise to a customary rule contemplating genocide not only as an individual crime, but also as a very serious international wrongful act of states. This explains why, when international criminal courts such as the ICTY, the ICTR, and the ICC were established in the 1990s, the definition of genocide was taken verbatim from the Genocide Convention without much discussion, and again inserted in all subsequent instruments instituting other international or mixed tribunals for the repression of international crimes. By contrast, at the time of the adoption of the Statute of the ICTY, the ICTR, and the ICC the notion of crimes against humanity was still highly controversial, as the Rome negotiations for the ICC made abundantly clear.

Box 12.5 Definition of genocide

Article II of the Genocide Convention defines genocide as:

> any of the following acts committed with intent to destroy, in whole or in part, a national, ethnical, racial or religious group, as such:

a. Killing members of the group;

b. Causing serious bodily or mental harm to members of the group;

c. Deliberately inflicting on the group conditions of life calculated to bring about its physical destruction in whole or in part;

d. Imposing measures intended to prevent births within the group;

e. Forcibly transferring children of the group to another group.

The list of the acts constituting genocide is exhaustive (practices such as ethnic cleansing are not included in the definition). In addition, only the four groups mentioned in the definition are groups protected by the commission of acts of genocide (political and cultural groups, for instance, are not protected by the Convention). Finally, the crucial element of genocide is the existence of a particular mental element on the part of the perpetrator, namely his/her intention to destroy a group 'as such' in total or in part.

Clearly, the crime of genocide does not require that the objective of the destruction of a particular group, in total or in part, is realized. On the contrary, genocide is perpetrated when an individual, by carrying out one of the prohibited conducts listed in Article II of the Genocide Convention, possesses the requisite special intent to destroy one of the protected groups, without this intent necessarily being accomplished. However, it is not clear whether genocide, as a criminal act entailing individual criminal accountability, also requires—as a legal constitutive element—the existence of a context of violence against a protected group (similar to the case of crimes against humanity, where the existence of a widespread or systematic attack against a civilian population is a legal ingredient of this class of crimes). The definition of genocide enshrined in the Genocide Convention does not provide for such an additional element, as the ICTY and the ICTR have stressed in their case law. However, at trial, the existence of such a context could help the prosecution to demonstrate that the person charged with genocide did possess the requisite genocidal intent.

The reasons for the different path of the international criminalization of war crimes with respect to crimes against humanity and genocide

One can speculate on the reasons why the process of international criminalization of crimes against humanity and genocide was different from that relating to war crimes. Arguably, for war crimes the 'national' origin of their international criminalization can be explained by taking into account that states had a narrowly defined self-interest in the criminal repression of these crimes within their national legal systems. Despite the humanitarian considerations behind the birth and development of the laws of war, it is a fact that these laws could apply solely within the context of an interstate relationship (i.e. they were conceived to regulate international armed conflicts), and hence were synallagmatic in nature. For a long time, no humanitarian reason was weighty enough to force or convince states to regulate civil strife as well. The notion of war crimes served various purposes: when it applied to national military servicemen, repression of violations of the laws of war served to impose military discipline and to protect the honour of armed forces; with regard to enemy combatants, such repression constituted an effective tool to discourage breaches of the rules of warfare by the belligerent enemy. The notions of crimes against humanity and genocide were born from a totally different seed: the concept that states are not the absolute owners of the lives and human dignity of their citizens, but that individuals' and groups' fundamental rights must be respected. At Nuremberg, for the first time, the right of the international community was proclaimed to lift the veil of state sovereignty and to interfere in the relationship between the state and its citizens when it is the state that systematically tramples upon their basic human rights. This was an unexpected revolution. True, the drafters of the Nuremberg Charter carefully tried to confine the notion of crimes against humanity to the historical events of World War II to avoid future interferences by the international community in their internal affairs as regards the treatment of their citizens; two US Military Tribunals sitting at Nuremberg even asserted that the notion of crimes against humanity could apply to extermination through euthanasia only if the victims were foreigners![4] A similar cautious development can be seen in the UN Charter; for example, the powers of the new organization in matters of human rights were originally limited to the adoption of general resolutions, while the passing of resolutions condemning a state for violating human rights was regarded as intervening in the domestic jurisdiction of each member state under Article 2.7 of the Charter. However, the seeds of the human rights doctrine had been sown. In the 1990s, this doctrine was embedded enough in the 'conscience' of the international community to allow the notion of individual criminal responsibility for large-scale violations of human rights to flourish and gain state support. The Rome negotiations for the ICC Statute and the adoption of Articles 6 and 7 of this Statute (on genocide and crimes against humanity) are the outcome of the process on the international criminalization of these two classes of crimes that started and developed, with some stops (for crimes against humanity), entirely at the international level.

The enforcement of international criminal law at the international level

The *ad hoc* criminal tribunals and the ICC: an overview

As noted above, the birth and assertion of international criminal law as a branch of international law is closely linked to the establishment of truly international criminal tribunals for the prosecution and punishment of international crimes. After the Nuremberg and the Tokyo Tribunals (which can be better described as common organs of the group of states which established them), the ICTY (1993) and the ICTR (1994) were the first international criminal tribunals ever created by Security Council Resolutions (see Chapter 8). The ICTY has jurisdiction over genocide, crimes against humanity, grave breaches of the 1949 Geneva Conventions, and other war crimes, committed on the territory of the former Yugoslavia after 1 September 1991. The ICTR has jurisdiction over genocide, crimes against humanity, and violations of common Article 3 of the 1949 Geneva Conventions. Its temporal jurisdiction is limited to conducts which took place between 1 January and 31 December 1994. Both Tribunals can only exercise jurisdiction over natural persons, and not over states or juridical persons.

These two *ad hoc* Tribunals were often accused of not being impartial. For instance, the decision by the Prosecutor of the ICTY not to launch an investigation over the alleged crimes committed by NATO during the bombing of Serbia in 1999 has attracted much criticism. Similarly, the lack of any indictment by the ICTR Prosecutor against any member of the Rwanda Patriotic Front (RPF)—which fought the war against the Hutu-led government—has been frequently raised to accuse the ICTR of being biased against the Hutu. In practice, those Tribunals have been accused of being 'partial' not only in the historical sense, because they have been set up to deal with crimes committed on a specific part of the globe and not elsewhere, but also at the level of their judicial activity.

Unlike the ICTY and the ICTR, the ICC is a permanent institution, established by way of a treaty (the Rome Statute, adopted on 17 July 1998) which can dispense justice for crimes after the entry into force of its Statute (1 July 2002). Its jurisdiction covers war crimes (committed both during an international and an internal armed conflict), crimes against humanity, and genocide. The ICC can also exercise its jurisdiction over the crime of aggression, provided that the member states of the ICC (i.e. the states which are party to the Rome Statute) will agree upon a definition of this offence in the future. The ICC prosecutor can start investigations *proprio motu* (*on his/her own initiative*, subject to an authorization by the judges of a pre-trial Chamber, i.e. subject to judicial control) or at the request of a state party to the Statute or of the Security Council (in which case, if the prosecutor decides to launch an investigation, there is no need to obtain an authorization by the pre-trial chamber). The ICC, however, can exercise its criminal jurisdiction only if the crime has been committed in the territory of a state party, *or* if the crime has been committed by a national of a state party. This exposes nationals of states not parties to the Rome Statute to the jurisdiction of the ICC, in so far as they can be accused of having committed crimes in the territory of a state party.

Box 12.6 International political support for the ICC

The creation of international criminal law is a puzzle for international relations and law scholars who hold that states would only commit to international institutions when the compliance costs are low. In the case of the ICC it is clear that the compliance costs are high as government officials, including heads of states, can be prosecuted and punished by the ICC for international crimes. As of 2009 over 100 states are parties to the ICC and a further forty have indicated intention to join it, but three out of the five permanent members of the Security Council, the United States, the Russian Federation, and China, are not yet parties to the ICC. What does the strong support from a large number of states and current lack of support from the United States, the Russian Federation, and China tell us about the future of this institution?

The United Nations Security Council and the International Criminal Court

The United Nations Security Council can exercise very broad powers with respect to the ICC. It can expand the jurisdiction of the Court over crimes committed by whomsoever and everywhere in the world (i.e. irrespective of whether the crimes have been perpetrated by the nationals of a state party or in the territory of a state party). It can also compress the exercise of the ICC jurisdiction, since Article 16 provides that 'no investigation or prosecution may be commenced or proceeded with . . . for a period of twelve months if the Security Council, in a resolution adopted under Chapter VII of the Charter of the United Nations, has requested the Court to that effect'. Such deferral 'may be renewed by the Council under the same conditions'. The Security Council has already used its authority with respect to the ICC in both ways. On 31 March 2005, it referred the situation in Darfur (Sudan) to the ICC prosecutor, therefore allowing the Court to exercise its jurisdiction over crimes committed in the territory of a state not party to the Statute. On two occasions, however, the Security Council has exercised its authority to halt the commencement of investigations by the ICC prosecution: on 12 July 2002, at the initiative of the US, it adopted Resolution 1422 whereby it requested the Court not to commence or to proceed with investigations or prosecutions with respect to members of UN peace-keeping forces, or forces acting on authorization by the Security Council, if such members were nationals of states not parties to the ICC Statute. This request was renewed on 12 June 2003, for twelve months, by way of Resolution 1487.

The powers that the Security Council can exercise with respect to the ICC risk putting into question the credibility of this Court as an independent judicial body, capable to dispense justice regardless of the political interests of the big powers sitting in the Security Council as permanent members (and therefore allowed to exercise a veto power) and their principal allies. These are genuine concerns, which, however, are not unique to the ICC. In various degrees, the risk of bending justice to politics may also affect national criminal courts. The danger that justice may be subject to, or at least contaminated by politics is inherent in any society. That is why a famous Italian criminal lawyer, Francesco Carrara, wrote more than a century ago 'When politics gets in by the door, justice is scared away through the window.'[5] International politics contributed to the establishment of international criminal courts and tribunals to prosecute and punish the persons responsible for odious crimes, such as genocide, crimes against humanity and war crimes. It also made it possible to build the temples of justice. It is now up to the judges, the investigators, the prosecutors of the international courts and tribunals, and also to all of us who believe in the rule of law, to make sure that politics stops outside the temple, leaving only justice inside. This position stands firmly in contrast to arguments which view international law and its institutions as subservient to international politics. Such arguments overlook the fact that once international institutions, such as the ICC, are created they strengthen the international normative frameworks by interpreting them and applying them. They further contribute to the socialization process of international criminal law amongst states (see also Chapter 2).

The pros and cons of international criminal proceedings

Criminal proceedings for the repression of international crimes before international courts have numerous advantages as opposed to national proceedings.

First, international courts apply international criminal law directly. For domestic courts, international criminal law often needs to be incorporated into the national legal order by virtue of the enactment of appropriate implementing legislation to be applicable. Therefore it may happen that international criminal law is 'lost in translation' because the national implementing legislation has incorrectly transformed the rule of international criminal law into the national one to be applied by the national judges. In short, international criminal courts are in a better position to know and apply international criminal law, and at the same time to guarantee a certain level of uniformity in the interpretation of this body of law.

Second, international criminal courts are in a better position to deal with the very complex legal issues raised by the prosecution and punishment of international crimes. These crimes are often committed in the context of widespread collective violence: the trial against a person accused of an international crime can prove very difficult, at the level of the establishment both of the determining of the facts and of the individual role played by the accused in the commission of crimes of a 'collective' nature. A special legal expertise is therefore needed in this regard, and such expertise is often lacking at the national level.

Third, and more importantly, international trials enjoy greater visibility than national proceedings. Therefore, they can better signal the will by the international community not to accept that individuals responsible for heinous crimes go unpunished. The hope is that the stigmatization of deviant behaviour at the international level and the great visibility of international criminal trials (especially those against political and military leaders) may also have a modicum of a deterrent effect, and prevent the commission of similar crimes in the future.

However, international criminal proceedings are not flawless. The major shortcoming is the need for international criminal courts to rely upon state cooperation for their judicial activity. Those courts are judicial organs not assisted by any enforcement power in the territory of any state. As a consequence, to collect one single testimony or other evidence, these courts have to request the relevant state to do so or to provide the necessary assistance for allowing the international investigators to collect evidence in its territory. As for the arrest and surrender of an accused person, again they have to rely upon the cooperation of the state where the accused is present. If the state does not comply with the request to assist the international criminal court, there is very little this court can do: usually, it can only make a judicial finding whereby it registers the lack of cooperation of the state. This judicial finding can be transmitted either to the Security Council (in the case of the ICTY and ICTR, or the ICC but only when its jurisdiction has been triggered by the Security Council), or—in the case of the ICC—to the Assembly of State Parties (which is the organ where all the states parties to the ICC are represented). Clearly, the necessity for international criminal courts and tribunals to rely upon state cooperation, and the lack of any effective enforcement mechanism in case of non-compliance by states, is among the weakest points of the current institutional system of international criminal justice. Here again politics rather than the existence of international obligations may heavily influence the decision of a state to cooperate, or not cooperate, with an international criminal court. However, international criminal courts and tribunals are relatively young institutions. Time is needed for them to grow up and to assert themselves as indispensable and more autonomous law enforcement mechanisms of the international community. The marriage between politics and international criminal justice is a difficult and highly problematic one, and will not last forever.

International proceedings also face hurdles of a practical nature in their day-to-day functioning. International criminal courts have working languages which often are not the languages of the suspects or the accused, nor of the state where the crimes have been committed. Every document or testimony must therefore be translated into all the official languages of the international court and/or in the language of the suspect or the accused. The same is true at the trial, where simultaneous translations are required. Language barriers slow down the proceedings which already tend to be very long because of the complexity of the facts and legal issues involved, and the difficulty in collecting evidence both for the prosecution and the defence. Finally, the length of the proceedings is enhanced by the adoption of the accusatorial model of common law systems: this model is based on the assumption that the evidence must be brought orally at the trial, and be subject to examination and cross-examination by the Prosecution and the Defence. This also means that a fact such as the weather conditions on a particular day at a particular place must be proven at trial 'orally' by witnesses, who will be examined and cross-examined on that specific issue.

The relationship between international criminal courts and national courts: primacy versus complementarity

The prosecution and punishment of international crimes by international criminal courts and tribunals does not rule out the possibility for national courts to exercise their criminal jurisdiction over the same crimes. A problem of coordination between the action of international courts and that of national courts therefore arises.

This problem has been solved differently by the statutes of the relevant international criminal court or tribunal. The two *ad hoc* Tribunals set up by the Security Council, the ICTY and the ICTR, have been given *primacy* with respect to national jurisdictions. This means that at any stage of the procedure, the *ad hoc* Tribunals may request the national courts of any state *to defer* a case they are dealing with to their competence. The two *ad hoc* Tribunals may issue a request for deferral when (1) the act being investigated or prosecuted at the domestic level is characterized as a domestic offence and not as an international crime (i.e. murder, and not war crime); (2) there is a lack of impartiality and independence of the domestic proceedings, which are carried out for the purpose of shielding the accused from criminal responsibility, or the case is not diligently prosecuted; (3) if the issue is closely linked, or involves significant factual or legal questions, which may have implications for investigations or prosecution by the international criminal tribunal.

On the contrary, the ICC is built on the assumption that its jurisdiction is *complementary* to that of national courts (including the national courts of states not parties to the Rome Statute). The ICC respects the sovereignty of states if they have a domestic judicial system which can guarantee that criminal proceedings are carried out genuinely. Complementarity means that cases before the ICC are admissible provided that the state possessing jurisdiction is unable or unwilling to genuinely carry out the criminal proceedings. In other words, under the ICC Statute, national courts have *priority of jurisdiction*: the ICC plays a subsidiary role, and steps in to exercise its jurisdiction only when domestic courts fail to do so. The ICC Statute provides that a state is unwilling to genuinely carry out the criminal proceedings when there is a lack of independence and impartiality by the domestic judicial courts that, in the circumstances of the case, is inconsistent with an intent to bring the person concerned to justice. With regard to inability, the ICC Statute establishes that a state is unable to genuinely carry out the proceedings when, due to a total or substantial collapse or unavailability of its judicial system, it cannot obtain the accused, or the necessary evidence and testimony.

The fact that the jurisdiction of international criminal courts and tribunals over international crimes is not exclusive, but rather concurrent with that of domestic courts, should come as no surprise in the current international system. International society operates horizontally and states have a primary role in the enforcement of international law. The principle of complementary is also sound policy. The fight against impunity needs to be conducted at all levels, national and international. In addition, the judicial authorities of every state (and not only those of the state most affected by those crimes, primarily the territorial state) should be ready to play a role in this regard. Complementarity is also conducive to national ownership of international criminal law. It enables the spread of a new ethos among nations and national judges. The international legal framework particularly empowers national judicial authorities to consider themselves as the guardians of universal values, protecting the life and limb and the dignity of human beings. International criminal law recognizes domestic judges as important actors who can enforce those values against those who, all over the world, and often by abusing their state authority and powers, trample upon them and strike at its very heart, the strenuous attempt to guarantee a world of peace and prosperity for all.

Box 12.7 Universal jurisdiction

National courts usually assert their criminal jurisdiction over a particular conduct provided that there is a link with that conduct, i.e. there is 'a jurisdictional link'. The most widely used and accepted jurisdictional link is that of territoriality, which is when the conduct is carried out on the territory of the state, or produces its effects in the territory of the state. Another accepted link is that of the nationality of the person, which enables the courts of a state to sit in judgment over the conducts carried out by the nationals of that state wherever in the world. These two jurisdictional links, however, may prove inadequate in the field of repression of international crimes. As noted above, those crimes are often committed by state officials and backed by the state apparatus. It is, therefore, unlikely that the courts of the state where the crimes have been committed will exercise their jurisdiction.

This is the reason why, for the repression of international crimes, another principle of jurisdiction should come into play: the universality principle. This principle would enable national judicial authorities to prosecute crimes regardless of the place of commission or the nationality of the offender. It can, therefore, be crucial in the matter of international crimes, for it would allow national judges to enforce universal values such as those protected by international crimes, without requiring a specific link with the crimes. It is still debated, however, to what extent the principle of universality is allowed under international law. There is a growing consensus among scholars that the universality of jurisdiction is always permitted, under customary international law, for the repression of the core crimes. Nonetheless, some states challenge this assertion and contend that the principle of universality is permitted only to the extent it is provided for in a treaty.

Conclusion

International law directly provides for the criminalization of some individual conducts, known as 'international crimes'. These crimes offend values common to the international community as a whole. The international criminalization of such individual conducts is a major achievement and it has radically reshaped the relationship between international law and national jurisdictions in the field of criminal law. International crimes are usually committed by individuals acting as state officials or backed by the state apparatus—and so are likely to escape domestic prosecution. Their international criminalization can thus be seen as a step towards ending impunity for all, and especially powerful, actors. International law still has to come to terms with some basic contradictions that have emerged from the process of international criminalization of individual conducts. In particular, the authority of the United Nations Security Council under Chapter VII of the United Nations Charter to expand and to express the exercise of criminal jurisdiction by the ICC has been criticized as yet another tool in the hands of powerful states to pursue their specific interests. Another concern has been that the international prosecution of powerful actors might sometimes stand in the way of national reconciliation after times of conflict. This debate emphasizes once more how international law and international politics are intertwined. Time will show to what extent the ICC with its international law approach can contribute to greater international justice, and to what extent its success depends on political and other considerations. It is to be hoped that in one way or another, the ICC will be able to assert itself as a credible institution, 'able and willing' also to prosecute the crimes committed by the nationals of the most powerful countries, and to dispense justice for all.

Questions

1. What is international criminal law?
2. When did this body of law start to develop and affirm itself?
3. Which crimes come under the scope of application of international criminal law?
4. What is the difference between international crimes and transnational crimes?
5. What role do international criminal courts and tribunals play to enforce international criminal law?
6. What are the merits and demerits of international criminal proceedings?
7. What is the role of national criminal courts in the repression of international crimes?

8. Can the criminal courts of a state assert their jurisdiction over international crimes under the universality principle?

9. What is the relationship between the Security Council and the International Criminal Court?

10. How do you evaluate the relationship between international politics and international criminal justice?

Further reading

Cassese, A. (2008) *International Criminal Law*, 2nd edn. (Oxford: Oxford University Press). *This book combines the classic common law and more theoretical approaches to the subject, it expounds the fundamentals of both substantive and procedural international criminal law, and provides a theoretical framework to understand the rules, principles, concepts, and legal constructs key to the subject.*

Cassese, A. (ed.) (2009) *The Oxford Companion to International Criminal Justice* (Oxford: Oxford University Press). *This book analyses and comments upon every aspect of international criminal justice and provides a complete overview of this emerging field.*

Cassese, A., Gaeta, P., and Jones, J.R.W.D. (eds.) (2002) *The Rome Statute of the International Criminal Court: A Commentary* (Oxford: Oxford University Press). *This Commentary takes a thematic look at the whole of international criminal law, appraising the contributions of international tribunals such as the Nuremberg and Tokyo Tribunals and the ad hoc Tribunals for Yugoslavia and Rwanda, as well as those of national courts.*

Cryer, R., Friman, H., Robinson, D., and Wilmshurst, E. (2007) *An Introduction to International Criminal Law and Procedure* (Cambridge: Cambridge University Press). *This book covers all aspects of international criminal law in a very accessible way, while setting out sophisticated and stimulating arguments to engage the reader.*

Gutman, R., Rieff, D., and Dworkin, A. (eds.) (2007) *Crimes of War: What the Public Should Know* (New York: Norton and Company). *This is an A-to-Z guidebook of the atrocities that are committed in wartime, written by distinguished experts from the media, military, law, and human rights groups.*

Lee, R. S. (ed.) (1999) *The International Criminal Court: the Making of the Rome Statute* (The Hague: Kluwer Law International). *A collection of commentaries on the negotiations which led to the adoption of the Rome Statute of the International Criminal Court written by some of the key players in the negotiations; it covers in a clear and detailed manner the various issues tackled by the drafters of the Statute.*

Mettraux, G. (2005) *International Crimes and the Ad Hoc Tribunals* (Oxford: Oxford University Press). *A comprehensive analysis of the case law of the International Criminal Tribunal for the former Yugoslavia and the International Criminal Tribunal for Rwanda.*

Peskin, V. (2008) *International Justice in Rwanda and the Balkans: Virtual Trials and the Struggle for State Cooperation* (Cambridge: Cambridge University Press). *A study focusing on the problem of state cooperation with international criminal courts and addresses the difficult relationship between Serbia, Croatia,* and Rwanda with the two ad hoc international criminal tribunals.

Schabas, W. A. (2004) *An Introduction to the International Criminal Court*, 2nd edn. (Cambridge: Cambridge University Press). *The book reviews the history of international criminal prosecution, the drafting of the Rome Statute of the International Criminal Court and the principles of its operation and addresses the difficulties created by US opposition, and analyses the various measures taken by Washington to obstruct the Court.*

Websites

http://www.icc-cpi.int/ *The website of the International Criminal Court offers information on the structure of the court, as well as cases, legal texts, and current news updates on its activities.*

http://www.icty.org/ *Among others, the website of the International Criminal Tribunal for the Former Yugoslavia contains a detailed database on the cases before the tribunal.*

http://avalon.law.yale.edu/subject_menus/imt.asp *The Avalon Project based at Yale Law School compiles all the relevant information and documents related to the Nuremberg Trials.*

http://www.un.org/ictr/ *This website gives access to detailed information related to the activities of the International Criminal Tribunal for Rwanda.*

http://www.ucl.ac.uk/laws/cict/ *The Centre for International Courts and Tribunals is the London home of the Project on International Courts and Tribunals (see Chapter 8)—on its website it announces current research and events related to it.*

Visit the Online Resource Centre that accompanies this book to access more learning resources www.oxfordtextbooks.co.uk/orc/cali/

Chapter endnotes

1. See the judgment of the Israeli Supreme Court of 29 May 1962 in the trial against *Eichmann*, where the Court stated: 'Not only do all the crimes attributed to the appellant bear an international character, but their harmful and murderous effects were so embracing and widespread as to shake the international community to its very foundations. The State of Israel therefore was entitled, pursuant to the principle of universal jurisdiction and *in the capacity of a guardian of international law and an agent for its enforcement*, to try the appellant. That being the case, no importance attaches to the fact that the State of Israel did not exist when the offences were committed' (emphasis added). The judgment is available online at http://www.nizkor.org. See also 36 *International Law Reports* (1968) 304.

2. Article 228 of the Treaty of Versailles provided as follows: 'The German Government recognizes the right of the allied and associated powers to bring before military tribunals persons accused of having committed acts in violation of the laws and customs of war . . .'

3. See the *Boudarel* case (*Sobanski Wladyslav*), decided on 1 April 1993 by the French Court of Cassation, in *RGDIP* (1994) 471–4.

4. See in this regard the cases reported in Cassese (2003: 88–9).

5. 'Quando la politica entra dalla porta, la giustizia fugge impaurita dalla finestra', *Programma del Corso di diritto criminale*, vol. VII, Lucca 1871.

Chapter 13
International human rights law

Basak Çalı

CHAPTER CONTENTS

- Introduction
- What makes up international human rights law and where do we find it?
- International human rights law institutions
- The relevance of international human rights law in international relations
- Compliance with international human rights law
- New international actors and international human rights law
- Conclusion

CHAPTER OVERVIEW

This chapter sets out international human rights law (IHRL), its institutions and the contribution that the corpus of international human rights law has made to our understanding of the international system. The chapter first addresses the question of where we find international human rights law and sets out a brief history of international human rights institutions. It then analyses the relationship between this body of law and state sovereignty in the fields of military intervention, the empowerment of individuals in the international system, the status of non-citizens and the states sovereign right to control its borders and state responsibility outside its own territory. The chapter finally discusses whether the state-focused IHRL is adequate in dealing with the rise of powerful economic actors and in what ways we can approach compliance with IHRL.

Introduction

Of the many concepts employed in international law and international relations, 'human rights' is one of the most controversial . Human rights, and its legal manifestation international human rights law (IHRL), are very complex domains of international theory and practice. Human rights initiates the most heated debates in international relations classrooms. It divides students along the lines of 'idealists' and 'realists', 'moralists' and 'pragmatists' or 'rationalists', and 'constructivists' (see Chapter 2). Students and scholars of international relations disagree about what human rights are, how important they are, what they do in international relations and whether they have any significant impact on state behaviour. When examined closely it becomes clear that simplifications about human rights are misleading, if possible at all. In the light of this complexity and controversy, the aim of this chapter is to make international human rights law and its effects on international relations more transparent and accessible. It will also look at the different ways IHRL figures in international relations theory and practice.

The chapter starts by describing what makes up IHRL and where it is found. It then discusses the relevance of IHRL in international relations by way of a three-level analysis setting out the relevance of human rights: (1) for debates on the character of the international system as a whole; (2) for what we expect from states as political agents; and (3) for new actors in the international system. It then discusses the ways in which we conceptualize compliance with IHRL.

What makes up international human rights law and where do we find it?

Box 13.1 What is IHRL?

IHRL is a system of international treaties and principles that aim to protect and promote the rights of individuals from state interference and state negligence.

International human rights law, like any other form of international law, is made up of treaties, customary international law and soft law. Multilateral treaties are the most common way of creating international human rights law. Both the United Nations and the regional organizations have a large number of human rights treaties. International human rights treaties can focus on a single right (for example, the United Nations Convention against Torture), they can have a long list of rights under a specific theme (for example, civil and political rights, or economic, social and cultural rights) or they can focus on protecting the rights of specific groups (for example, rights of the disabled, rights of migrant workers, rights of women, rights of children).

Box 13.2 Core international human rights treaties and monitoring bodies

United Nations human rights treaties

There are eight core international human rights treaties, each of which has a committee of experts to monitor implementation and compliance.

International Convention on the Elimination of All Forms of Racial Discrimination (ICERD), 1965.

International Covenant on Civil and Political Rights (ICCPR), 1966.

International Covenant on Economic, Social and Cultural Rights (ICESCR), 1966.

Convention on the Elimination of All Forms of Discrimination against Women (CEDAW), 1979.

Convention against Torture and Other Cruel, Inhuman or Degrading Treatment or Punishment (CAT), 1984.

Convention on the Rights of the Child (CRC), 1989.

International Convention on the Protection of the Rights of All Migrant Workers and Members of Their Families, 1990.

Convention on the Rights of Persons with Disabilities, 2008.

The interaction between international human rights treaties and customary international law of human rights is close. The recognition of a right in an international human rights treaty that is ratified by a large number of states, and not challenged by non-ratifying states, supports strong arguments about the customary nature of the provisions of those human rights treaties (see Chapter 6). Some of the human rights recognized in treaties are emblematic of a larger commitment to setting constraints on the use of state powers in international law. For example, the prohibition of torture is not just any law. It represents the boundaries of state-sanctioned power in the legal system. It is for this reason that some categories of human rights law are also considered as *ius cogens* norms (peremptory norms) and *norms erga omnes* (norms that create duties toward all) (see Chapters 5 and 6). This means that if state A and state B made an agreement to torture terrorist suspects to extract vital information, this agreement would be null and void in international law and it would be prohibited for third states to deport and extradite individuals to these countries.

The origins of international human rights law

It is common for international lawyers to start the history of IHRL with the United Nations Charter in 1945 and the Universal Declaration of Human Rights in 1948. While these dates do not tell us much about the history of human rights as an idea in philosophy, they are significant because they mark the international and political manifestation of the idea of human rights. The United Nations Charter in its preamble states that the peoples of the United Nations are determined to 'save succeeding generations from the scourge of war, which twice in our lifetime has brought untold sorrow to mankind' and 'reaffirm faith in fundamental human rights'. Article 1 of the United Nations Charter identifies 'promoting and encouraging respect for human rights and for fundamental freedoms for all without distinction as to race, sex, language, or religion' as one of the purposes of the United Nations along with maintaining international peace and security, to develop friendly relations, and to achieve international cooperation. The emphasis on human rights in post-World War II international politics and organization is closely related to the shortcomings of domestic laws and political processes in Europe to protect mass-scale discrimination and the subsequent Holocaust. The emphasis on human rights in the United Nations Charter signals that the treatment of individuals by states and the use of political powers are not simply domestic matters for individual states to deal with.

This emphasis on human rights within the United Nations Charter led to the creation of human rights bodies and declarations internationally and regionally. The Human Rights Commission was the first intergovernmental commission set up in 1946. It was given the aim of guiding the overall human rights work of the United Nations. It was while this Commission was working on a draft of the Universal

Declaration of Human Rights (UDHR), that the American Declaration of the Rights and Duties of Man was declared. Issued in April 1948, this was the world's first international human rights instrument of a general nature.

Box 13.3 Regional human rights treaties and implementation mechanisms

Regional human rights treaties

European Convention on Human Rights and Fundamental Freedoms (Council of Europe, 1950), compulsory European Commission on Human Rights and optional European Court of Human Rights (1959–1998), compulsory European Court of Human Rights since 1998.

American Convention on Human Rights (Organization of American States, 1969), Compulsory Inter-American Convention on Human Rights and Optional Inter-American Court of Human Rights.

African Charter on Human and Peoples' Rights (African Union 1979, 1986), Compulsory African Commission on Human and Peoples' Rights and optional African Court of Human and Peoples' Rights (latter established in 2006).

Arab Charter on Human Rights (Council of the League of Arab States 1994, revised 2004 and entered into force 2008).

On 10 December 1948 (now celebrated annually as Human Rights Day), the United Nations General Assembly voted for the Universal Declaration of Human Rights. Forty-eight votes fell in its favour, with Byelorussia, Czechoslovakia, Poland, Saudi Arabia, the South African Union, Ukraine, the USSR, and Yugoslavia abstaining. There was no vote in opposition. The UDHR was not presented as an international treaty, but a declaration of the General Assembly of the United Nations' states. This means that states are not legally bound to enforce the rights it proclaims. Nor does it provide for the enforcement of these rights. The UDHR states that human rights are 'a common standard of achievement for all peoples and all nations'. It provides a list of twenty-eight rights that are internationally recognized by the United Nations General Assembly. The significance and ongoing relevance of the UDHR in international law and relations lies in its originality and universal support it has attracted over the years. It was the first time the organized community of nations made a declaration on human rights and fundamental freedoms. The document received the backing by the United Nations as a whole and it inspired a generation of international human rights instruments and institution-building within the United Nations.

Box 13.4 Human rights institutions created by the United Nations

Human Rights Council

The **Human Rights Council** which replaced the Commission on Human Rights is an inter-governmental body within the UN system made up of forty-seven states responsible for strengthening the promotion and protection of human rights internationally. It was created by the UN *General Assembly* in 2006 with the main purpose of addressing situations of human rights violations and making recommendations on them.

One way in which the Council assesses human rights situations is through the **Universal Periodic Review mechanism.**

The **Universal Periodic Review** (UPR) involves a review of the human rights records of all 192 UN member states once every four years. The UPR is a state-driven process, under the auspices of the Human Rights Council, which provides the opportunity for each state to declare what actions they have taken to improve the human rights situations in their countries and to fulfil their human rights obligations. As one of the main features of the Council, the UPR is designed to ensure equal treatment for every country when their human rights situations are assessed.

The UPR was created through the UN General Assembly on 15 March 2006 by Resolution 60/251, which established the Human Rights Council itself. It is a cooperative process which, by 2011, will have reviewed the human rights records of every country. Currently, no other universal mechanism of this kind exists. The UPR is one of the key elements of the new Council which reminds states of their responsibility to fully respect and implement all human rights and fundamental freedoms. The ultimate aim of this new mechanism is to improve the human rights situation in all countries and address human rights violations wherever they occur.

Special procedures

'**Special procedures**' is the general name given to the mechanisms established by the Commission on Human Rights and assumed by the Human Rights Council to address either specific country situations or thematic issues in all parts of the world. Currently, there are thirty *thematic* and eight *country* mandates.

Special procedures' mandate holders are asked to examine, monitor, advise, and publicly report on human rights situations in specific countries or territories, known as *country mandates*, or on specific topics relating to human rights violations worldwide (*thematic mandates*). Various activities can be undertaken by special procedures, including responding to individual complaints, conducting studies, providing advice on technical cooperation at the country level, and engaging in general promotional activities.

Special procedures are either individuals (called 'Special Rapporteur', 'Special Representative of the Secretary-General', 'Representative of the Secretary-General' or 'Independent Expert') or working groups usually composed of five members (one from each region). Mandate holders of the special procedures do not receive salaries or any other financial compensation for their work, which is supposed to help secure their impartiality.

United Nations Office of the High Commissioner for Human Rights (OHCHR)

OHCHR has a mandate from the United Nations General Assembly to promote and protect all human rights. It is led by the High Commissioner for Human Rights, the principal human rights officer of the United Nations. The OHCHR aims ensure that international human rights standards are implemented on the ground in the United Nations member states. It provides leadership to United Nations agencies on human rights matters and builds and supports partnership with civil society and UN agencies. It also supports the work of the United Nations human rights mechanisms, such as the Human Rights Council and the core treaty bodies (see Box 13.1).

International human rights law institutions

If the UDHR is the point when the idea of human rights was universally proclaimed and recognized, the period since 1948 has seen the legalization, interpretation, and implementation of human rights ideals. This has happened in three different ways. First, states drafted a number of international human rights treaties under the auspices of a variety of international organizations—the United Nations, the Organization of American States (OAS), the Council of Europe (CoE), and the African Union (formerly the Organization of African Unity). These also established international mechanisms to oversee the implementation of these treaties.

Second, international organizations sought to mainstream human rights in their work in order to realize the human rights aims declared in the United Nations Charter. This led to the proliferation of guidelines, principles, soft laws, resolutions, and declarations created by the United Nations and regional international organizations. Third, the universal application and relevance of these rights led to the proliferation of non-governmental organizations (NGOs), which advocate human rights internationally. These NGOs have become an essential part of the international human rights protection and monitoring machinery (see Chapter 7).

These three developments are interrelated. Most of the political work of the international organizations has led to the drafting and coming into force of new international human rights law treaties. The very existence of legal commitments in the field of international human rights has empowered NGOs to legitimately claim these rights and to campaign for them. Because NGOs had an increased capacity to raise human rights problems internationally, the political organs of the United Nations and other regional organizations have raised a diversity of concrete and real life human rights problems as requiring international guiding principles (see Chapter 7). This latter development has also led to the understanding that many human rights principles are part of customary international law and therefore bind states who have not signed up to a particular treaty (see Chapter 6). Which human rights are part of customary international law is a debate in international law as there is no final authority which can confirm the precise list of these rights and their meanings. This does not mean, however, that this is not a convincing or futile debate. The (former) Commission on Human Rights, for example, affirmed that the ban on the imposition of the death penalty on juveniles and pregnant women as found in Article 6 of the ICCPR is customary international law (Commission on Human Rights Resolution 2005/59) and this has been used as a legal and campaigning tool in may countries.

The key distinction between international human rights treaty law and human rights as customary law is the type of legal consequences attached to the former. First, if a state has ratified an international human rights treaty it becomes much easier to identify the content of that state's international legal commitments. The state in question also cannot deny in principle that it has made legal commitments. Second, becoming a part of an international human rights treaty makes a state answerable to the monitoring body of that treaty. This means that there is a degree of international accountability to ensure that states keep their promises. The degree of accountability varies from regime to regime.

The United Nations human rights treaties, for instance, have the most universal coverage, but the weakest accountability provisions. All of these UN treaties require the state parties to submit periodic reports and enter into constructive dialogue with a monitoring body made up of experts who review state reports and issue 'concluding observations' on the state of implementation and further steps to be taken. Individuals are able to bring complaints against states, but only if a state explicitly agrees through signing up to an optional protocol to the treaty. When a treaty-monitoring body examines an individual complaint, it can only make recommendations to states if it determines a violation of the treaty provisions. Such recommendations are not legally binding.[1] UN treaty-monitoring bodies further issue interpretations of the provisions of the human rights treaties (such as the right to health, the right to privacy) in order to provide guidance to states.

The regional systems, on the other hand, provide for stronger forms of accountability. The Organization of American States and the African Union have Human Rights Commissions, which issue reports on human rights situations and where individuals can submit complaints of human rights violations by states. Both systems also have courts, but these courts are optional and not all states that are parties to the treaties are also parties to the court. The Council of Europe Human Rights system provides the strongest form of accountability and oversight. It has a permanent court, which is compulsory for all member states of the Council of Europe. The result is that, in the European system, over 800 million individuals have the right of access to a human rights court in order to bring cases against their states should they require.

Unlike international relations scholars, international lawyers see much of the human rights research problems as hidden in the detailed argument and analysis rather than in general patterns of compliance. This is due to the fact that the idea of human rights is in need of constant interpretation, reinterpretation, and concretization in order to have relevance and action-guiding effect in actual situations. International monitoring mechanisms (be they UN or regional) interpret human rights law to give it concrete application. For example, there is no human rights treaty that says 'water boarding' (pouring water over the face of a person when he/she is stretched on his/her back or hung upside down and his/her face/mouth is covered) is prohibited in international law, but the United Nations Committee against Torture interprets it to be torture, which is prohibited. Similarly, United Nations human rights treaties focus on specific categories of rights holders such as women, children, the disabled, migrant workers, or specific categories of rights such as freedom from racial discrimination and torture in order to clarify the specific duties of states for different categories of human rights concern. International human rights law, therefore, is a complex web of principles, interpretations, and institutions that react to emerging contexts and concrete events.

There is a relationship between the existence of external institutions with powers to monitor and enforce human rights law and how human rights are understood and supported in specific contexts. The more external interpretations of human rights law are viewed as authoritative and persuasive by states the easier it becomes to internalize human rights as objective international standards. It is also true, however, that commitment to human rights is an important factor for states to support the activities and interpretations of international human rights bodies. There is a danger that states make legal human rights commitments as a reputational move or as part of a political bargain. In doing so, they may enter a long list of reservations that means that most of the provisions of a treaty do not meaningfully apply to them. In such cases of half-hearted commitments, however, other states and non-governmental organizations gain legitimate grounds for criticizing a state with legal human rights commitments. It is for these reasons that the cross-cutting debates on international human rights law focus on creating strong international institutions that are seen to rise above the selective policy preferences of individual states. It is naïve to expect that human rights will not have a political dimension. It is, however, also necessary that the meaning and application of human rights are not fully subject to the political preferences of states.

Following the process of the legalization of human rights and the consolidation of the interpretations of treaty provisions, a number of general interpretive principles emerged with respect to what IHRL means:

1. IHRL assigns rights to individuals and duties to states;

2. states have both *negative* (the duty not to interfere with a right) and *positive* duties (the duty to protect individuals from third parties, the duty to plan policies to realize rights);

3. international human rights law applies in times of peace and war. States may derogate from some rights during war or civil conflict;

4. freedom from slavery, freedom from torture, and right to a fair trial are absolute rights and they should be protected at all times in a non-discriminatory way;

5. states must always show reasons for restricting rights. Arbitrary restrictions of rights are prohibited;

6. states must have long-term strategies for the realization of rights;

7. states should not take measures that will have retrogressive effects on human rights protections;

8. states may be responsible for the protection of the rights of individuals outside of their territory when they invade another country or when they have military operations overseas;

9. states may be responsible for the actions of third parties if they act negligently in preventing rights violations over which they have jurisdiction; and

10. states owe duties of humane treatment and due process to non-citizens in their territory, including asylum seekers and illegal immigrants.

The relevance of international human rights law in international relations

The relevance of IHRL in international relations needs to be tackled by differentiating between the different types of functions international human rights law has in international relations. There are three central ways to understand the relevancy of IHRL in international relations. First, provided that IHRL pronounces common standards for the treatment of individuals by all states, do states have a duty to act when another state fails to maintain these standards or deliberately acts to undermine them? Second, is IHRL a way of usurping state sovereignty? Third, given the prominence of the rise of non-state actors in international relations (be it transnational corporations or non-governmental organizations), is the state-focused IHRL really relevant in the current international system? These questions are challenging, but they are also basic to understanding the complex standing of IHRL in international relations.

IHRL and intervention in the internal affairs of other states

As discussed earlier in this chapter, human rights law can have the character of *ius cogens* and *erga omnes* norms. When we assert, for example, that the prohibition of slavery is *ius cogens* we also imply that any state that carries out slavery should face some consequences for engaging in it. When we assert that human rights norms are *erga omnes* we also imply that other states have an interest in putting an end to the breach of such a norm. Indeed, some international treaties (for example, the International Covenant on Civil and Political Rights, the Convention against Torture and the European Convention on Human Rights) incorporate this principle of third-party interest in human rights law violations. These treaties allow for a state to bring a complaint against another state for breaching human rights law. Real examples of this can be seen in the European Convention on Human Rights where cases have been brought against Greece (by Denmark and Sweden), the United Kingdom (by Ireland), Turkey (by Cyprus) and Russia (by Georgia). Interstate complaints have not been used before the United Nations Human Rights treaty monitoring bodies. Because of the character of the international system, usage of *erga omnes* human rights are viewed as political in character and in contradiction with the cornerstone principle of non-intervention in the internal affairs of states by other states. This is part of the reason why interstate complaint mechanisms are underutilized in international human rights law and when they are used there is scepticism about the motives for their use over and beyond their *erga omnes* character.

The international human rights law system responds to this interventionist scepticism by supporting multilateralism as the basic structure for the protection of human rights internationally. The response is to create a general, non-contradictory, and stable interpretative framework that applies to all states and that is transparent and accessible by way of international human rights bodies and courts. It is inevitable that there will be disagreements about the application of IHRL and whether a state has breached its obligations or not. Such disagreements are often about the application of principles to facts. Interpretive conflicts over human rights law make international human rights institutions an all the more important part in the implementation of human rights law. The creation of human rights special rapporteurs, country specific rapporteurs, fact-finding missions and working groups, treaty-monitoring bodies, and human rights courts serves to objectify the application of IHRL in the eyes of the states. This institutional development is by no means perfect and the charge against states of using IHRL for self-serving purposes can only stop if all the world's states fully support multilateral, independent human rights institutions rather than their own self-assessments of their own human rights records and those of other states.

There is a further interventionist element that is closely associated with human rights in international relations. That is the use of 'human rights violations' as a reason for military intervention in a state. This debate is not part of IHRL as such because breaches of IHRL have consequences for states only as long as states are plugged into the international human rights regime and these consequences are invariably legal. They are solved by asking states to remedy human rights violations, requesting them to ensure similar violations do not take place again and openly criticizing states for the breach of their duties under IHRL. Regional organizations (the AU, the OAS, and the CoE) have the powers to suspend membership, and serious breaches of international law may be a ground to use such a sanction. But the United Nations Security Council is the only legitimate international institution in international law that has the power to link breaches of international human rights violations with military measures (see Chapter 10). Under the Charter, the Security Council has the mandate to maintain international peace and security and it has linked serious violations of international human rights law with a threat to international peace and security when authorizing peace enforcement missions, for example as in the case of Sudan, Democratic Republic of Congo, and the former Federal Republic of Yugoslavia. However, in the practice of the Security Council only a specific category of rights is relevant to authorize the use of military force and those rights must be massively or systematically violated for such authorization to happen. In other words, only massive or systematic actual attacks on the lives of individuals would trigger military intervention and those attacks may be committed by state actors or non-state actors, and it is worth noting that the United Nations Security Council calls the former serious violations of international law and the latter serious violations of humanitarian law. If attacks on the lives of civilians reach a serious level of severity and are part of a policy, they could constitute crimes against humanity or genocide (see Chapter 12). In short, 'military intervention for human rights' is popular discourse. IHRL does not authorize such intervention. Together with international humanitarian law and international crimes, it provides a conceptual framework to assess when reasons to respect a state's sovereignty no longer exist.

IHRL and state sovereignty

The system of international human rights law rests on an apparent puzzle. On the one hand, it is argued that IHRL takes the sovereignty of states away and that this is not necessarily a good thing. On the other hand, IHRL exists because states have drafted and ratified international treaties and they continuously support multilateral action through international organizations and by attending human rights meetings, voting on human rights resolutions and declarations, and criticizing each other's human rights records. The way in which IHRL scholars approach this puzzle is not to ask whether IHRL *really* takes away the sovereignty of states. Instead, they seek to define the way we understand the very concept of sovereignty in the first place by drawing the boundaries of sovereign discretion. There is an apparent tension in this approach because IHRL aims to change the ways in which political power is employed by states, but it also accepts that sovereignty is a necessary institution. When the problem of sovereignty in IHRL is framed in this way the question is no longer whether human rights law trumps sovereignty, but what space is occupied by sovereign rights and IHRL respectively. There are a number of ways in which international human rights law accommodates the sovereignty of states, but at the same time it aims to place constraints on how that sovereignty is exercised.

Temporary derogation from IHRL

All major human rights treaties recognize that a state may temporarily limit some IHRL protections if there exists a public emergency threatening the life of a nation. In IHRL, this is called **derogation**. IHRL treaties also provide a list of rights where restrictions are not provided at any time. These are called **non-derogable** rights. International and internal conflicts, major terrorist threats, and natural disasters are some examples of public emergencies. The core idea behind derogation from IHRL is that public authorities may need to restrict the freedoms of individuals in certain times and places in order to protect the safety and well-being of the very same individuals. Temporary restrictions on the freedom of assembly where there are credible threats of terrorist attacks or imposition of curfews limiting the freedom of movement in certain places where an internal armed conflict is taking place are examples of such restrictions. Undoubtedly, derogating from IHRL is a highly sensitive matter and each derogation invites a discussion of whether the derogation is necessary and proportionate. IHRL bodies, for example the Human Rights Committee, recognizes this problem and demands that states provide public and detailed reasons for temporary derogations, how it addresses the specific emergency, and review such reasons regularly with the view of lifting the restrictions. Derogations, which discriminate amongst the population in terms of their effects, are not permitted.

Box 13.5 Procedural requirements for derogation and non-derogable human rights provisions under the ICCPR

International human rights law allows states to *derogate from* (that is, temporarily suspend) *rights* during periods of 'public emergency' under Article 4(1) of the ICCPR.

There is, however, a group of rights which can never be restricted nor derogated from. These **non-derogable rights** are:

- the rights to be free from arbitrary deprivation of life;
- torture and other ill-treatment;
- slavery; imprisonment for debt;
- retroactive penalty;
- non-recognition of the law; and
- infringement of freedom of thought, conscience, and religion (Article 4(2)).

ICCPR provisions underline the exceptional nature of derogations from rights guaranteed in the Covenant. Procedural conditions under which derogations from rights are permitted by international law are:

- evidence of existence of a threat to the life of the nation;
- official proclamation of the state of emergency;
- derogations to be strictly required by the exigencies of the situation;
- derogations not to be inconsistent with other international obligations of the state;
- derogations not be discriminatory; and
- non-derogable rights to be respected.

IHRL as last resort

If an international human rights treaty allows for individuals to make complaints against states, individuals have to exhaust all domestic remedies before they can bring such an international complaint. In IHRL this is called the '*exhaustion of domestic remedies*' principle. This principle says that a state's domestic courts are the first place where individual complaints about human rights violations should be heard. There are two reasons for this. First, when a state signs up to an international human rights treaty that treaty should become the law of the land. In other words, states should eliminate the discrepancies between their domestic laws and practices and international promises about human rights. This assumption places the onus on the state to be the first body to investigate and remedy allegations of violations of human rights law made against it. It is only in cases where a state is unwilling or unable to address violations, or when violations occur on a massive scale that international human rights bodies and international security mechanisms step in. This means that under normal circumstances of proper overall application of IHRL complaints, only a few of those will find their way to international human rights bodies and courts. This is why individual complaints are viewed as 'barometers' of political domestic systems. When states become more totalitarian or slip into internal conflict, their ability or willingness to observe international human rights protections significantly diminish. Complaints from individuals may also diminish because of the high risk to the individual's safety from making such complaints. Indeed, the United Nations has a special mechanism in the shape of the *Special rapporteur on human rights defenders*. The rapporteur's role is to monitor and report abuses and attacks against human rights defenders.

Box 13.6 Human rights cases

Human rights cases are the most popular ways of familiarizing with IHRL provisions. Individuals challenging states internationally is one of the most innovative developments in international law.

Each human rights court or treaty body has different procedures to admit and decide on in human rights cases. When a human rights court delivers a decision, it is legally binding. If a human rights court finds a violation of their human rights treaty, states may have to pay compensation to individuals, re-institute the situation of the individual, change legislation or policy, or prosecute state agents for their actions.

Three of the five permanent members of the Security Council—UK, France, and Russia—have accepted the compulsory jurisdiction of the European Court of Human Rights. The US and China have not accepted the right to individual petition before any regional court or international body.

IHRL and economic, social, and cultural policy

Political theorists, policy-makers, and international lawyers have long discussed whether economic and social rights can be adequately protected by IHRL. The discussion focuses on the resource implications of economic and social rights, such as the right to health, education, and food and difficulties of having common standards across countries with different levels of economic development and historically divergent views on economic and social policy. These discussions have had an effect on the drafting of the ICESCR. Compared to other treaties, ICESRC has a distinct approach which stipulates that states should 'take steps' towards the 'progressive achievement of the rights'. It, however, asks states to show that it is taking steps and report to the CESRC what these steps are. States, therefore, have a margin of discretion to decide on how best to implement IHRL on economic, social, and cultural rights. IHRL, nevertheless, introduces principles that block policy options of states and asks states to assist other state parties in the realization of economic, social, and cultural rights. States have also drafted an individual complaint mechanism for the ICESCR, which is open to adoption. The individual complaint is based on a dual principle that a person or a group has to show that they suffer significant disadvantage of their economic, social, and cultural rights and that the states must show that they have taken reasonable steps.

> **Box 13.7 IHRL constraints on domestic economic, social, and cultural policy**
>
> - Every state has a duty to prioritize minimum core obligations to ensure the satisfaction of, at the very least, minimum essential levels of each of the rights irrespective of the availability of resources.
> - States should not deny ESC rights in a discriminatory fashion.
> - When a state is unable to fulfil its obligations, it has the burden of proving this is the case.
> - States should sufficiently regulate non-state actors that have an impact on the enjoyment of ESC rights.
> - States should not take deliberate retrogressive measures.
> - States should not actively deny ESC rights.
> - State should have policies and plans in place for progressive realization of ESC rights.

IHRL, citizenship, refugees, and migrants

IHRL assigns rights to persons as individuals and not as citizens. The sovereign right to give citizenship to an individual, however, is untouched by this. A non-citizen does not have the right to become a citizen of any county he/she wishes. States, on the other hand, do not have the right to deny nationality to their own citizens as stated in Article 15 of the UDHR. A non-citizen is entitled to IHRL protection so long as he/she legally resides in another country. The UN Migrant Worker Convention further aims to specify the duties of states towards migrant workers and their families.

In contemporary international politics IHRL often comes into conflict with the rights of states to decide who enters and who remains in their territory. Political oppression and persecution, civil wars, poverty, and unemployment mean that millions of people are on the move in the world. IHRL sets out guidelines on how these people should be treated by states. The entry requirements into a country and standards for deportation are two areas where IHRL has had the most impact.

Article 14 of the UDHR gives everyone the right to seek and enjoy asylum from prosecution and wars. The Refugee Convention of 1950 and the 1967 Additional Protocol set out specific guidelines and obligations for states to process asylum applications. The minimum a state has to do is to assess the merits of the individual's claims, provide a fair hearing and decision-making process, and treat the person humanely during the waiting period. States have further obligations towards accompanied and non-accompanied minors seeking asylum with respect to their education and support. Apart from giving refugee status to an individual, states also have duties not to return individuals to countries where they may face torture or risk to their lives. This is called the ***non-refoulement*** principle. IHRL introduces constraints on the rights of states to admit or deport non-citizens. States not only have to consider why a person leaves his/her country, but also the situation he/she may return to when deported.

A non-citizen's right to remain in the country is at the discretion of the sovereign state. He/she is also vulnerable to deportation if he/she does not adhere to local laws. This view frequently clashes with states' immigration and security policies. Under IHRL a state cannot adopt a policy to expel a non-citizen without considering the ties the non-citizen has to that country and without assessing whether the non-citizen faces risk to his/her life in the country to which he/she would be expelled. Policies to deport individuals when they are viewed as security threats have become common in international relations and states view this as an integral part of their sovereignty. IHRL demands that states consider the life of the deported individual as an important part of any policy. This means that, in considering deportation, any risk to the life of the individual and his/her family needs to be part of the state's decision-making process and must be balanced against any perceived security risks of non-deportation.

Non-citizens (or aliens) face discrimination and disadvantage in civil, political, and economic life in the countries they reside. International human rights treaties, such as the Migrant Workers Convention and International Labour Organization

Conventions, aim to reduce arbitrary forms of discrimination and disadvantage towards non-citizens. These treaties, however, only apply to states that have ratified them. IHRL, therefore, has uneven impact on the treatment of migrants internationally.

IHRL outside of the territory of a state

A central contribution of IHRL to our understanding of sovereignty lies in how the former sees the latter as a functional entity. IHRL conceives states as carrying out politically sanctioned legislative, judicial, and executive functions. States have human rights responsibilities for the laws they enact, for the decisions its courts take, and for the actions of its executive bodies. States traditionally undertake all three functions in their own territory. But we also know that states carry out activities through their security forces and military outside of their own territories. The framework of IHRL requires states to fulfil their human rights law responsibilities even when acting outside their own territory. In IHRL, these are called **extra-territorial human rights obligations**. This becomes relevant when a state invades another state and starts effectively running that country, when a state establishes prisons or detention centres in the territories of other states, or when states engage in torture practices on planes, sea vessels, or in the territory of other states. It is for this reason that the Human Rights Committee, which is the monitoring body of the International Covenant on Civil and Political Rights, decided, for example, that Israel has human rights law obligations for individuals in its occupied territories (Concluding Observation of HRC on Israel 1999, UN Doc CCPR C/79/Add.93 at 10) and that the same obligations apply to Belgian forces operating under a UN peacekeeping mandate in Somalia (Concluding Observation of HRC on Belgium 1998, UN Doc CCPR C/79/Add.07 at 14).

Compliance with international human rights law

A central puzzle for international relations research concerns the degree of compliance states have with IHRL. This concern is empirical and asks questions about the effectiveness of IHRL to guide state behaviour. Given the complexity of IHRL, the numbers of treaties that exist under the auspices of different international organizations and the different types of obligations IHRL proscribe, the empirical analysis of compliance is not an easy matter. From the proceeding discussion, however, we can appreciate that compliance is not an 'either/or' question and it would not be factually accurate to divide the world into states complying with international human rights law versus states refusing to comply or disregarding international law. Compliance with IHRL is a matter of degree and context. Each human rights law regime has its own historical characteristics and institutional features that determine questions about compliance. The domestic preferences of the governments in power, the constitutional character of the state, the perceived authority of the external human rights institution that demands compliance, and the existence of coercion or incentives to comply with a specific human rights law directive are also relevant in measuring compliance with human rights treaties.

A further important issue when discussing empirical compliance is the subject matter of the international human rights treaty in question. It is relatively straightforward, for example, to identify whether states comply with the ban on the death penalty for juveniles if we can have access to worldwide statistics on this issue. It is not, however, as clear to identify compliance with freedom of expression, as the restrictions on the right to freedom of expression require adjudication based on the context of expression in order to identify whether the expression incites violence or hate or defames or insults private persons. The empirical analyses of compliance with international human rights law are also sensitive to the research designs employed. It is not possible to say empirically that no state complies with IHRL. Neither is it possible to empirically show that compliance is perfect. The empirical knowledge we have of compliance is time-specific, issue-specific, and inherently comparative in time or across countries.

Empirical difficulties in measuring compliance IHRL, however, are only one part of the compliance debate. There are also conceptual difficulties in analysing compliance. The general approach in the rationalist-realist tradition argues that compliance with international human rights treaties is inevitably weak because human rights are norms and therefore relatively inconsequential in international relations. This approach links up with a number of related assumptions about international law in general and what determines state behaviour. Given that IHRL is a very prominent part of international relations and a vast majority of the world's states are at least party to one international human rights treaty, international relations scholars with a more constructivist and institutionalist bent have used IHRL international human rights law as a test case to prove the rationalists and realists wrong. This approach links up with a number of related assumptions on the role of diffusion and socialization of norms through international agreements, customs, and usage and the ability of human rights regimes and networks to alter state preferences. What is to be expected empirically is a great degree of variation with respect to the explanatory power of these views. This is due to the important fact that there is not a simple and unified object called 'IHRL' that we can see being complied with in the real world. There are a number of international treaties, a long and demanding list of rights in each treaty, and a set of arguments about which rights constitute customary international law.

New international actors and international human rights law

There are a large number of non-state actors and intergovernmental actors that operate internationally and exert significant influence on states. This raises questions about how IHRL deals with these entities and whether actors other than states can have international human rights obligations. In contemporary international relations attention is focused on transnational corporations that operate in more than one state and have larger budgets than many developing states. International financial organizations, namely the World Bank and the IMF, have also received much attention because of the influence they have on the economic evolution of developing states and their fiscal policies. As discussed in the earlier sections of this chapter, IHRL assigns duties to states with respect to the treatment of individuals. States are the sole parties to international human rights treaties. Even though transnational corporations have economic and political powers, they do not have law-making and law-enforcement capabilities. In this respect, transnational corporations may be involved in serious crimes and assist human rights violating states but these crimes or wrongs, nevertheless, can only be remedied by domestic courts.

A clear exception to this logic is when a non-state entity governs a territory and/ or a people. An example of this is the United Nations Interim Administration in Kosovo (UNMIK) acting as the government of Kosovo after the NATO intervention of 1999. Indeed, the Human Rights Committee, which only monitors the human rights commitments of states under the covenant on civil and political rights, asked UNMIK to present a report about how it protected ICCPR rights of the individuals residing in Kosovo. This is an important development for understanding the impact of IHRL on how we understand international accountability. If we are able to point to an entity, which is not itself a state, but has taken on government-like functions with respect to a group of people, we have a plausible case to think about the applicability of IHRL to this entity.

In international practice, however, such cases are rare. Most often the problem arises not because a non-state entity replaces a state, but because it exerts influence on the actions of a state or becomes complicit in the human rights violations of states or because it commits human rights violations under the instructions or direction of states. There are two ways to advance the debate further in this field: first, how can we enable states to control powerful non-state actors and, if such control is not possible; second, what international mechanisms we would need to think about to hold powerful non-state actors to account?

The question of how we can ensure that states better control the human rights' impacts of the activities of non-state entities centres on the idea that states are not only responsible for refraining from committing human rights violations, but are also responsible for exercising due diligence to protect individuals from third parties. This idea calls on the state's legislative and judicial powers to be used to protect human rights. This could be done, for instance, by according primacy to IHRL obligations in the domestic constitutions of states when they conflict with investment agreements or IMF commitments. In cases of conflict between an investment agreement with a transnational corporation or a stand-by agreement with the International Monetary Fund, individuals should be able to challenge a government's policy choices from the perspective of compatibility with IHRL. Governments can also be called in to exercise powers over their companies acting in other countries. In cases of complicity with serious human rights violations, such as torture or killings, the home states of transnational corporations could accept cases against the parent companies of such corporations. The Alien Torts Claims Act in the US is an example of this practice. Affected individuals have brought cases against the US-based companies Chevron, Union Carbide Corporation, and Unocal for complicity in serious human rights violations in Nigeria, India, and Burma (Myanmar) respectively.

In the face of pressure from civil society organizations, multinational corporations and international organizations in the field of human rights have also turned to voluntary self-regulation. The World Bank, for example, has responded to the international human rights accountability gap in its operations by setting up the World Bank Inspection Panel. It accepts complaints from anyone, people or non-governmental organizations, who believe that they have been or are likely to be adversely affected as a result of the Bank's policies. The Panel has powers to recommend investigations to the World Bank's board, which takes the ultimate decision to compensate victims, to halt a project, or to carry out investigations. A United Nations-guided initiative has established the United Nations Global Compact and transnational corporations can voluntarily associate with this in order to show that they observe international human rights principles (as well as environmental and anti-corruption measures). The Global Compact has a mechanism called 'Communication on Progress', which is a reporting mechanism for transnational corporations about how they live up to their human rights promises. Transnational corporations are also asked to respond to queries from the Global Compact office about their performance within three months of the query being made. The Global Compact makes public its list of corporations which fail to do this.

A final discussion on international actors and their accountability for complicity in human rights abuses or serious impact on human rights protections concerns the ultimate effectiveness of state-based action towards these actors and the self-regulation of actors themselves. Economic activity in the international sphere is not under the control of international human rights law. International human rights law requires states not to violate human rights and guides them on how to regulate, prosecute, and punish the actions of non-state actors. But, as we have seen in previous discussions, one of the reasons for that was that there was such wide support for the Universal Declaration of Human Rights in 1948 that states were unable to protect human rights domestically. In cases where states are unable or unwilling to regulate non-state actors and these actors do not restrain themselves voluntarily, there emerges a serious accountability gap from the perspective of the individuals who are affected by the actions of states as well as non-state actors. The question then becomes whether international actors other than states should become directly accountable for their negative impact on human rights protections in international law? This is a new frontier for designing institutions in the international system, but one not without example. The International Criminal Court (ICC), established in 1999, has complementary jurisdiction over individuals who commit the most heinous international crimes that states have been unable or unwilling to prosecute (see Chapter 12). It is indeed a good time to think about an international tort court, which can have jurisdiction over powerful international actors whose harmful and criminal activities states have either failed or not wanted to regulate, prosecute, or punish. The international human rights law system is the vehicle behind this thinking as it enables us to view the international system not merely as a space for interstate interactions with immunity and impunity, but as a space where international responsibility is a natural extension of international conduct.

Conclusion

This chapter has set out IHRL and its institutions. It showed that IHRL is a complex web of international commitments legally recognized by states in varying degrees, but that many rights, such as those of right to life, freedom from torture, fair trial, and freedom from slavery are also regarded as customary international law binding on all states. The chapter then considered the relevance of international human rights law in contemporary international relations. It set out that IHRL bears on a number of cross-cutting debates in international relations, namely military intervention, the empowerment of individuals against states internationally, and the treatment of non-citizens, migrants, and refugees. The chapter further discussed the interrelationship between the rise of non-state actors and IHRL. The chapter finally addressed the question of compliance with international human rights law and the consequences that an issue-based, a treaty-based, or a rights-based approach may have on understanding compliance.

Case Study 13.1   IHRL and advocacy

You are approached by a local civil society organization, Arcadia Rights Centre (ARC), in Draconia with a small Arcadian minority. The ARC would like to advocate their rights by using IHRL before international human rights institutions and bodies as they feel that the Draconian state is not responding to their complaints of non-discrimination and accuse them of separatism by claiming rights. In particular, they tell you that:

- Arcadian Rights Centre activists are arbitrarily detained and tortured;
- a number of Arcadian newspapers have been banned; and
- Arcadians are forcefully evicted from their homes because of the Draconian inter-state highway project funded by major multinational corporations.

Draconia is a member of the United Nations, party to core UN human rights treaties, but not party to any of the regional courts or individual complaints mechanisms.

Advise ARC on which provisions of IHRL they can invoke and before which UN bodies they can bring their complaints.

Questions

1. What are the sources of international human rights law?
2. Why do states create and sign international human rights law treaties?
3. What is the difference between international human rights law and rights recognized in domestic constitutions and laws?
4. What does it mean to suggest that a human right is part of customary international law?

5. In what ways does human rights law affect our understanding of state sovereignty?

6. What is the relationship between a state's security policy and IHRL?

7. What is the relationship between IHRL and military interventions?

8. How does IHRL address the rise of powerful multinational corporations and their activities? Is this adequate?

9. In what ways should we approach the empirical compliance with IHRL?

10. In what ways does IHRL pose questions to realist understandings of international relations?

Further reading

Clapham, A. (2006) *Human Rights Obligations of Non-State Actors* (Oxford: Oxford University Press). *A seminal discussion of how armed groups, international organizations, and multinational corporations can be accountable for their involvement or complicity in IHRL violations.*

Conte, A. and Burchill, R. (2009) *Defining Civil and Political Rights: The Jurisprudence of the United Nations Human Rights Committee* (Farnham: Ashgate). *A comprehensive collection of the interpretation of international human rights law by the monitoring body of the International Covenant on Civil and Political Rights.*

Craven, M. (1998) *International Covenant on Economic, Social and Cultural Rights* (Oxford: Oxford University Press). *A comprehensive discussion of how IHRL protects economic, social, and cultural rights.*

Freeman, M. (2002) *Human Rights: An Interdisciplinary Approach* (Cambridge: Polity Press). *An introductory book to the idea of human rights and its international development.*

Harris, D., O'Boyle, M. and Warbrick, C. (2009) *The Law of the European Convention on Human Rights* (Oxford: Oxford University Press). *A right-by-right analysis of the case law of the European Court of Human Rights.*

Meckled-Garcia, S. and Cali, B. (eds.) (2006) *The Legalisation of Human Rights: Multidisciplinary Perspectives on Human Rights and Human Rights Law* (London: Routledge). *An edited collection that sets out the complex interaction between human rights as a moral ideal, as law, and as a political project.*

Mertus, J. (2009) *United Nations and Human Rights*, 2nd edn. (London: Routledge). *A comprehensive account of the work of all of the organs of the United Nations in the human rights field.*

Nickel, J. (2007) *Making Sense of Human Rights*, 2nd edn. (Oxford: Wiley-Blackwell). *A comprehensive discussion of international law and its justification and feasibility with a focus on economic, social, and cultural rights.*

Okafor, O. C. (2007) *The African Human Rights System, Activist Forces and International Institutions* (Cambridge: Cambridge University Press). *A constructivist account of how IHRL systems and NGO advocacy can affect attitudes towards human rights in domestic contexts.*

Steiner, H., Alston, P., and Goodman, R. (eds.) (2007) *International Human Rights in Context: Law, Politics and Morals*, 3rd edn. (New York: Oxford University Press). *A comprehensive resource book on a wide range of topics on international human rights law with excerpts from leading articles and documents.*

Websites

http://www.ohchr.org/ *The website of the Office of the High Commissioner for Human Rights contains a great wealth of information relating to human rights—such as on UN human rights bodies, human rights instruments, national human rights institutions, and country situations.*

http://www2.ohchr.org/english/law/ *All the international legal documents relating to human rights are compiled in this website.*

http://www.coe.int/ *The Council of Europe website provides detailed information on the European regional human rights system, and informs about the activities of the European Court of Human Rights, the Commissioner for Human Rights, as well as the Parliamentary Assembly and the Committee of Ministers.*

http://www.oas.org/oaspage/humanrights.htm *The website of the Organization of American States informs about the institutions of the Inter-American human rights system—the Inter-American Commission on Human Rights and the Inter-American Court of Human Rights.*

http://www.achpr.org/english/_info/news_en.html *This website informs about the activities of the African Commission on Human and Peoples' Rights which is charged with ensuring the promotion and protection of Human and Peoples' Rights throughout the African Continent.*

Visit the Online Resource Centre that accompanies this book to access more learning resources www.oxfordtextbooks.co.uk/orc/cali/

Chapter endnote

1. Some of the United Nations Treaty bodies have additional powers. The Sub-Committee on Prevention of Torture created under an Optional Protocol is able to make visits to state parties to monitor places of detention. The Committee on the Elimination of Racial Discrimination has early warning measures, which aim at preventing existing situations escalating into conflicts and urgent procedures to respond to problems requiring immediate attention to prevent or limit the scale or number of serious violations of the CERD.

Chapter 14

International law for environmental protection

David M. Ong

CHAPTER CONTENTS

- Introduction
- International treaties for environmental protection
- International environmental principles and the sustainable development paradigm
- Environmental treaty non-compliance mechanisms
- Non-state actors and environmental protection
- A mixed regime for international environmental law?
- Conclusion

CHAPTER OVERVIEW

This chapter examines the development of international environmental law in international relations. International environmental law draws from a diverse range of sources, namely, international treaties, soft law principles, compliance mechanisms, and voluntary self-regulation by non-state actors. The chapter analyses these sources in turn and discusses the implications of a diversity of sources and actors for the effective protection of the environment. The chapter puts a further emphasis on the coexistence of interstate commitments, regimes and non-state actor voluntary regulation in this field and the potential of incorporating non-state actors as standard setters in the field of environmental protection.

Introduction

Everyone—states, companies, individuals, civil society—agrees that the environment matters and that action has to be taken to protect it. All the more so because of increasing scientific evidence that the contemporary condition of the environment is one of degradation affecting the health and well-being of humans as well as the eco-systems of the world. It has also become clearer that human activities and choices are having direct effects on environmental outcomes. Despite this general agreement on its importance and the pressing need to protect or improve it, however, there is little agreement on what counts as an environmental issue or threat, what should be done, and who should do something about it and how. The environment is a difficult term to define. It covers a wide range of issues such as climate change, air pollution, the protection of eco-systems and endangered species, and the management of harmful substances, such as toxic chemicals. Furthermore, environmental threats are in constant need of assessment in the light of changing circumstances. The protection of the environment or the regulation of environmental issues presents a collective action problem both domestically and internationally. The uncoordinated actions of each actor, be they state or non-state actors, does not necessarily result in the best outcome in terms of protecting the environment. There is, therefore, an incentive for cooperation. But there are also disagreements on the best route of action and who should bear the costs involved in protecting the environment. This leads to attitudes to avoid cooperation and regulation.

This complex background is central for any approach to international environmental law in international relations and for understanding the development of international law that concerns the environment. There is no globally applicable multilateral instrument which defines any international law of environmental protection as there is, for example, in the case of international trade law (see Chapter 15). Instead, international environmental law has developed on three main fronts. First, states have met in a number of international conferences and articulated general principles aimed at guiding states towards ensuring environmental protection. These principles developed in the form of non-legally binding commitments or soft law (see Chapter 7). Second, specific treaty regimes have been created which have addressed particular environmental problems. These treaties have established detailed and technical international regulatory regimes aimed at controlling specific environmental threats. Third, non-state actors have created voluntary self-regulatory frameworks for environmental impact and risk assessment. These three strands of international environmental law-making together offer us an account of development of this dynamic field.

This chapter will first identify the international treaties that have been developed for the protection of the environment. It will then focus on the soft law environmental principles and discuss their content and status. The chapter will next address compliance mechanisms for international environmental law and the significance of the cooperation of non-state actors with states, as well as non-state actor efforts to self-regulate industries in order to achieve environmental protection. The chapter will conclude with a discussion of the limits for international cooperation for the protection of the environment and in what ways we can assess the involvement of non-state actors as voluntary standard-setters in the field of environment.

International treaties for environmental protection

The international law for environmental protection has mainly developed through the adoption of multilateral treaty regimes addressing specific environmental threats. There are two types of environmental law treaties. First, there are globally applicable, but issue-specific, treaties. Second, there are treaties that are

Table 14.1 Types of international environmental treaties

A. Global and issue-specific treaties	B. Regional regulatory frameworks of pollution
The 1973 Convention on International Trade in Endangered Species (CITES) Treaties with compliance mechanisms: The 1987 Montreal Protocol to the 1985 Vienna Convention on Substances that Deplete the Ozone Layer	The United Nations Environment Programme (UNEP) Regional Seas Programme, managed the 1976 Barcelona Convention for the Mediterranean Sea, the 1983 Cartagena Convention for the Wider Caribbean Region, and the 1985 Nairobi Convention for Eastern African Region
The 1989 Basel Convention on the Transboundary Movement of Hazardous and Other Wastes The 1992 United Nations Framework Convention on Climate Change	Independently managed: 1992 Bucharest Convention for the Black Sea, The 1981 Lima Convention for the Protection of the Marine Environment and Coastal Areas of the South-East Pacific,
The 1997 Kyoto Protocol to the 1992 Framework Convention on Climate Change The 1998 Aarhus Convention on Access to Information, Public Participation in Decision-Making and Access to Justice in Environmental Matters	Economic Commission for Europe (ECE) treaties such as the 1979 Geneva Convention on Long Range Transboundary Air Pollution, and its related Protocols

expressly confined to a clearly defined regional space, most usually in the form of a semi-enclosed sea, for example, but encompass within their overall regulatory framework several pollution sources in that region. These international treaties come with innovative procedural mechanisms to ensure compliance with these specific obligations and standards.

We can make two preliminary observations by looking at how international environmental treaties evolved in international relations. First, there are a lot of environmental treaties on a wide range of issues. Second, most of these treaties are specialized. The proliferation and specialization of international environment treaties has both positive and negative aspects from the perspective of environmental protection. It is possible to envisage a relatively seamless international regime consisting of general principles to guide state behaviour, together with individual treaty rules establishing specific legal obligations and standards. All of these obligations act to constrain the environmentally damaging effects of state activities. Indeed, it is possible to suggest that a gradual knitting process is underway here, with the global and regional regulatory threads becoming entwined over time to form a universal regulation (whether global and/or regional in form) covering all types of general and specific environmental threats.

It is, however, also possible to ask whether these multi-layered Multilateral Environmental Agreements (MEAs) are either necessary, or effective. There are important gaps both with regard to the participation of states in international environmental treaties, as well as with the coverage of environmental issues. Certain regions in the world are much better regulated than others. In particular, Western and Northern Europe and its marine regions are the subject of a wide range of regional environmental treaties.[1] In other parts of the world, this is not the case. Particularly in regions effected by economic underdevelopment, there is little prospect in the short-to-medium term timeframe for this regulatory gap to be bridged, at least in terms of the range of environmental threats covered by individual regional instruments. The third-party (*pacta tertis*) rule of international treaty law stipulates that non-party states, no matter how well-supported the treaty is, cannot have any treaty obligations. This means that none of the international environmental treaties achieves universal coverage—a *systemic* difficulty generally encountered by international environmental law.

A further problem for the effectiveness of international environmental law concerns the issue areas it covers. Whilst the present international regulatory framework of global and regional treaties covers a whole range of environmental threats (even though general and region-specific) these treaties cannot easily be expanded to cover newly perceived environmental threats. So the increase of specialized environmental treaties, often overlapping in subject matter with other instruments, tends to occur in full knowledge of such existing environmental treaty regimes.

There are difficulties in invoking general environmental principles before dispute settlement mechanisms. The World Trade Organization Panel in the *EC-Biotech Products* case, for example, decided that an international environmental treaty matters at this forum when *all* WTO members in the dispute are party to it.[2] In this case, this meant that neither the 1992 Biodiversity Convention, nor its 1999 Cartagena Protocol on Biosafety, was regarded as relevant to the dispute because the United States was not a party to those. This is a sign of a continuing sense of uncertainty among governments, judicial bodies, and international lawyers, both international and domestic, as to the legal status and scope of general principles of 'international environmental law' or customary international law and what inter-national environmental treaties tell us about these.

International environmental principles and the sustainable development paradigm

There are five central and well-accepted environmental principles in international law. They were recognized at the 1972 United Nations Convention on the Human Environment (UNCHE), held in Stockholm and further confirmed in 1992 at the United Nations Conference on Environment and Development by members of the United Nations. These are: (1) the environmental integration principle, entailing the inclusion of environmental considerations within socio-economic develop-ment activities; (2) the preventive and precautionary principles, providing that such activities do not cause environmental harm or damage; (3) the polluter-pays principle, requiring that polluters should pay for the environmentally damaging causes of their activities; (4) the environmental impact assessment (EIA) principle, providing that the environmental impact of proposed socio-economic activities is fully accounted for; and (5) the principle of public participation on environmental issues in decision-making processes relating to such socio-economic development activities. International public policy points to the overall goal of these principles as the achievement of 'sustainable development'. 'Sustainable development' was first authoritatively defined as: 'development that satisfies the needs of present generations without compromising the ability of future generations to meet their own needs' by the World Commission on Environment and Development (WCED) in 1987. Environmental principles recognize foremost that states have a right to exploit their own resources for the well-being of their citizens. States are also free to formulate their own environmental and developmental policies. The only substantive constraint on states' choice of environmental and development policy is the responsibility to ensure that activities within their jurisdiction or control do not cause damage to the environment of other states or of areas beyond the limits of national jurisdiction. The remaining environmental principles are of a procedural character and aim to guide states to put environmental concerns into the policy-making and implementation agenda. It is helpful to first go through these principles to identify their normative content and what kinds of interpretation and implementation problems they raise for policy-makers and international lawyers. We will then turn to the status of environmental principles and how they interact with international environmental treaties.

The integration principle

This principle provides for the integration of environmental considerations into socio-economic policies.

Box 14.1 Integration principle

Principle 4 of the 1992 Rio Declaration

'In order to achieve sustainable development, environmental protection shall constitute an integral part of the development process and cannot be considered in isolation from it.'

The duty this principle identifies is procedural. It requires governments to ask the 'environment question' when they engage with social and economic policy. There is continuing uncertainty over the extent to which the integration principle applies beyond the realm of the state or government policy-making, and especially whether it extends to non-governmental entities generally and companies, in particular. For example, should the integration principle be included in and applied to contractual arrangements between host states and investing companies for major infrastructure projects within so-called Transnational Investment Agreements (TIAs) or Host Government Agreements (HGAs) that are clearly part of the 'development process' for the countries involved in these state-investor agreements?

The preventive and precautionary principles

These two principles are increasingly taken together and constitute an imperative and the single most important principle for environmental protection embedded in environmental law: to take *a priori* measures to prevent harm to the environment, rather than *ex post facto*, reactive responses assigning responsibility and liability to compensate for damaged environments.

Box 14.2 Preventive and precautionary principle

Principle 15 of the Rio Declaration
'In order to protect the environment, the precautionary approach shall be widely applied by States according to their capabilities. Where there are threats of serious and irreversible damage, lack of full scientific certainty shall not be used as a reason for postponing cost-effective measures to prevent environmental degradation.'

In spite of the compromised language, ambiguous phrases and qualifying clauses contained within this statement of the principle, it nevertheless highlights the main thrust of current environmental law-making processes, for example, within the international climate change regime. Article 3(3) of the 1992 Framework Convention on Climate Change provides as follows: 'The Parties should take precautionary measures to anticipate, prevent or minimize the causes of climate change and mitigate its adverse effects. Where there are threats of serious or irreversible damage, lack of full scientific certainty should not be used as a reason for postponing such measures, taking into account that policies and measures to deal with climate change should be cost-effective so as to ensure global benefits at the lowest possible cost.'

Box 14.3 International treaties and negotiations on climate change

The Framework Convention on Climate Change (came into force in 1994)
This Convention sets an overall framework for intergovernmental efforts to tackle the challenge posed by climate change. The Convention enjoys near universal membership committing states to gather and share information on greenhouse gas emissions, national policies and best practices, launch national strategies for addressing greenhouse gas emissions, and adapting to expected impacts, including the provision of financial and technological support to developing countries, and cooperating in preparing for adaptation to the impacts of climate change.
The Kyoto Protocol to the Convention on Climate Change (came into force in 2005)

The Kyoto Protocol sets binding targets for thirty-seven industrialized countries and the European community for reducing greenhouse gas (GHG) emissions. The major distinction between the Protocol and the Convention is that while the Convention *encouraged* industrialized countries to stabilize GHG emissions, the Protocol *commits* them to do so. The Protocol places a heavier burden on developed nations under the principle of 'common but differentiated' responsibilities. The Protocol is ratified by 193 countries and the European Union.

Post-Kyoto negotiations

Negotiations are underway for a post-Kyoto instrument to be adopted at the next (15th) Conference of Parties to the Framework Convention on Climate Change at Copenhagen in December 2009. The Copenhagen meeting will continue to carry on the task of addressing human-induced greenhouse gas emissions, as well as the facilitation of mitigation and adaptation efforts for climate change generally.

Canada, France, Germany, Italy, Japan, Russia, the United Kingdom, the United States, Brazil, China, India, Mexico, and South Africa adopted the non-binding Washington Declaration on 16 February 2007 and agreed in principle to a global 'cap-and-trade' or greenhouse gases emissions trading system that would apply to both industrialized nations and developing countries.

The polluter pays principle

There are different conceptions of this principle, ranging from a simple, but arguably simplistic, interpretation requiring actual polluters to be liable for the environmental consequences of their activities, to the more sophisticated interpretation that envisages this principle as requiring the 'internalization' (a well-known concept in economics) of environmental costs incurred from polluting activities that would otherwise be left to society as a whole to absorb. Principle 16 of the Rio Declaration favours the latter approach.

Box 14.4 Polluter pays principle

Principle 16 of the Rio Declaration

'National authorities should endeavour to promote the internalisation of environmental costs and the use of economic instruments, taking into account the approach that the polluter should, in principle, bear the cost of pollution.'

Increasingly however, the emphasis of the polluter pays principle in legal terms is focusing also on liability for what is known as 'pure' environmental damage, or ecological damage, i.e. damage to natural elements of the environment, especially wildlife species and their habitats. Principle 13 of the Rio Declaration, for example, provides that 'States shall develop national law regarding liability and compensation for victims of pollution and *other environmental damage*' (emphasis added). This trend is also in line with a wider conception of what the phrase 'environmental protection' should entail. Multilateral treaties providing for civil liability on behalf of so-called ultra-hazardous industrial activities such as oil tanker shipping and nuclear power generation now expressly include the possibility of incorporating (as a separate liability heading) claims for clean-up measures aimed at restoring damaged aspects of the natural environment, in addition to the traditional tort liability headings of personal injury, property damage, and economic loss. A good example of the recent emphasis on compensating for the rejuvenation of wildlife damage is the inclusion of such claims under a separate liability heading under the European Community's Environmental Liability Directive. Compensation has also been a well-known concept in US federal environmental legislation, as the 1980 Comprehensive Environmental Response, Compensation and Liability Act (CERCLA) and related domestic case law show.

The principle of environmental impact assessment (EIA)

Box 14.5 Environmental impact assessment

Principle 17 of the Rio Declaration
  'Environmental impact assessment, as a national instrument, shall be undertaken for proposed activities that are likely to have significant adverse impact on the environment.'

This principle is now provided for in numerous multilateral, bilateral, and domestic environmental instruments. The almost universal application of this principle within developed, transitional and even developing country economies is a typical example of the progressive changes wrought by environmental regulation and their impact on general trade and investment relationships. An environmental impact assessment (EIA) exercise is limited in its punitive reach. It merely requires the assessment of effects on the environment, but does not necessarily oblige the entity whose activities are having a negative impact to mitigate such impacts. Nevertheless, the publication of EIA information fulfils the transparency requirements of both the principles of access to environmental information and public participation in environmental decision-making.

The importance of greater transparency for ensuring better accountability is especially pertinent in situations where infrastructure projects have negative impacts on wildlife habitats. While local communities can reasonably be expected to make use of public consultation mechanisms provided for them under the EIA process, such mechanisms will clearly not be useful to the wildlife without well-organized, grassroots support networks among local community raising the issue of potential destruction of such wildlife habitat by the planned infrastructure projects. Of course, relying on local support for wildlife habitat preservation where impoverished communities are being offered relatively large sums of money for the sale or use of their land may not be very effective.

The tension between immediate or mid-term benefits of economic development and environmental protection has led to the development of the concept of strategic environmental assessment (SEA). SEA represents a progressive evolution in the standard EIA exercise and is now required on a regional basis within the member states of the European Union, especially in the context of marine environmental protection within their offshore jurisdictions. While the EIA process embodies a proactive approach, the SEA operates on a much larger scale than the individual projects that are subject to EIAs. Moreover, each SEA exercise is both comprehensive in its coverage of nearly all aspects of development projects with environmental implications, as well as subject to review by stakeholder groups, to ensure the final version of the SEA is as up to date and as accurate as possible.

The principles of access to environmental information, public participation in the environmental decision-making process, and access to environmental justice

Box 14.6 Environmental information

Principle 10 of the Rio Declaration
'Environmental issues are best handled with the participation of all concerned citizens, at the relevant level.'

This principle has three aspects: (1) the duty to give access to environmental information, especially in respect of hazardous activities; (2) the duty to provide opportunities for public participation; and (3) the duty to allow effective access to judicial proceedings to seek redress for any failings in respect of the first two aspects.

All these elements are present in a range of regional environmental treaties. For example, the 1991 Espoo Convention on Transboundary Environmental Impact Assessment provides that each state party must establish an Environmental Impact Assessment procedure that permits public participation in respect of the proposed activities listed under Appendix I that are likely to cause significant adverse transboundary impact. Such public participation includes notification and consultation. Building on the successful entry into force of the Espoo Convention, the Economic Commission for Europe (ECE) adopted the 1998 Aarhus Convention which is regarded as being the most advanced international treaty on public participation in environmental issues so far. Article 4 of this Convention provides for access to 'environmental information', with a broad definition of what this constitutes under Article 2(3). It then follows this up with a fairly comprehensive right to public participation in various environmental decision-making processes described under Articles 6, 7, and 8, and particularly in relation to certain activities specified in Annex I to the Convention, as well as activities that 'may have a significant effect on the environment.' Especially significant in this context is the fact that the definition of 'the public concerned' (i.e. the public affected, or likely to be affected by environmental decision-making processes) envisages Non-Governmental Organizations (NGOs) to play an important role. However, both of these regional treaties are ECE Conventions and thus geographically limited in their application only to certain European and North American states. Their progressive application of the principles of access to environmental information, public participation, and even judicial review of environmental decision-making processes must be replicated within other regional or bilateral agreements across the world before it can be argued that their present formulations transcend their individual instruments to inform the development of, and moreover, contribute to the customary sources of international environmental law.

The rights to environmental information, public participation, and access to justice, are procedural, rather than substantive, rights. A substantive right to a healthy or clean environment is not as well-established under international law as the procedural rights enumerated above. Moreover, procedural environmental rights suffer from a major defect as they rely on the presence of well equipped and informed environmental NGOs and facilitation of their role in policy-making. Explicit legal recognition of such a role for environmental NGOs has so far been mainly confined to the legal systems of a handful of developed or industrialized countries.

Status of environmental principles in international law

All these principles are now well accepted by states as international environmental norms, but the legal authority of these norms is a subject of debate. This has a knock-on effect on their specific implementation, both between and within states. The continuing legal difficulties raised by these principles for the progressive development of international environmental 'rules' (as opposed to 'principles') of law are twofold in nature. First, they are usually articulated in non-legally binding international instruments such as Declarations, Resolutions and Programmes of Action. Secondly, the question arises as to whether these environmental 'principles', currently articulated in 'general' terms within these international instruments, have developed into much more normatively significant 'rules' of customary international law, containing specific rights and duties for individual states in the environmental protection field.

> **Box 14.7 Soft law or custom?**
>
> The 1992 Rio Declaration on the Environment and Development is a non-legally binding international instrument. In 2002 the World Summit on Sustainable Development reaffirmed commitment to the Rio Declaration.
>
> Does this continuing support for the principles make them binding under customary international law?

The status of environmental principles in international law and what duties these principles trigger for states is an important discussion in international law. We can identify three perspectives about the function of these principles: a legal, a political, and usage-oriented perspective. The first one emphasizes the legal relevance of the principles and the duties of states to take them into account. The emphasis here is that environmental principles are a very important form of law, which may be 'soft', but which should not be confused with 'non-binding' law (Boyle 1999: 907).

The political perspective points out that environmental principles enable conforming states to put political pressure on dissenting states to comply with the soft law norms contained within these instruments. This pressuring process is political rather than legal because of the lack of express legal consent of states to the principles. Shelton therefore concludes that 'nonbinding norms and informal social norms can be effective and offer a flexible and efficient way to order responses to common problems. They are not law and they do not need to be in order to influence conduct in the desired manner' (Shelton 2006a: 322). The flexibility of such environmental principles, due to the non-legally binding nature of their sources and their hortatory rather than imperative language, does however come at a price. This price is their uncertain legal status under international law: Are they general 'principles' or specific customary 'rules' of international environmental law?

The usage oriented perspective looks at whether and how states use the principles before dispute settlement mechanisms. Indeed several of these environmental principles have been invoked by states in the context of legal claims against other states adjudicated before international tribunals. Boyle observes in this respect that these principles '. . . may lay down parameters which affect the way courts decide cases or the way an international institution exercises its discretionary powers. They can set limits, or provide guidance, or determine how conflicts between other rules or principles will be resolved' (Boyle 1999: 901). The use of environmental principles before international judicial organs, however, also comes with limitations. Judicial pronouncements from international tribunals seized of environmental issues do not have the capacity to confirm the global application of these principles as rules of customary international law above and beyond the environmental treaty regimes where these principles are re-iterated as specific rules. Indeed, the analysis of a number of significant cases before different international tribunals, namely, the International Court of Justice (ICJ), the WTO Panels and Appellate Body and the International Tribunal for the Law of the Sea (ITLOS), suggests that there is a lack of confirming jurisprudence in favour of the application of significant environmental principles, such that there is arguably a lack of a certain 'animating spirit' within international environmental law. This lack of an 'animating spirit' does not allow these undoubtedly well-accepted, but generally-worded and in themselves non-binding, environmental principles to be applied in such a way that they can transcend their specific articulation within individual environmental treaties, and facilitate their transition to rules of customary international law providing for environmental protection.

A final consideration about the status of the environmental principles is that there is little evidence of long-standing state practice pointing to observation of these general environmental principles fully, both as between themselves, and within their domestic legal regimes. This is so even where these principles are now articulated more specifically in individual treaty regimes, addressing particular environmental problems identified for concerted action by these very same states. State practice does not reflect uniform implementation of these principles. This suggests that states take the principles merely as guidance for their domestic environmental policies, rather than implement them within their environmental laws.

This analysis shows that the really critical questions regarding the legal status and application of these general environmental principles remain unanswered. It is still a debate, therefore, whether successful transition from 'political slogans to legal rules' have been made when it comes to the protection of the environment (Sadeleer 2005). There are significant differences between regarding general environmental principles as mere guidelines for state behaviour in the environmental policy-making field, or as obligatory rules of customary international law both legally and politically. Legally, only obligatory legal principles can trickle down to domestic legal system and can be invoked in interstate disputes about the environment effectively. Politically, it is difficult to level the playing field internationally when states give conflicting signals as to what their mutual expectations are. The very nature of the issues at stake in environmental protection also poses important problems. It is difficult to argue that the environment as a whole can be protected by bilateral agreements, which are generally more conducive to protect reciprocal state interests and preferences (except for the principle that states have an obligation not to inflict transboundary environmental damage). Some international lawyers insist that environmental principles should be conceived as multilateral rules entailing *erga omnes* obligations owed by each state to every other state, on the basis that *all* states have an interest in global environmental protection. So a state would be able to bring proceedings against another state merely on the basis that the latter is harming the global environment. The International Court of Justice declined an opportunity to enunciate on this very issue in respect of the Australian application to intervene in the 1995 *Nuclear Tests* case, brought by New Zealand against France. Moreover, the further question as to whether *erga omnes* obligations (even where they can be proved to apply to a particular situation) in turn give rise to the exercise of an *actio popularis* right by any state to enforce such obligations was also not addressed by the ICJ in the initial, 1974 *Nuclear Tests* cases.[3] The approach by the Court is not surprising, given that the concept of *ius cogens* norms is still nascent in its development even within general international law.

Environmental treaty non-compliance mechanisms

The reality is that few, if any, of the environmental principles have been applied in such a way as to directly constrain the environmentally degrading actions of states. International environmental law pursued an alternative pathway in order to achieve compliance by establishing non-compliance mechanisms. The first of the treaty-based non-compliance procedures was introduced in the 1987 Montreal Protocol to the 1985 Vienna Convention on Substances that Deplete the Ozone Layer. More recently, these non-compliance mechanisms have arisen in the context of the 1997 **Kyoto Protocol** to the 1992 Framework Convention on Climate Change, and the 1989 **Basel Convention** on Transboundary Movement of Hazardous and Other Wastes. These mechanisms aim at securing the cooperation of states to first accept and then act upon their non-compliant behaviour. The emergence of these mechanisms implicitly highlights the shortcomings of the dispute settlement systems established by the multilateral environmental agreements (Churchill and Ulfstein 2000). However, in any case, traditional judicial dispute settlement mechanisms are not necessarily well-suited to prevent environmental harm, as they are usually only engaged after the alleged non-compliance has already led to damage (Fitzmaurice and Redgewell 2000: 43–4).

Non-compliance mechanisms are formulated as alternatives rather than replacements for the traditional means of international law enforcement through peaceful dispute settlement. These procedures have two important characteristics. First, they monitor all parties to a treaty equally in order to increase the protection of the environment multilaterally. Second, their aim is to facilitate and increase cooperation amongst states rather than increase confrontation (Churchill and Ulfstein 2000: 644–5).

Indeed, with the exception of the Kyoto Protocol, which established enforcement as well as facilitative branches in the Compliance Committee, these environmental treaty compliance mechanisms do not include provisions for exerting sanctions against the non-compliant states. They are designed to play mainly facilitative, rather than enforcement, roles in ensuring compliance with specific environmental treaty obligations. For example, all these compliance regimes adopt, as an alternative to the traditional confrontational style of international judicial dispute settlement, the possibility for a 'confessional'-type procedure. When a state party realizes that it may not be able to comply with its international obligations under the specific environmental treaty regime, it can present itself before the compliance committee/commission and request assistance to achieve compliance. The cooperative model underlying the confession approach is in contrast to coercive models, which is characteristic of international sanctions.

It appears at first glance that international environmental law has developed an innovative means to ensure compliance with substantive rules and standards provided within the individual environmental treaty regimes. However, these individual non-compliance mechanisms are not able to inform the general development of international environmental law, and so do not contribute to the development of optimum standards for state compliance with environmental rules and standards. This is because non-compliance procedures developed within specific treaty regimes do not apply to state parties. They also cannot cover emerging environmental threats. The autonomous nature of each compliance procedure also means that it is not possible for innovative best practice within one of these regimes to be applied to any other treaty compliance regimes.

Box 14.8 The Aarhus Convention non-compliance procedure: a model for future environmental protection?

The United Nations Economic Commission for Europe (UNECE) *Convention on Access to Information, Public Participation in Decision-Making and Access to Justice in Environmental Matters* was adopted on 25 June 1998 in the Danish city of Aarhus.

The Aarhus Convention extends the right to complaint against a state party's alleged non-compliance to individual members of the public and also to environmental and/or human rights non-governmental organizations. The complainants do not have to prove a direct interest in the environmental information requested. Moreover, any person complaining need not be a citizen of the state party concerned, nor in the case of an NGO complaint, need it be based in the state party concerned.

As of April 2009, Aarhus Convention has forty-two state parties.

Non-state actors and environmental protection

Contemporary international relations under the condition of economic globalization has witnessed an increase in the numbers of transnational corporations, private investment banks, and financial institutions as well as agreements between states and these actors in order to facilitate trade and investment. In order to understand the role of non-state actors in environmental protection, it is helpful first to identify types of actors and agreements. Two types of non-state actors are significant for the protection of the environment: international organizations and transnational corporations (TNCs).

Table 14.2 Non-state actors and environmental protection

International organizations	Profit-making actors
Examples:	Examples:
The World Bank Group	Transnational corporations
International Maritime Organization	Private banks lending money for investment projects

First, there are international organizations created with the agreement of governments, and whose sphere of activity has an effect on the protection of the environment. Two examples of such international organizations are the **World Bank** and the *International Maritime Organization*. The World Bank is a collection of organizations that offer loans, credits, and grants to developing countries for a wide array of purposes that include investments in education, health, public adminis- tration, infrastructure, financial and private sector development, agriculture. The International Maritime Organization (IMO) is an intergovernmental organization with the task to develop and maintain a regulatory framework for shipping—its remit includes environmental concerns, legal matters, technical cooperation, mari- time security, and the efficiency of shipping. In the case of the World Bank, major development projects have significant environmental consequences. In the case of the IMO, maritime pollution is an important source of environmental degradation. Both the World Bank and the IMO have codes, standards, and procedures that aim to reduce environmental risks in their sphere of activities. One way of seeing these organizations is as standard setters for states. World Bank development projects are subject to environmental impact assessments and the IMO takes the lead on air pollution by shipping vessels, safety of oil tankers, and ship recycling. Furthermore, the World Bank Group's Environmental, Health and Safety Guidelines (also known as the EHS Guidelines) indicate that when host country regulations differ from the levels and measures presented in the EHS Guidelines, projects are expected to achieve whichever is *more* stringent. Another way of seeing these non-state actors is in terms of their lack of accountability for the decisions they take affecting the envi- ronment. A central question in this regard is whether those actors should be legally bound by environmental principles when designing policies and procedures—a question all the more difficult to answer as the issue of bindingness has not yet even been resolved with regard to states.

Second, there are the profit-making non-state actors, which operate in more than one country. These are known as transnational corporations (or multinational cor- porations), but we can also include private banks in this category. TNCs carry out their economic activities by signing agreements with states in which they oper- ate. These are called host government agreements or state/non-state actor tran- snational investment agreements, and they accord reciprocal rights to states and TNCs. Disputes between host states and TNCs are not subject to domestic laws, but to international dispute settlement. Unlike states, TNCs have no international law obligations to protect the environment. They are bound by the terms of the contract they sign with host states. A host government agreement which brings together a state that is unable or unwilling to take international environmental law obligations seriously and a TNC with no regard to environmental impact or environmental risk is a recipe for environmental disaster. States may be unable to negotiate effectively with TNCs because of civil war, corruption, or lack of technical knowledge about environmental risks—as in the case of the logging contracts issued in the Congo Basin Forest (the world's second largest rain forest, located in the Democratic Republic of Congo) by TNCs trading rain forest timber. In most cases, however, the environmental impact of TNC activity can be subtle and complex and requires detailed analysis and consultation. Because most developing states regard foreign investment as central to economic development they may be unwilling to scare off investment by imposing environmental requirements on TNCs.

Self-regulation by TNCs in the field of environment: the Equator Principles

An important development for the protection of the environment is the emergence of self-regulation by TNCs. In this section, we will focus on the Equator Principles drafted by a group of commercial lending banks which, along with the World Bank Group's International Finance Corporation (IFC), established a banking industry framework for addressing environmental and social risks in the project finance sector.

There are a number of factors that have made TNC self-regulation possible in international relations. The first factor has to do with the structure of transnational project finance. Project finance is a bank lending method whereby the lender relies primarily on the revenues generated by a specific project run by a project company, as the source of repayment for the original loan, as well as the security for the exposure of the lending bank itself.[4] Finance-type projects entail a high exposure to risk on the part of the lending bank and are more likely to be located in higher risk countries. Such commercial lending practices to firms that are often located in foreign jurisdictions have given the banks concerned a more significant stake in the borrowers' financial performance. This relationship in turn provides the banks with not only a financial, but perhaps more importantly, a reputational motive in the overall success of the project. Second, there has been increased attention on TNC activities, especially in countries with civil wars and authoritarian regimes, by environmental and human rights organizations. Public and media attention have created a strong reputational incentive for TNCs to consider the environmental, social (and other) risks. This is especially the case where the projects involve large-scale extractive and/or infrastructure-type development activities, such as oil and gas exploration, mining, dam building, and the laying down of highways/motorways, etc. Both the scale and impacts of these projects are the central focus of campaigning environmental and human rights NGOs.

Three reasons explaining why private sector actors voluntarily place limits on their environmental behaviour (even if these limits are not very constraining and, perhaps more significantly, weakly enforced) have been put forward. These are: (1) risk reduction; (2) reputation enhancement; and (3) learning (Haufler 2001). From the last of these reasons, namely, corporate 'learning', we can discern a shift in attitude and strategy from 'defensive reaction' to 'opportunity grasping'. Indeed, many private actors have departed from the reactive or responsive attitudes of their peers and clearly hope to achieve a number of implicit or even explicit goals in their private or self-regulatory efforts. In this respect, there are also positive effects of 'clubbing together' by business corporations in the field of environment (Prakash and Potoski 2006: 17–27 and 34–80). As these authors note, '(e)ffective green clubs induce participating firms to incur the private costs of undertaking progressive environmental action beyond what they would take unilaterally' (Prakash and Potoski 2006: 17).

The Equator Principles were decided in June 2003. By mid 2007 the Principles had been agreed to by fifty-one Equator Bank countries accounting for nearly 90 % of emerging market project finance. The Principles represent a common set of environmental and social policies and guidelines that are applicable globally and across all industry sectors. Each participating financial institution has adopted the Principles individually and declared that it will put into place internal policies, procedures, and processes that are consistent with these Principles. Notwithstanding the explicitly 'soft' or non-binding nature of these Principles, they have arguably become the standard for assessing and managing environmental and social risk within project financings. There are also close links between these Principles and the environmental, social, and health and safety guidelines and conditionalities utilized by the state-funded multilateral/global financing institutions such as the World Bank. This is because many of these projects ultimately rely on a mixture of public and private sources for funding and credit provision, especially when they concern the building and operation of large infrastructure projects. The Equator Principles represent the establishment of a common framework for the *private* PF industry based on external and respected benchmarks established by *public* sector international financial institutions, namely, the World Bank and IFC Guidelines.

A mixed regime for international environmental law?

International environmental law exposes some of the most significant implications of economic globalization for international law. In the sphere of economic activity, the role of the traditional nation state is changing. Previous governmental functions are increasingly being undertaken by quasi-public, mixed, public-private, or even entirely private, non-state actors. Where these non-state actors remain within the territorial jurisdiction of just one state, they can arguably still be effectively controlled by the domestic legal regime. However, many of these actors, especially when they are in the form of transnational business entities, now traverse the world in pursuit of their economic goals. This phenomenon gives rise to a dilemma for international environmental law (and general international law), since in formal terms this legal discipline only binds states and creates limited rights and obligations for non-state actors only when states agree to this. On the other hand, when private, non-state actors' activity with direct impact on the protection of the environment takes place with the agreement of states, transnational actor practice can arguably also be seen as contributing to the process of international norm formation, despite its non-state origins. Non-state actor self-regulatory practice in the field of environment, therefore, has potential to contribute to the development of a mixed regime of international environmental law.

A danger in encouraging self-regulation of non-state actors in the field of environment is the negative consequences of this for state responsibility and regulation. Even though it is desirable that all non-state actors, TNCs and international organizations follow the same standards for environmental protection, states still remain the key actor with prescriptive powers to hold actors to account and allow citizen participation. States therefore still fulfil an important regulatory and accountability task at domestic and international levels. Special interest non-governmental organizations (NGOs), especially in the environmental, human rights, and labour standards fields, have campaigned against the perceived takeover, especially by private entities, of what had previously been conceived as state-controlled fields, or areas, of regulation.

From an international legal policy perspective one can argue that the self-regulation of non-state actors is a welcome development given that states themselves have been unable to create a globally applicable regime. There are wide discrepancies in states' environmental protection practices and developing states are known to be less willing to impose high environmental costs on state or non-state-led economic development processes. The self-regulatory transnational law forms part of an internalization or socialization process (as opposed to a regime based on threat of sanctions) of principles concerning the protection of the environment. Due to the multi-faceted nature of the problem of the protection of the environment, and the complexity of the actors involved in potentially damaging or improving it, it is positive that there are parallel processes of law-making. The challenge of coordinating states as well as non-state actors in coherently interpreting the environmental principles, however, remains.

Conclusion

In this chapter we have identified that international environmental law suffers from both *substantive* and *systemic* difficulties. There are general environmental principles, but they are enunciated in non-binding international instruments, such as the 1992 Rio Declaration. There are international environmental treaties, but these are either sector specific in their orientation or regional in their scope of application. This developmental gap between general environmental principles and specific treaty rules points towards a *substantive* failing within international environmental law as a viable regulatory framework. Environmental treaty compliance procedures, while performing a valuable role in ascertaining compliance with the specific treaty regime concerned, do not yield authoritative judgments contributing to an understanding of the application of the accepted environmental principles for the wider international community as decisions of international courts and tribunals would do.

Environmental protection through international law also suffers systemic difficulties in the international system. The lack of an equally comprehensive treaty covering all major environmental threats is due to the lack of disagreements about the appropriate concrete collective steps to be taken to protect the environment internationally. States at different stages of economic development have different views on international action. The significant capacities of non-state actors, in particular, international organizations and TNCs, further complicate the picture for international coordination for action. An important development in this regard is the increasing numbers and strength of patterns and networks of international environmental *governance* with its focus on the prevention of environmental harm, rather than the allocation of fault, blame, and liability for its remediation. This alternative regulatory approach offers a possibility for the internalization of international environmental principles and standards by non-state actors, especially when these environmental principles have not been fully implemented within domestic legal regimes.

Questions

1. What are the sources of international environmental law?
2. What types of environmental treaties are there?
3. What is the status of environmental principles in international law; why does this matter?

4. What is the relationship between environmental principles and sustainable development?

5. The protection of the environment is a global phenomenon. Why is there not a global environmental treaty?

6. In what way do non-compliance mechanisms guide state behaviour in the field of environment?

7. What is a confessionary proceeding? What is its use?

8. What role do non-state actors play in environmental protection?

9. Why are there self-regulatory non-state actor regimes?

10. What is the relationship between international law and transnational law for the protection of the environment?

11. What are the prospects for a more comprehensive and effective regulation in the field of environment?

Further reading

Abbott, K. W., Keohane, R. O., Moravscik, A., Slaughter, A.-M., and Snidal, D. (2000) 'The Concept of Legalisation' *International Organization* 54/3: 401–19. *This paper, along with several other articles within this Special Issue, all draw from different theoretical perspectives and approaches of political science to examine the relationship between international relations and international law.*

Birnie, P., Boyle, A., and Redgwell, C. (2009) *International Law and the Environment*, 3rd edn. (Oxford: Oxford University Press). *Arguably the pre-eminent textbook on international environmental law, now fully updated in its third edition.*

Bodansky, D., Brunnee, J., and Hey, E. (eds.) (2007) *The Oxford Handbook of International Environmental Law* (Oxford: Oxford University Press). *Excellent volume of essays offering a comprehensive and yet also in-depth individual treatment of a whole range of issues and written by the pre-eminent authors in this field.*

Broude, T. and Shany, Y. (eds.) (2008) *The Shifting Allocation of Authority in International Law* (Oxford: Hart). *This volume brings together the thoughts of several eminent international lawyers on this theme: 'the allocation of authority in international law' and in doing so allows them to reappraise basic concepts such as 'sovereignty' and 'authority' within international law and consider their relationship with newer concepts such as 'governance', 'fragmentation', and 'subsidiarity'.*

Djelic, M.-L. and Sahlin-Andersson, K. (eds.) (2006) *Transnational Governance: Institutional Dynamics of Regulation* (Cambridge: Cambridge University Press). *Explores the relationships between states, international and transnational organizations in the regulation of certain fields.*

Hall, R. B. and Biersteker, T. J. (eds.) (2002) *The Emergence of Private Authority in Global Governance* (New York: Cambridge University Press). *One of the first volumes of essays devoted to describing and explaining the growth in private authority supplementing* and potentially superseding public (state) authority in the global governance of certain fields.

Jessup, P. (1956) *Transnational Law* (New Haven: Yale University Press). *Possibly the first monograph to introduce the term 'transnational' law for the consideration of the implications of the whole range of legal relationships between states, as well as between states and other international or 'transnational' actors, including private entities.*

Koh, H. (1996) 'Transnational Legal Process' *Nebraska Law Review* 75: 181–206 *This seminal article appraises the evolution of 'transnational law' and makes a sustained case for its recognition as a further normative impulse within states and their 'transnational' private actors.*

Slaughter, A.-M., Tulumello, A. S., and Wood, S. (1998) 'International Law and International Relations Theory: A New Generation of Interdisciplinary Scholarship' *American Journal of International Law* 92/3: 367–97 *An attempt by eminent international lawyers to assess the potential value of theories of international relations to explain the normative relationships between states, as well as between states and other international actors.*

Winter, G. (ed.) (2006) *Multilevel Governance of Global Environmental Change: Perspectives from Science, Sociology and the Law* (Cambridge: Cambridge University Press). *Multi-disciplinary approaches exploring the problem of effective management of global environmental change.*

Websites

http://unfccc.int/kyoto_protocol/items/2830.php *The website of the Kyoto Protocol offers access to documents, informs about the Kyoto mechanisms, emission targets, the status of ratifications, and other related issues.*

http://www.unep.org/Documents.Multilingual/Default.asp?DocumentID=78&ArticleID=1163 *Here the United Nations Environment Programme publishes the Rio Declaration on Environment and Development as well as related resources.*

http://www.imo.org *The International Maritime Organization provides access to its documents and news related to the environmental protection of oceans.*

http://www.ifc.org/sustainability *The International Finance Corporation of the World Bank has developed principles on environmental sustainability which you can find in detail on this website.*

http://www.equator-principles.com/index.shtml *Here you can find the 'Equator Principles', an industry approach for financial institutions in determining, assessing, and managing social and environmental risks in project financing.*

Visit the Online Resource Centre that accompanies this book to access more learning resources www.oxfordtextbooks.co.uk/orc/cali/

Chapter endnotes

1. For example, the 1976 Barcelona Convention on Mediterranean Sea, the 1979 Geneva Convention on Long Range Transboundary Air Pollution, the 1991 Espoo Convention, the 1992 Paris Convention, the 1994 Baltic Convention, the 1998 Aarhus Convention, as well as their related Protocols. There are also environmental protection Regulations and Directives promulgated by the relevant European Union institutions, to be implemented and enforced within each of the member states of the EU.

2. Full title: *EC-Biotech Products, US, Canada, Argentina v EC*, WT/DS291R, WT/DS292R, WT/DS293R, 29 September, 2006.

3. *Nuclear Tests Cases* (*Australia v France, New Zealand v France*) (1974) *ICJ Reports* 253, at 387.

4. This is distinguished from corporate finance-type projects, whereby the lending bank's capital exposure is secured *both* on the corporate assets of the investing company (usually a foreign TNC) as well as the project company assets and revenues.

Chapter 15

World trade and international law

Thomas Sebastian

CHAPTER CONTENTS

CHAPTER OVERVIEW

This chapter describes the international law relating to international trade, focusing specifically on the World Trade Organization (WTO) treaty system. In broad terms, countries conclude trade treaties in order to obtain access to each other's markets. The WTO provides a forum within which countries can conclude such agreement and monitor compliance. The basic WTO disciplines are geared towards facilitating the negotiation of commitments to limit protectionism and ensuring that those commitments are not undermined. These disciplines leave countries with considerable freedom to regulate. However, advanced disciplines, introduced more recently, constrain the ability of countries to regulate in a variety of important areas, such as intellectual property policy and risk regulation.

Introduction

In 2007, countries imported goods worth approximately 14 trillion dollars and commercial services worth 2 trillion dollars (WTO 2008: 11–15). This flow of goods and services is only possible because individual governments have allowed it to occur. This chapter examines how international law has contributed to making this flow of goods and services possible. It explores how governments have used international law as a means to facilitate cooperation on matters of trade policy, the limitations they have accepted on their sovereignty, and the institutions they have built to serve their objectives.

We begin by examining the rationale for trade treaties and main types of trade treaties. We then turn to the WTO Agreements and examine the structure and functions of the institution created by that treaty. Following this, we review the major disciplines, a set of interlinked obligations which limit state action, established by the WTO Agreements as well as the major exceptions from these disciplines. We finally examine certain criticisms of the WTO regime and conclude.

The rationale for trade treaties

Take two countries, A and B. Both of them have car industries. For whatever reason, B's car industry is more competitive than A's industry. Cars from country B are cheaper, more reliable, and perform better than similar cars from country A. Sensing a good commercial opportunity, B's car industry wants to export cars to country A. A's car industry reacts to this threat (to its profits and market share) by lobbying its government to take steps to make it more difficult for B's car industry to compete in the domestic market. In other words it lobbies for 'protection' from imports. The obstacles that the government of A (the importing country) can impose on imports of cars from B can take a variety of forms:

1. *Import prohibitions*: The most extreme step that A can take is to prohibit imports of cars altogether. An import prohibition would completely insulate A's domestic car industry from foreign competition. B's car industry would then face an insurmountable barrier to trade; it simply could not enter the market for automobiles in A.

2. *Import quotas*: Less extreme would be for A to impose quotas on imports of cars. Quotas are numerical limits on the amount of imports that can enter a country in a given year. Assume that the annual demand for new cars in A is around 100,000 cars. A can impose a 50,000 annual quota on imported cars. Effectively, this means that half of the automobile market is reserved for A's domestic car industry. Depending on how much of the domestic market it insulates from competition, a quota can present a significant obstacle to trade.

3. *Tariffs*: A could also impose tariffs on imports of cars from B. A tariff is a tax levied on goods when they cross an international border. For instance it could impose a tariff of 20% of the price of every car imported from B. This effectively would raise the costs of cars imported from B by 20%. Because A's domestic car industry does not pay any tariffs, this measure delivers a competitive advantage to A's domestic car industry equal to the value of the tariff paid by B's car industry. Regardless of level, all tariffs operate as obstacles, high or low, to market access.

4. *Discriminatory internal taxes and regulations*: A could decide to protect its domestic industry by imposing higher internal taxes on imported cars. So if the sales tax on a domestically produced car is 20%, A could levy a substantially higher sales tax on imported cars, say 40%. The 20% tax differential confers a competitive disadvantage on B's domestic car industry in precisely the same way as a 20% import tariff does. A could also impose discriminatory regulatory requirements on imported cars. For instance, A could specify that imported cars have to be fitted with expensive pollution control technology while exempting domestically produced cars from this requirement. The consequence is that B's car industry would have to incur costs that the domestic car industry in A can completely avoid.

5. *Production subsidies*: A could decide to protect its domestic industry by giving it subsidies, i.e. giving cash payments to domestic car producing firms. Unlike tariffs or discriminatory internal taxes or regulations which have the effect of increasing the costs borne by imported cars, the effect of a subsidy is to reduce the costs borne by domestic producers. If subsidies are high enough domestic car producers can reduce their prices to a level where it becomes impossible for B's car industry to compete. Accordingly, subsidies can also operate as obstacles to international trade.

Box 15.1 Examples of the use of policy instruments to protect domestic economies

These five policy instruments are the ones most frequently utilized by governments when they attempt to protect domestic economic actors from foreign competition. Thailand prohibited imports of cigarettes until the early 1990s which helped its local cigarette manufacturers. The United States imposed quotas on textile imports from China from 2006 to 2008 to protect textile producers in North Carolina and other states. India currently imposes tariffs of around 100% on imported wine with the aim of protecting its emerging domestic wine industry. At one time Japan taxed imported alcoholic beverages more heavily than their locally produced competitors while Canada subjected imported alcohol products to more onerous regulatory requirements. The European Union famously protects its farmers by giving them massive subsidies under the Common Agricultural Policy. While all of these examples relate to trade in *goods*, analogous policy instruments are deployed to protect domestic *service* providers from foreign competition. For instance, a Chinese construction firm cannot bid for a construction project in Switzerland and march its employees into Switzerland to do the building work at Chinese wage levels. Swiss immigration laws would act as a bar to such a transaction—in much the same way as an import prohibition acts as a bar to trade in goods.

Going back to the car industry in country B which hopes to enter the market in country A, can international law assist country B in its endeavour of removing these obstacles to trade?

To begin with, it is important to note that under customary international law, every state has an absolute right to restrict trade with other countries and to discriminate against foreign goods and services (Schwarzenberger 1971: 163–5).[1] States are free, under customary international law, to deploy the five instruments discussed above. Constraints on the ability of states to impose obstacles on international trade cannot be derived from customary international law; instead they must be derived from treaties, from obligations voluntarily assumed as part of an agreement with another state.

The potential for a treaty bargain in these circumstances seems clear. If under customary international law the United States is free to impose tariffs on imports of *cars* from Japan, the converse is also true—Japan is equally free to impose tariffs on imports of, for instance, *computers* from the United States. The United States may commit to reduce or eliminate restrictions on trade from Japan in exchange for similar commitments by Japan to reduce or eliminate restrictions on trade from the United States.

This basic structure—an exchange of commitments on market access—underlies all trade treaties. State A agrees to provide access to its market in exchange for a corresponding commitment by state B. Exporting enterprises in one state benefit from improved market access opportunities in the other state. A given state will enter into a given trade treaty as long as the benefits that it receives as a result of the treaty exceed its costs of compliance.

However, from an economic point of view there is a difficulty with this description. Under standard economic theory, a state will always benefit from reducing trade barriers, so it should do so regardless of whether or not other states grant market access under a trade treaty.

Box 15.2 A puzzle for economists

The puzzle for economists is why countries would need trade treaties to commit to a policy (free trade) that is in their own interest. Indeed, on this standard view, there should not be any trade treaties because states should not have any market access barriers to begin with. In the words of Krugman (1997: 113) 'if economists ruled the world there would be no need for a World Trade Organization'. On the standard view, the explanation for the persistence of trade barriers comes from political economy factors: because producer interests are fewer and better organized than consumers they are in a better position to influence political officials. Political officials adopt trade restrictive policies which benefit these producer interests. In this environment, market access barriers will persist and, consequently, there is a role for trade treaties.

Economists explain that trade treaties eliminate 'time-inconsistency problems' by reducing the likelihood that politicians will reinstate protectionism in response to domestic political pressure. Trade treaties alter the domestic political calculus: exporters will lobby for domestic liberalization as a means of obtaining and maintaining access to the markets of treaty partners and it becomes difficult for politicians to respond to domestic rent-seeking groups without hurting an exporting constituency.

It is important to note that there are contrary views on all of this. The notion that free trade policies are invariably welfare-enhancing and associated with economic growth has come under attack from a dissident strain of economic scholarship (Rodrik 2007; Chang 2008). Moreover, policy-makers (and displaced workers) have always had a difficult time digesting this notion.

Types of trade treaties

Trade treaties come in several forms.

First, there are *bilateral trade treaties*. These are trade treaties between *two* countries. The earliest trade treaties were bilateral. Two states would enter into agreement slashing tariffs on each others imports. A contemporary example is the US-Australia Free Trade Agreement concluded in 2004. Under this treaty Australia and the United States made commitments on a broad range of issues, for instance the duties to be applied on lamb imports to the United States, permissible levels of export subsidies and the content of regulation in the telecoms and financial services sectors.

Second, there is an in-between category of trade treaties which we will call *regional trade treaties*. These are trade treaties that are concluded between more than two countries (so they are not bilateral trade treaties) but less than all 153 WTO members. The most prominent contemporary example is the treaty establishing the European Union, the so-called Treaty of Rome concluded in 1957, which currently binds twenty-seven countries. As part of this treaty, all twenty-seven member states of the European Union have agreed not to impose barriers on trade in each other's goods and services. Another example is the North American Free Trade Agreement between Canada, Mexico, and the United States. It should be noted that regional trade treaties, as we have used the term, also encompasses treaties between three or more countries that are not in the same geographical area. An example is the EFTA-SACU free trade agreement which binds thirty countries in Europe and five countries in Africa.

Third, there are *multilateral trade treaties*, i.e. the WTO Agreements. These are treaties between *all the 153 member countries of the WTO*. Any country in the world can apply to become a member of the WTO so in theory these treaties are open to all countries. All the major economies, with the exception of Russia, are now members of the WTO. As a consequence, almost all of world trade is conducted under the WTO Agreements. Moreover, none of the four major trading powers, the United States, the European Union, Japan, and China, have entered into bilateral or regional trade treaties with each other. For these reasons, the multilateral trade treaties are the most significant category of trade agreements.

From a legal point of view, bilateral and regional trade treaties are treated as a single category distinct from the multilateral trade treaties. Whenever a WTO member enters into a bilateral or regional trade treaty it must ensure that the treaty meets a set of complex requirements set out in the WTO Agreements.

Countries frequently use all three types of trade treaties to achieve their trade policy goals. So going back to our previous example, B could obtain market access for its car industry by including market access for cars in A's WTO commitments, negotiating a bilateral trade treaty with A or entering into a regional trade treaty which includes A. Which route offers the best prospects of success is ultimately a matter of political judgement. This chapter does not examine the content of the approximately 400 bilateral and regional trade treaties currently in force. Instead, our focus is limited to the regime established under the multilateral trade treaties, i.e. the WTO Agreements.

The WTO: negotiating forum and monitoring institution

The WTO was established in 1995 and currently has 153 member states. Countries agreed to create the WTO at the conclusion of the Uruguay Round of trade negotiations that lasted from 1986 to 1994. The Uruguay Round negotiations were conducted under the auspices of the General Agreement on Trade and Tariffs (GATT) and the WTO is the successor organization to the GATT.

The GATT was signed in 1947 by twenty-three countries (eleven of which were developing countries) and was originally meant to be an interim arrangement but it persisted and eventually gave rise to an informal organization, also called the GATT, which became the dominant institution for cooperation on trade policy in the postwar period. In the forty-eight years between the signing of the GATT and the creation of the WTO, eight rounds of multilateral negotiations were held under its auspices—Geneva (1947), Annecy (1948), Torquay (1950), Geneva (1956), the Dillon Round (1960–1), the Kennedy Round (1964–7), the Tokyo Round (1973–9) and the abovementioned Uruguay Round (1986–94). In this period the GATT grew from 23 to 125 countries. Earlier rounds focused exclusively on tariffs but later rounds tackled non-tariff barriers as well.

Like the GATT, the WTO has two primary functions: (1) it facilitates negotiations between its members on trade policy matters, (2) it monitors compliance with relevant treaty obligations. Before examining how the WTO carries out those functions it is worth dealing with the decision-making process.

As a formal matter every member has one vote and there is no weighted voting in the institution. Moreover, in practice, almost all decisions in the WTO are taken on the basis of consensus. For this reason, the WTO is often described as a 'member driven organization'. The implication often drawn is that it is not possible to attribute agency to the WTO; to blame 'the WTO' for a misguided decision is somewhat like blaming a parliamentary building, as opposed to legislators, for a misguided piece of domestic legislation. As we shall see, although all members have equal rights, it does not necessarily follow that every member wields equal power.

Facilitating bargains

The WTO is first and foremost a negotiating forum. Its 153 members gather to strike bargains on trade policy, as Collier (2008: 170) puts it '[the WTO] is not a purposive organization but rather a marketplace. The WTO Secretariat is there merely to set up the stalls each day, sweep the floor each evening, and regulate the opening hours. What happens is determined by bargaining'. In the current Doha Development Round countries are negotiating on a broad range of issues, from the level of tariffs on agricultural goods to how national patent systems should approach inventions embodying particular types of genetic resources. Negotiating with a broad range of countries and to a common timetable permits countries to reach agreements that they could not reach bilaterally or in small groups.

A key feature of the WTO is that no member can be bound by the results of a negotiation unless it agrees with them and formally accepts the resulting treaty. There is no formal mechanism in the WTO to impose a treaty obligation on a country that is unwilling to accept it. In this sense, even the smallest WTO member has control, at least in theory, over the content of its treaty obligations. Consequently, all WTO rules can be traced back to a unanimous agreement between members.

Bargaining at the WTO, like bargaining anywhere, is conducted on the basis of reciprocity. This means that if a participant does not contribute something of interest to its negotiating partners then it risks getting nothing of interest from those partners. The 'currency' of these negotiations is typically market opening and closing. As a consequence, countries with large import markets tend to have greater bargaining power. The European Union has much more bargaining power than Malawi, simply because of the greater size, and hence importance, of its import market. Bargaining power differences were very much in evidence at the conclusion of the Uruguay Round. At that point, the major economies of the GATT, the United States, the European Union, and Japan, presented developing country participants with a choice—accept the Uruguay Round package they proposed (including massively controversial disciplines on intellectual property and services) or they would withdraw from the GATT. Facing the prospect of a complete loss of access to major import markets the developing countries folded and accepted the Uruguay Round package paving the way for the creation of the WTO (Steinberg 2002: 359–60).

Monitoring compliance

The WTO not only facilitates the process of bargaining, it also monitors compliance with bargains reached under its auspices. At the core of the institution are the set of agreements reached at the end of the Uruguay Round of negotiations—collectively known as the WTO Agreements. The WTO Agreements actually consist of a variety of instruments, best understood as chapters of a single treaty, dealing with different aspects of trade policy. Box 15.3 lists the structure of the WTO Agreements:

Box 15.3 The structure of WTO Agreements

Institutional

1. Agreement Establishing the World Trade Organization
2. Understanding on Rules and Procedures Governing the Settlement of Disputes (DSU)

Goods

1. General Agreement on Tariffs and Trade (GATT)
2. Agreement on Agriculture
3. Agreement on the Application of Sanitary and Phytosanitary Measures (SPS Agreement)
4. Agreement on Textiles and Clothing
5. Agreement on Technical Barriers to Trade (TBT Agreement)
6. Agreement on Trade-Related Investment Measures
7. Agreement on Implementation of Article VI of the General Agreement on Tariffs and Trade 1994
8. Agreement on Implementation of Article VII of the General Agreement on Tariffs and Trade 1994
9. Agreement on Preshipment Inspection
10. Agreement on Rules of Origin
11. Agreement on Import Licensing Procedures
12. Agreement on Subsidies and Countervailing Measures (SCM Agreement)
13. Agreement on Safeguards

Services
General Agreement on Trade in Services (GATS)

Intellectual property
Agreement on Trade-Related Aspects of Intellectual Property Rights (TRIPS Agreement)

A key function of the WTO is to facilitate the monitoring of compliance with these agreements. It does so in two ways.

First, the WTO allows for information sharing and review through the committee system. Members have to make regular notifications and respond to specific queries on their trade policies before various specialized committees in the WTO. For example, the Committee on Agriculture receives notifications from every member on the amount of subsidies provided in a given year. These notifications help other WTO members to assess compliance. The process of discussion before the committee permits members to obtain a better understanding of each others positions and allows for a form of 'naming and shaming' pressure to be exerted on members that are demonstrably in breach of their commitments. This process of 'cooperative regulation' has been remarkably successful (Scott 2007: 41–75).

Second, the WTO provides for binding dispute resolution. Any WTO member that considers another member to be not in compliance with its treaty obligations can initiate a complaint. A three-person tribunal, called a 'panel', hears the complaint and issues its ruling on the basis of the submissions of both parties and third party WTO members. Either party can appeal against the panel's ruling to a standing body, called the 'Appellate Body', which can reverse a panel ruling if the ruling is based on erroneous interpretations of the WTO Agreements. If a WTO member is found to be in breach of its obligations under the WTO Agreements the only remedy that a panel can order is that the member halt its illegal conduct within a 'reasonable period of time'. Panels cannot impose broader remedies such as monetary damages to compensate for losses or order refunds of improperly collected tariffs.

After the reasonable period of time expires there is often disagreement as to whether the violating member has actually halted its illegal conduct, i.e. brought itself into compliance. The original panel resolves this question in so-called compliance proceedings. If the compliance proceedings conclude with a finding that the violating member has not brought itself into compliance then the member which brought the complaint (and no one else) can proceed to take retaliatory measures. Retaliatory measures usually take the form of increased tariffs on imports from the violating country but they can take other forms like the temporary expropriation of intellectual property. The level of these retaliatory measures is carefully regulated and, if necessary, the original panel may actually give a ruling on the appropriate magnitude of these measures.

The dispute resolution system of the WTO is different from that which prevailed under the GATT. The GATT operated what was essentially a consensual mediation system; countries could avoid dispute settlement by refusing to consent to adjudication or by refusing to accept a panel report. In the WTO system, members have no such veto right. In summary, the WTO has a far stronger system of enforcement. Indeed, the WTO Agreements certainly rank as one of the most stringently enforced multilateral treaties. In an influential study of the functioning of the WTO dispute settlement system in its first ten years, Davey (2005: 48) concluded that members comply with adverse WTO rulings in 83% of cases. Nevertheless, there are significant cases of non-compliance. In this regard it must be emphasized that retaliation by a country with a small import market is unlikely to be of much consequence to a larger WTO member such as the United States and the European Union. Accordingly, it is arguable that countries with small import markets lack enforcement power in the WTO. The introduction of binding dispute settlement under the WTO has not made power differences between countries irrelevant.

Having reviewed the rationale for trade treaties, the different types of trade treaties and the manner in which these treaties are created and enforced in the WTO context we now examine the actual content of the WTO Agreements.

Basic disciplines: limiting protectionism

In this section we review a series of interlinked obligations whose common rationale is to ensure that commitments to limit protectionism are adhered to and not undermined. These basic obligations are to be found in the GATT and date back to 1947. One could argue that almost all of the obligations imposed under the original GATT ultimately had their justification in the desire to keep protectionism within negotiated limits.

Limits on the forms of protection

At the beginning of the chapter we reviewed five different types of policy instruments that a government could deploy to confer protection on local producers. The WTO Agreements limits the freedom of governments to utilize these instruments. Article XI:1 of the GATT imposes an obligation on WTO members to refrain from utilizing import prohibitions and import quotas as tools of protection. Article III of the GATT prohibits the use of discriminatory internal taxes and regulations. Articles 5 and 6 of the SCM Agreement as well as several provisions of the Agreement on Agriculture curtail the ability of governments to use production subsidies in particular circumstances.

These provisions imply that the only instruments of protection that a government can utilize to protect local producers of goods are tariffs and, to a lesser extent, production subsidies. This limitation on the form of protective instruments facilitates bargaining because trading partners can easily assess the magnitude of protection granted—all they have to observe is the tariff applied at the border (and, where necessary, the magnitude of subsidies). In general terms, the obligation to resort to a single instrument of protection permits trade negotiators to concentrate their energy on a single issue—reducing the magnitude of tariffs applied at the border—rather than a host of other issues.

Limits on the magnitude of protection

The basic tool of trade liberalization is the tariff binding: a commitment not to impose tariffs higher than a specified level on imports of specified goods. To revert to our previous example, a tariff binding on cars could take the form of a promise by country A not to levy tariffs greater than 10% of the value of the imported car. In WTO parlance, country A's 'bound rate' on cars is 10%. This tariff binding is inscribed in a document called a schedule of concessions. Each WTO member has its own schedule of concessions that sets out the bound rates that apply for particular products. Article II of the GATT imposes an obligation to ensure that tariffs imposed on imports of a given product do not exceed these bound rates.

In essence, a tariff binding controls the magnitude of protection that a country can deliver to its domestic constituents or, conversely, the extent of market access it must grant to its trading partners. Tariff bindings are carefully negotiated by WTO members. In the early years of the GATT they were negotiated on a product-by-product basis but in later years they were often negotiated on the basis of across the board reduction formulas (i.e. the negotiators reach agreement that all participants reduce bound tariffs by specified percentages). GATT negotiations led to steady and significant reductions in bound tariff levels for industrial goods in developed countries. However, liberalization proceeded much less steadily for agricultural goods. Moreover, developing countries as a group did not reduce bound tariff levels to the same extent as developed countries.[2]

In the case of trade in services, the mechanism for ensuring market access is different. As a result of negotiations, individual WTO members designate particular sectors and modes of supply as subject to market access commitments in their schedules. Once a service sector and mode of supply are designated as subject to market access commitments then, under Article XVI of the GATS, the member concerned must refrain from imposing specified categories of measures in that sector—such as quantitative restrictions or limitations on the types of entities that can provide services—even if the measures apply equally to domestic service providers.

Non-discrimination

There are two principles of non-discrimination—the principle of most-favoured nation ('MFN') treatment and the principle of national treatment.

The MFN principle is about treating all trading partners equally. It is reflected in Article I of the GATT, Article II of the GATS, and Article 4 of the TRIPS Agreement. The MFN rule specifies that a product or service coming from one WTO member should be treated as well as comparable products or services ('like products or services' in

WTO parlance) coming from any other country. This means that if the United States wants to provide duty free access for cut flowers from Colombia it has to provide the same duty free access to cut flowers from other WTO members such as Venezuela and China. It cannot favour allies or disfavour countries which adhere to different values. The right to MFN treatment is one of the major incentives for countries to join the WTO because it guarantees equal competitive opportunities in export markets.

One important consequence of the MFN principle is that it creates free-rider problems for trade negotiations. Because tariff reductions have to be extended to all WTO members, regardless of whether or not they made tariff reductions in return, individual members can, in theory, 'free-ride' and reap the benefits of a negotiation without having to make concessions of their own. They can delay making concessions on their part, hoping to benefit from the results of other members' concluded negotiations. In practice, this problem is somewhat mitigated by carrying out negotiations in coordinated rounds—when concessions are made simultaneously each participant can withhold its concessions until other participants make adequate concessions of their own.

The national treatment principle is about treating foreigners and locals equally. This principle is reflected in Article III of the GATT, Article XVII of the GATS, and Article 3 of the TRIPS Agreement. The rule is that imported and domestic goods/services should, in principle, face equal internal tax and regulatory burdens. So if India imposes higher sales taxes on foreign cars than on equivalent domestically produced cars then this amounts to a clear breach of the national treatment principle. In this illustration, the WTO member explicitly distinguishes between products on the basis of their origin.

However, there can be more complex cases where a WTO member does not explicitly distinguish on the basis of nationality. Imagine that India imposes higher sales taxes on cars that have a horsepower in excess of a specified level but all of the high horsepower cars 'happen' to be imported and all of the low horsepower cars 'happen' to be domestically produced. Whether the national treatment obligation prohibits this type of tax policy is a far more complex question. Panels are still grappling with the issue of how to interpret the national treatment principle in a manner that forbids disguised protectionism but leaves governments free to distinguish between products when this is warranted for policy reasons. Some tests focus on the effects of the measures while others focus on the policy intent. Another complex area is whether WTO members may distinguish between products on the basis of how they are produced; for instance imposing higher internal taxes on goods produced in factories that fail to adhere to particular labour or environmental standards. This type of tax policy would encourage foreign producers to adhere to the labour and environmental standards prescribed by the importing country. Opinion is divided on whether these types of policies, in WTO-parlance, distinctions based on 'process and production' methods, are valid and the issue has not yet been the subject of a definitive ruling by the Appellate Body.

The disciplines described in this section, disciplines dating back to the GATT, leave governments with considerable freedom to regulate. Particular regulatory outcomes are not prescribed and the focus is on controlling the types of policy instruments that a country can utilize (Roessler 2000: 109–17). The essential substantive constraint imposed is that internal regulation should not be protectionist, i.e. imported and domestic goods and services should be given equal competitive opportunities on the internal market. We now turn to disciplines that impinge on the regulatory prerogatives of WTO members in a more profound way.

Advanced disciplines: constraints on regulatory freedom

While the GATT essentially sought to control protectionism, the WTO has gone beyond this and imposes further constraints on how its members can regulate and even prescribes particular regulatory outcomes in areas such as intellectual property policy and risk regulation.

The most conspicuous example of this shift is the SPS Agreement. Article 2.2 of the SPS Agreement obliges WTO members to ensure that certain measures adopted for the purpose of protecting human, animal, or plant health are based on sound science. A perfectly non-discriminatory measure, for instance a prohibition on producing and selling hormone-treated beef, can be challenged on the ground that it is not based on sufficient scientific evidence.[3] This obligation constrains the ability of a government to regulate risks as it deems fit and can force governments to run risks that they would prefer not to shoulder. For example, even if there is an overwhelming consensus within a country that genetically modified organisms should not be introduced or marketed within its borders this preference cannot be given effect to if it is utterly devoid of any scientific basis. The fact that there is no protectionist intent behind the policy is irrelevant. To this extent, the SPS Agreement constrains the ability of members to adopt precautionary regulatory policies. The extent to which the SPS Agreement curtails the scope of action in situations of scientific uncertainty is an issue which panels and the Appellate Body continue to struggle with.

Another example is the TRIPS Agreement. It requires WTO members to adopt specified intellectual property policies. Prior to the creation of the WTO, countries followed diverse intellectual property policies based on what was suited to their particular context. For instance, many developing countries did not permit the patenting of pharmaceutical products and imposed local working requirements as a condition for obtaining intellectual property protection. The TRIPS Agreement requires all WTO members to adhere to certain minimum standards of protection; standards that more or less reflect the intellectual property policies prevailing in developed countries at the time of the Uruguay Round. As a consequence, developing country WTO members have had to make major adjustments to their intellectual property policies. For instance, they now have to grant patents on pharmaceutical products and have to provide adequate remuneration to rights holders when they issue compulsory licences. These changes are associated with significant increases in the cost of medicines. The TRIPS Agreement also affects the ability of developing countries to respond to pandemics and provide life-saving drugs at affordable prices to their citizens. The example of HIV/AIDS in Africa shows that these constraints on regulatory autonomy can inflict heavy costs on developing countries.

Further examples of this trend can be observed in the GATS. As noted above, Article XVI of the GATS obliges WTO members to refrain from limiting the number of market participants in service sectors for which they have agreed to assume market access commitments. In effect, countries have to provide for unrestrained competition in those sectors. The GATS also contains an Annex on Telecommunications which imposes disciplines on regulatory policy in the telecoms field, in particular on access to public telecommunications, transport networks and services.

Finally, both the SPS Agreement and the TBT Agreement contain obligations requiring WTO members to pursue their regulatory goals using the least trade restrictive means available. [4] The SPS and TBT Agreements also contain soft obligations to use international standards as the basis for regulation in specific circumstances. [5] The use of international standards reduces regulatory heterogeneity which can act as a barrier to trade; after all the need to adapt products to different regulatory standards can generate additional costs for producers.

The GATT, in contrast to the roughly contemporaneous regional trade treaty establishing the European Union, did not require its member countries to adopt similar regulatory policies. As we have seen the WTO Agreements mark a departure from this earlier position. The shift from tackling protectionism to ensuring that regulatory choices facilitate trade or are 'reasonable' or 'scientific' is a significant one and one which places the WTO in the midst of delicate and difficult debates. While traders may prefer regulatory harmonization because it reduces the costs of doing business, governments may find themselves unable to implement policies which reflect their unique preferences.

Loopholes and exceptions

The WTO Agreements contain a wide variety of exceptions from the disciplines sketched out above. Giving WTO members legal permission to deviate from their obligations in specified circumstances can be more rational than requiring compliance. It is rational, for instance, to permit deviation in circumstances where compliance would impose unduly high costs (e.g. requiring members to permit the transit of arms to an adversary during a time of conflict). Similarly, deviation can be sanctioned where it would confer benefits to some WTO members without significant costs to others (for instance a bilateral trade treaty which does not involve trade diversion but creates trade between the parties). A further means of dealing with unduly high compliance costs is to allow countries to renegotiate their commitments. Article XXVIII of the GATT allows a WTO member to unilaterally alter its tariff bindings to a higher level; affected trading partners can alter their own bindings in response or can choose to accept compensation. Article XXI of the GATS is the corresponding provision for services.

Significant exceptions contained in the WTO Agreements are: (1) security exceptions;[6] (2) exceptions for preferences granted under regional and bilateral trade treaties;[7] (3) exceptions for preferences granted to developing countries under the auspices of the generalized system of preferences;[8] (4) exceptions for measures taken to address balance of payments problems;[9] and (5) exceptions for measures taken to protect a domestic industry against serious injury on account of unforeseen import surges.[10]

In addition, the general exceptions provided for in Article XX of the GATT and Article XII of the GATS are of particular importance. These provisions allow countries to resort to WTO-inconsistent measures when needed to achieve non-economic objectives such as health, environmental protection, and public morals. One requirement is that the measures in question must not result in 'arbitrary or unjustifiable discrimination' between countries and should not be 'disguised restrictions' on international trade. The interpretation of these provisions generates some of the most complicated issues in WTO law: whether countries can use these exceptions to defend measures which seek to protect resources or persons outside their territory, whether measures which are merely likely to achieve the objective sought can be deemed to be necessary, etc. The case study extracted below describes one case in which a panel and the Appellate Body were called upon to interpret Article XX and arrived at opposite results on a crucial interpretative issue.

Case Study 15.1 The *US Shrimp* case

Under the Endangered Species Act, the United States requires that domestic shrimp fish-ermen outfit their fishing nets with devices called 'turtle extruder devices'. These devices protect certain species of endangered sea turtles from incidental capture. US shrimp trawl-ers have to use these 'turtle extruder devices' whenever they fish in areas where there is a high likelihood of encountering these sea turtles.

In 1989, the United States adopted further legislation banning the import of shrimp from countries which did not impose similar regulatory requirements on their own fishermen. This meant that in order to export shrimp to the United States, a country would have to require its fishermen to use similar 'turtle extruder devices'. Obviously, this created a strong incentive for shrimp exporting countries to regulate shrimp harvesting activity in the same manner as the United States. This in turn can be expected to reduce the risk of extinction of these sea turtles while raising the costs of production for fishermen in the countries that adopt these requirements.

In 1997, India, Malaysia, Pakistan, and Thailand brought a joint complaint against the import ban imposed by the United States. The United States did not dispute that its meas-ures contravened its obligation under Article XI of the GATT to refrain from utilizing import prohibitions. However, it attempted to justify its measures under the general exception in Article XX(g) of the GATT which permits measures 'relating to the conservation of exhaust-ible natural resources if such measures are made effective in conjunction with restrictions on domestic production or consumption'.

The panel rejected the United States' argument. It interpreted Article XX(g) as limited to measures taken to protect natural resources located within the territory of the member invoking the exception, i.e. within US territory. Here the import ban served to protect tur-tles located on the high seas or within the territorial waters of exporting countries rather than turtles located within the United States.

However, the Appellate Body reversed the panel's interpretation. It ruled that a WTO member could, in principle, condition access to its market on the basis of whether or not an exporting country adhered to a set of regulatory policies that it deemed necessary to protect environmental resources located outside its territory. It then concluded that there were some minor problems with the manner in which the United States had implemented its policy. These problems were easily fixed. The United States continues to condition access to its shrimp market on whether or not exporting countries have adopted regulations to safeguard endangered sea turtles.

In effect, the Appellate Body opened the door to using sanctions as a means of influencing the environmental policy choices of trading partners. This shifts bargaining power towards countries that have large import markets. Moreover, the limits are unclear: can WTO members impose sanctions against those countries that refused to comply with unilaterally prescribed limits on greenhouse gas emissions? What if these unilaterally set limits are more stringent than the limits contained in a multilateral agreement like the Kyoto Protocol? Can a country that decides that vegetarianism is the solution for global warming impose sanctions on countries that permit the marketing and consumption of meat products?

In contrast, the panel's interpretation would have prohibited the use of sanctions as a means of altering the environmental policies of trading partners. However, it would leave individual countries powerless when faced with environmentally irresponsible conduct by their trading partners, even where the conduct breaches a multilateral environmental treaty negotiated outside the WTO. On the panel's approach, only when a significant proportion of WTO members support the use of sanction (3/4 of the 153 Members of the WTO would have to approve any decision granting a waiver to permit trade sanctions), can the international community act against countries that fail to respect the environment.

Criticisms of the WTO: a biased forum?

The WTO has been the subject of sustained criticism from a variety of quarters. Indeed, WTO ministerial meetings often attract large-scale protests from civil society groups. The criticisms levelled are fairly heterogeneous and need not be internally consistent. It is not possible to review all of them.[11] Instead, we will have to be selective and focus on allegations that the WTO is a biased forum.

One persistent criticism is that the WTO Agreements are biased against developing countries. There are two strands here: the first is that the WTO *permits* developed countries to pursue a series of policies that have adverse effects on developing countries, the second is that the WTO *constrains* the ability of developing countries to pursue policies that are in their interest.

An example of the first strand is the argument that the WTO does not do enough to constrain policies such as the European Union's Common Agricultural Policy or the United States' policy of granting subsidies to its cotton farmers. It is argued that these policies depress prices for a number of commodities, thereby destroying the livelihoods of vulnerable developing country farmers. Likewise, the WTO permits these countries to impose high tariffs on exports of goods of interest to developing countries which greatly impairs the ability of people in these countries to escape from poverty.

An example of the second strand is the argument that obligations under the WTO Agreements prevent developing country governments from adopting appropriate policies. For instance, TRIPS Agreement obligations force developing country governments to grant patent rights which increase the prices of medicines while bloating already stretched public health budgets and obligations under the Agreement on Agriculture preventing developing country governments from imposing minimum price schemes to protect their farmers from price swings.

Criticisms of this type usually raise complex empirical questions. For instance, although the Common Agricultural Policy drives down global prices and thereby affects the returns to farmers it also arguably helps food consumers in net food importing countries by reducing the cost of food. Similarly, on intellectual property obligations, it can be argued that unless developing countries protect intellectual property there will be no incentive to invest in research into diseases that disproportionately affect their populations, for instance malaria. It is impossible to make sweeping conclusions about these matters. However, it is certainly naïve to hold the view that all WTO rules serve the interests of developing country members. After all, these rules emerged from a process of competitive bargaining.

A related criticism of the WTO is that its decision-making is not transparent or democratic and that a few countries are in position to impose their will on all other members. At first blush this appears to be an implausible claim: unlike in the IMF, the World Bank, and even the United Nations, in the WTO there are no preferred members with greater votes than others or veto power over important decisions. As noted above, every member has one vote and, in theory every member can block a consensus. However, organizations like Oxfam (2002: 250–8) have argued that the United States, the EU, and Japan wield considerable 'informal power' through their ability to set the agenda in closed meetings. Also, as has been pointed out above, depending on the size of their markets, some states have greater bargaining power than others. Whilst there may be considerable disparities in power, the questions of whether it is possible to eliminate these disparities or how to do this do not have clear answers. Should the WTO switch to weighted voting by population or share in world trade? No particular alternative is likely to be acceptable to all participants.

Conclusion

The WTO as an institution has been successful in enabling countries to cooperate on issues of trade policy. International law has been a fundamental in facilitating this cooperation. Indeed, even the United States and the European Union, both of whom can dictate terms to most of their trading partners, have regularly altered their policies in order to comply with adverse WTO rulings. However, the example of the WTO illustrates that international law constantly reflects international politics. Arguably, the large trading powers have consistently shaped WTO law in a manner that advances their interests—from the TRIPS Agreement to the Agreement on Agriculture. This is to be expected, after all, when law is based on consensual bargains it must reflect, to a greater or lesser extent, differences in bargaining power.

Questions

1. Why do states enter into trade agreements?

2. What instruments do states typically use when they seek to protect domestic producers from foreign competition?

3. What are the different types of trade agreements?

4. How are decisions in the WTO taken?

5. Does it make sense to criticize the WTO as opposed to its member states?

6. How is WTO law enforced?

7. What factors motivate states to comply with WTO law?

8. Can WTO member A impose higher tariffs on goods from member B on the grounds that member B allegedly fails to respect human rights? What principle does member A violate?

9. Should countries be able to use trade sanctions or internal taxes to encourage their trading partners to adopt particular environmental and labour standards?

10. Does WTO law impede the ability of states to tackle environmental problems in other countries and/or globally?

11. Has the GATT/WTO system led to significant trade liberalization?

Further reading

Barton, J.H. et al. (2006) *The Evolution of the Trade Regime : Politics, Law and Economics and the GATT and WTO* (Princeton: Princeton University Press). *This book is a multidisciplinary account of the GATT/WTO system.*

Jackson, J. (1969) *World Trade and the Law of the GATT* (New York: Bobbs Merrill). *A classic account of the GATT from a leading scholar.*

Journal of International Economic Law (Oxford: Oxford University Press); *World Trade Review* (Cambridge: Cambridge University Press);

and *Journal of World Trade* (Amsterdam: Kluwer). *These are the major academic journals in this area.*

Mavroidis, P (2007) *Trade in Goods* (Oxford: Oxford University Press). *A more recent account of WTO law relating to trade in goods.*

Van Den Bossche, P. (2008) *The Law and Policy of the World Trade Organization*, 2nd edn. (Cambridge: Cambridge University Press). *A well-organized introductory textbook on WTO law.*

Websites

http://www.wto.org/ *The website of the World Trade Organization provides information on activities and trade law.*

http://www.wto.org/english/tratop_e/dda_e/dohaexplained_e.htm *This site provides information on the Doha Development Rounds and gives access to the Doha documents.*

http://www.unctad.org/ *The United Nations Conference on Trade and Development website provides research, data, and policy analysis on trade and development.*

http://www.oecd.org/ *The Organisation for Economic Co-operation and Development website provides policy briefs, reports, and working papers on world trade.*

http://globaltradealert.org/ *A leading information site on world trade organization law.*

Visit the Online Resource Centre that accompanies this book to access more learning resources www.oxfordtextbooks.co.uk/orc/cali/

Chapter endnotes

1. Judicial confirmation can be found in the ICJ judgment in the *Nicaragua* case: '[a] state is not bound to continue particular trade relations longer than it sees fit to do so, in the absence of a treaty commitment or other specific legal obligation' *Military and Paramilitary Activities in and against Nicaragua*, Merits, (1986) ICJ Reports 14.

2. See the views set out Subramanian and Wei (2007) and the contrary literature discussed therein.

3. See Article 2.2 of the SPS Agreement. See also Appellate Body Report, *EC Measures Concerning Meat and Meat Products (Hormones)*, WT/DS26/AB/R, WT/DS48/AB/R, adopted 13 February 1998, DSR 1998:I, 135.

4. See Article 5.6 of the SPS Agreement and Article 2.2 of the TBT Agreement.

5. See Article 3 of the SPS Agreement and Article 2.4 of the TBT Agreement.

6. See Article XXI of the GATT and Article XIV bis of the GATS.

7. See Article XXIV of the GATT and Article V of the GATS.

8. See the Enabling Clause of 1979.

9. See Articles XII and XVIII:B of the GATT.

10. See Article XIX of the GATT.

11. See Singer (2002), chapter 3, for an interesting set of critiques of the WTO.

Chapter 16

Global social justice and international law

Saladin Meckled-Garcia

CHAPTER CONTENTS

- Introduction
- What kinds of problems does social justice address?
- What is justice and where does it apply?
- Does international law have the right profile for social justice to apply to it?
- Can international law be used to advance the cause of social justice?
- What standards of justice are applicable to inter*national* affairs?
- Conclusion

CHAPTER OVERVIEW

This chapter gives the student an analytical framework for understanding the relationship between conceptions of social justice, international law, and international relations theory. This is done by first explaining the notion of social justice, and the prerequisites for applying that notion to political institutions (for institutions being considered 'social justice-apt'). An analysis is then given of international law explaining its point and limits in terms of four functions. The chapter shows that because the four functions are state-centred, international law is not social justice-apt. The chapter then considers what different notion of justice other than social justice might be applicable to international legal institutions.

Introduction

Is there a place for justice in international relations studies? And, if there is, what is its relationship to international law? This chapter identifies important questions of international justice that have begun to find their place in the international relations literature (through the 'International Society' or the 'English' school of thought in international relations theory), but at the same time also shows what the limits on international (versus domestic) social justice are given the limits of international legal practice.

The chapter first identifies the problems that justice theory is thought to respond to in the domestic and international spheres, contrasting normative justice theory with descriptive approaches to international relations and giving some examples of justice theory. An explanation is given as to why a certain type of agency (political authority with assignment jurisdiction) is needed for standards of social justice to apply to a domain of human relationships. The chapter then shows how this type of agency is not present in the international sphere, and how that is reflected in the nature of international law. The consequence of this for matters such as global poverty, economic competition, and global effects is that they are not subject to the same standards of justice as domestic affairs. The chapter then describes three different kinds of cosmopolitan theory that respond to the international normative scenario described. The weaknesses of these responses are described as well as one alternative to the cosmopolitan view.

What kinds of problems does social justice address?

Justice in the domestic context finds its way into debates about the most appropriate way to organize institutions. There are many ways to understand this question, such as, for example, in terms of how institutions might best function so as to perpetuate themselves efficiently. Justice, and here, we are concentrating on social justice, however, is the matter of what arrangement of institutions treats the members of a society correctly: with the concern and respect which is appropriate to them. Is a society in which tax institutions favour the rich and punish the poor a just society? Is health and education provision according to need more just than provision according to ability to pay?

> **Box 16.1 Theories of social justice**
>
> Theorists of justice have developed a number of theories that aim to answer what it is for social institutions to treat members of a political community correctly, including the utilitarian idea that justice is where institutions are organized so as to maximize the social good and the contrasting idea that justice is where institutions must respect key rights and liberties. The point, however, is that accounts of what justice consists in are offered in the form of standards of behaviour (rules) which are backed up with arguments appealing to key values that express the notions of equal concern and respect for members of society.

Whether one believes a society should act justly or not, theories of justice are meant to answer the conditional question: if society is to act justly then according to which principles should its institutions be organized. That question cannot be answered by merely looking at the way states organize themselves and act, or their citizens behave, but rather a normative approach is needed.

In the study of international relations different theories vie with each other to explain international affairs and to engage in 'normative analysis.' The term normative here is used in a descriptive way: they seek to identify and explain what norms of behaviour are present in international interactions. Some headway has, however, been made to introduce properly normative, or prescriptive, issues into international relations theory. The *Liberal Realist* or *Rationalist* school has found modern expression in *International Society Theory* (also known as the English School) and in particular those elements of international society theory that have been called *Solidarist* (Wheeler 2000). This view sees international society as a society of states in which ethical concepts such as democracy, human rights, and humanitarianism do, and should, structure international relations. However, questions of international justice reach deeper into the debate on global responsibilities, with organizations like the *United Nations Development Programme* and numerous NGOs appealing to the ethics of global justice as a solution to poverty in a globalized world and international institutions with economic powers playing important roles in economic development, poverty alleviation, and financial assistance to states. These views and institutional practices raise key questions regarding how international institutions should be organized, given their far-reaching effects on the lives of persons, effects which reach across borders.

The same question asked above of domestic institutions can be asked of these international institutions: how should these institutions function if we are to say they are acting in conformity with social justice? Should we consider international interactions as beyond the reach of principles, a 'state of anarchy' in which standards of social justice have no place (in contrast with the domestic sphere)? When international trade institutions allow free trade in biofuels and this produces food shortages, is this an injustice because it does not benefit the least advantaged? Is poverty an international matter subject simply to principles of assistance and rescue, or to principles of distributive justice imposing obligations on affluent states and their citizens to redistribute wealth to the global poor until the least well off have their condition improved? Is the international economic order missing a tax system to redistribute wealth from affluent countries to poor and enforce equal concern for all individuals across the face of the globe?

Box 16.2 Cosmopolitanism and alternatives

The school of thought which says that international relations are subject to the same fundamental standards of justice as domestic relations is called **cosmopolitanism**. Some alternatives to cosmopolitanism argue that justice does not apply internationally because political societies constitute communities which have stronger links between their members than their members have with people outside of their state and these links should be respected; others argue that states have a right to self-determination which would be violated by imposing demands of global justice; and still others argue that standards of justice only properly apply between persons who live under common coercive (non-voluntary institutions) and that no such common institutions exist in international relations.

The way in which justice needs to be achieved in the domestic sphere is through the assignment of rights and duties to persons and their associations in a way which produces the *desired pattern of distribution*. If the theory of justice we favour is one in which the least advantaged are made as well off as they possibly could be, then the state must assign rights and duties through its system of laws and institutions in such a way that the least advantaged will be benefited. The property regime, the taxation system, the laws of contract and civil claim, as well as public institutions regulating or providing health, education, and other forms of welfare have to be designed with this aim in mind. Such a project implies an authority must exist capable of acting through its legislative system (and the executive extension of that system) to distribute rights and duties. These features of domestic states make them into *subjects of justice* and I shall briefly explain why that is, below. This also, however, poses a question for international relations. If these are relevant features of domestic states making them subject to principles of justice, are those same features present globally?

What is justice and where does it apply?

International relations theorists offer different explanatory models of interaction between types of agents in order to explain global states of affairs and their domestic repercussions. In doing so, the explanatory models offered are descriptive and pre-dictive (see Chapter 2). When international relations theories seek to move beyond description and prediction, however, and become prescriptive, their pretensions can be challenged for doing so. That is, when the model used is not only an account of how things are but is used to judge, say, the rationality or adequacy of actions, then it has overstepped its mark; prediction moves to prescribing types of aims and goals, international relations theory steps into the territory of theories of moral standards of behaviour. In that territory purely self-interest-driven motives will be in com-petition with other standards (e.g. ones advancing equal concern and respect for individual persons). It can, of course, be held that there are no normative standards of behaviour; that morality is an illusion, and that international justice beyond the descriptive models of international relations theory is an empty category. In this chapter, however, it is being assumed that we can have an idea of what justice is in the domestic context: principles of action for state agents which, when those agents act on the duties they prescribe, entail the agents showing equal concern and respect to all members of a society. One such principle is to distribute goods and burdens (resources towards living a good life or a life of one's choice, and the cost of produc-ing those goods in the form of taxation or limits on property rights) in such a way as to only allow inequalities if these are of benefit to the least advantaged in society (this principle from John Rawls is famously known as the 'Difference Principle'). If it is indeed assumed that we can have such principles and use them to judge domes-tic institutions, then the question is *whether the same principles can or should be used to judge institutions which go beyond the domestic level*. Of course, we cannot convince someone who does not believe there can be standards of justice even in the domestic case about their relevance in international relations.

That said, we ask what the specific point might be of standards of behaviour which are candidates for what we call 'justice'. There are many types of human relationship to which standards of one type or another can apply. Between private persons, relationships of friendship or family can arise which have their own stand-ards of behaviour, invoking notions of special (rather than equal) concern. What is it that singles out some areas of human life for treatment in terms of social justice and leaves others to their own standards? The approach in this chapter is to say that what marks out any relationship as distinctive (distinctively requiring standards for action) is the presence of distinctive goods and costs. The goods and costs available in the relationship of friendship which set that relationship apart from other types include the goods of loyalty and faithfulness, of commitment and constancy. The costs are the associated burdens that those pursuing friendship must take on, such as the sacrifices implied by loyalty and constancy, to produce the goods. Given these goods have their own character, standards of behaviour requiring persons to act in ways which go against this character would be self-defeating. If we applied, for example, a standard that appealed to equal concern for all persons to friendship the very impartiality of equal concern for all would undermine the point of enjoy-ing goods such as loyalty and constancy and the practice of friendship would lose coherence. Regulation of these goods, and their associated burdens, then needs to appeal to a master value which is appropriate to those goods and costs and appro-priately expresses the relationship.

Each domain of human relationships then is defined by the special goods and bur-dens available within it and any theory of standards of behaviour for that domain will employ values appropriate to those goods and the relationship. This goes for justice too. The goods and costs involved in social justice are those general goods usable in the pursuit of a conception of the good life, whatever that conception might be, and the socially contextualized costs associated with the supply of such goods. That means the resources, both material and social, that a society can make available such as wealth, status and opportunities, as well as the contribution to producing those resources which includes accepting social rules regulating behav-iour and ownership.

What sets aside state institutions with regard to justice is their monopoly on *political authority*. This means the power to assign rights and duties to persons in a society so as to produce social effects, such as the effect of redistribution. Rights and duties are assigned through laws and orders in a state and who has the power to create such laws and issue such orders will be a matter for a political community to establish. When a new tax law is passed, for example, this imposes new obliga-tions on citizens to pay tax in a certain way. Whilst many types of agent, ranging from individual private persons through shopkeepers, to corporations and political parties, can in some way affect the distributions of goods and costs in a society, their effect is of a different order to political authority. Their effects are varied, unpredict-able, and cumulative. The investment by a particular company in a particular indus-try can have knock-on effects for persons which are neither fully predictable nor the aim of the initial action. Investing in biofuels might increase food prices, thereby negatively affecting the most vulnerable in society. Yet it is not the intention of any one biofuel investor that his or her actions have this effect and certainly there is no coherent way of separating out his or her contribution to the outcome and assign a corresponding share of the blame. Many, if not all, of the most innocent actions and interactions between individual persons and their associations in a society have this character: they have consequences over time that cannot be coherently assessed in terms of individual responsibility, even if some of the negative consequences can be foreseen. Of course, some actions are not innocent to begin with, being clearly directed at either causing direct harms or seeing direct harms done, and these are the paradigmatic actions dealt with by criminal law. But even those actions that are *in themselves* well intentioned, or at least not malicious, can have devastating cumulative consequences in terms of the relative position of people in society.

Justice is the standard of behaviour we use to guide the actions of an agency that can stand aside from all these specific interactions and whose fundamental role is to adjust distributions of goods and costs in line with some master value expressing equal concern for all, such as the value of fairness in distribution. What allows an agency to stand apart in this way is its monopoly on the power to assign rights and duties in a society in a way which can adjust for the accumulated effects of people's actions. This capacity is political authority, exclusive to states. It is the power to adjust the background of duties and rights so as to produce patterns of distribution or a background against which individuals can act without worrying about the accumulated consequences of each and every one of their actions. Standards of justice impose absolute obligations on agencies with this capacity so that they do not simply have a fair distribution as a desirable aim but rather are obliged to aim at such distributions as a matter of legitimacy for their power.

In sum, then, it is having this power of political authority, and therefore the ability to adjust for accumulated effects of personal actions, that makes an institution or set of institutions **social justice-apt**: open to judgements as to whether it is or is not just (in the sense of social justice).

So for any sphere of human relationships we must ask what principles, expressing which master values and regulating the distribution of which goods and costs are appropriate to that sphere. Only where relationships have the features associated with political authority as mentioned above can they be said to be social justice-apt (meaning that they can be judged as just or unjust). If, instead, the relationships in question have different characteristics, then different standards might be applicable in that context.

To establish whether standards of social justice normally applied in the domestic case are directly applicable internationally we must establish, then, whether political authority exists in the international sphere, or if it does, what form it takes. The important question here is whether political authority is present in such a way as to be able to maintain a pattern of distribution of benefits and costs for individual persons across the globe in such a way as to offset the cumulative effects of all agents' actions. To broach this question, the next section provides an analysis of international legal relations. Legitimate (valid) legal obligations which are not domestic can only be created through the practice of international law. Perhaps these norms, and the institutions they empower, represent a way of creating background adjustment globally. If they can, then there is a case for saying that international institutions are social justice-apt.

Does international law have the right profile for social justice to apply to it?

Of course, like any legal system, the international system functions according to principles which define it and give it its particular identity. Those principles, which include principles on how laws can be made (rights and duties created) and on whom obligations can fall, must be the basis for any analysis of international law. However, it is not this sense of justice (internal to the functioning of the legal order) that we are interested in when asking whether international law is justice-apt. Otherwise, the question in the above heading would be tautological: it would ask 'Does the system of justice called international law have the right profile for justice to apply to it?' What we are asking, however, is more substantive: whether, given all its presuppositions and the principles of operation that define it, there is anything in international law that essentially clashes with the aim of implementing at the global level (and through international legal provisions) the same standards appropriate to domestic justice?

In order to properly answer that question it must first be asked what defines the specific point and purpose of international law: its distinctive role as a practice. In what follows it shall be shown that the fundamental principles which define international law are in essence unable to offer the kind of background adjustment that would make international institutions justice-apt. The system of decision-making in place in international law which allows the production and assignment of rights and duties to specific agents is limited by statist constraints (see Chapter 14). The point of international legal institutions and the practices they enshrine can be summed up in four types of aim: (1) establishing substantive cooperative agreements between states; (2) principles and institutions which facilitate substantive cooperative agreements between states; (3) principles and institutions defining agency (those empowered to enter into substantive cooperative agreements) in international law; and (4) principles and institutions which maintain international public order (against the background of which substantive cooperative agreements can be pursued). These principles correspond to, and express, the key values of interstate (inter-political community) cooperation, interstate dispute resolution, status specification, and peace and security.

The first question that should be asked about international law, before characterizing its point and purpose, is: what does it do? For the purposes of this chapter, a purely formal definition can be used: international law can be understood as the provisions of decision-making institutions which assign obligations to specified agents the validity of which are not directly sensitive to domestic legislative decisions. The world contains a number of political communities with their own institutions and laws, commonly referred to as municipal law and what sets international law apart from these is this feature of its validity. Thus, the international duty of the UK government to accept asylum seekers is not an obligation which can be revoked simply by an act of the UK domestic legislature. The UK government would have to extricate itself from its commitments under the 1951 Convention and the 1967 Protocol Relating to the Status of Refugees. There are some international obligations from which states cannot extricate themselves (or their citizens) even by such special procedures, such as *ius cogens* norms (see Chapter 5).

Now, at a superficial level we can find statements defining international law in terms of its sources and processes (treaty, custom, judicial reasoning and decisions, the opinion of scholars), these being the sources of validity for its claimed provisions (see Chapters 5 and 6). Yet all that this tells us is *how* international law functions; a relatively formal characterization. It does not tell us whether there are significant limits on how international law can be used. That requires an analysis probing deeper into the principles which give international law its point and purpose; explaining its distinctive features and limits: what its different parts do and why.

To understand this point it needs to be set against the background of a specific thesis. We can call this 'statism'. That thesis says that the background of political authority relations inherent in international law is one in which political authority is fundamentally state-bound. Being state-bound means that there exist distinctive political authorities with jurisdictions (the right to assign rights and duties) over a specific group of persons which are themselves, as a community, identified by reference to a territory.

> **Box 16.3 Types of jurisdiction**
>
> Any other type of political authority is in one way or another derivative of this kind of political authority. Now it should be made clear here that there are different types or concepts of jurisdiction, and that the statist thesis focuses on one. Those persons over whom an authority can assign (create, define, prescribe, etc.) rights and duties are its '*assignment jurisdiction*'. On the other hand, those over whom an authority can enforce duties (for example through prosecution for illegality) are its '*enforcement jurisdiction*'. The statist thesis made above is about assignment jurisdiction, not enforcement jurisdiction. It is assignment that matters in the first instance when considering the kind of authority that can produce just distributions of goods and costs (through the distribution of rights and duties). *Assignment-jurisdiction* should also not be confused with that jurisdiction in terms of when a state is responsible for the effect of its actions on a person (*responsibility-jurisdiction*)—when persons can claim special rights against it.

The international legal system is fundamentally statist. That is not to say that entities other than states cannot have some degree of political authority, it is however to stress that any political authority with assignment jurisdiction belongs to states, derives from state authority, or from the background necessary to facilitate the cooperation of state authorities. Now, this view might be thought to clash with some theories of international law, as it seems to claim that only states exist. However, statism here is not a view about what exists, or even which entities can have effects in international relations. It is rather a view about what entities have assignment jurisdiction. Its distinctiveness is that it says that only independent, individual state institutions have political (assignment) authority, and that authority is bound to particular persons identified by reference to the territory of the state. On the other hand, as will be seen below, the statist view does present some problems for liberal and rationalist (international society) approaches to international relations.

To round off discussion of the statist thesis it is important to clarify what statism as defined is and is not: Statism is simply the view that political authority (with assignment-jurisdiction) in the international sphere is either state-bound or derives from the need to facilitate the cooperation of state-bound authorities. It is not or does *not* entail any of the following: (1) only states exist as international agents; (2) only state agency can affect the international legal order; (3) only state interests (understood narrowly as advancing limited goals: as per the realist literature on international law) are integrated into international legal standards; (4) only states have legal subjectivity, status, or responsibility in international law; (5) only concepts referring to states and their features can be employed in international law; (6) states can only enter into relationships with other states; (7) the political authority of states over citizens is unlimited (this latter thesis is about the notion of state sovereignty, its legitimate extent and limits, which is a different issue from the question of statism in terms of assignment jurisdiction).

Is statism true? Instead of going through all the areas and aspects of international law, one way to test this is to ask: is there any form of assignment jurisdiction which is recognized in any area of international law which is not itself a case of either: (a) state-bound assignment jurisdiction, or (b) validated by reference to state-bound assignment jurisdiction (e.g. by the facilitation of its exercise)? As was said above, the provisions of international law can be analysed as expressing four distinctive types of aim: (1) the actual pursuit of substantive cooperation between states; (2) the facilitation of substantive cooperation; (3) the establishment of status (which kinds of entities count as states or can engage in the creation of international legal provisions); and (4) the maintenance of international public order (peace and security).

The only plausible challenge to the statist thesis we might derive from the list (1)–(4) above would be finding a principle in international law which either empowered non-state (and non-state-derived) entities to create international legal provisions or which imposed legal provisions on states (and others) which did not respect state-bound authority. The latter would have to involve international legal provisions that did not derive from substantive state cooperation or from the aim of facilitating state cooperation, but from some other consideration. Now, clearly (1) and (2) above are indelibly stamped with the mark of statism (state-bound assignment authority), for (1) allows the creation of provisions (the assignment of obligations) for states by engaging in substantive agreements (see Chapter 5). It is therefore limited by their agreements and therefore by respect for state-bound assignment authority, whilst (2) establishes the creation or assignment of provisions derivative from facilitating such agreements.

Substantive cooperation between states can range from bilateral treaties between states to the creation of multilateral organizations for more universal purposes, such as the United Nations (the explicit aims of which are the furtherance of cooperation between states and maintaining peace and security). It can also give rise to supra-national institutions with powers to create laws assigning new duties such as the European Union. However, in this case the authority to assign comes from the agreement of states to join or constitute the association in question in an understanding of its mandate. That is to say, supra-national authority in such cases is derivative, resting on state-bound authority. Where international courts exist, these can establish duties falling on states and their citizens. The point of such bodies is precisely to settle disputes over the provisions of treaties. Their points of reference, then, are not just any considerations but rather the terms of treaties as well as general principles of law that allow these bodies to operate as adjudicative organs (see Chapter 8).

As we can see, then, the provisions that can emerge as a matter of functions (1) and (2) of international law do not obviously challenge statism and in fact can be seen as being constitutive of statism in international law. Where there are provisions that seem to go beyond statist forms of duty assignment, these are in turn explicable either as derivative from substantive agreement, and so from state-bound jurisdiction, or by the needs of facilitating statist aims (through adjudication), rather than by aims which go beyond statism. So, any powerful challenge to statism would have to come from the imports of functions (3) and (4).

Function (3) is the definition of *agency* in international law, which should not be confused with subjectivity in international law. *Legal subjectivity* is the question of which types of entity can be subject to or feature in the provisions of international law. As we shall see, this ranges from states to individual persons. Individuals can be subjects of international law in terms of being the focus of the provisions of international criminal law (see Chapter 12), they can also be subjects when empowered through substantive state agreements to make claims against states in the enforcement of treaty provisions (see Chapter 13). Agency in international law, on the other hand, is the question of what types of agent can be involved in the creation of provisions (the assignment of duties) of international law. If it could be shown that those agents accepted as makers of international law were not limited to state-bound jurisdictions, then there would be a case for saying that international law was not statist. Yet, whilst states can enter into relations with other types of entity, it is clearly only state parties that can establish international obligations through agreement. Whilst some routes to the making of such law are less straightforward than others (customary versus treaty-based, for example: see Chapter 5 and 6), there is no other type of entity whose decisions (without the adjoined decisions of a state) can actively create obligations through agreement. That is not to deny the existence of organs deriving their authority from state parties through agreement, or of organs attempting to facilitate substantive agreement between state parties that can actively establish international legal provisions. Nevertheless, the capacity of these latter to establish obligations, as has been set out above, is derivative from the aim of substantive cooperation.

Another way one might challenge statism in regard of agency would be by asking whether the agents of international law, whilst involving states, are truly statist, in the sense of representing genuine cases of state-bound assignment jurisdiction.

Perhaps control over the definition of status by other organs and institutions can also imply control over jurisdiction. So, for example, the status of membership of the UN, or collective recognition by other states, can be seen as a source of status as an equal sovereign power. Yet in the objective sense of objective statehood the status of states depends on their properties. A state is treated as a state for the purposes of conducting international affairs when other states address themselves to its government and respect its territory. Customary international law recognizes having a government, a permanent population, a territory, and a capacity to enter into relations with other states as objective signs of statehood (see for example *The Montevideo Convention on Rights and Duties of States*, 1933, Articles 1 and 2). Each of these features effectively expresses an element of state-bound jurisdiction, fitting very well with the statist thesis. The other sense of statehood is where status is officially recognized. In that sense an entity might have the four characteristics identified above, yet not be recognized for the purposes of membership of the United Nations, for joining international associations and organizations (such as the WTO) in full capacity or for the purposes of official diplomatic recognition by other states. So, for example, the Republic of China (Taiwan) has the four objective features of statehood, but is not recognized by some states for full diplomatic purposes, has to date not been granted member status at the UN, and is represented in a limited capacity at the WTO. However, not obtaining that sense of statehood does not challenge a state having statehood in the first sense, which is an objective measure, and it is that sense in which (for example) statehood is relevant to signing a treaty, establishing customary law, or participating in adjudication. And it is that sense of statehood which is explicable in terms of a capacity to assign rights and duties to its citizens. Treaties and voluntary methods of arriving at obligations only make sense if one sees states as having powers over their citizens which allow them to see the treaties adhered to and implemented. It is also for that reason that the method of government in a state is not a condition of recognizing it as an equal in the international terrain, as all that is relevant for the sake of substantive cooperation is a state's power to assign rights and duties to a specified group.

This brings us to the area of international law which presents the greatest challenge to the statist thesis. That is the area I have called 'international public order' (4 above). This area is composed of some related notions: international criminal law, the peremptory norms known as *ius cogens* norms, and principles of mutual peace and security, as well as the special organs which act on these principles. The reason this particular function of international law is a challenge to the statist thesis is that here we have what appears to be an area in which non-state-bound jurisdiction is rife.

Not only are there international criminal courts and tribunals that have a mandate to try individual persons for recognized international crimes, some of these crimes are considered to be of such a significance as to justify states instituting procedures to exercise *universal jurisdiction* (see Chapter 12) which allows their domestic legal organs to indict and try persons charged with those international crimes, whether they are citizens or not and whether or not the criminal actions are alleged to have occurred on the state's own territory or a territory over which it exercised control. This practice is bound up with the doctrine of *ius cogens* norms and the doctrine of obligations *erga omnes*, which is the idea that some actions harm members of the international legal community as a whole (all states).

Now, it appears that the notion of international crime implies a jurisdiction over individual persons which challenges state-bound jurisdiction. Yet, those actions that can count as international crimes are not unlimited, or in the hands of any specific authority to extend or reduce. What counts as an international (or transnational) crime is limited to a specific kind of purpose. The list of currently recognized international (and transnational) crimes includes: piracy, genocide, crimes against humanity, war crimes, torture, slavery, and apartheid (see Chapter 12). It is clear from this list that it is not simply the effect on individual persons that defines an international or transnational crime. The list includes actions which, if permitted, can threaten the function of international property regimes, and threaten states' ability to regulate their own citizens, such as slavery. In the case of war crimes, placing limits on the form that armed conflicts can take it addresses questions important to all states with respect to their citizens and their property as well as the treatment of their captured personnel. So, war crimes provisions focus on regulating inter-action between states in specific and extreme circumstances, and on structuring post-conflict claims, in order to limit the consequences of war. Laws of war can, to that extent, be understood in terms of the needs for preserving some of the conditions for state-bound jurisdiction in the face of armed conflicts. With genocide, crimes against humanity, torture and apartheid, the actions do not have any necessary *direct* impact on states other than those in which they occur. There are potential effects of crimes against humanity and genocide as attacks against minorities that can impinge on other states, where the populations involved have affiliations with populations in other states, or refugee flows are caused by their persecutions and spill over into the territories of states not directly involved.

However, these, and the relatively new crime of apartheid (included in the *Rome Statute of the International Criminal Court*), are not the only features of these actions that are relevant to their being internationally banned. They also represent standards of behaviour in the use of state power that are provocative to other members of the community of states. They are the limits beyond which the conscience of states cannot be expected to remain impassive (crimes which 'shock the conscience of mankind' in the words of the *Genocide Convention*), and consequently which challenge international peace and security (because of a propensity to intervene in such events). The important point, however, is that there is no necessary connection between the nature of an action in terms of its effect on an individual person and its featuring in the list of internationally proscribed crimes. The significant element is what consequences that action has for international public order (otherwise simple murder would be an international crime).

What is clear, however, is that international criminal provisions are not designed to govern states' internal affairs, they merely place limits on the exercise of assignment authority and do so for the sake of maintaining international order. Furthermore, the jurisdiction that derives from these standards is not an assignment jurisdiction, but an enforcement one. International criminal courts have specific mandates listing specific international crimes, with limits on how they can exercise jurisdiction for the sake of enforcement (limited to specific territories, persons or states). In all these cases, however, it is not in the power of any judicial enforcement institutions to create new crimes or remove old ones from the list of what counts as an international criminal offence.

The international criminal provisions just discussed overlap with a special set of international norms known as *ius cogens* norms (see Chapters 5 and 6). *Ius cogens* norms are distinguished by (1) rendering some of the provisions of some treaties as non-derogable, and (2) by their power to nullify a treaty which violates them. The list of what comprises these norms is controversial, but lists often include the prohibitions on piracy, slavery, crimes against humanity, torture, racial discrimination, as well as attacks on self-determination, genocide, and war crimes. But once again, nobody has the power to create such standards by a decision (although international courts can adjudicate and enforce them), and in each case, as in the case of international criminal provisions, it is the public order element of norms that elevates them so highly.

The public order function also extends to specific organs, such as the Security Council of the United Nations (SC) which is charged with preserving peace and security for member states. It derives its mandate from the United Nations itself, but interprets its mandate according to the public order aims of peace and security. Some of the Security Council resolutions, however, can be seen as challenging the statist thesis. It has, for example, established *ad hoc* criminal tribunals (for the former Yugoslavia and for Rwanda), and more recently in the case of Darfur, Sudan, it referred the situation to the prosecutor of International Criminal Court through a resolution (*Resolution 1593*). The SC resolution made references to the need to 'promote the rule of law, protect human rights and combat impunity in Darfur'. However, it also determined in the same resolution that the situation in Sudan posed a threat to 'international peace and security' and thereby justified its own actions as acting under *Chapter VII* of the *UN Charter*. This action appears to suspend state-bound jurisdiction. Similarly, in the case of the former Yugoslavia the SC declared the territory of Kosovo an administrative territory in which a special UN agency (UNMIK) would take control of central governance functions.

Yet as radical a departure as these actions might seem from statist principles they do not really challenge the statist thesis. The actions of the SC derive validity primarily from the consent of member states: the referral of Sudan to the ICC can be justified by the SC's treatment of Sudan as a UN member state together with the SC's public order mandate. Similarly, the special cases of the SC initiation of actions to reconfigure territories, and states are validated by its public order mandate (see Chapter 10). Of course, the decisions of the SC may and have been interpreted as politically motivated in many instances and can be seen as stretching the remit of its mandate for such purposes, but, here, the question is what its actual mandate is. That the mandate is to establish international peace and security remains unchallenged.

Finally, it is worth referring to international institutions which engage with economic distribution of some kind. There are first the international finance and trade institutions (World Bank, IMF, and WTO) and also UN treaties, instruments, and organs dealing with socio-economic aims, such as the International Labour Organization and the International Covenant on Economic, Social and Cultural Rights and its Committee, the United Nations Development Programme and the UN General Assembly (with its *Declaration on the Right to Development* and the *Millennium Development Goals*). We will discuss what might be achieved through substantive cooperation, including cooperation through such organizations, below. For now it is important to see that these organizations operate against the background of state-bound political authority (jurisdiction). None of them has assignment jurisdiction, for they all work as associations whose mandate either derives from the authority of those that consent to their terms (and those who constitute them), or from public order aims. The World Bank, for example, has its origins as a reconstruction organization aiming at economically patching up states whose post-war situation was precarious, and so to shore up stability. The *Declaration on the Right to Development* does not assign any specific obligations and certainly does not empower any authority with international redistributive powers (which would require the power of assignment authority), the work of the UNDP is fundamentally consensual, and the *Millennium Development Goals* are aspirations with no clear associated obligations assignable to any agent. Finally, the Committee of the ICESCR, whilst dealing with socio-economic effects, does not have the authority to enforce aims beyond what signatory states have agreed. Like other human rights treaties, it treats implementation as a state-bound idea and is not comparative—seeking distributive patterns across different states. It also leaves decisions on implementation in the hands of states themselves.

Table 16.1 International cooperation and social justice

Institution	Functions	Key instruments
United Nations Security Council	Preserving peace and security, can authorize use of force, establish international protectorates, freeze assets of companies.	Country-specific and legally binding Security Council Resolutions.
United Nations General Assembly	Making recommendations and providing guidance to states on domestic social justice, interstate justice, and the duty to assist the poorest states.	Articles 1 and 55 of the United Nations Charter Declaration on the Right to Development. Millennium Development Goals.
United Nations Peace-building Commission	Advising on and proposing strategies for post-conflict countries for economic recovery by marshalling resources and bringing together donors, international financial institutions, and the post-conflict states.	Peace-building fund providing or facilitating funding for short- and medium-term projects.
Committee on Economic, Social and Cultural Rights	Making recommendations to the states parties to the ICRESC on how to fulfil their obligations domestically and with respect to international assistance of poor countries.	ICESCR Concluding observations with respect to state reports. General comments advising states on protecting the worst off and carrying out their duties of social justice responsibly.
World Bank	Providing economic resources to developing and least developed states.	Project funding for economic and social development projects.
International Monetary Fund	Providing fiscal and monetary assistance to states with balance of payment problems.	Offering fiscal packages to states to improve financial stability.

Table 16.1 *(Continued)*

Institution	Functions	Key instruments
World Trade Organization	Facilitating free trade across borders.	International trade agreements though allowing some exceptions for states to regulate their economies.
United Nations Development Programme	Providing technical assistance to states on development with the aim of protecting the worst off and the most vulnerable.	Human Development Projects, technical assistance programmes.
United Nations Special Rapporteur on Human Rights and Extreme Poverty	Reporting to states on how the rights of the worst off in societies can be protected and promoted.	Annual reports to the Human Rights Council.

We can see that from the four different types of function that international legal norms play, (1) allows provisions to be created through substantive cooperation between political authorities with state-bound assignment jurisdiction, whilst (2) and (3) are background functions which facilitate that cooperation and define entities that can create new obligations through substantive cooperation. The three functions, then, do not challenge the statist thesis. Function (4), the international public order function, is the function that would seem to most strongly challenge the statist thesis. Yet the point of that function is not to challenge the norm of state-bound assignment jurisdiction, but rather to preserve conditions of security in which substantive cooperation can occur. So whilst this function can at times require the suspension of state-bound jurisdiction, it is not for the purposes of arrogating that jurisdiction by a different type of entity. To summarize this: whilst the functions of international law may provide for the suspension of a particular state's jurisdiction, and may allow for the enforcement of some obligations in a way that challenges absolute state jurisdiction, they do so in ways that reflect statist aims rather than challenge them. No institutions of international law have, or claim, a non-statist governance function.

Can international law be used to advance the cause of social justice?

The above analysis has shown that the principles and functions defining international law do not constitute an authority that has assignment jurisdiction, but rather that assignment jurisdiction remains fundamentally statist, as per the statist thesis. This means that international law and its institutions, as it stands, is not social justice-apt where justice means social justice.

Cosmopolitanism, the idea that domestic principles of justice should, as a matter of consistency, apply to international institutions, needs, then, to approach international justice differently. It cannot claim that existing practices of international law represent the same kind of institutional order as a domestic state. In the latter case there is a political authority with assignment jurisdiction. That authority can use the distribution (assignment) of rights and duties across persons to adjust for the accumulated effects of people's interactions. If people buy less of a product and that leads to weakness in a given market sector, with resulting unemployment or loss of wages, the political authority can redistribute tax burdens and benefits to assist those in a position of disadvantage. If there is an accumulated inequality in life chances and opportunities, due to lower income, inheritance, and social-background patterns, the state can invest in education and infrastructure, and regulate inheritance, to address these problems. The state may not be able to prevent economic crises, but it has a responsibility to make sure their effects are continually fairly distributed across persons rather than primarily falling on the least advantaged.

Yet, as we have seen, such an authority does not exist internationally. Rather, separate state authorities exist together with a legal order facilitating their cooperation. In order to show that social justice (of the same kind applying to domestic institutions) applies internationally, cosmopolitans would need to show that continuous redistributive adjustment is still possible without a single unitary political authority. To do so they would need to show that there are specific principles of action that independent political authorities can follow in all their activities (regulation of internal markets, external trade, cooperative agreements, currency coordination, public sector investment, social service supply, as well as foreign investment, transfers, projects, and intervention) which will have the continuous coordinating effect of producing a pattern of distribution across the globe in which the least advantaged are as well off as they could be. That would seem to be quite a challenge, given also the potential conflict of such a wide-ranging and perpetual activity for states with the aim of producing justice for their own citizens. Can cosmopolitans show this is possible?

It is not the aim of this chapter to answer that question, call it the question of 'cosmopolitan coordination'. The coherence of this idea is disputed in the literature. Rather, the question here is whether principles of justice can apply to international law, not whether states can coordinate to produce justice by whatever means. To claim international law is itself subject to justice principles—that it can be used to codify obligations for the purposes of governance in line with social justice for persons rather than justice betweens states—it needs to be shown that international law can be used in ways going beyond the statist functions outlined above. That means either adopting a position of subverting the existing practices of international law or of reforming them.

This aim can broadly be called 'legal **cosmopolitanism**': the idea that international law can and should be moved in a direction that makes it more social justice-apt. An important question here is how radical this notion should be. One approach, the most radical, would be to propose that moving in the direction of a world state (a global and universal political authority with assignment jurisdiction) is an ethical obligation for all agents. That means that all legal agents (whether judiciaries or states themselves) when presented with opportunities to move towards the centralization of global power should do so. Yet, quite apart from the question of the desirability of such a concentration of power, this approach is not a legal approach as such. It has consequences for international law by default, not because of changes in the nature of international law itself. If global political authority (and assignment jurisdiction) is effectively centralized, then there ceases to be a need for international law and the statist principles at its heart.

The only kind of alternative to such a conception of legal cosmopolitanism is the idea that legal agents have duties to subvert the institutions of international law. Subversion, in turn, must be in a non-statist direction. If this is possible, then it would seem those agents (states and judiciaries) have an obligation to act so as to assign rights and duties in a way not subject to statist constraints. Courts like the ICJ and treaty bodies, as well as international bodies like the Security Council of the UN would have to act so as to centralize obligation assigning authority (taking it out of the hands of states themselves for certain purposes). For example, one of these organs (or states acting through this organ, as in the case of the SC) could order the creation of an International Redistributive Commission. This would impose taxes on affluent persons or industries internationally so as to redistribute resources to the least advantaged across the globe. It would do so irrespective of state agreement.

Again, it is not the point of this chapter to discuss whether such an idea is even economically coherent. Instead the question before us is whether it is legally coherent—achievable using international law. One would need to show not only that decision-makers acting *ultra vires* (outside of any context which gives legal validity to their decisions) can take actions outside the legal limits of international law. The question is whether they could make decisions which mobilized international law to assign rights and duties to specific persons and other agents for governance purposes. That is, can they generate valid obligations in international law in a non-statist way?

This brings us back to the status of the four functions this chapter has identified with international law. If these are taken to be simply a description of where international law happens to be right now, then nothing seems to stand in the way of introducing new functions into it. That would be a significant change to the limits of what can be achieved in the legal medium. The analysis that has been offered, however, is not of these functions as contingencies, or transient policies of international law. They explain the role of international law in a world of states. They are in effect both bases and limits of validity: the sole sources of legitimacy in international law. Outside of what these functions authorize the only other kind of political authority with assignment jurisdiction is that of states themselves. Decisions which run against the principles defining these functions, then, are not legally valid decisions. The creation of the International Redistributive Commission mentioned above takes power from states for economic governance purposes and claims an authority to assign rights and duties. That authority cannot be itself derivative of state assignment authority, substantive cooperation, or the conditions which make these possible. Its claim to authority is in fact in conflict with those functions of international law.

A decision which aims to be both legally valid (thereby imposing international obligations) yet undermining these four functions would imply a contradiction. On the one hand it would be claiming its authority from principles which only give statist mandates. On the other it would be claiming this authority to use in decisions which conflict with those very underlying principles. It would be reasonable to ask in such cases what the source of validity is for the decision, and the answer would be that nothing in international law validates it. It represents a usurpation of power which international law recognizes as legitimately belonging to states alone. As such it poses a direct threat to international public order, and so should be considered not only invalid but illegal.

One strategy to avoid this problem might be to argue that international legal decisions derive validity both from formal principles of legality (the four functions) and from substantive principles found within the law. The latter include principles of human rights standards, for example, and these might sanction a non-statist decision where the human rights of persons are involved. The problem with this approach is that substantive principles of international law are validly applied only to the extent that they fit the four functions. Consider the principles at the heart of the International Covenant on Economic Social and Cultural Rights, for example. The treaty assigns obligations to states with respect to their citizens. The obligations are not comparative and do not aim at maintaining a relational distribution between states. If the treaty body associated with the ICESCR sought to assign obligations in a different way, seeking distributions of costs across signatories say, to help the least advantaged states that would violate the terms of the treaty. The imposition of distributive obligations across states would have no legal source of validity.

The very meaning of the term 'human rights' might be thought to imply considerations going beyond statism. It might be thought that states substantively agreeing to a human rights treaty cannot limit the obligations of the treaty to their understanding of it or of human rights, when signing. Even if at the time of signing a state did not understand that the human right to non-discrimination extends to gays and lesbians, a court can arrive at that conclusion validly from the notion of non-discrimination. Can this same kind of reasoning be used to extend provisions to redistribution? To begin with, treaty provisions are clear that their point is to assign obligations; not to pursue a general aim with obligations simply flowing, as and when necessary, from that aim. The treaty does not aim at say, universal health provision in the world, and leave the assignment of responsibilities for this as a matter to be tailored to differing obstacles faced in achieving the aim. Further, making a treaty comparative would necessarily make it aim-based and so bring in a governance function for the treaty body. It is that kind of function that is avoided by having treaties assigning clear duties which respect state-bound jurisdiction.

It should be clear from the above that given the point of international legal relations, there is no room to use international law for purposes which fundamentally clash with that point.

What standards of justice are applicable to inter*national* affairs?

This chapter has not aimed at showing that international law is so limited that no conception of justice and just interactions can apply to it, other than those internal to the legal system itself. To restrict international justice to jurisprudential justice would be to ignore that the international system is a facilitation system, a set of institutions and laws that make cooperation possible. A central question with respect to international law, then, is what are the limits of cooperation within the constraints of its role?

It has been left open as to whether states acting together against this legal background could *coordinate their actions to produce social justice* (although there are difficulties with this idea). All that has been ruled out is the idea that global social justice can be 'enforced' through international law acting as an instrument of governance. What does that leave? It certainly does not rule out states seeking substantive cooperative agreements on the basis of fair and equitable relations. Nor does it rule out states cooperating to rescue and assist nations and people in emergency circumstances. The idea that it is legitimate to criticize finance institutions like the IMF for giving advantages to some economies and disadvantages to others, or for ravaging social services within developing economies, are ideas that remain intact even given the above analysis of international law. It is just that the criticism cannot be that these activities are illegal by the standards of international law. On the other hand, a state signatory to the ICESCR which agrees measures with a finance institution that will undermine its own ability to fulfil its ICESCR obligations can be seen as failing in its international obligations.

If we rule out the idea of world government, and think that substantive cooperation cannot achieve the level of coordination needed for continuously maintaining a just pattern of distribution across all persons, then what this leaves is fairness in state cooperation. A great many of the problems which are identified with international justice, such as the problem of poverty, can be addressed as matters of fairness in the rules of international cooperation, especially at the level of finance (assistance) and trade institutions. It is clear that states have ethical obligations in this regard that they more often than not ignore. In that sense of justice the international legal system creates opportunities, even if it does not impose obligations. Citizens of states are becoming increasingly aware of the ways in which their governments gain advantage at the expense of fairness in international agreements. International justice is in this context a criticism of governmental foreign policy according to principles of fair dealing with other states. This level of criticism, however, is still firmly within the bounds of inter*national* (rather than global social) justice.

Conclusion

This chapter began by identifying questions of social justice and asking whether (as some campaigners have had it) international law is itself subject to such standards in the form of global social-justice principles. It then gave an analysis of what kind of institutions are apt for judgement in terms of social justice and why. That analysis showed that institutions need to exhibit a special kind of political authority (one with assignment jurisdiction) in order to be social justice-apt. The chapter then asked whether international law (its principles and organs) possessed this kind of political authority. The analysis of international law according to its four defining functions showed that it is not social justice-apt in this way. Ways of making international law justice-apt were then presented under the heading of 'legal cosmopolitanism' and the problems for these were highlighted. Finally, a different notion of standards of international justice (rather than global social justice) was outlined.

Questions

1. What kind of questions are questions of social justice?

2. What might make institutions apt for applying principles of social justice to them?

3. What kind of entities have (or are taken to have) the ultimate authority to assign political obligations to persons?

4. What kind of entities can legitimately engage in the creation of international legal provisions?

5. What are the central functions of international law?

6. Are there limits on what kind of international legal provisions can be created?

7. When international institutions intervene to prevent war, is that because they have a mandate to help individual persons?

8. Is international law a 'governance' institution?

9. Is the status of a norm as a *ius cogens* norm due simply to how ethical it is?

10. Is fair dealing betweens states the same as social justice?

Further reading

Beitz, C. (1999) *Political Theory and International Relations*, 2nd edn. (Princeton: Princeton University Press) and Pogge, T. (2002) *World Poverty and Human Rights* (Cambridge: Polity Press). *These are two cosmopolitan approaches to international justice.*

Mapel, D. R. and Nardin, T. (eds.) (1999) *International Society, Diverse Ethical Perspectives* (Princeton: Princeton University Press). *A good introduction to different approaches to International Society Theory in international relations.*

Meckled-Garcia, S. (2008) 'On the Very Idea of Cosmopolitan Justice: Constructivism and International Agency' *Journal of Political Philosophy* 16/3: 245–71. *This offers a critique of cosmopolitan theory.*

Rawls, J. (1971) *A Theory of Justice* (Oxford: Oxford University Press) and Dworkin, R. (2000) *Sovereign Virtue* (Cambridge, Mass.: Harvard University Press). *These are two of the most influential contemporary theories of social justice.*

Tesón, F. (1998) *A Philosophy of International Law* (Boulder, CO: Westview Press). *A strongly 'interventionist liberal' approach to international law.*

Wheeler, N. (2002) *Saving Strangers: Humanitarian Intervention in International Society* (Oxford: Oxford University Press). *A representative of the Solidarist school of International Society Theory.*

Websites

Written by eminent scholars in their respective fields, the Stanford Encyclopedia of Philosophy provides overviews of topics in political theory. Of particular interest for this chapter will be the contributions on:

International Justice:

http://plato.stanford.edu/entries/international-justice/

Distributive Justice:

http://plato.stanford.edu/entries/justice-distributive/

Cosmopolitanism:

http://plato.stanford.edu/entries/cosmopolitanism/

Nationalism (esp. Section 3 on the moral debate):

http://plato.stanford.edu/entries/nationalism/

Egalitarianism:

http://plato.stanford.edu/entries/egalitarianism/

Visit the Online Resource Centre that accompanies this book to access more learning resources www.oxfordtextbooks.co.uk/orc/cali/

CONCLUSION

Chapter 17

International law in international relations: what are the prospects for the future?

Başak Çalı

CHAPTER CONTENTS

- Introduction
- The political (in)stability of international law
- Institution-building for international law
- The breadth of international law
- Complexity and differentiation of international law regimes
- Non-state actors and international law
- Conclusion

CHAPTER OVERVIEW

This chapter invites students for a final discussion on how we should conceive the role and future of international law in international relations. Will international law be respected more in the future? Is there going to be more international law in the future? What new institutions does international law need, if any? We can approach these questions in three different ways: by focusing on states, on institutions and the very nature of international law. First, a central question on the future of international law is how to stabilize the attitudes of states towards it. What factors will lead to an international order that respects international law more? Second, we can focus on the role of institutions in shaping the behaviour of actors: domestic and international courts are two such actors that are playing an increasingly important role. Finally, we can focus on the nature of the laws themselves and discuss their ability to pull towards compliance and the challenges that non-state actors bring to international law.

Introduction

As we have seen in previous chapters, diverse topics of social, economic, moral, and political significance are subject to some form of international legal regulation. International law as a set of ideas, practices, and institutions is very much part of international relations in our contemporary world—a world that is characterized by global interdependence and the interaction of states as well as of groups and individuals. Global interdependence is a defining feature of international relations not only because states have common problems, but also because most states agree that domestic political choices must be subject to some constraints by international law. It is no longer a widely held view that states have an absolute right to act in any way they please in their domestic or international affairs. The need for collective decision-making and acceptance of international values presents cooperation as a necessity rather than a mere choice in international relations. States have made treaties in areas as diverse as international trade, the protection of the environment, protection of human rights, regulation of the sea and space, international crimes, and the exploitation of our world's resources. There is, furthermore, a widespread consensus that there are ground rules that constrain the terms of cooperation (*ius cogens* constraints on international agreements), the terms of the interaction between states (principle of sovereign immunity of states) and domestic laws and practices (human rights law and international criminal law).

Despite this diversity in regulation and the existence of ground rules for cooperation, international laws are under constant danger of being ignored, downplayed, trivialized, diluted, and disagreed upon in everyday international politics. Politicians in many states turn a blind eye to international law when they believe that it does not serve their policy objectives. They succumb to domestic pressures, even if this means violating international legal commitments. Legal advisers to foreign ministries provide conflicting interpretations about what international rules say on a subject or what route a treaty negotiation should follow and, in the absence of a final adjudicative authority to settle matters, they agree to disagree on some of the most important problems of our times, such as the environment, the protection of natural resources, and alleviation of poverty.

The future of international law in international relations lies in this dynamic of ever propagating international law and the unstable attitudes political actors have towards international law while pursuing politics in the territorially divided political entities we call states. Given what we now know about international law, this final chapter aims to analyse in what ways we can best approach this dynamic by setting out three discussion questions:

1. Is political instability a structural characteristic of international law?

2. Shall we have more, less, or a different type of international laws?

3. What is the place of non-state actors in international law?

The first question deals with the problem of how to make international cooperation, the defining characteristic of international law, deeper, and more sustainable. The second question addresses the very nature of the international laws themselves: Do we have too few or too many? Which subject matters are in need of further international law? How do the different bodies of international law relate to each other? The final question requires a sound understanding of our globalized world and its problems. At first glance, it may look like the first question concerns the student of international relations and the second of international law and the final question seems to concern both. The questions, however, are interrelated. In order to make international law longer lasting, future decision-makers need to advance international laws that will receive widespread levels of support without being accused of imposing values, or being unrealistic. So the future of international law depends on the relationship between the quality of international laws and the support they attract in a horizontal, interstate system.

The political (in)stability of international law

The political instability of international law has long occupied international relations scholars and international lawyers. In effect, the classical realist Morgenthau was himself an international lawyer who was disillusioned with the political instability of international law in the aftermath of World War II. He, therefore, dismissed international law altogether as an unrealistic project. This historically grounded reaction to international law left an important legacy in the discipline of international relations: a suspicion of any stable cooperation between states which not only pursue different agendas, but also are willing to pursue their agendas at the expense of international law. This legacy has *two important dimensions*. First, there is the argument that international law is and will be ignored by states because there is a structural weakness in the international system. When international law is not ignored it is only because states' self-interests and laws happen to overlap. Second, international law is and will continue to be very difficult to pin down, as it will always be interpreted through the individual preferences of each and every state. The second dimension makes a much deeper and more troubling claim about international law. It implies that the very content of international law is subservient to international politics. If we add to this picture that, in decentralized orders, 'might is right', we can simply say that international law is and will continue to be a mere reflection of the preferences of the most powerful states and their dominant lobbies international relations. This paints a grim picture and is a powerful critique of international law. But does this picture adequately capture the way in which international law and international relations work?

One way of approaching this critique is to say that the international rationalist-realist camp got it right all along. One does not need to have too much wisdom to say that the future of international law is not going to be very different from its present or its recent past in terms of how international law is made, applied, and enforced. So long as the international system is made up of sovereign states, international law will be a horizontal system (treaty law and customary international law) with a number of international organizations facilitating cooperation. There is no denying that even the strongest and most influential states need to cooperate with others. In such instances, pockets of international law will emerge, as they have in the areas of trade, sovereign immunity, diplomatic protection. And precisely because there is a strong overlap between preferences of the strong and the influential, agreements will be adhered to, and international lawyers will have a good deal of interpretive work to do. This does not and will not mean, however, that adherence to agreements will be subject to a cost–benefit analysis and their endurance will be connected to benefits that outweigh costs. So, international law will remain relatively stable if: (1) it reflects the interests of the powerful and influential and (2) it will not impose high costs on politicians domestically or internationally.

Another way of approaching this critique is to look at the very practice of states and see whether the above is an accurate description of the international system and whether it is indeed the case that states only comply with agreements that have low costs for them. If this is not the case, we can make further inquiries into how and under what conditions international law is embedded in the belief systems of states.

The international law respecting state: an idealist category?

Empirically speaking it is difficult to make a list of states which solely aim to advance 'their own interests' through mutual cooperation and those which simply respect international law because politicians regard this as 'the right thing' to do. State actors behave both in interest–maximizing rational ways and normatively motivated ways in different circumstances—in fact, the two types of considerations may not always be easy to distinguish as normative considerations often play an important role in defining states' interests in the first place (Checkel 2005). Consider the example of the first interstate case before the European Court of Human Rights: *Ireland v United Kingdom* (1978) where Ireland complained that United Kingdom was violating the human rights of terrorist suspects in the UK. On one account, we can say that Ireland seriously risked its own interests by bringing a case against its greatest trading partner and influential neighbour. On another account, we can say that the Irish case against the UK was in the broader interests of Ireland insofar as the detained were Irish citizens. We can, however, also see that the existence of an international treaty, the European Convention on Human Rights, and an international adjudication body, the European Court of Human Rights, made a very important difference in the way in which relations between these two states were shaped at that time. International law and its institutions in this respect play an interest-shaping role by providing institutional opportunities for states to interact in certain ways and enable them to frame relationships in terms of rights and responsibilities.

This brings us to an important point of international relations constructivists. International law and institutions influence the ways in which domestic and foreign policy is formulated and processes through which such policy is pursued (Kratochwil 1989; Barnett and Finnemore 2004). If it becomes possible to have a critical mass of states that foster a strong international law-respecting attitude, it may indeed be possible to alter the unstable political nature of international law. An international law-respecting state is one where domestic decision-makers recognize that states have duties to cooperate, respect agreements, assist each other, and act collectively to protect the international public order. This does not mean that instrumentalist and cost–benefit analysis type calculations would disappear for good. It means, however, that such instrumentalist forms of reasoning by politicians will take place in the shadow of international law rather than at the expense of it.

There are two historically constrained obstacles to this. First, there is the problem of instability of domestic political regimes themselves, be they democratic or not, with respect to their attitudes towards international law. In each political community, some political groups and parties are more international law-respecting than others. This means that changes of government at elections can jeopardize the attitude of respect for international law. The instability of international law is risked further if and when major powers in the international system have governments with indifferent or hostile attitudes towards international law. This often has a knock-on effect, pushing other states to follow suit either because of coercion, incentives, or ideological similarities. Two contemporary examples of this have been, first, the large number of countries following the United States' lead on torturing terrorist suspects or helping the US despite the well-recognized *ius cogens* character on the prohibition of torture and, second, the countries following the European Union lead on returning ships carrying asylum seekers in territorial seas without processing their asylum applications.

Authoritarian states, facing alienation, sanctions, or threats also clash with international law because these states exhibit strong anti-interventionist tendencies towards the outside world and may adopt isolationist policies that see them refusing to cooperate with or respect well-established principles of international law. The sanctions imposed on such states may have further negative effects on the respect for international law domestically. Both democratic and authoritarian forms of government, therefore, are capable of breeding hostile attitudes towards international law. In both cases, international law is equated with the 'imposition of values' from the outside. Such imposition is characterized as either: (1) that international law is the imposition of the rule of the strong over the weak or (2) that international law is the imposition of rules over nations/people.

In sum, international law's political stability is clearly rooted in the attitudes of decision-makers and such attitudes are a function of particular socio-political contexts. The stability of international law can be cultivated by increasing the number and distribution of international law respecting states so that the rest of the international community would find it embarrassing, uncomfortable, and difficult to jeopardize international law. This is because a horizontal system like international law only works if all states comply with the rules most of the time and are compelled by a duty to comply with international law. International lawyers would argue that the existence of international law on a subject matter gives state officials a special and distinct reason to act in specific ways. An ideal statesman in international law terms is someone who asks 'what is the international law on this matter' before deciding on a particular course of action. This is clearly a political process rather than a legal one with domestic and international dimensions.

International relations and law scholars have pointed out that increasing the number and quality of democratic regimes must be part of the political process to increase respect for international law (Franck 1997, Roth and Fox 2000). International law does not require each member of the state system to be democratic, but many international agreements promote democratic values. An obvious connection between democratic forms of government and international law is that non-democratic governments are more prone to violating laws of international human rights, such as, among others, the right to fair trial, freedom from unlawful detention, freedom of expression, and freedom from discrimination. The democratization of domestic polities, therefore, enables more domestic respect for international human rights law. Becoming a democratic state, however, does not in itself guarantee respect for international law. The ideal international law respecting state, therefore, needs not only to be internally democratic, but also rule of law respecting internationally.

Institution-building for international law

An important insight from sociology is that institutions can have effects on actors' attitudes. Two institutional developments in contemporary international relations come to mind in this respect: the proliferation of international institutions and domestication of international law. The central question about these institutions is whether they can depoliticize and stabilize attitudes towards international law amongst states.

The creation of international organizations, courts, tribunals, and expert bodies

As we have seen in previous chapters, international law in many instances creates international institutions, be these compliance procedures, international courts, or expert bodies. These bodies take their authority from the consent of states that have agreed to establish them. They are, however, dynamic institutions as they have to interpret what the states have consented to in order to fulfil their roles. The existence of these organizations complicates the descriptive picture of international law as a purely interstate phenomenon. These bodies provide concreteness and precision to general rules of international law by their decisions. They allow the participation of non-governmental organizations and individuals in the interpretation of international law (see Chapters 7 and 13). They further provide access to citizens around the world on complex international public policy issues through their public investigations, decisions, and reports. The descriptive functions of these bodies should not be confused with their authority (see Chapter 16). These bodies do not have the authority to enforce their decisions. The consent and cooperation of states, therefore, is necessary for the decisions of these bodies to be implemented.

This point aside, one can also ask whether the conduct of international relations would have been the same if we had no international organizations, courts, and other bodies at all. In this sense international institutions provide new opportunities for states to act in certain ways (i.e. taking another state to court, giving evidence on domestic policy before an international body, allowing visits of international experts into the country), open up international law processes to non-state actors (i.e. bringing a case against a state, writing shadow reports to international bodies criticizing states), and enables views to emerge on concrete international law debates that have persuasive authority amongst decision-makers (e.g. definition of rape as a war crime).

Box 17.1 Imagining new forms of cooperation

The ability of international institutions to change the terms of international debate and to increase, deepen, and normalize cooperation is attractive for internationalist decision-makers and NGOs. A number of proposals are worth mentioning for future discussion here:

A *World Court for Human Rights* is an idea that aims to increase the binding force of international human rights law internationally. Currently, there are only regional courts and UN human rights bodies that have recommendatory powers. Such a court is hoped to play a role in the depoliticization of human rights as a foreign policy tool and to set minimum standards applicable to all states.

An *International Environmental Court* is proposed to bring coherency to interpretation of environmental principles and develop them further to promote awareness of environmental interdependency, provide guidance, and set standards.

An *International Tort Court* tries to address the accountability gap for multinational corporations, which operate in so many countries and escape responsibility for their complicity in serious human rights abuses, environmental damage, international crimes, and labour law violations. Similar to the subsidiary logic of international criminal law, an international tort court can hear cases against major corporations when states are unwilling or unable to prosecute them. The threat of prosecution may enable multinational corporations to adopt and adhere to strict business ethics standards and may signal corrupt or authoritarian regimes that they will not have support from private economic actors.

Domestic courts and international law

Domestic courts have not been important actors in international law and international relations. This is partly because international law has been more readily associated with foreign ministries and diplomats and partly international law manifests itself in very different ways in the domestic systems of states.

Domestic courts often do not have a legal mandate to scrutinize a government's foreign policy and international commitments because of the separation of powers doctrine. This is also reflected in how international law is placed in the domestic legal systems. In international law, states are often divided as **monist** and **dualist** with reference to how their domestic legal systems position themselves towards international law. A monist state is one that sees the international law and the domestic law as one order and when a treaty is ratified by a state it automatically becomes part of domestic law (e.g. Germany, the Netherlands). Monist states differ in how they view an international law in the hierarchy of domestic laws. Some see international laws as equal to domestic laws, others say they are equal to constitutional provisions. Dualist states on the other hand maintain a strict separation between domestic legal systems and international law (e.g. the United Kingdom, Ireland). The latter can only be a part of the former if it is *incorporated* into the system by an Act of Parliament. Some states also have a mixed regime: some customary international laws and treaties are directly applicable, whereas other treaties require domestic legislation (the USA).

In both monist and dualist states, however, domestic judges were traditionally cut off from international law as most international treaties concerned interstate relations and domestic judges have had no role to play in such foreign policy matters.

In the contemporary institutionalization of international law, the picture is—again—more complex due to the emergence of international human rights law, international criminal law, *ius cogens* norms, and expanding grounds for universal jurisdiction. Domestic courts are now being asked to rule on how armies and security forces conduct themselves in faraway lands. They receive demands to arrest and prosecute suspected foreign war criminals travelling to their country. They also are asked to review investment agreements that states make with multinational corporations and international financial institutions. These developments are not taking place evenly in all parts of the world and the domestic reception of international law and the opportunities available for using domestic courts change radically from one place to the other. There is, however, a trend towards recognizing the domestic courts as actors of international law implementation.

The insertion of domestic judges into the processes of international law imposes an institutional limitation on the behaviour of governments towards international law and it makes governments accountable domestically for the decisions they take as a matter of international policy. Given that there is no centralized authority to oversee government behaviour internationally, domestic courts offer an alternative model to increase the input of international law considerations in international relations.

The breadth of international law

An important observation about international law is that there is a lot of it. It regulates more issue-areas and it interferes in the domestic law-making processes. We can approach this development first considering the negative scenario: would it be desirable to have as little international law as possible? The international lawyer's answer to this question is simple: the absence of international law is clearly negative for international relations. It is a sign of instability, conflict, exploitation, and injustice. International law may not always be able to remedy these, but the existence of international law is a constant reminder that there are laws that apply to all states and state action is subject to assessment and judgment by virtue of the existence of these rules.

This perspective, however, does not answer the question of *how much* international law we should have and which areas should be adequately regulated in the international sphere. The topics we have discussed in this book give us a fairly good idea of matters for international concern; (1) matters that arise distinctly from international interactions (e.g. wars, armed conflicts, prisoners of war, dispute settlement); (2) matters that are regarded as ground rules for interactions (e.g. rules of treaty making, principles of exercising jurisdiction); and (3) matters that are defined as part of international public interest (e.g. prohibition of genocide, protection of the environment).

It is often the third category that sparks discussion as different actors define matters that are part of international public interest in different ways. As we see in the cases of international criminal law and international human rights law, it is relatively easy to focus on prohibitive behaviour in international law, such as the prohibition of war crimes or torture, but it is more difficult to get agreement amongst states on prescriptive behaviour, such as the regulation of multinational corporations. For some, this is a failure of international law. There is not enough international law on some of the most salient issues of contemporary societies. For others, international law is not an adequate tool to regulate on important issues (see Chapter 16). This is an important debate for the future of international law as it goes to the heart of effective institutional design for international commons. International policy-makers all around the world recognize a broad list of issues ranging from poverty to the environment, the regulation of capital to the protection of health of common concern for international society. Recognition of the political importance of these issues, however, does not translate into regulative principles internationally or when they do, they are weak, voluntary, or disputed. This does not mean that such regulative efforts are completely futile, but it means that it does take time for attitudes to converge on fine-tuned principles.

Such convergence is more difficult in some areas than in others. International law enables states to contest different proposals on future cooperation. The United Nations bodies, regional human rights courts, human rights law monitoring mechanisms, environmental law compliance procedures, trade law dispute settlement mechanisms, and the International Criminal Court are all outcomes of such contestation. All of these institutions have been advocated and campaigned for longer than they have existed. The regulation of issues of common concern by international law, therefore, is an active and dynamic process, which relies on increasing and negotiating agreement between states through mechanisms of socialization.

The message here is not to be a relentless advocate of the international legal regulation of international affairs. Over-regulation by international law is also a problem that is subject to backlash. Political groups in different states may view international law as too deep an intervention into domestic political and legal processes or the imposition of one set of values over the rest. This would very easily spark anti-international law attitudes.

In our discussions of topics we have seen that international law is a nuanced system rather than a collection of blunt statements of international rules. In trade law, environmental law, as well as human rights and criminal law, there are exceptions to rules and space is left for domestic processes to pursue different policy options. The healthy relationship between domestic and international processes is more central to the future of international law than extensiveness of international law. The question is, therefore, to discuss which international laws to pursue rather than to have international law on all matters of importance.

Complexity and differentiation in international law regimes

When looking at the future of international law institutions, international lawyers often emphasize the need to rationalize and harmonize the operation of existing international law regimes. This debate is important for international lawyers because of the parallel development of a number of specialized areas in international law and the creation of overlapping institutions and regimes. This is indeed a sign of the maturity and the complexity of international law. It also means that there may as well be potential conflicts between different competing objectives of different bodies of law.

The potential conflicts between different specialized regimes of international law can be approached as systemic problems and as political problems. The first identifies regime conflict as a function of the lack of an overarching international authority that could intervene and adjust when such conflicts arise. The second sees this in terms of the relative political power states have in dictating a particular preference for the resolution of such conflicts. A central example by which to discuss these perspectives is the possible conflict between investment laws and international human rights protections for economic, social, and cultural rights. As we have seen earlier, IHRL demands states to regulate non-state actors that may impact on the enjoyment of rights. Bilateral investment treaties, on the other hand, demand that foreign direct investment is immune from domestic regulation. Due to the lack of an international constitutional order, neither of these obligations legally trump each other. The political perspective on this issue would highlight that this is more a clash of ideologies (economic development through foreign direct investment versus human rights protections) rather than a technical problem of international law.

It seems that the complexity of international law and regime conflicts will be an important feature of international law in the future. This means that international policy-makers will focus more on questions of international public order, and new principles will emerge to address or deal with any conflicts. This will remain an important issue to be addressed by non-governmental organizations in their campaigns, domestic judges, and international courts and tribunals.

Non-state actors and international law

We have seen in the course of this book that nobody disputes that the international system is made up of *more than* states. Alongside international organizations, there are also other non-state actors such as multinational corporations, non-governmental organizations, and terrorist networks. Non-state actors are diverse and they become relevant under international law in different ways. We can identify three potential ways that non-state actors figure in and challenge international law—first, as potential law-makers, second, as subjects of regulation and, finally, as threats to international law.

Non-state actors as potential law-makers?

As we have seen throughout this book, the making of international law requires collective decision-making by states. International organizations and non-governmental organizations participate in international law-making processes, influence state actors, but they do not make the law. We have also seen that in areas such as the environment and human rights, multinational corporations are creating their own codes of conduct. They operate in similar ways to state actors in regulating their activities. Pointing to the economic power of multinational corporations and their self-regulative activities in the international sphere, some commentators argue that we should start thinking about international law-making not solely as a domain for states. Two arguments are generally mobilized in support for this view: (1) many economic non-state actors are more powerful than many states; and (2) incorporating multinational corporations and non-governmental actors in international law-making can increase the effectiveness of international laws in areas such as the protection of the environment. Thinking about non-state actors not as actors that influence law-making processes, but as law-makers in their own capacity, however, runs into a number of important problems. Firstly, there is the question of whether the influence of these actors make them fit for the task of law-making. Multinational corporations are profit-seeking entities and it would make little sense for them to promote international laws that would decrease their profit. Non-governmental organizations are unequally distributed both geographically and thematically and it would be difficult to determine which of the thousands of them should participate directly in law-making. Secondly, there is the question of the legitimacy and accountability of non-state actors as law-makers. Multinational corporations are accountable to their stakeholders and the accountability for non-governmental organizations varies from accountability to their members to accountability to their funders. In the case of states—even in non-democratic ones—there is accountability through political processes and states derive their legitimacy as international actors from this public accountability process. It is for this reason that we regard states as possessing a title to speak for a population and a territory. In this respect, the effectiveness argument stands in strong contrast to arguments of legitimacy and accountability. It is, however, also true that powerful non-state actors are able to influence states' preferences more than non-profit interest groups and there may be a case for including these quieter voices in international law-making. The creation of an assembly of a global civil society to the United Nations is one proposal along these lines. As we have seen in Chapter 7, in some areas, notably human rights, non-state actors are able to influence the law-making process.

Non-state actors as subjects of regulation

The regulation of non-state actors is one of the most important challenges for international law. Currently, international law regulates the conduct of individuals in the context of armed conflicts and when they commit an international crime. Warlords, terrorists, and crime networks are all subject to prosecution within the framework of international criminal law. International law relies on domestic courts to regulate violent non-state actors in the first place. The fact that these actors can be prosecuted in any country where the crimes are committed or the victim resides or where the perpetrator resides creates a strong judicial net and significantly affects the number of countries in which such individuals can reside.

The regulation of collective actors—most notably multinational corporations—remains an important challenge as no judicial system exists that can regulate in the event of wrongdoings by such actors. Multinational corporations operate in a number of countries and they are subject to diverse sets of domestic laws and regulations depending on the country in which they have activities or special contracts they sign with states. This means that they are able to operate in ways that maximize their profits. Civil society activists often complain about the freedom multinational corporations have to play states against each other in order to secure the most profitable deals and the lack of accountability these organizations have due to their complex administrative structures. Despite broad criticisms, however, it is not clear in which ways multinational actors should be regulated in the international arena. The lack of agreement between states on areas such as environmental regulation and labour standards further complicate questions of multinational corporation regulation. Recent years have witnessed large amounts of litigation against multinational corporations in domestic courts for being complicit in human rights violations or international crimes. In the future, this is an area where we can expect more accountability regimes to emerge.

Non-state actors as threats to international law

Globally organized violent non-state actors pose a threat to the stability of international law. This threat is rooted in the reactions states have to the activities of non-state actors. Violent non-state actors generally do not respect international laws, including humanitarian laws, the use of weapons, or the treatment of captured persons. The terrorist attacks in the United States of September 2001, directly led the US government to argue that violent non-state actors, most notably terrorists, who have no regard for international law do not need to be treated under the rules of international law. This has been a dangerous development for international law as this not only leads to the application of international laws being diluted, but also provides an example for other states to follow. Violent non-state actors do not respect international law (or any domestic law for that matter) because they are criminal actors and they are engaged in criminal acts. Levelling down states with such actors has the serious consequence that states start behaving like criminal actors rather than as public actors with international law obligations.

The development of the military capabilities of non-state actors cause further problems in areas such as prohibited weapons and means of warfare in international relations. International law is unable to deter a non-state actor that is able and willing to use prohibited weapons. This has the dangerous potential of conflicts where there is little regard for international law and potentially prolonged armed conflicts (such as in Afghanistan) at the expense of civilians.

Conclusion

We identified three broad approaches to analysing the role of international law in international relations to assess whether the role of international law will change or not in the future. The first perspective is to view international law as a product of the structural condition in the international system. In accordance with this view, international law plays a constant role in international relations and its role is the product of—and thus limited by—this structure. The second perspective is to view international law as a producer of relationships in the international arena. This means that international law can create deeper and more stable cooperation between states by enabling international law respecting attitudes to emerge. This has the potential of making cooperation effective, long-lasting, and even habitual. We have also highlighted, however, that the political sources of anti-international law attitudes (in the form of prioritizing self-selected objectives) exist both in democratic and non-democratic states. This shows the very close relationship between political conditions and the future of international law.

A very striking finding about international law is that there is a lot of it and a wide range of actors participate in the making, interpretation, and implementation of it. These actors range from politicians, elected or otherwise, non-governmental organizations, international organizations created by international agreements, to domestic judges. Even individuals can, by bringing individual cases against governments, contribute to the interpretation of international treaties. When we approach international law as a set of processes, we have to study the large number of complex relationships that exist between actors, domestic and international. Non-state actors in international law pose regulatory challenges. They also affect the ways in which existing rules are interpreted by states. In sum, the future of international law will be a fertile land for political and institutional analysis and it will host political struggles both domestically and internationally about the future of international relations.

Questions

1. Is international law structurally a weak system?

2. Why are political attitudes towards international law unstable?

3. What factors contribute to more stable and respectful attitudes towards international law amongst decision-makers?

4. What role do international organizations, courts, and expert bodies play in strengthening the commitment to international law?

5. In what ways do domestic courts complicate the definition of international law as rules regulating interstate relations?

6. Are new international law regimes needed and feasible to establish in international relations? Discuss with reference to: (a) a world court of human rights; (b) an international environmental court; and (c) an international tort court.

7. Does international law contain conflicting legal systems?

8. Should non-state actors have a law-making role in international relations?

9. In what ways does international law regulate non-state actors?

10. In what ways do violent non-state actors threaten the stability of international law?

11. How do you assess the future of international law in international relations?

Further reading

Chimni, B. S. (2007) 'The Past, Present and the Future of International Law: A Critical Third World Approach' *Melbourne Journal of International Law* 8/2: 499–515. *A critical analysis of international law as reflecting power inequalities across the globe and proposing an approach to future regulation.*

Guzman, A. (2007) *How International Law Works: A Rational Choice Theory* (Oxford: Oxford University Press). *An account of how international law succeeds in the absence of coercive enforcement.*

Slaughter, A. M. and Burke-White, W. (2006) 'The Future of International Law is Domestic (or The European Way of Law)' *Harvard International Law Journal* 47/2: 327–52. *An analysis of what roles domestic courts play in the implementation of international law and how this affects domestic political processes.*

Websites

Visit the Online Resource Centre that accompanies this book to access more learning resources
www.oxfordtextbooks.co.uk/orc/cali/

Table of cases

Table of major multilateral international treaties and documents

Treaties

African Charter on Human and Peoples
Rights (1984)
American Convention on Human Rights (1978)

Charter of the United Nations (1945)
Convention on the Pacific Settlement
of International Disputes (1904)
Convention on the Prevention and Punishment
of the Crime of Apartheid (1973)
Convention on the Prevention and Punishment
of the Crime of Genocide (1948)
Convention on the Suppression of Terrorist
Bombing (1997)

European Convention on Human Rights and
Fundamental Freedoms (1950)

General Agreements on Tariffs and Trade (1994)
Geneva Convention for the Amelioration
of the Condition of the Wounded and Sick
in the Armed Forces in the Field (First) (1948)
Geneva Convention for the Amelioration
of the Condition of Wounded, Sick and
Shipwrecked Members of the Armed Forces
at Sea (Second) (1949)
Geneva Convention Relative to the Protection of
Civilian Persons in Time of War (Fourth) (1949)
Geneva Convention Relative to the Treatment
of Prisoners of War (Third) (1949)

Hague Convention IV on the Laws and Customs
of War on Land (1907)

International Convention against Torture
and Other Inhuman Degrading Treatment
or Punishment (1984)
International Convention on the Law of the Sea
(1984)
International Covenant on Civil and Political
Rights (1966)
International Covenant on Civil and Political
Rights (1966)
International Covenant on Economic, Social
and Cultural Rights (1966)

International Covenant on Economic, Social
and Cultural Rights (1966)

Kellogg-Briand Pact (1928)

Montevideo Convention on the Rights
and Duties of States (1933)

Nuclear Non-Proliferation Treaty (1968)
Nuclear Safety Convention (1994)

Protocol Additional to the Geneva Conventions
of 12 August 1949 and relating to
the Protection of Victims on Non-International
Armed Conflicts (1977) (Also 2nd Additional
Protocol)
Protocol Additional to the Geneva Conventions
of 12 August 1949, and relating to the
Protection of Victims of International Armed
Conflicts (1979) (Also known as 1st additional
protocol)

Statue of the International Criminal Court
(1999)

The Agreement Governing the Activities
of States on the Moon and Other Celestial
Bodies (1984)
The Framework Convention on Climate Change
(1994)
The Kyoto Protocol to the Framework
Convention on Climate Change (2005)

UN Convention on Conventional Weapons
(1981)
United Nations Convention on Chemical
Weapons (1993)

Vienna Convention for the Protection of the
Ozone Layer (1985)
Vienna Convention on Diplomatic Relations
(1961)
Vienna Convention on the Law of Treaties (1969)
Vienna Convention on the Secession of States
with Respect to Treaties (1978)

Declarations

Universal Declaration of Human Rights (1948)

United Nations Declaration on Permanent Sovereignty over Natural Resources (1962)

United Nations Declaration on Principles of International Law Concerning Friendly Relations and Co-operation among States in Accordance with the Charter of the United Nations (1970)

United Nations Declaration on Granting Independence to Colonial Countries and Peoples (1960)

United Nations Declaration on the Right to Development (1984)

Stockholm Declaration on Human Environment (1972)

United Nations Declaration of the UN Conference on Environment and Development (1992)

United Nations Declaration on the Rights of Persons Belonging to National or Ethnic, Religious and Linguistic Minorities (1992)

United Nations Declaration on Millennium Development Goals (2000)

United Nations Declaration on the Rights of Indigenous Peoples (2007)

Glossary

Aarhus Convention The international environmental treaty which famously links government accountability and environmental protection and establishes that environmentally friendly development can only be achieved through the involvement of stakeholders.

Accession A state becoming party to a treaty which is already in force among other states.

Admissibility Rules stipulated in the founding document of each international court or tribunal regulating whether or not the court shall adjudicate the substantive part of the dispute. Admissibility is a filtering mechanism of cases.

Adoption Expression of agreement by negotiating state parties to the final text of an international treaty. Adoption of a treaty is not binding unless otherwise specified.

Advanced disciplines Interlinked obligations in international trade law that aim to intervene in domestic trade policy.

Advisory Opinion A legal pronouncement delivered by an international court on a particular question of international law. They are aimed at clarifying a legal position and are not legally binding as such for states, but carry persuasive authority.

Advocacy Pursuit of influencing outcomes in domestic and international public policy.

Agreement The basis of an international treaty if reached between two or more state parties. Some treaties may also be named as an 'agreement'.

Alien Tort Claims Act A piece of US legislation that gives the authority to US domestic courts to hear tort cases committed by a non-US citizen in non-US territory for violations of the law of nations or a treaty of the United States.

Anarchy Lack of a central political authority.

Anticipatory self-defence The international law doctrine which holds that states do not need to wait for an actual armed attack to happen in order to use their right to self-defence.

Apartheid The charge for prohibited acts which are committed in the context of systematic oppression and domination of one racial group over any other and with the intention to maintain such oppression or domination.

Arbitration A process undertaken outside legal courts to settle disputes between states or between states and non-state actors. Involves a third-party arbitrator whose decision all parties agree to accept and are binding on the parties.

Armed attack Use of force against the territory, ships, air force, or army bases of a state.

Asylum seeker A person who fled her/his own country to find a safe place elsewhere. Asylum seekers have an entitlement to make an asylum application under the 1951 Convention on Refugees and its 1967 Protocol.

Authentication Certification by the state parties that the text of a treaty for adoption is the definitive and the authentic text. States, however, may still propose technical or substantive changes before signature.

Balance of power Stability between competing forces or a just equilibrium in international relations that prevents any one state from getting sufficiently strong to impose its will on other states.

Basel Convention The Convention on the Control of Transboundary Movements of Hazardous Wastes and their Disposal. It is the most comprehensive global environmental agreement on hazardous and other wastes.

Basic disciplines Interlinked obligations in international trade that aim to offset domestic protectionist trade policies.

Berlin Conference Conference of 1884–5 attended by European powers, Russia, and the Ottoman Empire deciding the regulation of European colonization and trade in Africa.

Bilateral investment treaty An interstate agreement which establishes the terms and conditions for private investment of citizens of one state in the territory of another.

Binding The quality of a duty or obligation, which commands adherence regardless of the subjective views of the states on that duty or obligation.

Campaigning An organized effort to influence public opinion and decision-making processes.

Chapter VII authorization The Chapter of the United Nations Charter which gives the right to the Security Council to authorize the use of force against a member state which threatens international peace and security.

Charge Criminal accusation based on a combination of assessment of acts, intentions, and/or consequences.

Charter Another name for an international treaty, the most famous one is the United Nations Charter of 1945.

Citizenship Membership in a political community which confers exclusive rights and obligations to a person vis-à-vis that community.

Civil war See non-international armed conflict.

Civilian Any individual who is not a combatant in a theatre of armed conflict.

Cold War The name that is given to the relationship predominantly between the USA and the USSR that emerged after World War II, which was marked by conflict, tension, and competition between these two superpowers.

Collective action problem A situation under which the uncoordinated actions of each actor within a collective may not result in the best outcome each actor can achieve.

Combatant Members of armed forces or groups that may be considered prisoners of war if captured by enemy forces.

Common Article 3 The common article of all four Geneva Conventions of 1949, which sets out minimum standards of treatment of individuals in times of any conflict.

Complementarity The doctrine of international law that states that international courts are subsidiary to domestic courts and they exercise jurisdiction when domestic courts are unwilling or unable to do so.

Compliance Indicators through which the adherence to international laws by states are assessed and measured.

Computer Network Attack (CNA) Attacks taken via computers to disrupt, deny, degrade, or destroy the information within computers and computer networks and/or the computers/ networks themselves. If such an attack occurs within the context of armed conflict such attacks come within the scope of IHL rules.

Concluding observations Reports issued by UN Human Rights treaty-monitoring bodies assessing how state parties comply with human rights treaty obligations.

Constructivism A collection of approaches in international relations that concerns itself with the role of non-material factors, such as ideas, norms, and interactions in understanding state behaviour, the international system, and the relationship between the two.

Consultative status A status accorded by international organizations to non-governmental organizations which allows the latter to contribute in the proceedings of intergovernmental meetings and make official submissions.

Convention Another name for an international treaty.

Cooperation The rationale which motivates a multiple number of actors to reach a mutually acceptable outcome and framework of relationship.

Cosmopolitanism The normative theory that holds that human beings are the central unit of moral concern. In the case of global justice, it is the view which holds that international relations ought to be subject to the same fundamental standards of justice as domestic relations.

Countermeasures Measures short of use of force that states are entitled to take against other states which fail to fulfil their international legal obligations.

Covenant Another name for an international treaty.

Crimes against humanity The charge for prohibited acts which have a widespread and systematic element pointing out a policy on the part of the perpetrators.

Criminal jurisdiction over nationals The principle which holds that domestic courts can exercise criminal jurisdiction over persons who are nationals of that state, regardless of where the offence is committed.

Criminal jurisdiction Principles of jurisdiction that determine under what conditions domestic judges can prosecute an individual for crimes. It has four traditional grounds: the territorial principle, the national principle, the protective principle, and the universal principle.

Critical legal studies A school of thought in international law and in law generally that concerns itself with the indeterminacy of the meanings of laws and the role of political struggles underpinning the dominant interpretations of law.

De facto regimes Political entities that have control over territory and people, but lack recognition and title of statehood from the international community.

Declaration on the Right to Development United Nations General Assembly Declaration of 1986, which recognized that individuals and peoples have a right to development. This is a composite and process-oriented right to participate in, contribute to, and enjoy economic, social, cultural, and political development.

Derogation An act of temporarily restricting IHRL rights in cases of states of emergency threatening the life of a nation.

Descriptive statism The descriptive claim that states are the major unit of analysis in international relations.

Descriptive theory A theory that aims to explain processes, mechanisms, and relationships that are established by individuals and collectives.

Difference principle The principle developed by political philosopher John Rawls, which permits inequalities in the distribution of goods in a political community only if those inequalities benefit the worst-off members of society.

Diplomatic immunity An international law principle that ensures that diplomats are given safe passage and they are not prosecuted for their actions before the courts of host states.

Discipline A set of interlinked obligations which limit state action in the field of international trade.

Dispute settlement Institutional provisions in international treaties that provide mechanisms for settling differences in the application and implementation of treaties.

Doha Development Rounds The current trade negotiation round of the World Trade Organization, which started in 2001. It aims to lower trade barriers to increase international trade.

Dualism International law doctrine which regards domestic law and international law as two separate systems.

Economic globalization The rapid increase in economic activity taking place across national boundaries altering the power relations in nation states.

English School The school of thought that holds that anarchical system and international law respecting behaviour are both important features of international relations.

Equator principles Non-governmental code of conduct and benchmarks for the transnational financial industry to manage social and environmental issues in project financing.

Extra-territorial human rights obligations Those obligations that states have to respect even when they are acting outside of their territory, often by way of presence of their security forces or intelligence agents.

Feminism A collection of approaches to social, political, and legal theory that concerns itself with structures, processes, and discourses that oppress, and undermine women and normalize a male-centred version of reality.

Game theory A branch of mathematics and economics, which explores strategic interaction amongst interest-maximizing rational actors.

General comments Documents issued by human rights treaty monitoring bodies laying out interpretations of specific treaty provisions.

General principles of law A source of international law recognized by the Statute of the International Court of Justice. It aims to assist in the application of international law before courts.

Geneva Conventions The shorthand for the four Geneva Conventions of 1949 which regulate the conduct of armed conflicts.

Genocide The charge for prohibited acts, which have been committed with the intention to annihilate an ethnic, religious, or social group.

Globalization A historical process involving rapid increase of social, political, cultural, and economic activity taking place across national boundaries and altering the nature of power relations in societies.

Grave breaches List of prohibited acts contained in the Geneva Conventions and Additional Protocols for which states have a duty to repress and individuals have criminal responsibility.

Greenhouse gas emissions The release of greenhouse gasses into the atmosphere causing climate change.

Greenhouse gases Types of gases in the earth's atmosphere that can have dangerous effects on the climate system.

Hague Regulations A generic name given to regulations contained in 1899 and 1907 Hague Treaties.

Hard law A shorthand for describing binding obligations of states created either through treaties or customary international law.

Hors de combat Literally meaning 'out of the fight' in French and refers to soldiers who are no longer able to fight. *Hors de combat* have prisoner of war status in international armed conflict.

Human Rights Council The chief intergovernmental political body responsible for promoting and protecting human rights at the United Nations.

Hybrid courts Courts that are composed of international and domestic judges and apply a mix of international and domestic law in the course of their proceedings.

Idealism An approach to international relations that holds that ideas can have important causal effect on events in international politics.

Import prohibitions A tool to protect domestic industries by prohibiting the import of certain goods and services into a country.

Import quotas A tool to protect domestic industries by imposing limits on imports.

Institutionalist theories An approach to international relations which holds that under anarchy, institutions can shape expectations and constrain the activity of rational state actors.

Interim measures See provisional measures.

Internal armed conflict A conflict taking place in the territory of a state between its armed forces and dissident armed forces or other organized armed groups which, under responsible command, exercise such control over a part of its territory as to enable them to carry out sustained and concerted military operations.

International armed conflict A situation that involves two or more states engaged in an armed conflict.

International crimes Crimes that are exclusively defined by international law and the prosecution of which the whole international community has an interest in.

International expert bodies Bodies composed of well-known experts, which are created by a decision of an international organization or by an international treaty to monitor or investigate international law obligations.

International financial institutions The generic name given to financial and economic policy bodies that are not subject to regulation by a single state. The most well-known ones are the World Bank Group, and the International Monetary Fund.

International instrument A generic name given to international treaties as well as non-legally binding documents that set out international standards of conduct.

International legal positivism A collection of theories that derive the validity of international laws from the explicit or implicit consent of state to laws.

International Monetary Fund An international organization that monitors and assists countries on macroeconomic policy, especially on balance of payments and exchange rates.

International norms The international relations terminology to refer to accepted rules in the international system without making any distinction between legal or non-legal status of such norms. International norms mostly overlap with international laws, but they generally refer to more generalized statements of such laws.

International personhood The exclusive right to have a legal standing in international relations which corresponds to having obligations, as well as the right to enter into international agreements. States have full, and international organizations have limited, personhood in international relations.

International standards A shorthand to refer to compilation of international regulation composed of treaties, customary international law and soft law documents in a specific area, for example, international standards on the use of firearms by security forces.

Ius ad bellum Laws regulating the reasons for waging for war.

Ius cogens Supernorms of international law that no interstate agreement can change and with the effect of overriding all agreement that is concluded in contrary to such norms.

Ius in bello Laws regulating the conduct of war.

Ius puniendi The right to punish. Traditionally only states had the right to punish, but now international criminal courts and tribunals also exercise this right under specific circumstances. A state does not have the right to punish another state.

Jurisdiction Authority granted to a formally constituted legal or political body to make decisions, to adjudicate or enforce decisions within a defined area of responsibility.

Just war theory A collection of theories that aims to develop criteria for justifiable and unjustifiable uses of organized armed forces and permissible and impermissible acts during conflicts.

Kyoto Protocol Shorthand for the Protocol to the Framework Convention on Climate Change, which intends to stabilize greenhouse gas concentrations in the atmosphere by targeting industralized countries.

Legal cosmopolitanism The idea that international laws should be interpreted to advance the equal moral worth of individuals.

Liberalism An approach to international relations theory which holds that domestic preferences of states determine the international behaviour of states.

Mandate system A system that regulated the governance of territories of the defeated world powers by the victors of Word War I.

Merits The assessment of the rights and wrongs in a court case.

Millennium Development Goals A set of international commitments and specific targets set by the United Nations member states in 2000 on poverty reduction, education, maternal health, gender equality, and aim at combating child mortality, AIDS, and other diseases.

Military objective A target that makes an effective contribution to military action of the enemy. Any direct attack upon the civilian population, or upon any places, localities, or objects used solely for humanitarian, cultural, or religious purposes such as hospitals, churches, mosques, schools, or museums are immune from being a military objective as long as they are not used for enemy military purposes.

Mitigating circumstances Conditions which do not excuse unlawful conduct, but are considered out of mercy and have an effect on the final judgment of penalties for the conduct.

Monism International law doctrine which regards domestic law and international law as belonging to one system of law.

Monitoring Bodies Expert bodies created by institutional provisions of international treaties in order to monitor and report on the compliance of states with their treaty commitments.

Most Favoured Nation clause The rule that stipulates that a product or service coming from one WTO member should be treated as well as comparable products or services coming from any other country.

Multinational corporation A corporation that manages its production and delivery of services in more than one country.

Natural law Laws that are thought to exist prior to human choices and theories that study and justify those laws.

Negotiation The process of treaty-making where states, and increasingly non-state actors, are influential in determining the provisions of a treaty.

New Haven School See Process school.

Non-aligned Movement A collection of states that did not regard themselves officially aligned to any major bloc during the Cold War. It is also an international organization founded with the same name in 1955.

Non-binding instrument An agreement that is agreed by states in a political forum and does not have legal effect as such. Some non-binding instruments may be as detailed as treaties, and others may reflect political aspirations or goals.

Non-derogable rights International human rights treaty rights of which no derogation is permitted in times of states of emergency.

Non-discrimination A central principle of international human rights law that requires states to show equal concern and respect to individuals in their treatment.

Non-governmental organization A diverse range of organizations created by private individuals in order to pursue a collective aim. In the international law literature, international NGOs generally refer to not-for-profit organizations that pursue social, humanitarian, or political agendas at the international level.

Non-international armed conflict An armed conflict taking place between a state and a non-state armed group or between non-state armed groups only.

Non-refoulment principle An international law principle (with basis both in treaty law and customary international law) that states that no individual should be returned to a country where he/she faces risk of persecution or torture.

Non-retrogressive measures A principle of international human rights law that requires states not to adopt policies that would negatively affect the protection of economic and social rights.

Non-state actors A term widely used to refer to actors that operate internationally, but are not states. It covers international organizations, multinational corporations, non-governmental organizations, armed groups, or criminal organizations.

Normative statism The normative claim that states are the only institutions with the legitimate authority to make and enforce laws.

Normative theory A theory that purports to establish independent standards of conduct and evaluation of conduct.

Obligations *erga omnes* Latin for 'in relation to everyone or toward all' is an international law principle that holds that states owe some obligations to the international community as a whole rather than to individual states.

Opinio iuris Latin for 'an opinion for law' is the subjective view held by states that they act in a certain way in international relations because they think this is required by law.

Optional protocol Treaties that are made to strengthen an existing treaty, but making it optional to the original state parties to ratify it.

Pacta sunt servanda Latin for 'agreements must be kept' is a central principle of international law and the basis for international treaties.

Pacta tertis The rule stipulating that non-parties to a treaty cannot have legal obligations under that treaty.

Passive personality principle The principle which holds that states can exercise criminal jurisdiction to try a foreign national for offences committed abroad that affect its own citizens.

Peacekeeping A diverse range of military and civilian activities carried out with the consent of parties in order to assist countries after inter- or intra-state conflicts to return to conditions for sustainable peace.

Persistent objector A doctrine which argues that a state persistently objecting to an emerging customary rule should not be bound by it.

Piracy The charge for acts committed by non-state actors against the territory, property or nationals of states at sea, river, or on shore.

Policy-oriented school See Process school.

Precautionary Principle See principle of precaution.

Principle of distinction The IHL principle which prohibits attacks that are indiscriminate in nature and therefore cannot distinguish civilians and combatants.

Principle of national treatment The international trade law principle that stipulates that national and foreigners should be treated equally.

Principle of precaution An international law principle widely used in international humanitarian law and international environmental law. For the former body of law, it requires that all fighting parties take preventative measures to ensure that civilian population and civilian objects are spared. For the latter, it demands that states anticipate, prevent, and minimize the causes of environmental damage.

Principle of proportionality The IHL principle which holds that even if there is a clear military target it is not possible to attack it if the risk of civilians or civilian property being harmed is larger than the expected military advantage.

Prisoner of war The status accorded to a captured combatant granting immunity from prosecution, the right to be treated humanely during imprisonment, and the right to return home once hostilities come to an end.

Private Military Company (PMC) Companies that provide specialized military services, such as training, logistics, or active combat to state and non-state actors.

Process school The theory which defines international law as an authoritative process of decision-making within which current decisions are constrained by past political and legal practices.

Project finance A bank lending method that enables the lender to rely on the revenues generated by a specific project run by a project company, as the source of repayment for the original loan, as well as the security for the exposure of the lending bank itself.

Protocol An additional treaty to an existing one, which purports to expand the scope of states' obligations or create monitoring mechanisms.

Provisional measure An order given in the course of international legal proceedings demanding a state to halt its activities that are the subject of the dispute because of the assessment that consequences of the actions could be irreversible when the proceedings are complete. It is also known as an interim measure.

Ratification The international legal act of accepting international treaty obligations, often through acceptance of a treaty by domestic parliaments.

Rational choice A framework for understanding and predicting the behaviour of agents, who are motivated to maximize their own interests.

Realism The school of thought in international relations which holds that the international system is one of anarchy and that states, therefore, will behave in ways to protect and promote their survival in the system.

Rebus sic stantibus Latin for 'things thus standing', the legal doctrine that allows

an exception to *pacta sunt servanda* when a state can show that there has been fundamental change in the circumstances effecting the terms of an international agreement.

Recognition A unilateral act by states to recognize a political entity as having statehood for the purposes of international relations.

Refugee A person whose asylum application is well-founded due to evidence that the person has fled his/her country due to political persecution.

Regimes A set of norms or institutions that enable interstate cooperation and the convergence of expectations of behaviour amongst states.

Reservation A mechanism that allows a state to become party to a treaty, but also to exclude the legal effect of some of the provisions of that treaty.

Rio Declaration The 1992 Declaration on the Environment and Development pronouncing general principles of international environmental law.

Rome Statute Shorthand for the Statute of the International Criminal Court which was adopted in Rome, Italy, in 1999.

Secession The act of separating from an existing state with the view to establishing a new state.

Self-defence The inherent right of states to defend themselves when they face an armed attack.

Self-determination The doctrine stipulating the right of a people to govern themselves without interference from any other country. In cases of colonial or alien domination, international law recognizes that right to self-determination provides for a right to secede.

Signature Signing of a treaty by the head of state or foreign minister indicating a commitment to ratify the treaty.

Social justice The assignment of rights and duties to persons and associations by a political authority in a way that produces the desired pattern of distribution of benefits and burdens.

Social justice-apt The ability of an institution to adjust for accumulated effects of personal actions, that makes the institution open to judgements as to whether it is or is not socially just.

Soft law A collection of international documents, such as declarations and guidelines, that do not have legally binding, but persuasive effect, in international and domestic politics.

Sovereign immunity The international law principle that bars any state from prosecution before any court without its consent.

Sovereignty The right to exercise authority over a territory and the status to enter into international agreements.

Special procedures Independent expert persons appointed by the United Nations Human Rights commission to investigate and report on a human rights theme or human rights situation in a specific country.

State conduct An action, decision, or omission carried out by state actors that carries international law significance.

State party A state that has ratified a treaty.

Statehood The right to exercise jurisdiction domestically, enter into international relations regulated by international law.

Succession Transfer of rights and obligations of one state to another one based on the historical relationship that the new state has with the old state.

Sustainable development An economic development paradigm that holds that development policies need to be designed in such a way that both meets present human needs and protects the environment for succeeding generations.

Tariff A tax or duty applied to a good when it passes political boundaries. This is usually applied to a good imported from one country to another, although it can apply to an exported good.

Terra nullus Latin for 'empty land' is a doctrine employed by colonizers to claim legal title to land occupied by indigenous peoples.

Territorial criminal jurisdiction The principle which holds that domestic courts can exercise criminal jurisdiction over persons who commit offences in the territory of the state, regardless of their citizenship.

Terrorist attack Attacks carried out to create fear, accompanied by an ideological goal, and are indiscriminate in terms of its effects. Terrorist attacks are criminal acts according to the United Nations Security Council and in the domestic laws of almost all nations.

Third World approaches to international law A critical and historically informed approach to international law that addresses the effects of, and injustices perpetrated by, colonization on the theory and practice of international law.

Transnational crimes Crimes that take place across national borders that states have mutually agreed to cooperate to suppress.

Treaty-monitoring body An expert body created by a multilateral treaty to monitor state compliance.

Unilateral humanitarian intervention The international legal doctrine that stipulates that states should militarily intervene in other states in order to save massive loss of human lives under imminent or ongoing threat.

United Nations High Commissioner for Human Rights The chief public official with a mandate of protecting and promoting human rights worldwide.

United Nations High Commissioner for Refugees The United Nations agency mandated to safeguard the rights and well-being of refugees worldwide by ensuring that an individual can exercise the right to seek asylum and find safe refuge in another state, with the option to return home voluntarily, integrate locally, or to resettle in a third country.

United Nations Peace-building Commission An intergovernmental advisory body of the

United Nations that supports peace efforts in countries emerging from conflict, in particular through assisting with institution-building and economic development.

Universal Declaration of Human Rights A General Assembly Resolution which declared human rights protections as common aspirations of all states in 1948.

Universal jurisdiction A criminal jurisdiction principle which enables a state to prosecute an individual for an offence even though the offence has no link to the nationals or the territory of the state.

Universal periodic review The mechanism under which each member of the United Nations goes under peer review for its human rights performance before the Human Rights Council.

Universality In international law, it means the applicability of a rule to all states, regardless of their individual consent to the rule.

Uti possidetis Latin for 'as you possess' is the international law principle that territory remains with its possessor after a conflict, unless there is an explicit agreement to transfer the title of the territory.

Vattel The Swiss philosopher, diplomat, and international lawyer (1714–57) who defended a natural law account of the sovereignty doctrine in international law, stressing the freedom and independence of states as a moral value.

Vittoria The Spanish philosopher, theologist, and classic international lawyer (1480–1546) who famously held that international law is founded on natural law and its principles not only governed relations between European states, but also with non-European peoples.

Voluntarism A doctrine of international law which holds that no state can be bound by international laws that it has not agreed to.

War crimes The charge for prohibited acts, which are committed within the context of an armed conflict.

Westphalian system The international system that is characterized by sovereignty of states within their own territory and recognition of international law and diplomacy as a way to manage interstate relationships.

Westphalian sovereignty Concept of sovereignty based on exclusive jurisdiction of each state within its territory.

Will theories A positivist branch of international law theories that holds that international laws stem exclusively from the will of the states.

Wilson principles Principles of self-determination, democratic government, collective security, international law, and a league of nations proposed by the US President Woodrow Wilson as the basis for the post-World War I order.

World Bank A shorthand used for the World Bank Group that offers loans for, and advice on, economic development to developing and the least developed countries.

World Bank Inspection Panel A three-member body that was created in an attempt to increase the accountability of the World Bank. The Panel is available as a forum for locally affected people who believe that they have been, or are likely to be, adversely affected as a result of the Bank's social and environmental policy violations.

References

Books and Articles

Abbott, K. (1989) 'Modern International Relations Theory: A Prospectus for International Lawyers' *Yale Journal of International Law* 14/2: 335–411.

Abbott, K. W. and Snidal, D. (2000) 'Hard and Soft Law in International Governance' *International Organization* 54/3: 421–56.

Abbott, K. W., Keohane, R. O., Moravscik, A., Slaughter, A.-M., and Snidal, D. (2000) 'The Concept of Legalisation' *International Organization* 54/3: 401–19.

Akehurst, M. (1974–5) 'Custom as a Source of International Law' *British Yearbook of International Law* 47: 1–53.

Alexandrowicz, C. H. (1973) *The European-African Confrontation: A Study in Treaty Making* (Leiden: A.W. Sijthoff).

Alston, P. (2004) 'Core Labour Standards and the Transformation of the International Labour Rights Regime' *European Journal of International Law* 15/3: 457–521.

Amerasinghe, C. F. (2009) *Jurisdiction of Specific International Tribunals* (Leiden: Nijhoff Publishers).

Anand, R. P. (1987) *International Law and the Developing Countries: Confrontation or Cooperation?* (The Hague: Kluwer Law International).

Anderson, K. (2000) 'The Ottawa Convention Banning Landmines, the Role of International Non-Governmental Organizations and International Civil Society' *European Journal of International Law* 11/1: 91–120.

Anghie, A. (2005) *Imperialism, Sovereignty and the Making of International Law* (Cambridge: Cambridge University Press).

Anghie, T., Chimni, P., and Mickelson, K. (2004) *The Third World and International Order: Law, Politics and Globalization* (The Hague: Kluwer Law).

Arendt, A. C. (1999) *Legal Rules and International Society* (Oxford: Oxford University Press).

Art, L. J. and Waltz, K. (2008) *The Use of Force: Military Power and International Politics*, 7th edn. (Lanham, MD: Rowman and Littlefield Publishers).

Aust, A. (2007) *Modern Treaty Law and Practice*, 2nd edn. (Cambridge: Cambridge University Press).

Austin, J. (1832) *The Province of Jurisprudence Determined*, edited by Rumble, W. E. (1995) (Cambridge: Cambridge University Press).

Axelrod, R. (1984) *The Evolution of Cooperation* (New York, NY: Basic Books).

Bagwell, K. and Staiger, R. (2002) *The Economics of the World Trading System* (Cambridge: MIT Press).

Ball, G. (1967) 'The Promise of the Multinational Corporation' *Fortune* 75/6: 80.

Banani, D. (2003) 'International Arbitration and Project Finance in Developing Countries: Blurring the Public/Private Distinction' *Boston College International and Comparative Law Review* 26/2: 355–84.

Barton, J. H., et al. (2006) *The Evolution of the Trade Regime: Politics, Law and Economics and the GATT and WTO* (Princeton: Princeton University Press).

Bass, G. (2000) *Stay the Hand of Vengeance: The Politics of War Crimes Tribunals* (Princeton, NJ: Princeton University Press).

Bayefsky, A. F. (ed.) (2000) *Self-Determination in International Law: Quebec and Lessons Learned* (The Hague: Kluwer).

Beckett, J. (2001) 'Behind Relative Normativity: Rules and Process as Prerequisites of Law' *European Journal of International Law* 12/4: 627–50.

___ (2005) 'Countering Uncertainty and Ending Up/Down Arguments: Prolegomena to a Response to NAIL' *European Journal of International Law* 16/2: 213–38.

___ (2006) 'Rebel Without a Cause? Martti Koskenniemi and the Critical Legal Project' *German Law Journal* 7/12: 1045–88.

___ (2008) *The End of Customary International Law?* (Saarbrücken: VDM Verlag).

Bederman, D. (2001) *International Law in Antiquity* (Cambridge: Cambridge University Press).

Beitz, C. (1999) *Political Theory and International Relations*, 2nd edn. (Princeton: Princeton University Press).

Bianchi, A. (2008) 'Human Rights and the Magic of Jus Cogens' *European Journal of International Law* 19/3: 491–508.

Biersteker, T., Spiro, P., Sriram, C. L., and Raffo, V. (eds.) (2006) *International Law and International Relations: Bridging Theory and Practice* (London: Routledge).

Birnie, P., Boyle, A., and Redgwell, C. (2009) *International Law and the Environment*, 3rd edn. (Oxford: Oxford University Press).

Bodansky, D. (2007) 'Legitimacy' in D. Bodansky, J. Brunnee, and E. Hey (eds.), *The Oxford Handbook of International Environmental Law* (Oxford: Oxford University Press), 704–23.

Bolton, J. (2000) 'Should We Take Global Governance Seriously?' *Chicago Journal of International Law* 1: 205–22.

Borgen, C. J. (2007) 'Imagining Sovereignty, Managing Secession: The Legal Geography of Eurasia's "Frozen Conflicts"' *Oregon Review of International Law* 9: 477–536.

___ (2008) 'Introductory Note to Kosovo's Declaration of Independence' *International Legal Materials* 4: 461–8.

van den Bossche, P. (2005) *The Law and Policy of the World Trade Organization* (Cambridge: Cambridge University Press).

Boyle, A. (1999) 'Some Reflections on the Relationship of Treaties and Soft Law' *International and Comparative Law Quarterly* 48/4: 901–13.

Boyle, A. and Chinkin, C. (2007) *The Making of International Law* (Oxford: Oxford University Press).

Broude, T. and Shany, Y. (eds.) (2008) *The Shifting Allocation of Authority in International Law* (Oxford: Hart).

Brownlie, I. (2003) *Principles of Public International Law*, 6th edn. (Oxford: Oxford University Press).

Brunsson, N. and Jacobsson, B. (eds.) (2000) *A World of Standards* (New York: Oxford University Press).

Buchanan, A. (2003) *Justice, Legitimacy and Self-Determination* (Oxford: Oxford University Press).

___ (2004) *Justice, Legitimacy and Self-Determination: Moral Foundations for International Law* (Oxford: Oxford University Press).

Buchanan, A. and Keohane, R. (2006) 'The Legitimacy of Global Governance Institutions' *Ethics and International Affairs* 20/4: 405–37.

Bull, H. (1977) *The Anarchical Society: A Study of Order in World Politics* (New York: Columbia University Press).

de Búrca, G. and Weiler, J. H. H. (2001) *Collected Courses of the Academy of European Academy of Law, 10–1* (Oxford: Oxford University Press).

Carr, E. H. (1939) *The Twenty Years' Crisis, 1919–1939* (London: Macmillan).

Cassese, A. (1995) *Self-Determination of Peoples: A Legal Reappraisal* (Cambridge: Cambridge University Press).

___ (2008) *International Criminal Law*, 2nd edn. (Oxford: Oxford University Press).

___ (ed.) (2009) *The Oxford Companion to International Criminal Justice* (Oxford: Oxford University Press).

___ (2003) *International Criminal Law* (Oxford: Oxford University Press).

Cassese, A., Gaeta, P., and Jones, J.R.W.D. (eds.) (2002) *The Rome Statute of the International Criminal Court: A Commentary* (Oxford: Oxford University Press).

Chang, H. (2008) *Bad Samaritans: The Myth of Free Trade and the Secret History of Capitalism* (London, Bloomsbury Press).

Charlesworth, H. and Chinkin, C. (2000) *The Boundaries of International Law: Feminist Analysis* (Manchester: Manchester University Press).

Charney, J. I. (1985) 'The Persistent Objector Rule and the Development of Customary International Law' *British Yearbook of International Law* 56: 1–24.

Charnovitz, S. (2006) 'Nongovernmental Organizations and International Law' *American Journal of International Law* 100: 348–72.

Charny, D. (2001) 'Regulatory Competition and the Global Coordination of Labour Standards' in D. C. Esty and D. Geradin (eds.), *Regulatory Competition and Economic Integration: Comparative Perspectives* (Oxford: Oxford University Press), 311–29.

Checkel, J. T. (2005) 'International Institutions and Socialisation in Europe: Introduction and Framework' *International Organization* 59/3: 801–26.

Chimni, B. S. (2007) 'The Past, Present and the Future of International Law: A Critical Third World Approach' *Melbourne Journal of International Law* 8/2: 499–515.

Churchill, R. and Ulfstein G. (2000) 'Autonomous Institutional Arrangements in Multilateral Environmental Agreements: A Little Noticed Phenomenon in International Law' *American Journal of International Law* 94/4: 623–60.

Clapham, A. (2006) 'Human Rights Obligations of Non-State Actors in Conflict Situations' *International Review of the Red Cross* 88/863: 491–523.

Clapham, A. (2006) *Human Rights Obligations of Non-State Actors* (Oxford: Oxford University Press).

Collier, P. (2007) *The Bottom Billion* (Oxford: Oxford University Press).

Conte, A. and Burchill, R. (2009) *Defining Civil and Political Rights: The Jurisprudence of the United Nations Human Rights Committee* (Farnham: Ashgate).

Cox, R. W. (1981) 'Social Forces, States and World Orders: Beyond International Relations Theory' *Millennium: Journal of International Studies* 10/2: 126–55.

Craven, M. (1998) *International Covenant on Economic, Social and Cultural Rights* (Oxford: Oxford University Press).

Crawford, J. (1979) *The Creation of States in International Law* (Oxford: Clarendon Press).

___ (2006) *The Creation of States in International Law*, 2nd edn. (Oxford: Oxford University Press).

Cresswell, J. (2003) *Research Design: Qualitative, Quantitative and Mixed Method Approaches* (London: Sage).

___ (2003) *Research Methods: Qualitative, Quantitative and Mixed Methods Approaches* (Thousand Oaks: Sage).

Cryer, R., Friman, H., Robinson, D., and Wilmshurst, E. (2007) *An Introduction to International Criminal Law and Procedure* (Cambridge, Cambridge University Press).

Cutler, A. C., Haufler, V., and Porter, T. (eds.) (1999) *Private Authority and International Affairs* (Albany: State University of New York Press).

Davey, W. (2005) 'The WTO Dispute Settlement System: The First Ten Years' *Journal of International Economic Law* 8/1: 17–50.

Detter, I. (2000) *Law of War* (Cambridge: Cambridge University Press).

Dinstein, Y. (2005) *War, Aggression and Self-Defence* (Cambridge: Cambridge University Press).

Djelic, M.-L. and Sahlin-Andersson, K. (eds.) (2006) *Transnational Governance: Institutional Dynamics of Regulation* (Cambridge: Cambridge University Press).

Doyle, M. (1983) 'Kant, Liberal Legacies, and Foreign Affairs' *Philosophy and Public Affairs* 12/3: 205–35 and 12/4: 323–53.

Dworkin, R. (2000) *Sovereign Virtue* (Cambridge, MA.: Harvard University Press).

Enloe, C. (1992) *Bananas, Beaches and Bases: Making Feminist Sense of International Politics* (Berkeley, CA: University of California Press).

Falk, R. (1966) 'On the Quasi-Legislative Competence of the General Assembly' *American Journal of International Law* 60: 782–91.

Finnemore, M. (2004) *The Purpose of Intervention: Changing Beliefs about the Use of Force* (Ithaca, NY: Cornell University Press).

Finnemore, M. and Barnett, M. (2004) *Rules for the World: International Organizations in Global Politics* (New York: Cornell University Press).

Finnemore, M. and Sikkink, K. (1998) 'International Norm Dynamics and Political Change' *International Organization* 52/4: 887–917.

___ and ___ (2005) 'International Norm Dynamics and Political Change' *International Organization* 52:4: 887–917.

Finnemore, M. and Toope, J. (2001) 'Alternatives to "Legalisation": Richer Views of Law and Politics' *International Organization* 55/3: 741–56.

Fitzmaurice, M. and Redgewell, C. (2000) 'Non-Compliance Procedures and International Law' *Netherlands Yearbook of International Law* 31: 3567.

Fox, G. and Roth, B. (2008) *Democratic Governance and International Law* (Cambridge: Cambridge University Press).

Franck, T. (1990) *The Power of Legitimacy Among Nations* (Oxford: Oxford University Press).

___ (1995) *Fairness in International Law and Institutions* (Oxford: Oxford University Press).

___ (2003) *Recourse to Force: State Action against Threats and Armed Attacks* (Cambridge: Cambridge University Press).

Franck, T. and Rodley, N. (1973) 'After Bangladesh: The Law of Humanitarian Intervention by Military Force' *American Journal of International Law* 67/2: 275–305.

Frank, M. (1997) 'The Development of Environmental Law Management Systems and the Legal Compliance Audit as Part of the Eco Audit' in M. Swart (ed.), *International Environmental Law and Regulations*, Vol. I (Chichester: John Wiley & Sons), 117–30.

Freeman, M. (2002) *Human Rights: An Interdisciplinary Approach* (Cambridge: Polity Press).

Frowein, J. A. (1992) 'De Facto Regime' in R. Bernhardt (ed.), *Encyclopedia of Public International Law*, Vol. 1 (Amsterdam: North-Holland).

___ (1992) 'Non-Recognition' in R. Bernhardt (ed.), *Encyclopedia of Public International Law*, Vol. 3 (Amsterdam: North-Holland).

Fukuyama, F. (2006) *After the Neocons: America at the Crossroads* (London: Profile Books).

Furger, F. (2001) 'Global Markets, New Games, New Rules: The Challenge of International Private Governance' in R. P. Appelbaum, W. L. Felstiner, and V. Gessner (eds.), *Rules and Networks: The Legal Culture of Global Business Transactions* (Oxford: Hart), 201–45.

Gardiner, R. (2008) *Treaty Interpretation* (Oxford: Oxford University Press).

Geir, U. (2008) 'A World Court for Human Rights?' in O. Bring, O. Engdahl, and P. Wrange (eds.), *Law at War: The Law as it was and the Law as it should be: Liber Amicorum* (Leiden: Brill), 261–72.

Gheciu, A. (2005) 'Security Institutions as Agents of Socialization: NATO and the "New Europe"' *International Organization* 59/4: 973–1012.

Gill, S. (1992) *American Hegemony and the Trilateral Commission* (Cambridge: Cambridge University Press).

Goldstein, J., Kahler, M., Keohane, R., and Slaughter, A. (eds.) (2000) Special issue devoted to 'Legalization and World Politics' *International Organization* 54/3.

Goodman, R. (2002) 'Human Rights Treaties, Invalid Reservations and State Consent' *American Journal of International Law* 96: 531–60.

Goodman, R. and Jinks, D. (2003) 'Measuring the Effects of Human Rights Treaties' *European Journal of International Law* 14: 171–83.

Grant, T. D. (1999) *The Recognition of States: Law and Practice in Debate and Evolution* (Santa Barbara, CA: Praeger Publishers).

Gray, C. (2008) *International Law and the Use of Force* (Oxford: Oxford University Press).

Grewe, W. (2000) *The Epochs of International Law* (Berlin: Walter de Gruyter).

Gutman, R., Rieff, D., and Dworkin, A. (eds.) (2007) *Crimes of War: What the Public Should Know* (New York: Norton and Company).

Guzman, A. (2008) *How International Law Works: A Rational Choice Theory* (New York: Oxford University Press).

Hall, R. B. and Biersteker, T. J. (eds.) (2002) *The Emergence of Private Authority in Global Governance* (New York: Cambridge University Press).

Hannum, H. (1996) *Autonomy, Sovereignty, and Self-Determination: The Accommodation of Conflicting Rights* (Philadelphia, Pennsylvania: University of Pennsylvania Press).

Harris, D. and Livingstone, S. (eds.) (1998) *The Inter-American System of Human Rights* (Oxford: Clarendon Press).

Harris, D., O'Boyle, M., and Warbrick, C. (2009) *The Law of the European Convention on Human Rights* (Oxford: Oxford University Press).

Hart, H. L. A. (1961) *The Concept of Law* (Oxford: Clarendon Press).

Hathaway, O. (2002) 'Do Human Rights Treaties Make a Difference?' *Yale Law Journal* 111/8: 1935–2042.

Haufler, V. (1993) 'Crossing the Boundary between Public and Private: International Regimes and Non-State Actors' in V. Rittberger (ed.), *Regime Theory and International Relations* (Cambridge: Cambridge University Press), 94–111.

___ (2001) *A Public Role for the Private Sector* (Washington, DC: Carnegie Endowment for International Peace).

Haverland, C. (2000) 'Secession' in R. Bernhardt (ed.), *Encyclopedia of Public International Law*, Vol. 4 (Amsterdam: North-Holland).

Henckaerts, J. M. (2005) 'Study on Customary International Law: A Contribution to the Understanding and Respect for the Rule of Law in Armed Conflict' *International Review of the Red Cross* 87/857: 175–212.

Henckaerts, J. M and Doswald-Beck, L. (2005) *Customary International Law*. Vol. 1: The Rules (Cambridge: Cambridge University Press).

Higgins, R. (1994) *Problems and Process: International Law and How We Use It* (Oxford: Oxford University Press).

Hobson, J. (2000) *The State and International Relations* (Cambridge: Cambridge University Press).

Holzgrefe, J. L. (2003) *Humanitarian Intervention: Ethical, Legal and Political Dilemmas* (Cambridge: Cambridge University Press).

Huntingdon, S. P. (1973) 'Transnational Organizations in World Politics' *World Politics* 25/3: 333–68.

International Council for Human Rights Policy, International Commission of Jurists, and International Service for Human Rights (2006) *Human Rights Standards: Learning from Experience* (Geneva: International Council for Human Rights Policy).

Jackson, J. (1969) *World Trade and the Law of the GATT* (New York: Bobbs Merrill).

Janis, M. W. (ed.) (1992) *International Courts for the Twenty-first Century* (Leiden: Nijhoff Publishers).

Jayasuriya, K. (1999) 'Globalization, Law and the Transformation of Sovereignty' *Indiana Journal of Global Legal Studies* 6: 425–56.

Jenks, C. W. (1972) 'Multinational Entities in the Law of Nations' in W. Friedmann, L. Henkin, and O. Lissitzyn (eds.), *Transnational Law in a Changing Society: Essays in Honour of Philip C. Jessup* (New York: Columbia University Press), 70–83.

Jennings, Sir R. and Watts, Sir A. (eds.) (1992) *Oppenheim's International Law*, 9th edn. (Oxford: Oxford University Press).

Jessup, P. (1956) *Transnational Law* (New Haven: Yale University Press).

Jurgensmeyer, M. (2002) 'The Global Dimension of Religious Terrorism' in R. B. Hall and T. Biersteker (eds.), *The Emergence of Private Authority in Global Governance* (Cambridge: Cambridge University Press), 141–57.

Keck, M. and Sikkink, K. (1998) *Activists Beyond Borders: Advocacy Networks in International Politics* (Ithaca, NY: Cornell University Press).

Keohane, R. (1984) *After Hegemony: Cooperation and Discord in the World Political Economy* (Princeton, NJ: Princeton University Press).

Keohane, R. and Martin, L. (1995) 'The Promise of Institutionalist Theory' *International Security* 20/1: 39–51.

Keohane, R., Moravcsik, A., and Slaughter, A.-M. (2000) 'Legalized Dispute Resolution: Interstate and Transnational' *International Organization* 54/3: 457–88.

Kimball, L. A. (1996) *Treaty Implementation: Scientific and Technical Advice Enters a New Stage* (Washington, DC: American Society of International Law).

King, C. (2008) 'The Five-Day War: Managing Moscow after the Georgia Crisis' *Foreign Affairs* 87/2: 2–11.

Kingsbury, B. (2002) 'Legal Positivism as Normative Politics' *European Journal of International Law* 13/2: 401–36.

Koh, H. (1996) 'Transnational Legal Process' *Nebraska Law Review* 75: 181–206.

Kohen, M. G. (ed.) (2006) *Secession: International Law Perspectives* (Cambridge: Cambridge University Press).

Kolben, K. (2007) 'Integrative Linkage: Combining Public and Private Regulatory Approaches in the Design of Trade and Labor Regimes' *Harvard Journal of International Law* 48/1: 203–56.

Korey, W. (2001) *NGOs and the Universal Declaration on Human Rights* (New York: Palgrave).

Koskenniemi, M. (1990) 'The Politics of International Law' *European Journal of International Law* 1: 4–32.

—— (1989, 2000) *From Apology to Utopia: The Structure of International Legal Argument* (Cambridge: Cambridge University Press).

—— (2000) *The Gentle Civilizer of Nations: The Rise and Fall of International Law 1870–1960* (Cambridge: Cambridge University Press).

—— (2005) *From Apology to Utopia: The Structure of International Legal Argument* (Cambridge: Cambridge University Press).

—— (2007) 'The Fate of Public International Law: Between Technique and Politics' *Modern Law Review* 70: 1–30.

Krasner, S. (ed.) (1983) *International Regimes* (Ithaca, NY: Cornell University Press).

Kratochwill, F. V. (1989) *Rules, Norms and Decisions: On the Conditions of Practical and Legal Reasoning in International Relations and Domestic Affairs* (Cambridge: Cambridge University Press).

Krugman, P. (1997) 'What Should Trade Negotiators Negotiate About?' *Journal of Economic Literature* 35: 113–20.

Ku, C., Diehl, P. F., Simmons, B., Dallmeyer, D. G., and Jacobson, H. K. (2001) 'Exploring

International Law: Opportunities and Challenges for Political Science Research: A Roundtable' *International Studies Review* 3/1: 3–23.

Lalonde, S. (2002) *Determining Boundaries on a Conflicted World: the Role of Uti Possidetis* (Montreal: McGill-Queens's University Press).

Landman, T. (2000) *Issues and Methods in Comparative Politics* (London: Routledge).

____ (2006) *Issues and Methods in Comparative Politics: An Introduction* (London: Routledge).

Lee, R. S. (ed.) (1999) *The International Criminal Court: the Making of the Rome Statute* (The Hague: Kluwer Law).

Lindblom, A. (2005) *Non-Governmental Organisations in International Law* (Cambridge: Cambridge University Press).

Loya, T. A. and Boli, J. (1999) 'Standardization in the World Polity: Technical Rationality over Power' in J. Boli and G. M. Thomas (eds.), *Constructing World Culture: International Nongovernmental Organizations Since 1875* (Stanford: Stanford University Press), 169–97.

Lynch, D. (2004) *Engaging Eurasia's Separatist States: Unresolved Conflicts and De Facto States* (Washington, DC: United States Institute of Peace Press).

MacMillan, M. (2002) *Paris 1919: Six Months that Changed the World* (London: Random House).

Mapel, D. R. and Nardin, T. (eds.) (1999) *International Society, Diverse Ethical Perspectives* (Princeton: Princeton University Press).

Martens, K. (2006) *NGOs and the United Nations: Institutionalization, Professionalization and Adaptation* (New York: Palgrave)

Mattli, W. (2001) 'International Governance for Voluntary Standards: A Game-Theory Perspective' in G. A. Bermann, M. Herdegen, and P. Lindseth (eds.), *Transatlantic Regulatory Competition* (Oxford: Oxford University Press).

____ (2001) 'Private Justice in a Global Economy: From Litigation to Arbitration' *International Organization* 55/4: 919–47.

Mattli, W. and Büthe, T. (2003) 'Setting International Standards: Technological Rationality or Primacy of Power?' *World Politics* 56: 1–42.

Mavroidis, P. (2007) *Trade in Goods* (Oxford: Oxford University Press).

McCoubrey, N. and White, H. (1996), *The Blue Helmets: Legal Regulation of United Nations Military Operations* (Sudbury, MA: Dartmouth).

McDougal, M.S., Lasswell, H.D., and Reisman, W.M. (1981) 'The World Constitutive Process of Authoritative Decision' in M. S. McDougal and W. M. Reisman (eds.), *International Law Essays: A Supplement to International Law in Contemporary Perspective* (Mineola, NY: The Foundation Press).

McQueen, N. (2006), *Peacekeeping and the International System* (Oxford: Routledge).

McRae, D. (1978) 'The Legal Effects of Interpretative Declarations' *British Yearbook of International Law* 49: 155–98

Meckled-Garcia, S. (2008) 'On the Very Idea of Cosmopolitan Justice: Constructivism and International Agency' *Journal of Political Philosophy* 16/3: 245–71.

Meckled-Garcia, S. and Cali, B. (eds.) (2006) *The Legalisation of Human Rights: Multidisciplinary Perspectives on Human Rights and Human Rights Law* (London: Routledge).

Meron, T. (1998) *War Crimes Law Comes of Age: Essays* (Oxford: Oxford University Press).

____ (2000) 'The Humanization of Humanitarian Law' *American Journal of International Law* 94: 67–121.

Mertus, J. (2009) *United Nations and Human Rights*, 2nd edn. (London: Routledge).

Mettraux, G. (2005) *International Crimes and the Ad Hoc Tribunals* (Oxford: Oxford University Press).

Moravcsik, A. (1997) 'Taking Preference Seriously: A Liberal Theory of International Politics' *International Organization* 51/4: 513–53.

_____ (2000) 'The Origins of Human Rights Regimes: Democratic Delegation in Postwar Europe' *International Organization* 54/2: 217–52.

Morgenthau, H. (1948) *Politics Among Nations: The Struggle for Power and Peace* (New York: Alfred A. Knopf).

Morrison, J. and Roht-Arriaza, N. (2007) 'Private and Quasi-Private Standard Setting' in D. Bodansky, J. Brunnee, and H. Hey (eds.), *The Oxford Handbook of International Environmental Law* (Oxford: Oxford University Press), 498–527.

Nardin, T. and Mapel, D. (2000) *International Society: Diverse Ethical Perspectives* (Princeton: Princeton University Press).

Nickel, J. (2007) *Making Sense of Human Rights*, 2nd edn. (Oxford: Wiley-Blackwell).

Nollkaemper, A. (2006) 'Responsibility of Transnational Corporations in International Environmental Law: Three Perspectives' in G. Winter (ed.), *Multilevel Governance of Global Environmental Change. Perspectives from Science, Sociology and the Law* (New York: Cambridge University Press), 179–99.

Norton, J. J. and Shams, H.M. (2005) 'Privatisation in Modern Banking Regulation: Selective Supervisory and Enforcement Dimensions' in M. Likosky (ed.), *Privatising Development: Transnational Law, Infrastructure and Human Rights* (Leiden: Martinus Nijhoff), 173–218.

Nussbaum, A. (1954) *A Concise History of the Law of Nations* (New York: Macmillan).

O'Connell, M. E. (1999) 'New International Legal Process' *American Journal of International Law* 93: 334–51.

_____ (2006) *International Dispute Resolution: Cases and Materials* (Durham, NC: Carolina Academic Press).

Okafor, O. C. (2007) *The African Human Rights System, Activist Forces and International Institutions* (Cambridge: Cambridge University Press).

Ong, D. M. (2008) 'International Environmental Law's Customary Dilemma: Betwixt General Principles and Treaty Rules' *Irish Yearbook of International Law*, Vol. I (Oxford: Hart), 3–60.

Orakhelashvili, A. (2006) *Peremptory Norms in International Law* (Oxford: Oxford University Press, 2006).

Orentlicher, D. (2004) 'Unilateral Multilateralism: United States Policy Towards the International Criminal Court' *Cornell International Law Journal* 36: 415–34.

Oxfam (2002) *Rigged Rules and Double Standards: Trade, Globalization, and the Fight Against Poverty* (Oxford: Oxfam Publications).

Paust, J. J. (2007) *Beyond the Law: The Bush Administrations Unlawful Responses in the 'War' on Terror* (Cambridge: Cambridge University Press).

Pellet, A. (1992) 'The Normative Dilemma: Will and Consent in International Law Making' *Australian Journal of International Law* 12: 22–53.

Peskin, V. (2008) *International Justice in Rwanda and the Balkans: Virtual Trials and the Struggle for State Cooperation* (Cambridge: Cambridge University Press).

Pogge, T. (2002) *World Poverty and Human Rights* (Cambridge: Polity Press).

Posner, E. A. (2002) *A Theory of the Laws of War* (Chicago: The Chicago Working Paper Series).

Potoski, M. and Prakash, A. (2004) 'Regulatory Convergence in Nongovernmental Regimes? Cross-National Adoption of ISO 1401 Certifications' *Journal of Politics* 66/3: 885–905.

Prakash, A. and Potoski, M. (2006) *The Voluntary Environmentalists: Green Clubs, ISO 14001, and Voluntary Environmental Regulations* (Cambridge: Cambridge University Press).

Ratner, S. and Slaughter, A.-M. (1999) 'Appraising the Methods of International Law: A Prospectus for Readers' *American Journal of International Law* 93: 291–301.

Rawls, J. (1971) *A Theory of Justice* (Oxford: Oxford University Press).

____ (1999) *A Theory of Justice*, 2nd edn. (Oxford: Oxford University Press).

Redgwell, C. (1993) 'Universality or Integrity? Some Reflections on Reservations to General Multilateral Treaties' *British Yearbook of International Law* 64: 245–82.

____ (2006) 'Reservations, Non-Compliance Procedures and the "Policing" Role of Treaty Institutions' in M. Craven et al. (eds.), *Interrogating the Treaty: Essays in the Contemporary Law of Treaties* (Nijmegen: Wolf Legal Publishers).

Reus-Smit, C. (ed.) (2004) *The Politics of International Law* (Cambridge: Cambridge University Press).

Reuter, P. (1995) *Introduction to the Law of Treaties*, 2nd edn. (Geneva: Presses Universitaires de France).

Risse, T., Ropp, S., and Sikkink, K. (1998), *The Power of Human Rights: International Norms and Domestic Change* (Cambridge: Cambridge University Press).

Roberts, A. (2008) 'The Equal Application of the Laws of War: A Principle Under Pressure' *International Review of the Red Cross* 90/872: 931–62.

Rodley, N. and Cali, B. (2007) 'Revisiting Kosovo: Humanitarian Intervention on the Fault-lines of International Law' *Human Rights Law Review* 7/2: 275–97.

Rodrik, D. (2007) *One Economics, Many Recipes* (Princeton: Princeton University Press).

Roessler, F. (2000) *Essays on the Legal Structure, Functions and Limits of the World Trade Order* (London: Cameron May).

Romano, Cesare (1999) 'The Proliferation of International Judicial Bodies: The Pieces of the Puzzle' *New York University Journal of International Law and Politics* 31/4: 709–51.

Russett, B. (1994) *Grasping the Democratic Peace: Principles for a Post-Cold War World* (Princeton: Princeton University Press).

de Sadeleer, N. (2002) *Environmental Principles: From Political Slogans to Legal Rules* (Oxford: Oxford University Press).

Sands, P. (ed.) (1999) *Manual on International Courts and Tribunals* (London: Butterworths).

Sands, P. and Klein, P. (2001) *Bowett's Law of International Institutions*, 5th edn. (London: Sweet & Maxwell).

Schabas, W. A. (2004), *An Introduction to the International Criminal Court*, 2nd edn. (Cambridge: Cambridge University Press).

Schachter, O. (1989) 'Entangled Treaty and Custom' in Y. Dinstein (ed.), *International Law at a Time of Perplexity: Essays in Honour of Shabtai Rosenne* (Dordrecht: Martinus Nijhoff), 717–38.

____ (1991), *International Law in Theory and Practice* (Dordrecht: Martinus Nijhoff).

Schemers, H. G. and Blokker, N. M. (2004) *International Institutional Law: Unity within Diversity*, 4th edn. (Leiden: Martinus Nijhoff).

Schwarzenberger, G. (1971) 'Equality and Discrimination in International Economic Law' *British Yearbook of World Affairs* 25: 163–81.

Scobbie, I. (1997) 'The Theorist as Judge: Hersch Lauterpacht's Concept of the International Judicial Function' *European Journal of International Law* 264–98.

____ (2007) 'The Approach to Customary International Law in the Study' in E. Wilmshurst (ed.), *Perspectives on the ICRC Study on Customary International Humanitarian Law* (London: Chatham House).

Scott, J. (2007) *The WTO Agreement on Sanitary and Phytosanitary Measures* (Oxford: Oxford University Press).

Shaw, M. N. (2008) *International Law*, 6th edn. (Cambridge: Cambridge University Press).

Shelton, D. (2006a) 'Normative Hierarchy in International Law' *American Journal of International Law* 100/2: 291–323.

____ (2006b) 'International Law and Relative Normativity' in M. D. Evans (ed.), *International Law* (Oxford: Oxford University Press), 159–86.

Simma, B. and Paulus, A.L. (1999) 'The Responsibility of Individuals for Human Rights Abuses in Internal Conflicts: A Positivist View' *American Journal of International Law* 93: 302–16.

Simmons, B. and Steinberg, R. H. (eds.), (2006) *International Law and International Relations* (Cambridge: Cambridge University Press).

Sinclair, I. (1994) *The Vienna Convention on the Law of Treaties*, 2nd edn. (Manchester: Manchester University Press).

Singer, P (2002) *One World: The Ethics of Globalization* (New Haven: Yale University Press).

____ (2007) *Corporate Warriors: The Rise of the Privatised Military Industry* (Ithaca: Cornell University Press).

Slaughter Burley, A.-M. (1993) 'International Law and International Relations Theory: A Dual Agenda' *American Journal of International Law* 87/2: 205–39.

____ (2001) 'Agencies on the Loose? Holding Government Networks Accountable' in G. A. Bermann, M. Herdegen, and P. Lindseth (eds.), *Transatlantic Regulatory Competition* (Oxford: Oxford University Press), 521–46.

Slaughter, A.-M. and Burke-White, W. (2006) 'The Future of International Law is Domestic (or The European Way of Law)' *Harvard International Law Journal* 47/2: 327–52.

Slaughter, A.-M., Tulumello, A. S., and Wood, S. (1998) 'International Law and International Relations Theory: A New Generation of Interdisciplinary Scholarship' *American Journal of International Law* 92/3: 367–97.

Spiro, P. (2006) 'NGOs in International Environmental Lawmaking: Theoretical Models' *Temple University Legal Studies Research Paper Series*, 26.

____ (2009 forthcoming) 'NGOs and Human Rights: Channels of Power' in *Research Handbook on Human Rights* (Cheltenham: Edward Elgar).

Steinberg, R. (2002) 'In the Shadow of Law or Power? Consensus-Based Bargaining and Outcomes in the GATT/WTO' *International Organization* 56: 339–74.

Steiner, H., Alston, P., and Goodman, R. (eds.) (2007) *International Human Rights in Context: Law, Politics and Morals*, 3rd edn. (New York: Oxford University Press).

Strange, S. (1996) *The Retreat of the State* (Cambridge: Cambridge University Press).

Summers, J. (2007) *Peoples and International Law: How Nationalism and Self-Determination Shape a Contemporary Law of Nations* (Leiden: Martinus Nijhoff).

Snyder, J. and Vinjamuri, L. (2003/4) 'Trials and Errors: Principles and Pragmatism in Strategies of International Justice' *International Security* 28/3: 5–44.

Subramanian, A. and Wei, S. (2007) 'The WTO Promotes Trade Strongly, But Unevenly' *Journal of International Economics* 72/1: 151

Tamanaha, B. (2004) *On the Rule of Law* (Cambridge: Cambridge University Press).

Tasioulas, J. (1996) 'In Defence of Relative Normativity: Communitarian Values and the *Nicaragua* Case' *Oxford Journal of Legal Studies* 16: 84–128.

Tesón, F. (1998) *A Philosophy of International Law* (Boulder, CO: Westview Press).

Thirlway, H. (1989) 'The Law and Procedure of the International Court of Justice, 1960–1989 (Part One)' *British Yearbook of International Law* 60: 4–56.

Thürer, D. (2000) *Self-Determination* in R. Bernhardt (ed.), *Encyclopedia of Public International Law*, Vol. 4 (Amsterdam: North-Holland).

Tomuschat, C. (2006a) 'Secession and Self-Determination' in M. G. Kohen (ed.), *Secession: International Law Perspectives* (Cambridge: Cambridge University Press).

_____ (2006b) *The Fundamental Rules of the International Legal Order: Jus Cogens and Obligations Erga Omnes* (Leiden: Martinus Nijhoff).

Ulfstein, G., Marauhn, T., and Zimmermann, A. (eds.) (2006) *Making Treaties Work* (Cambridge: Cambridge University Press).

Vincent, R. J. (1986) *International Relations and Human Rights* (Cambridge: Cambridge University Press).

Vosko, L. F. (2004) 'Standard Setting at the International Labour Organization: The Case of Precarious Employment' in J. J. Kirton and M. J. Trebilcock (eds.), *Hard Choices, Soft Law: Voluntary Standards in Global Trade, Environment and Social Governance* (Aldershot: Ashgate), 135–52.

Voyiakis, E. (2003) 'Access to Court v. State Immunity' *International & Comparative Law Quarterly* 52: 297–332.

Wallerstein, I. (1974) *The Modern World-System* (San Diego, CA: Academic Press).

Waltz, K. (1979) *Theory of International Politics* (New York, NY: McGraw-Hill).

Walzer, M. (2006) *Just and Unjust Wars: A Moral Argument with Historical Illustrations* (New York: Basic Books).

Weeramantry, C. G. (2005) *Universalizing International Law* (Leiden: Martinus Nijhoff).

Weil, P. (1983) 'Towards Relative Normativity in International Law?' *American Journal of International Law* 77: 413–38.

Weller, M. and Metzger, B. (eds.) (2008) *Settling Self-Determination Disputes: Complex Power-Sharing in Theory and Practice* (Leiden: Martinus Nijhoff).

Wendt, A. (1992) 'Anarchy is What States Make of It: The Social Construction of Power Politics' *International Organization* 46/2: 391–425.

_____ (1999), *Social Theory of International Politics* (Cambridge: Cambridge University Press).

Wheeler, N. (2002) *Saving Strangers: Humanitarian Intervention in International Society* (Oxford: Oxford University Press).

Wight, M. (1992) *International Theory: The Three Traditions* (London: Holmes and Meier).

Wilde, R. (2008) *International Territorial Administration: How Trusteeship and the Civilizing Mission Never Went Away* (Oxford: Oxford University Press).

Wildhaber, L. (2006) *The European Court of Human Rights, 1998–2006 : History, Achievements, Reform* (Kehl: Engel).

Winter, G. (ed.) (2006) *Multilevel Governance of Global Environmental Change: Perspectives from Science, Sociology and the Law* (Cambridge: Cambridge University Press).

Woodward, B. K. (2006) 'Global Civil Society and International Law in Global Governance: Some Contemporary Issues' *International Community Law Review* 8/2–3: 247–355.

WTO (2008) *International Trade Statistics 2007* (Geneva: World Trade Organization Reports).

Zifcak, S. (2005) 'Globalizing the Rule of Law' in S. Zifcak (ed.), *Globalisation and the Rule of Law* (Abingdon: Routledge).

Government and UN Documents

Declaration on Principles of International Law Concerning Friendly Relations and Co-operation among States in Accordance with the Charter of the United Nations, General Assembly Res. 2625, Annex, 25 UN GAOR, Supp. (No. 28), U.N. Doc. A/5217 at 121 (1970).

Eleventh Report of the Special Rapporteur, U.N. Doc. A/CN.4/574, ILC Report, A/62/10, 2007.

International Council for Human Rights Policy, International Commission of Jurists, and International Service for Human Rights (2006), Human Rights Standards: Learning from Experience (Geneva: International Council for Human Rights Policy).

Kosovo Declaration of Independence, 47 ILM 467 (2008).

Montevideo Convention on the Rights and Duties of States, Dec. 26, 1933, 49 Stat. 3097, 165 U.N.T.S. 19

Security Council Res. 367, U.N. Doc. S/RES/367 (March 12, 1975)

Security Council Res. 541, U.N. Doc. S/RES/541 (Nov. 18, 1983)

Security Council Res. 1244, UN Doc S/RES/1244 (1999)

The Aaland Islands Question: Report Submitted to the Council of the League of Nations by the Commission of Rapporteurs, League of Nations Doc. B7/21/68/106 (1921)

Index

Entries in bold are also in the glossary.